COLONIAL
LATIN AMERICA

COLONIAL LATIN AMERICA

Mark A. Burkholder
Lyman L. Johnson

New York   Oxford
OXFORD UNIVERSITY PRESS
1990

Oxford University Press

Oxford   New York   Toronto
Delhi   Bombay   Calcutta   Madras   Karachi
Petaling Jaya   Singapore   Hong Kong   Tokyo
Nairobi   Dar es Salaam   Cape Town
Melbourne   Auckland

and associated companies in
Berlin   Ibadan

Copyright © 1990 by Oxford University Press, Inc.

Published by Oxford University Press, Inc.,
200 Madison Avenue, New York, New York 10016

Library of Congress Cataloging-in-Publication Data
Burkholder, Mark A., 1943–
Colonial Latin America / Mark A. Burkholder, Lyman L. Johnson.
     p.   cm.   Bibliography: p.   Includes index.
ISBN 0-19-504542-4.
—ISBN 0-19-506110-1 (pbk.)
1. Latin America—History—To 1830.
I. Johnson, Lyman L.
II. Title.   F1412.B96   1990   980—dc20
89-32558   CIP

2 4 6 8 9 7 5 3 1
Printed in the United States of America

For the Teachers
who started us on the path to this book
especially
Juan Alonso
William L. Fisk
Hugh M. Hamill, Jr.
and Taylor Stults

ACKNOWLEDGMENTS

We first discussed writing a textbook on colonial Latin America in the delightful setting of Poogan's Porch during a Southern Historical Association meeting in Charleston, South Carolina, in 1983. Subsequently, we have learned much from the work of hundreds of colleagues, only some of whom could be mentioned in our suggestions for additional reading. To all, however, we are grateful. We have benefited in particular from the timely publication of three useful and important works: the multivolume *Cambridge History of Latin America* edited by Leslie Bethell, *Early Latin America* by James Lockhart and Stuart B. Schwartz, and *Spain and Portugal in the New World 1492–1700* by Lyle N. McAlister.

We want to single out for special appreciation those persons who took time away from their own research to critique, sometimes trenchantly, early drafts of our manuscript. Dauril Alden, Kenneth J. Andrien, Jacques A. Barbier, Kristen Burkholder, Paul D. Escott, Asunción A. Lavrin, William S. Maltby, and James S. Saeger helped us immeasurably with their incisive and thoughtful comments. Whatever flaws remain in the manuscript, however, are ours alone.

We owe a special debt of gratitude to Asunción A. Lavrin in particular for graciously providing us with most of the illustrations that appear in this volume.

We thank Vice Chancellor for Academic Affairs James H. Werntz and the Foundation of the University of North Carolina at Charlotte for travel funds as well as the financial support needed for the production of the illustrations and maps. We also thank the Department of Geography and Earth Sciences at the University of North Carolina at Charlotte for producing the maps.

At the University of Missouri-St. Louis, Dean E. Terrence Jones and the College of Arts and Sciences and Dean Donald H. Driemeier and the School of Business Administration made available the word processing equipment used in preparing the manuscript. Anne Butler, Judy Camigliano, Joan Lorson, and Diane Piskulic graciously provided the technical information necessary to make the equipment work properly. Steven C. Hause offered encouragement and friendship throughout the project. We thank them all for their continued support.

Suzanne Hiles Burkholder provided not only technical assistance on the manuscript but also an incomparable working environment. Without her patience and willingness to delay her own work, this manuscript would not yet be completed. Sue Johnson showed equal forbearance, and her support and encouragement were invaluable throughout the duration of the project.

Nancy Lane of Oxford University Press was both receptive to our original proposal and supportive throughout the long preparation of the manuscript. We greatly appreciate her confidence.

Coauthoring a lengthy manuscript offers numerous challenges as well as benefits. We can truly say, however, that this book is jointly authored and only we know who is responsible for any errors in fact or interpretation.

St. Louis, Mo.   M. A. B.
Charlotte, N.C.   L. L. J.
April 1989

CONTENTS

COLONIAL
LATIN AMERICA

ONE

IBERIA AND AMERICA BEFORE THE CONQUEST

Amerindian Civilizations on the Eve of European Conquest

The history of Latin America must begin with its earliest inhabitants. America's first inhabitants migrated from the Asian mainland across the Bering Strait between 40,000 and 25,000 B.C. and were almost completely dependent on hunting for food, relying on stone-tipped weapons and fire-hardened projectiles. Except for small dogs, no domesticated animals participated in the long trek from north-central Asia.

It took millennia to occupy the enormous open spaces of the Western hemisphere. Archaeological evidence suggests that some areas of the Caribbean Basin and the plains of South America were occupied less than two thousand years before the voyage of Columbus. On the other hand, human societies had been present in the central highlands of Mexico, Central America, and the high valleys of the Andes since approximately 10,000 B.C. These regions contain evidence outlining the dawn of agriculture and the emergence of sophisticated civilizations. By 1492 the indigenous population may have reached 35 million to 45 million.

Although the Aztecs and Incas are the civilizations best known during the age of conquest, they constituted only a minority of the total Amerindian population and resided in geographic areas that together comprised only a small portion of Latin America's landscape. Araucanians, Arawaks, Caribs, Chibchas, Chichimecas, Ge, Guaraní, Mapuche, Otamí, Maya, Quibaya, Taino, Tepanecs, and Tupí joined a host of other peoples and linguistic groups that inhabited the Americas; together they formed a human mosaic whose diverse characteristics greatly influenced the ways in which colonial Latin America developed.

By 1500 over 350 major tribal groups, 15 distinct cultural centers, and more than 160 linguistic stocks could be found in Latin America. Despite the variety suggested by these numbers, in general terms there were only

The Great Aztec Temple, reconstructed by Ignacio Marquina from descriptions of Spanish conquerors and surviving Aztec monuments

Inca ruins and terraces, Machu Picchu, Peru

three kinds of Indian cultures. One was a largely nomadic group that relied on hunting, fishing, and gathering for subsistence; its members had advanced little over the people who first made stone points in the New World in about 10,000 B.C. A second group was sedentary or semisedentary and depended primarily on agriculture for subsistence. More advanced technologically than the nomadic peoples, its members benefited from the domestication of plants that had taken place after about 7200 B.C. The third group featured dense, sedentary populations, surplus agricultural production, greater specialization of labor and social differentiation, and large-scale public construction projects. These complex civilizations were located only in Mesoamerica and western South America. The civilizations of Teotihuacán, Monte Albán, Tiahuanaco, and Chimu were among its most important early examples.

In both Mesoamerica and the Andean region, early Amerindian civilizations mastered sedentary agriculture, constructed irrigation systems, engaged in cultural and sometimes political imperialism, and lived in socially stratified societies. Extensive urban and ceremonial centers reveal the centrality of religion in daily life and could not have been built without the surplus produced by sedentary agriculture. In the century before the Spaniards arrived, two militaristic and demanding civilizations—the Aztec and the Inca—built on the legacies of their predecessors and dominated central Mexico and much of western South America.

The Aztecs

Although the Spaniards encountered Amerindians from Columbus's initial voyage onward, the first highly developed civilization they found was that of the Aztecs, to use the name commonly given to the last preconquest cultures resident in the Valley of Mexico. When the sixteenth century began, the Aztecs were at the height of their power: Only the swiftness of their defeat exceeded the rapidity with which they had risen to prominence. Indeed, for the century before the arrival of Cortés, they were unquestionably the most powerful political force in Mesoamerica.

Among the many Chichimec peoples who pushed south in the wake of Tula's collapse were the Mexicas, a fierce, Nahua-speaking people. The most powerful of the invaders who formed the Aztec state, the Mexicas adopted elements of the political and social forms they found among the advanced urbanized agriculturalists. After 1246 this emerging Chichimec elite forged a dynastic link with the surviving Toltec aristocracy of Culhuacán. This infusion of the northern invaders invigorated the culture of central Mexico and eventually led to a new period of political dynamism. The civilization that resulted from this cultural exchange, however, was more militaristic and violent than that of its predecessors.

The Mexicas became important participants in the conflicts of the Valley of Mexico while the city of Atzcapotzalco was the dominant political power. Valued for their military prowess and despised for their cultural backwardness, Mexica warriors served as mercenaries. They initially received permission to settle in Chapultepec, now a beautiful park in Mexico City, but jealous and fearful neighbors drove them out. With the acquiesence of their Tepanec overlords in Atzcapotzalco, the Mexicas then moved to a small island in the middle of Lake Texcoco where they could more easily defend themselves from attack. Here in 1325 or soon afterward they began to build their capital of Tenochtitlán. Despite their improved reputation, they continued for nearly a century as part-time warriors and tributaries of Atzcapotzalco.

By 1376 the Mexicas had moved from a political organization based on clans *(calpulli)* to a monarchy. Their first king *(tlatoani)*, Acampichtli, claimed descent from the Toltec dynasty of Tula. After a period of consolidation, the new state undertook an ambitious and successful campaign of military expansion. Under Itzcóatl, the ruler from 1426 to 1440, the Mexica allied with two other city-states, Texcoco and Tlacopan, located on the shore of Lake Texcoco. In a surprise attack this triple alliance conquered the city of Atzcapotzalco in 1428 and consolidated control over much of the valley. During Moctezuma I's rule from 1440 to 1468, the Mexicas gained ascendancy over their two allies, pushed outward from the valley, and established control over much of central Mexico. Following an interlude of weaker, less effective rulers, serious expansion resumed during the reign of Ahuitzotl from 1486 to 1502, and Aztec armies conquered parts of Oaxaca, Guatemala, and the Gulf coast. By the early sixteenth century, few pockets of unconquered peoples, principally the Tarascans of Michoacán and the Tlaxcalans of Puebla, remained in central Mexico.

When Moctezuma II took the throne in 1502 he inherited a society that in less than a century had risen from obscurity to political hegemony over a vast region. Tenochtitlán had a population of several hundred thousand persons, many of them immigrants, and the whole Valley of Mexico was home to perhaps 1.5 million. Social transformation accompanied this rapid expansion of political control and demographic growth. Before securing their first *tlatoani,* the Mexica society had a relatively egalitarian structure resting on the *calpulli,* a socioeconomic unit originally based on kinship that was common throughout Mesoamerica. This fundamental social unit, normally a group of families residing in one place, had its own patron deity, temple, and school. It provided military service and controlled access to the land on which its members lived and to other resources such as fishing and hunting rights. The *calpulli's* ability to redistribute land held jointly by its members was more important to rural and semirural areas than to urban centers. There also were noteworthy differences in wealth, prestige, and power within each *calpulli* and among all *calpullin.* The *calpulli's* leader, however—always elected from the same family—handled the local judicial and administrative affairs with the advice of a council of elders.

After the triple alliance conquered Atzcapotzalco—the critical event in the evolution of the Mexica and the Aztec empires—Itzcoatl removed the right of selecting future rulers from the *calpullin* councils and gave it to his closest advisers, the newly established "Council of Four" from which his successors would be selected. The power and independence of the ruler continued to expand as triumphant armies added land and tribute to the royal coffers. In the late fifteenth century the ruler also served as high priest: Moctezuma II took the final step by trying to equate himself with Huitzilopochtli, the Mexicas' most important deity.

The appearance of a hereditary nobility, the *pipiltin,* followed the selection of Acamapichtli as the Mexicas' first *tlatoani.* Acamapichtli had many wives and concubines who were the daughters of the most prominent Mexica warriors and priests. Through their father, the children claimed descent from the Toltecs and Quetzalcóatl and thus a divine lineage. In the 1420s, according to later Mexica propaganda, the *pipiltin* used the imminent conflict with Atzcapotzalco to strike a bargain with the commoners, or *macehualtin,* who preferred to surrender rather than fight. If defeated, the *pipiltin* would henceforth obey the *macehuales;* if victorious, the *macehualtin* would obey them. The alleged bargain justified the *tlatoani's* and *pipiltin's* seizing most of the lands and tribute taken in the defeat of Atzcapotzalco. This victory expanded the nobility's status and widened the social and economic gulf between them and the commoners. The *pipiltin* participated actively in the later military campaigns and, by virtue of birth and military service, won many of the ensuing benefits, such as land, office, and labor.

The *pipiltin* received a share of the lands and tribute in from the conquered areas, the amount apparently related to their administrative position and rank. They staffed the highest military positions, the civil bureaucracy, and the priesthood. Their sons went to schools to prepare them for careers of service to the state. Noblemen had one principal wife and numerous concubines. This polygyny resulted in a disproportionate growth in the number of nobles and helped promote military expansion as a means of sustaining their pretensions.

Except for those in Tenochtitlán, the *macehuales*—commoners who owned land or who lived in urban *calpulli*—benefited comparatively little from conquest. Instead, as the backbone of the agricultural labor force, they remained subject to work demands by the state and the nobility as well as to military service. Moreover, the advent of a powerful hereditary nobility reduced the commoners' ability to influence political decisions. Although a few *macehuales* advanced in society by means of success on the battlefield or service in the priesthood, the potential for upward social mobility was much diminished after the initial period of imperial expansion.

At the base of Aztec society were the vanquished commoners and slaves. *Mayeques* were commoners whose *calpullin* had lost their lands in war and thus had to work for their conquerors. They formed perhaps 30 percent of the population of central Mexico by the early sixteenth century, whereas slaves numbered perhaps 5 percent. Slaves were most often found around Tenochtitlán, where the Mexicas often received them as tribute. In addition, judges punished certain criminal acts by enslaving the offender; prisoners of war were also enslaved. And adults often voluntarily gave up their freedom to ensure themselves food, housing, and clothes. But even though slaves were regarded as property, their children did not inherit this status.

Another group in Mexica society was the craftsmen—goldsmiths, jewelers, and featherworkers—who were urban commoners but ranked above other *macehuales*. A more specialized group of merchants, the *pochteca*, lived in Tlatelolco, an island city adjoining Tenochtitlán. Rich and powerful, they tried unsuccessfully to wrest control from the ruler Axayacatl in 1473, thereby losing many of their privileges until Moctezuma II restored all except their exemption from tribute. The *pochteca* handled long-distance trade with areas outside Aztec control. Not only did they play an important economic role, but they also provided information to the emperor about unconquered peoples and restive subjects. Despite their aid to and benefits from Aztec expansion, the *pochteca* were excluded from high-ranking administrative and political positions.

The gap between the hereditary aristocracy and the commoners grew during the fifteenth century. The dominant *pipiltin* subjected the rest of society to an increasingly harsh regime. A growing problem with drunkenness may have been one result of commoners' inability to adjust to the new social and economic realities. At the same time, most of the nobles lost power relative to that of the ruler and his court.

The economy of Mesoamerica rested on agriculture; with most of the people engaging in the cultivation and harvest of maize, beans, squash, chilies, and a variety of garden vegetables. Under Aztec rule, however, the *pochteca* traded with peoples living as far away as Central America, exporting embroidered cloth, blankets made from rabbit fur, obsidian knives, jewelry, medicinal herbs, and dyes in exchange for unfinished goods that included semiprecious stones, quetzal and other feathers, pearls, and untanned animal skins. The state forbade them, however, to trade in tribute items: cotton, cotton cloth, gold, and cacao beans.

The biggest market in central Mexico, in Tlatelolco, daily served tens of thousands of buyers and sellers. The stalls were in neat rows, with foodstuffs dominating the market. Jewelry, feathers, and precious stones were in one row, slaves in another, and cooking utensils and building materials in still another. Although neither a monetary system nor credit was used for these transactions, cacao beans often were.

Religious rituals overseen by a large and powerful priesthood ruled public life in Tenochtitlán. The Mexicas worshiped a complex mix of deities and spirits, including Quetzalcóatl, the culture god associated with Teotihuacán; Tezcatlipoca, the war god of the Toltecs; Tlaloc, the ancient Mesoamerican rain god; and Tonatiuh, the warrior sun. The center of the

Aztecs' religious life, however, was the cult of Huitzilopochtli, a demanding tribal god that the Mexicas had worshiped before making the long journey south to the Valley of Mexico. As the Mexicas grew in might and wealth after 1428, the cult of Huitzilopochtli expanded as well, and Huitzilopochtli became the most important god of the pantheon, absorbing qualities previously associated with other deities and continually requiring human sacrifices. Most importantly, the Mexicas used Huitzilopochtli to justify their military expansion and the creation of a tribute empire. The imposition of this bloody cult accompanied each new conquest.

The Mexicas believed that only the daily sacrifice of human hearts could provide the magical substance necessary for the sun to rise and the world to survive. Although human sacrifice had been common in Mesoamerica for centuries, if not millennia, the Aztecs practiced it on an unprecedented scale. Continued warfare and the provision of sacrificial victims to Huitzilopochtli to sustain the sun became sacred duties, and as the Mexicas' power grew, bloody public sacrifices to other gods, such as the fertility deity Xipe Totec, were added to their religious practice. The Mexicas' special mission justified and required conquest and tribute, they believed, and drew fanatical energy from noble and commoner warriors alike. Capturing enemies in battle brought tangible rewards, whereas perishing in battle or on an enemy's sacrificial stone secured an afterlife of luxury and pleasure.

War captives, criminals, slaves, and persons supplied by subject peoples as tribute fell victim to the obsidian sacrificial blade atop the great pyramids. After a victory ceremony, warriors often provided a feast for friends and relatives, in which the sacrificed captives' flesh was served in a stew. But by the mid-fifteenth century the Aztecs' military expansion had slowed and, with it, the supply of sacrificial victims. To solve this shortfall, the Mexicas resorted to "flower wars," conflicts with limited political objectives that were fought with nearby peoples also anxious for sacrificial victims. After taking their prisoners to Tenochtitlán, the Mexicas brought in aristocrats from Tlaxcala and other rival states to witness the sacrifices, which might include their own people. Seated in flower-covered boxes, the guests learned a political lesson that transcended the ceremony's religious content: Rebellion, deviance, and opposition to the Aztec state were extremely dangerous. Indeed, in 1487 the Mexicas dedicated the new temple of Huitzilopochtli in Tenochtitlán by sacrificing more (some sources say many more) than twenty thousand persons.

Even the conquered peoples' gods' images went to Tenochtitlán, where they were kept in a pantheon of captive deities. In short, the Aztecs fully exploited their conquered peoples, giving—commoners at least—nothing in return. Not surprisingly, such exploitation fostered deep hostility toward the Aztecs in much of central Mexico.

The Aztecs united their conquered territories through taxation and tribute rather than strong cultural or political institutions. Resident tribute collectors were the sinews of the empire and received tribute payments every eighty days. This tribute was in addition to what the commoners already paid their local rulers. Behind the tax collectors stood the army, the ultimate weapon to enforce the payment of taxes and to suppress dissension within the empire. The ruling families in conquered areas well knew that Aztec favor was indispensable to their survival, and in addition, cooperation brought them economic benefits and support for their continued rule. Although their children often married Aztec nobles—thus admitting spies to their midst—this also strengthened their authority.

While recognizing the human cost of their empire, one must also appreciate that the Aztecs did accomplish much. They built magnificent temples, created a generally effective army, and developed an elaborate ideology that tied together warfare, human sacrifice, and religion. The construction and provisioning of Tenochtitlán, the development of extended commercial routes and large-scale markets, the creation of an effective educational and propaganda system, and the spread of Nahuatl as a common tongue throughout the region also were noteworthy achievements.

The Incas

The Incas created the largest indigenous empire in the Americas and developed the most sophisticated political and administrative structure found among the native peoples there. In the thirteenth century the Incas were one of many competing military powers in the southern highlands of Peru. Then, in less than a century, they extended their empire, Tawantinsuyu or "land of the four quarters," from the Valley of Cuzco on to the northern border of what is now Ecuador and to the Maule River in Chile. The ruler Pachacuti (1438–71) was the prime architect of this territorial expansion and the Incan administrative structure. He first conquered the highland regions near Cuzco and, with his son and successor Topa Inca, pushed the empire's borders into the highlands of northern Peru. Topa Inca (1471–93) later conquered the Chimu and extended the Incas' control over the vast coastal plain and the southern highlands. Huayna Capac (1493–1525) then made the final additions to the empire in successful campaigns against the peoples of present-day Ecuador.

From the beginning, the Incas' power was rooted in the efficient organization and administration of their resources. Indeed, their conquest and later control of distant regions depended more on their ability to organize and supply large fighting forces than on new military technology or tactical innovations. Relying on nobles for officers, the Incas used conscripted peasants for the bulk of the army, but they also employed mercenaries. After conquering a region, they conscripted its male population and advanced farther into historically hostile adjacent regions, promising the new subjects an opportunity to even old scores and gain the spoils of victory. Unlike the Aztecs, Incan armies were not interested in taking prisoners, and thus death in battle was more common. But the Incas' frequent successes were a powerful lure in enlisting defeated peoples for participation in future conquests.

An excellent road system in the Andes and along the coast, the maintenance of a network of runners for communication over long distances, and a system of state-organized warehouses of clothing, food, and weapons facilitated the Incas' military readiness and political control. The empire had over 25,000 kilometers of road, much of it predating the Incas. Relay runners could carry messages from Lima to Cuzco in three days and from the capital to Quito in less than a week. In the absence of writing, they carried *khipus (quipus)*, multicolored, knotted strings that served as memory aids.

The omnipresent llamas gave the Incas both draft animals and a mobile meat supply. In addition, every district of the empire reserved some portion of its production—maize, potatoes, wool, cotton, or other goods—for hard times and also for the Incan army and bureaucracy.

The Incas were superb organizers rather than great innovators; unlike the Mexicas, they sought to centralize their empire around its capital in Cuzco. They divided it territorially into four major regions, eighty provinces, and more than twice that many districts, each with a number of *ayllus*, the smallest territorial units. At each level were officials who reported to superiors, the entire pyramidal system culminating in the Sapa Inca, or emperor. Such a system of communication also functioned as a chain of command emanating from the emperor. Close relatives of the emperor administered the four quarters, and other Incan nobles, the eighty provinces. Local and regional chieftains, or *kurakas*, headed the smaller units and formed the local political bases. The Incas generally used the existing political structures and established elite groups at the local level. Even when rebellion or insubordination forced changes in the administration, the Incas preferred to appoint officials drawn from the families of the deposed rulers.

The imperial social structure largely reflected pre-Inca social organization under a growing and more demanding hereditary nobility related to the Incan rulers. The basic social unit above the family was, again, the *ayllu*, a kin group that had a common ancestry and a hereditary chieftain or *kuraka* advised by village elders. *Ayllu* members worked on the same property, helped one another in a system of mutual obligation, and labored for their leaders, who provided reciprocal benefits in accord with long-standing Andean tradition. Individuals unattached to *ayllus* were known as *yanacona* and were employed by the Incan rulers to maintain themselves, favored nobles, deities, and the cult of royal mummies.

Ancestor worship and *huacas*—sacred items, persons, or places—were central to Andean life long before the Incas appeared. Each *ayllu* had its own deities and shrines supported by land farmed to provide sacrifices to them. On matters of import, the villagers consulted prominent ancestors—rulers, the founders of *ayllus,* and *kurakas*—whose mummies were carefully preserved in necropoli and brought out during ritual celebrations. The demands of ancestor and *huaca* worship were originally modest—periodic gifts of food, beverage, and textiles—and the preimperial *ayllus* had little difficulty in meeting them. But then Pachacuti introduced royal ancestor worship on a scale that had far-reaching consequences for the empire.

When an emperor died, his chosen heir, a son born to his principal wife, inherited the office and responsibilities of the Sapa Inca but not his father's wealth. The deceased emperor's other male descendants, the *panaca,* received his physical possessions as a trust to maintain his mummy and cult. This living court treated the dead emperor as though he were alive, a holy object tangibly linked to the Inca pantheon. Because the *panaca* continued to hold the emperor's personal possessions after his death, the share of the state's wealth devoted to the royal mummy cults increased. Consequently, the new Incan emperor had to secure his own resources for support in life and death; by raising taxes or expanding the empire and thus the base for tribute. It was the royal mummy cults and the system for their support, therefore, that led to the Incas' dramatic territorial expansion.

Religion was central to the Incas' life. In its upper pantheon was a sky god of innumerable distinct aspects that Spanish chroniclers mistakenly considered to be independent deities. The three principal manifestations of this sky god were Viracocha, a creator god of ancient origin; Illapa, the god of thunder and weather; and Inti, the sun god. Because the Incan rulers claimed descent from one manifestation of Inti, he held the central place in the state's ancestor cult, providing the Incan rulers with links to divinity and the Incan people with a sense of identity and, ultimately, confidence in a mission of expansion. The Incas transported the idols of their conquered peoples to Cuzco where they were kept in the sun temple. In return, they spread Inti's cult as part of their conquest, constructing temples to him throughout the empire. Compared with that of central Mexico, the Incas' priesthood was modest in size. Human sacrifice, moreover, was rare and designed to win the deities' goodwill rather than to maintain the universe. Instead, animals, food, fine textiles, and beverages were the usual sacrifices.

In most of their conquered lands, the Incas maintained the existing productive practices. The peoples of the Andes had long valued collective labor to farm, mine, weave, build, and maintain essential services; reciprocal rights and obligations and custom largely defined the nature of an individual's labor. Before the Incas arrived, the region's inhabitants had developed complex administrative and territorial structures to organize labor for irrigation and cultivation and to provide for the exchange of specialized goods across ecologically distinct zones. Called by some the "archipelago" pattern, the hamlet kinship groups, *ayllus,* placed settlers in distinct ecological zones so as to ensure their access to a range of products—maize, potatoes, cotton, llamas, and coca, among others. The expansion of the imperial bureaucracy, the requirements of the army, and the maintenance of the royal ancestor cults, however, meant that the state had to control any surplus production.

The Inca levied a rotational labor tax, the *mita,* on *ayllus* to secure workers for agricultural lands held by the state and its religious cults, as well as to engage them in the construction of roads, bridges, fortresses, temples, palaces, terraces, and irrigation projects. Terracing and irrigation brought previously uncultivated and, at times, marginal lands into production, usually to grow maize. Expanding on an earlier Andean practice, the Incas sent groups of colonists from their homes to produce ecologically specialized products in conquered regions. These *mitmaq* also helped secure subject territories militarily.

The state stored in numerous regional warehouses the goods produced by labor taxation and specialized craftsmen. Administrators distributed them to state employees, to *mita* laborers as payment for their service, and to other persons as the need arose. Shared labor and economic redistribution existed in the Andes long before the rise of the Inca state; the Incas' innovation was to organize the resources over a much larger area and thus mitigate the effects of drought and other natural disasters. There was no form of money in the central Andean highlands, and private trading was limited to Peru's north and central coasts and Ecuador's highlands.

The Incas' advances in economic and political organization eroded the local autonomy and social equality in the Andes; in fact, the imperial elite and the expanding state bureaucracy became almost completely cut off from the masses of agricultural workers and craftsmen. At the same time, the *kurakas* were increasingly separated from the Indian masses.

The Incas' cultural achievements were largely derived from those of earlier Andean civilizations. Their monumental architecture featured superb stone masonry, but the absence of arches and vaulting gave the buildings a squat appearance. The Incas' exquisite textiles and ceramics and silver and gold work also continued older traditions. Although astronomical observation was a central concern of the priestly class, as in Mesoamerica, the Incas' calendric system has been lost, but their astronomy appears to have been inferior to that of the Mayas. Likewise, the Mesoamerican glyphs and pictographs were clearly superior to the Incas' *khipus* for non-oral communication. Instead, Andean superiority over Mesoamerica was most evident in political organization and the expansion of agricultural productivity through terracing and irrigation. In addition, the Incas contributed more to the peoples they defeated than did the Mexicas. Increased agricultural production in parts of the highlands; the introduction of llamas, mainly in northern Peru; and the economic benefits of peace throughout the empire were among the Incas' most important contributions. Moreover, they attempted to centralize their empire through political organization, the use of religion and ideology, the adoption of the Quechua language, and the resettlement of peoples.

The complexity of the Inca and Aztec empires and their cultural attainments were unparalleled in the Americas in 1500. Yet these high cultures shared a number of characteristics with the area's other indigenous peoples: All New World societies lacked iron and hard metal tools, with the exception of a small amount of bronze used by the Incas. Aside from llamas and their relatives in the Andes, there were no large domestic animals available for transport, food, or clothing. Humans transported goods without the benefit of wheeled vehicles. And religion and belief in the supernatural were widespread. Despite these commonalities, however, these various New World societies were marked more by their diversity of cultural, economic, and political achievements, a fact that profoundly affected the course of Iberian conquest and settlement.

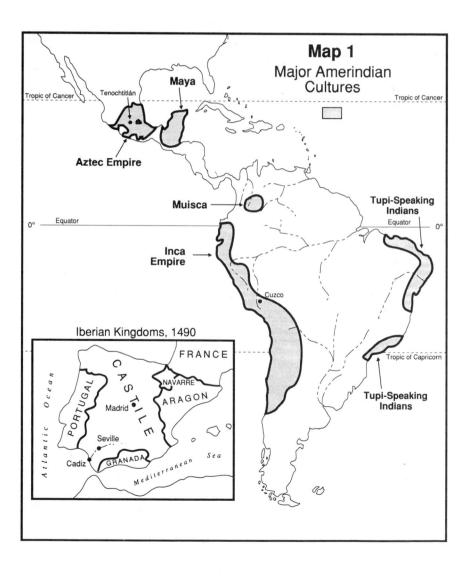

Map 1

Major Amerindian Cultures

The Iberian World in the Late Fifteenth Century

The Iberian peninsula, from whence the conquistadors and settlers of the New World came, is but a fraction of the size of the erstwhile Spanish and Portuguese empires in the Americas. Long a part of the Roman world, Iberia endured centuries of political dislocation following the Germanic invasions that began in the fifth century. The repeated failure to resolve the problem of monarchical succession and bitter conflicts among Christian sects rendered the Visigothic kingdom incapable of withstanding the Muslim invasion launched in 711. Divided by differing regional, political, cultural, and linguistic identities, the Iberians carried to the New World attitudes formed during the Reconquest, nearly eight centuries of intermittent conflict with the Islamic civilizations that had overtaken the peninsula. The Iberians' own social, cultural, and geographical diversity enabled the conquistadors to perceive, and to manipulate to their own benefit, a similar diversity in the loose collection of cultures that they found in Mesoamerica and the Andes.

With the exception of the Pyrenees Mountains that form its northern boundary with France, Iberia is surrounded by water. The Mediterranean Sea on the east and south extends to the Straits of Gibraltar, the narrow expanse that separates the peninsula's southern tip from Africa by 10 miles. The Atlantic Ocean and the Cantabrian Sea encircle the remainder of the peninsula. Just over 225,000 square miles in area, Iberia is slightly smaller than the states of Arizona and New Mexico combined. Its landscape is dominated by mountains whose mean altitude is higher than that in any western European country except Switzerland. Although flatlands can be found, mainly on the Portuguese coast, range after range breaks Iberia's terrain into a patchwork of distinct regions. Coupled with few navigable rivers, the mountains make transportation and communication difficult and obstruct political and economic integration. Although its northern and northwestern parts receive substantial rainfall, much of Iberia is dry. A Spanish proverb summarizes the weather of the great central tableland as "nine months of winter and three months of hell."

The Reconquest

The Reconquest created a cultural legacy that the conquistadors and settlers carried to the New World. Although Christians and Muslims struggled intermittently to control Iberia, from about 718 to 1492, the most active years were between about 850 and 1250. During this time, Christian knights and settlers pushed south from their initial redoubt in the mountains of northern Spain. Although the Reconquest is often labeled a crusade, its religious zeal only complemented the more mundane and important objectives of securing additional grazing and agricultural land. Military action was most frequently a raid for booty, including slaves. But slowly and sporadically the Christians pushed the frontier south.

In 1147 Lisbon was recovered, and in 1179 the pope recognized Alfonso I of the House of Burgundy as the first monarch of the independent kingdom of Portugal. By the mid-thirteenth century the Portuguese had taken the southern coastal region known as the Algarve and expelled the Muslims from their territory. A change of dynasty in 1384 brought the House of Aviz to the throne, and during an almost fifty-year reign, the first monarch, John I, consolidated his position and set the stage for the creation of Portugal's overseas empire.

But with the Castilian seizure of Seville in 1248, Islamic domination was reduced to the kingdom of Granada. Although subsequent Christian princes occasionally engaged the Muslims in battle, the final phase of the Reconquest did not begin until 1482. In that year Isabella and Ferdinand responded to a Muslim attack on a Christian town and launched a war that lasted until the city of Granada surrendered on January 2, 1492.

Royal families, valorous warriors, a militant Church, and military orders founded to spearhead the Christian advance reaped the initial rewards of land, booty, and tribute. Military prowess brought lordship over subject peoples and immediate economic gain; thus serving a king in arms became the Iberian Christians' preferred route to wealth and honor. As the Reconquest progressed, Christian settlers entered the conquered frontier regions, often locating in former Muslim cities and villages. But with the consolidation of territorial gains, the pressure of a growing population for additional land renewed the cycle of military conflict.

The final triumph over the Muslims in Granada reinforced the booty mentality that the Iberian Christians had developed during the long Reconquest: The victorious Christians enslaved fifteen thousand Muslim inhabitants of Malaga. Nobles who had contributed to victory gained jurisdiction over areas with large Muslim populations. Commoners received land and in some cases ennoblement for their valor, through royal grants that again confirmed the importance of military service for social advancement. Conveniently, the Christians saw their triumph as evidence that their God actively supported their cause, a belief that they carried into battle against the native civilizations of the Americas.

Iberia in the Age of Ferdinand and Isabella

In the mid-fifteenth century five independent kingdoms occupied Iberia. Portugal, whose boundaries approximated those of the modern country, had a population of perhaps 1 million persons in the late fifteenth century. Thus it was only slightly less populous than the Crown of Aragon, which held sway in the northeast and maintained long-standing territorial and commercial interests in the Mediterranean, including ties to Italy, Byzantium, and the east. Granada, the remaining Muslim stronghold located in the southeast, had some 500,000 persons; Navarre, a small kingdom in the western Pyrenees, had fewer than 200,000. At the center of the peninsula lay Castile, whose area was more than triple that of either Portugal or Aragon and whose population of perhaps 4.5 million persons was roughly four times as large. This geographic and demographic dominance increased even more when Castile conquered Granada in 1492 and annexed Navarre in 1512.

The most significant domestic event in Iberian history between the mid-fifteenth century and the fall of Granada was the marriage in 1469 of Isabella of Castile and Ferdinand of Aragon. In 1468 Isabella had been reluctantly recognized by her half-brother Henry IV as the heir to Castile; such was the price of peace in his realm. Henry's reluctance can be traced to his wife's daughter Juana. Juana is also known to historians as La Beltraneja, after Beltran de la Cueva, who was her mother's lover and—according to Isabella's supporters—Juana's father. Although the charge was probably baseless, Henry, a weak monarch, was cursed with the epithet "The Impotent," and Isabella made the most of her opportunity. Aided by a forged papal bull permitting her to marry a close relative, she wed Ferdinand, heir to the throne of Aragon. Isabella was clearly a woman of strong will, who had already rejected marriage to the widowed King Alfonso of Portugal and the French suitor Charles of Valois. Ferdinand of Aragon was the energetic and ambitious son of John II, who saw in Castile the resources necessary to combat French designs on his kingdom's border.

After Henry IV died in December 1474, Isabella declared herself the queen of Castile. In response, Juana claimed the throne in May 1475 with military support from Portugal and an anti-Aragonese faction at the court of Castile. The ensuing civil war ended in Isabella's victory in 1479. When his father died in the same year, Ferdinand became the king of Aragon, and the "union of the crowns" and a "double monarchy" became reality. For the following quarter-century, the "Catholic Kings"—as the couple were later dubbed by Pope Alexander VI—jointly ruled the largest and wealthiest area of Iberia.

The name Spain is often used to describe the realms of Isabella and Ferdinand, but the term erroneously implies a nonexistent unity. Both Castile and Aragon maintained separate economies, political institutions, monetary systems, customs barriers, and life-styles. Even though the two monarchs worked together so closely that a chronicler recorded, for example, "the king and queen, on such and such a day, gave birth to a daughter," they never, as did their counterparts elsewhere in Europe, sought political unification of their kingdoms. Although their grandson Charles V inherited both crowns, the creation of a single Spanish polity awaited the abolition of the traditional rights *(fueros)* of the Crown of Aragon in the early eighteenth century.

Earlier, during the unhappy reign of Henry IV (1454–74), the most powerful noble families of Castile exerted a political influence that rivaled the Crown's. Henry accordingly attempted to strengthen his power in ways that anticipated actions by the Catholic Kings: He employed *corregidores,* royal agents assigned to major towns, to provide justice and secure compliance with the Crown's will. He also reorganized the Holy Brotherhood (Hermandad), a league of law officers hired by municipalities, and increased the appointment of university-educated officials. Henry's open-handed grants of land, jurisdictional rights, offices, and incomes in an effort to buy the loyalty of high aristocrats ultimately failed, however, and consequently Isabella inherited serious financial and political problems.

Isabella's victory over La Beltraneja enabled her to consolidate and extend her royal authority within Castile. Substantial military and political support from many powerful families during the civil war emphasized their importance as allies and the threat they posed if discontented. Consequently the queen moved carefully to maintain their continued support. By confirming most of Henry's grants to them, she ensured the nobility's economic and social preeminence, but at the same time, she worked to curb their political strength.

The queen used a further reorganized Hermandad to end the anarchy plaguing Castile and bring peace to the countryside. Its agents captured

Punishment of a thief in sixteenth-century Spain

malefactors and meted out justice. The imposition of royal justice restored order in rural areas, and the destruction of castles held by nobles who had sided with La Beltraneja was further evidence of the queen's intention to rule as well as reign. In 1480 the Catholic Kings resolved to increase the number of *corregidores* and to send them into all the major cities. As Henry IV had, they turned to men with a university education to staff many of the royal offices. Both Henry and Isabella turned their personal attention to administering justice—the essence of kingship—and enlarging the judicial system to make it more accessible and effective. In addition, they reorganized the Council of Castile. The queen appointed to this supreme advisory, judicial, and administrative body university-educated jurists who were lower-ranking aristocrats or commoners rather than more illustrious nobles. Taken together, the monarchs' actions strengthened the Crown of Castile's authority and increased its ability to implement diplomatic, economic, fiscal, and religious policies.

The Portuguese monarchy in the late fifteenth century was heir to a tradition of strong centralized rule occasionally disrupted by high-ranking nobles eager to enhance their wealth and power. The unprecedented revenue resulting from the Crown's monopoly over trade with newly discovered lands, however, enabled John II (1481–95) to reassert the royal authority lost by his predecessor. John expanded the judicial system and increased the number of provincial administrators *(corregedores)*. In addition, he executed for treason the duke of Braganza, the richest and most influential noble in the realm, and enlarged the royal patrimony in the process. Centralization was again ascendant, although, as in Castile, the aristocracy retained social and economic dominance.

Society

Society in Castile and Portugal shared many characteristics: Each kingdom recognized three estates—clergy, nobility, and commoners—and a number of corporate bodies with special legal privileges. Birth and family normally determined an individual's place in the social hierarchy. Ties created through godparentage and client–patron relationships also were important to both societies. Each kingdom contained Jews, Muslims, Italians and other foreigners, and black slaves, and neither had many professionals or merchants.

At the top of the Castilian and Portuguese social hierarchies were a few great families that bore titles of duke, marquis, or count. In Castile the greatest nobles controlled half of the kingdom's land, and in Portugal a similar group of about fifteen families also held noble titles, extensive lands, and economic power. Other titled nobles, often indistinguishable from the first in resources, formed a second tier of Castile's hierarchy. In Portugal some two thousand nontitled nobles received land grants and incomes from the monarchy and constituted an upper-middle nobility. Together these groups were at the apex of their respective social orders.

From 1505 onward, high-ranking Castilian nobles could create entailed estates, or *mayorazgos,* which enabled the preservation of property in perpetuity and formed the basis for consolidating through marriage still larger estates.

The remainder of the nobility were knights known as *caballeros (cavaleiros)* or gentlemen, *hidalgos (fidalgos).* In Castile they used the prefix *don* and proudly displayed coats of arms. Their status exempted them from direct taxation and provided additional privileges denied to commoners. The *hidalgos'* economic resources varied considerably: The wealthiest in Castile were indistinguishable from the poorer titled nobles, whereas the poorer *hidalgos* possessed less than did well-to-do commoners. Commoners coveted nobility for both its social cachet and its privileges. Recognizing their desire for noble rank, Castilian monarchs gave and, from the 1520s, sold to them patents of nobility. Thus in both Castile and Portugal a trickle of new families continuously entered the most privileged class in society.

Commoners accounted for over 90 percent of the Iberian population. Most engaged in agricultural or pastoral activities. Although many owned land, frequently it was just a garden plot. Most commoners worked a noble's land for remuneration that at best provided subsistence. A few commoners held professional positions, serving in the clergy, practicing law, or engaging in commerce. Not a bourgeoisie or true middle class, their highest ambition was ennoblement. Though few succeeded, some of the wealthiest did make the transition. Below them were artisans, themselves divided into guilds ranked by prestige, with silversmiths the most honored and cobblers the least.

Although few in number, successful foreign merchants and their descendants formed colonies in Iberia's commercial centers. For example, Genoa's commercial families had their largest Spanish colony in Seville. Their compatriots and other Italian merchants also resided in Lisbon and other Portuguese ports, from which they controlled the kingdom's long-distance trade. Although Iberian merchants were active in Burgos, Medina del Campo, Barcelona, Lisbon, Oporto, and other trading centers, the noble values of the Reconquest—valor and virture, land, warfare, and religion—stigmatized trade as demeaning for aristocrats. It required the overseas expansion of the fifteenth and sixteenth centuries to modify this attitude.

Slaves constituted a small segment of society, though slavery had long been known in Iberia, as captives taken in the Reconquest fighting frequently were enslaved. But when Portuguese traders began importing slaves from Africa in 1441, they transformed the nature of slavery on the peninsula. By 1492 more than 35,000 black slaves had reached Portugal. Although some remained in servitude there, many were reexported. By the late fifteenth century, both Seville and Valencia had large slave populations and active slave markets. Most slaves worked as domestic servants or as unskilled laborers, and the association of dark skin with slavery had become firmly established before the settlement of the New World.

Although by the time of the Reconquest Iberia contained Christians,

Muslims, and Jews, religious tolerance had disappeared by the early sixteenth century. Isabella and Ferdinand followed up the victory over the
Muslim minority in 1492 by giving the Jews four months either to convert
to Christianity or emigrate. Perhaps 80,000 of the 200,000 Jews in Castile
and Aragon fled rather than give up their faith. But they took with them
knowledge and skills that the kingdoms could ill afford to lose, although
the remaining *conversos* continued in their occupations as tax collectors,
financiers, physicians, and the like. Spain's loss was Portugal's gain, as John
II allowed the exiled Jews to enter his kingdom and remain for some
months in return for monetary payments. After the prescribed period
ended, the wealthiest Jews purchased permits allowing permanent residence. In 1497, however, John's successor Manuel I (1495–1521) ordered
the conversion or expulsion of all Jews in his kingdom. Some accepted
baptism and remained, but others returned to Spain or emigrated to Holland and other countries. Those who remained in the peninsula joined the
converso or New Christian minorities.

As the final blow in creating religious homogeneity, Isabella and Ferdinand in 1502 ordered the expulsion or conversion of the remaining Muslims in Castile. Approximately 200,000 had already emigrated after the fall
of Granada. But because the terms of the 1502 measure made exile tan-
tamount to the confiscation of their property, nearly all of the remaining
Muslims accepted baptism. In Portugal Manuel I had ordered the small
number of free Muslims to leave in 1497, thus establishing a single religion
for his realm as well.

Although the expulsions imposed a superficial religious homogeneity,
the new converts still suffered discrimination because of their religious
background and ancestry. "Old Christians" had viewed the *conversos* with
suspicion for many years. Systematic discrimination against the "New
Christians" in some jobs and universities then began in mid-fifteenth-cen-
tury Castile and continued for centuries. The sudden increase in the number of *conversos* in Portugal also created social and religious tensions that
resulted in riots, pogroms, and an official discrimination policy forbidding
New Christians to hold public offices, receive honors, or marry nobles.

Suspicion that the *conversos* were secretly practicing their former religion led Isabella in the 1470s and the Portuguese in 1547 to establish tribunals of the Inquisition to investigate the genuineness of the *conversos'*
Christianity. Indeed, the Spanish Inquisition proved so effective in prosecuting Judaizers that by 1500 it had largely met its initial goal of eliminating them.

Noble or commoner, wealthy or poor, Iberians preferred to reside in
cities, towns, and villages rather than in widely scattered dwellings in the
countryside. As the Christians moved south during the Reconquest, the
monarchs chartered towns and granted privileges to entice occupation and
settlement. Town coucils were routinely established and aldermen and officials selected. Within Castile seventeen towns (eighteen after Granada was
conquered) were represented in the Cortes, or parliament.

Cities, towns, and villages housed clerics, local officials, merchants, and artisans. Even nobles with rich estates normally spent much of the year in town houses. For the majority of the population—*labradores* who worked the small properties they owned or rented and wage-earning day laborers who worked in agriculture or pastoral activities—towns and villages were home. Most walked to fields in the adjoining countryside each workday and spent few nights away from home.

The settlement pattern of clustered residences fostered pride in the local region, the town and adjacent rural lands that fell within its jurisdiction. Kinship ties supplemented by bonds created through godparentage resulted in tight extended family groups that were the primary social units, with political and economic overtones. Individuals tended to maintain a strong allegiance to their native region as well as to their families. Local residents regarded outsiders with suspicion; it required years of residence and the development of social and economic ties for an outsider to enter the local society.

Economy

In the late fifteenth century only Seville, Granada, Toledo, and Lisbon had populations in excess of thirty thousand persons. Thus numerous smaller communities provided many of the cultural activities and social and economic opportunities without which Iberians considered civilization nonexistent and living conditions intolerable. Urban centers were the locus of local economic exchange and social contact.

Agricultural and pastoral activities were the foundation of the Iberian economies. Although the yield was low, grain production on the Castilian plateau was ample enough in good years to permit exporting a surplus to the poorer regions of Galicia, Asturias, and Vizcaya to the west and north. In lean years, however, even Castile had to import grain from abroad, and beginning in 1502 the Crown started to fix the maximum price of grain. Portugal was chronically short of wheat and other cereals, and by 1500 imports of grain were commonplace. In contrast, Andalusia exported grain, first to Aragon and later to the New World. Olive orchards and vineyards completed the traditional triad of Mediterranean agriculture in Spain. In Portugal, wine, fruit, cork, olive oil, salt, and fish were the major products.

High-quality wool from merino sheep dominated Castile's exports in the mid-fifteenth century and continued to do so for many years. Vast numbers of sheep held by members of the mesta, or sheep owner's guild, migrated annually from summer pastures in Aragon to winter forage in Andalusia and Extremadura. Great aristocrats, monasteries, and small private owners sent their sheep on the great walks that traversed Castile but even more sheep stayed home. Although restrictions prohibited owners from letting their sheep wander through planted lands, the immense size of the flocks necessarily reduced the amount of land available for agriculture. The pattern of exporting raw materials (wool) and importing finished goods (textiles) was firmly established before Henry IV ascended the Castilian throne. But lacking a solid industrial base on the eve of empire, Castile failed to develop one in the next three centuries.

Engaging in substantial foreign trade joined northern Castilians with merchants of Barcelona, Seville, and Lisbon in an international mercantile system. The Portuguese, long involved in international trade, in the second half of the fifteenth century were exporting slaves, gold, ivory, and sugar brought from Africa and the Madeira Islands as well as salt and other domestic products in exchange for finished goods. With important bases in Seville and Lisbon, Genoese financiers and merchants comprised an influential foreign presence in Iberian commercial circles.

The Castilian Crown employed a plethora of taxes and tariffs, but the principal source of revenue during the reign of Ferdinand and Isabella was the *alcabala,* a sales tax frequently farmed out to city councils for collection. Although the amount of regular revenue increased more than tenfold during their reign, it was never enough to support the court, the army, and Ferdinand's foreign ventures. Consequently the Crown resorted to borrowing, a recourse that ultimately had disastrous results for the succeeding Habsburg monarchs. The revenue of the Portuguese Crown also rose in the late fifteenth century, but its expenses also repeatedly exceeded its normal tax income.

The Iberian world of the late fifteenth century remained fragmented politically but had become substantially stronger through the union of the crowns of Castile and Aragon and the conquest of Granada. In addition, the forced conversion or exile of non-Christians, the Inquisition's activities against suspected heretics, and the imposition of royal justice had brought a unity to Castile that rivaled that achieved earlier in Portugal. The centralization of royal authority had increased in both kingdoms. The Iberian population was expanding as it continued to recover from the ravages of the fourteenth-century Black Death. The African trade and early exploitation of the Atlantic islands was benefiting Portugal. And with technological advances in sailing vessels and sailors' increased confidence in their ability to undertake lengthy voyages, the way was opened for the great era of exploration.

Exploration and the Caribbean Experiment

The Portuguese capture in 1415 and continued possession of Ceuta across the Strait of Gibraltar opened an era of exploration, trade, conquest, and settlement for the Iberian kingdoms. A little over a century later, the survivors of Ferdinand Magellan's expedition had circumnavigated the globe. Between these two events the Portuguese developed a thriving trade with West Africa, reached India via the Cape of Good Hope, created a successful sugar economy in the Madeira Islands, and discovered Brazil. Columbus led four voyages to the New World, and other subjects of the Crown of Castile settled the Caribbean islands, Central America, and the northern coast of South America and conquered the Aztec Empire in Central Mexico.

Several years after the victory at Ceuta, Prince Henry, the energetic, ambitious, and wealthy younger son of John I (1385–1433), began to promote the exploration of the west African coast—earning from later generations but not contemporaries the nickname "The Navigator," despite his sailing personally only to Morocco. Progress accelerated after 1434 when an expedition finally rounded Africa's fearsome Cape Bojador. By the prince's death in 1460, Portuguese ships had pushed 1,500 miles down the African coast and discovered (or rediscovered) Madeira, the Azores, and the Cape Verdes. The tempo then slowed for two decades as attention focused on exploiting Africa's slaves, ivory, and gold through trade. During the reign of John II (1481–95), Portuguese exploration proceeded with renewed vigor as the young king sought to secure the African lands confirmed as Portuguese by the Treaty of Alcaçovas signed in 1479 with Castile. When Bartholomeu Dias rounded the Cape of Good Hope in 1488, a sea route to India and its spices was open at last.

Discovery of the New World

Within this seafaring environment, an obscure Genoese seaman named Christopher Columbus appeared in Lisbon in 1476. Having already sailed in the Mediterranean and as far north as Iceland, he now joined the mariners most advanced in long-distance travel. He sailed with the Portuguese, married the daughter of one of Prince Henry's sea captains, and for a time lived in the Madeiras. A stubborn, brave man, Columbus believed that God had selected him to spread Christianity throughout the unconverted world and assumed that glory and wealth would crown his success. Unable to admit his own faults, he was loath to recognize his subordinates' virtues. Thus despite being a capable seaman, Columbus would prove hopelessly unsuited for administrative responsibilities.

Portugal, England, and France rejected Columbus's appeals to support his scheme to reach the Indies by sailing west. His failure lay in both his demand for substantial personal rewards and an accurate scholarly appreciation that he was grossly underestimating the distance to Asia. Bartholomeu Dias's voyage further reduced Portugal's interest in the project.

Then Columbus's luck changed. Euphoric after defeating the Muslims and securing Granada, Isabella and Ferdinand agreed to support his enterprise, in the hope of great gains for God and Castile. Striking a bargain with the mariner, the monarchs granted him a patent of nobility, the offices of admiral of the ocean sea and viceroy and governor of the lands found, and a tenth of the gold, silver, spices, and other valuables obtained, in the event he was successful.

With three ships and fewer than ninety men, Columbus sailed first to the

Canary Islands, confirmed as a Castilian possession in the Treaty of Alcaçovas but still not fully conquered or settled. He set forth again in early
September with a year's provisions. After sailing more than three thousand
nautical miles, the gamble paid off when on October 12, 1492, Columbus
and his men sighted an island in the chain later named the Bahamas.

Further exploration revealed Hispaniola and Cuba, the two largest
islands in the Greater Antilles. On Hispaniola Columbus found the gold
he sought and a docile Arawak population. He lavished praise on the
natives—"affectionate people and without covetousness. . . . [They] are
always smiling"[1]—whom he dubbed "Indians" as a result of believing that
he had reached Asia. The Arawaks, also called the Taino, had a peaceful,
sedentary, stratified society. They cultivated yucca, sweet potatoes, maize,
beans, squash, and other plants and harvested fish, turtles, fowl, and other
wildlife. Initially the Arawaks shared their food with the Spaniards and,
under their leaders' direction, provided voluntary labor as well. This
proved especially valuable when the *Santa María* struck a reef and the dis-
mantled wreck was used to build a fort at Navidad. Thirty-nine sailors
remained there while the *Niña* and the *Pinta* returned to Spain in early
1493.

Columbus obtained enough gold through barter on Hispaniola to
ensure a warm reception when he met Isabella in Barcelona in 1493.
Although certain he had reached Asia as intended, Columbus found his
sovereigns dubious but anxious for dominion over whatever land he had
reached. Following medieval custom and a more recent Portuguese precedent, they asked Pope Alexander VI, a protégé of Ferdinand, for title to
the newly discovered territory in return for undertaking the Christianization of its inhabitants. The pope acceded and in a bull dated May 3, 1493,
designated the lands as "islands and firm land" located in "the western
parts of the Ocean Sea, toward the Indies," an identification that neither
confirmed nor denied that the lands were Asiatic. A later bull gave Castile
title to the lands west of a north-south demarcation line one hundred
leagues west of Cape Verde and the Azores.

This papal donation limited Portugal's ambitions, thus causing John II
to react strongly. Faced with the threat of war, in 1494 Castile signed the
Treaty of Tordesillas. Under its terms Portugal received all lands east of a
line of demarcation 370 leagues west of the Cape Verde Islands. Lands
west of the line would belong to Castile, thus giving Portugal title to a
portion of the as-yet-undiscovered Brazil.

Columbus's voyage inaugurated a burst of exploration that quickly
enlarged Europe's geographical knowledge of the New World and the
winds and currents most favorable for sailing to and from it. The intrepid
admiral led three more voyages, the last ending in 1504. During these
same years, a Portuguese expedition headed by Vasco da Gama reached
India by sea. In 1500 Pedro Alvares Cabral followed da Gama's instructions for reaching India by sailing far southwest of Africa to catch the best
winds for rounding the Cape of Good Hope. Voyaging farther west than

planned, he accidentally made contact with the Brazilian coast. This unexpected development proved the wisdom of John II's insistence on revising the papal donation, although for decades the economic benefits of the Brazilian landfall were modest. In 1501 a small fleet that included the Florentine Amerigo Vespucci sailed along the southern coast of Brazil. Numerous coasting expeditions also proceeded north and south from the Caribbean, but the hoped-for strait across the landmass proved elusive. By the mid-1520s ships had coasted from Nova Scotia in the north to Tierra del Fuego in the south. Added to Magellan's voyage, the explorations provided a view of the world's geography that differed greatly from that of a century earlier. In addition, better knowledge of winds and currents reduced the normal travel time necessary to sail to and from the Old and the New Worlds.

Early Settlements

During the same years that exploration illuminated much of the New World's geography, the first confrontations between Spaniards and Indians took place on Hispaniola and the other islands of the Greater Antilles. The quarter-century of experience on the islands revealed problems that recurred over and over when the mainlands were conquered and settled. The different realities of the New World forced the modification of Castilian institutions. Accordingly, the years between 1492 and 1519 were a period of experimentation and capital accumulation that prepared the immigrants for the advance to the mainland.

Columbus reached the Caribbean islands expecting to trade with the inhabitants and to establish factories, or fortified trading stations. This focus on commerce rather than colonization was characteristic of the earlier Genoese and Portuguese expansion in Africa and the Atlantic islands. The Castilian tradition of colonization and settlement used in the Reconquest, however, quickly came to the fore. In late 1493 Columbus returned to Hispaniola with 1,500 men who included seamen, officials, and the first clerics to venture to the New World. The second voyage was organized to establish a permanent settlement, and so the men brought animals, seed, tools, and trading goods, but no European women.

Most of the early immigrants to the islands were from Andalusia. Soon, however, men from Extremadura and the remainder of Castile joined them. Although their backgrounds varied, commoners predominated, and high-ranking noblemen were conspicuously missing. As a group the immigrants had left Spain in the hope of bettering their lot. Though some sought adventure and glory, most pursued the more mundane objective of wealth. Gold or other riches would open the way to social ascent and the trappings that signified the good life as Castilians viewed it: a large residence, horses, retainers and servants, a Spanish wife, and always the ability to offer hospitality to relatives and friends. To fulfill this dream the settlers asserted control over the native labor.

Spaniards who went to the New World expected the natives to work for them. Upon his return to Navidad in 1493, Columbus found that the excesses of the men left behind had resulted in the destruction of their small settlement. The men had physically abused the natives and seized their women; revenge had followed. This incident strained future relations between the Spaniards and the Arawaks, although Columbus did distinguish between "good" or friendly Indians and those that were hostile. But the Spaniards' pillage of foodstuffs during a famine in 1494 and repeated acts of violence eventually drove the natives into a hopeless rebellion. The victors subsequently began punitive expeditions, enslaving the natives and demanding tribute payments from the remaining population.

Columbus had organized his expeditions as a monopoly company. He promised salaries but in fact paid his men irregularly. Dissatisfied with their lot, perhaps half of the settlers on Hispaniola joined Francisco Roldán in a revolt against the authority of the Columbus family. When the admiral returned to the island on his third voyage in 1498, he found his brother Bartolomé's authority challenged. To establish peace, Columbus recognized the grants of Indians that his rivals had made to individual Spaniards.

These allocations, or *repartimientos,* assigned a chieftain and his people to an *encomendero,* as the recipient was known, to work whatever mines and properties he held. Because they guaranteed access to needed labor and gave the recipient high status, *repartimientos* were coveted by the early Spanish settlers. With modification this basic institution for organizing labor followed the conquistadores to the American mainlands as *encomienda,* a term long associated with nobility and conquest and its rewards in Spain. It persisted as a major labor institution for decades in some regions and for centuries in others.

Both the *repartimiento* laborers and the enslaved Indians separated from their communities were forced to toil in the fields as well as in placer gold mines. Both forms of work produced hardships. The available gold was limited in quantity, and quickly the streams played out. Accustomed to producing only enough foodstuffs for their own subsistence, the natives proved unwilling or incapable of growing enough to feed the Spaniards as well. Food shortages, malnutrition, and death resulted. The Spaniards' disillusionment was so great that when Columbus offered them the chance to return to Iberia in 1498, three hundred did so, each with an Indian slave.

Subjected to new, harsh working conditions and at times enslavement, abused by the Spaniards, their society disrupted, their diet altered, and the prospect for improvement nil, the native population of perhaps one million in 1492 quickly began to decline, and by the mid-sixteenth century the Arawaks of Hispaniola had virtually disappeared.

This disastrous depopulation occurred for a variety of reasons. Spanish rule had turned the idyllic paradise that Columbus had described into a living hell for the natives. Nearly everything the Spaniards did created havoc on the indigenous population, but the demands they placed on the

Early representation of an American Indian

food supply and the conditions under which they made the natives live and labor were the main causes of the decline. Legislation to improve the natives' working conditions and to halt the decline came to nothing. There also is <u>some</u> evidence that disease accompanied Columbus on his second voyage, although smallpox apparently did not arrive until 1518, by which time there were fewer than thirty thousand natives still alive.

The Dominicans in particular protested the Spaniards' abuse of the indigenous population, and in 1511 Father Antonio Montesinos condemned the Spaniards for their abominable callousness and exploitation of the Indians. "Tell me," he queried in the famous sermon, "by what right or justice do you hold these Indians in such cruel and horrible slavery? By what right do you wage such detestable wars on these people who lived idly and peacefully in their own lands, where you have consumed infinite numbers of them with unheard-of murders and desolations?"[2] Later, Bartolomé de las Casas (1474–1566), a former *encomendero* who had witnessed the devastation of the Caribbean islands, angrily excoriated, in an endless stream of publications, his compatriots' abuse of the natives and pushed the Crown toward reform.

Critics of the Spaniards' treatment of the Indians posed the fundamental question of Spain's right to conquer and rule in the New World. The response, duly furnished by learned scholars convened by King Ferdinand, was that the papacy could, as it had done in the bulls of 1493, confer dominion over the pagans to their Christian rulers who then would have the responsibility to convert them. If they refused Christianity and allegiance to the Castilian Crown, the Spaniards could declare a "just war" on them. After 1512 Spaniards were required to read the *requerimiento* to natives before battle. The document stated: "We protest that the deaths and losses which shall accrue from this are your fault, and not that of their highnesses, or ours, or of these soldiers who came with us."

Although the Spaniards' devastation of the native cultures of Hispaniola and other islands is beyond dispute, equally apparent was the rapid appearance of Spanish institutions in the Caribbean. In August 1496 construction began on the city of Santo Domingo. Rebuilt in 1502 after a destructive cyclone, it quickly became the first true city in Spanish America. Modeled after Santa Fe, where Isabella and Ferdinand had based their troops during the siege of Granada, Santo Domingo was built on a gridiron pattern that would be the standard form for future Spanish cities in the Americas.

Spanish society in Hispaniola centered increasingly in Santo Domingo. Although the urban focus was prevalent in Spain, it became even more pronounced in the colonies. A city provided both stability for the Spaniards' lives and social relations and the amenities of civilization that the settlers tried to reproduce wherever they went. In addition, a municipality enjoyed the important right of communicating directly with the monarch. As the center of government, Santo Domingo housed the governor of the island and, after 1511, the first high court, or *audiencia,* in the Indies. A city council, or *cabildo* (sometimes called an *ayuntamiento*), made up of local citizens *(vecinos)* appeared immediately. A cathedral was constructed in the city, and a university, the first in the Americas, was founded by 1540. As Spaniards moved to other islands in the Caribbean and then to the mainland beyond, they immediately founded municipalities. Without exaggeration one can consider the municipality, and especially its largest variation, the city, as the base for Spanish life and rule in the Indies.

The Imposition of Royal Authority

Unrest and discontent among the settlers was revealed vividly in the Roldán revolt and Columbus's failure to prevent the mistreatment of the natives or to deliver the riches he had promised. After having had these complaints investigated, Isabella and Ferdinand relieved the admiral of his administrative responsibilities on Hispaniola. They also licensed expeditions to explore and trade in the Indies, and in August 1500 a royal governor, Francisco de Bobadilla, arrived on the island to find yet another revolt. Sent to replace Columbus, who was still in Hispaniola, the new governor acted immediately. Soon he had the admiral bound in chains and on his way to Castile in disgrace. The Crown had begun to assert its authority in the New World and to regain the prerogatives bartered away in the 1492 agreement with Columbus.

Under Bobadilla's rule, gold production increased, and the several hundred Spaniards who still remained on Hispaniola enjoyed greater prosperity. Neither the settlers nor the natives revolted, although the expanded mining brought greater disruption to Indian society and probably accelerated the population decline. A drop in royal income from the mines, because Bobadilla allowed the settlers a generous share of the gold, spurred the Crown to replace him in 1502 with Nicolas de Ovando, an experienced administrator from Extremadura.

Ovando left Spain with an expedition of 2,500 persons, including many from his native province, which henceforth became an important source of conquistadors and colonists. The largest group yet to depart for the Indies, it included a broader cross section of Castilian society than had earlier expeditions, and even some families. The availability of free native labor, antipathy toward agricultural labor, and the possibility of rapid enrichment combined to lure most new arrivals to the gold fields instead of settling into the more stable and sedentary existence the Crown had wanted.

Within two years of his arrival, Ovando extended Spanish authority throughout Hispaniola. He took the *residencia* of Bobadilla, introducing to the Indies this Castilian check on officials' conduct. Charged by the Crown to promote the natives' conversion and good treatment, he relied on the *encomienda* to fulfill this end. The *encomenderos* paid far more attention to the Indians' obligation to work, however, than to their own responsibility to instruct or take care of them. With all natives now encompassed by the institution, the level of exploitation rose and the population decreased as countless labor gangs were sent to the gold mines. Ovando established fifteen Spanish towns on the island and implemented a policy restricting Spaniards to their own municipalities and segregating them from the Indians, whose own villages were at times combined as their populations fell. This policy of "two republics" or separate existences for Spaniards and Indians followed the colonists throughout the New World but was never fully successful, as the populations were forced to become socially and economically dependent on each other.

The Ovando years from 1502 to 1509 brought prosperity to a rapidly growing number of Spaniards. No longer did the settlers face crises of subsistence. Livestock had arrived with Columbus in the 1490s and multiplied in the following decade. Grazing pigs, cattle, and horses disrupted Indian agriculture and thus hastened the demise of the native population, which in turn opened more land to unchallenged grazing. Gold mining facilitated by forced Indian labor brought fortunes to some Spaniards.

Others grew rich from trade as the growing number of colonists imported more goods from Spain. In 1508 forty-five ships were involved in the transatlantic trade. Successful entrepreneurs, for example, the merchants Diego de Nicuesa and Rodrigo de Bastidas, accumulated capital that was used to expand Tierra Firme, the continental southern rim of the Caribbean.

Beyond Hispaniola

The pressures and incentives to move beyond Hispaniola were several. By 1509 little gold remained on the island, and the colonists were anxious to find precious metals elsewhere. The larger Spanish population of perhaps eight thousand to ten thousand, moreover, meant a greater demand for native labor at a time when the supply was rapidly disappearing. In 1503 the Crown permitted natives to be enslaved only if they had engaged in cannibalism. This restriction was frequently ignored, however, and settlers turned to other islands and the mainland as sources for Indian slaves during Ovando's tenure. The conquest of Puerto Rico began in 1508, and the enslavement of its inhabitants followed. The islands known since the seventeenth century as the Bahamas fell next to the demand for labor, and by 1513 they were depopulated. Cuba followed suit in 1511 after a successful invasion led by its governor-to-be Diego Velázquez de Cuellar, an experienced old hand who had sailed with Columbus in 1493. The island had some gold, and the Spaniards again employed *encomienda* labor to mine it. The consequence for the Indians imitated the experience on Hispaniola. Within a decade, few remained. European livestock—pigs, cattle, and some horses—took their place.

In 1500 the exploration of Tierra Firme began. These early expeditions were generally disastrous for the Spaniards. Mortality was high, and survival rather than gold, pearls, or slaves often became the adventurers' principal concern. By the end of 1510 the Indian town of Darién in Panama became the base of operation in Tierra Firme for the few Spaniards who had survived. Vasco Núñez de Balboa, an Extremaduran who had reached the Indies in 1500, emphasized control over his men and cordial relations with the natives. Unlike many of his contemporaries, he realized that good treatment rather than enslavement, *encomienda,* or demands for excessive tribute from the natives would serve himself and his men better in the long run. But Balboa, despite claiming the Pacific Ocean for Castile in 1513, lost out to more rapacious men.

Pedro Arias de Avila (Pedrarias) arrived from Spain in 1514 as governor of Castilla del Oro, as Tierra Firme was then known, with an expedition of at least 1,500 men. He settled at Darién where illness and famine immediately struck, and one contemporary reported that within months two-thirds of the newcomers had died. Under Pedrarias's misrule, greed and cruelty prevailed. Balboa's policy of peace with the Indians was shattered, and he himself was executed in 1519 on trumped-up charges.

In their search for easily extracted wealth by 1519, the Spaniards had devastated the Caribbean and much of Tierra Firme. Despite a few protesting voices, the native population had been annihilated in some places and barely clung to a precarious existence in others. Despite the destructiveness of this early phase, the outline of colonial economic and political relations was in place. Trade lines to Seville were firmly established. Indian labor was organized in the *repartimiento,* and European crops and livestock had been introduced. The appointment of Crown officials and the development of religious institutions restricted the authority of discoverers and early settlers. Experienced Indian fighters were numerous. Havana, itself the result of a conquest based in Santo Domingo, was ready to serve as the base for a major advance to the North American mainland. The town of Panama would similarly serve as the initial base for expeditions to western South America. The island phase was over; the great age of conquest was at hand.

Notes

1. Carl Ortwin Sauer, *The Early Spanish Main* (Berkeley and Los Angeles: University of California Press, 1966), p. 32.
2. Charles Gibson (ed.), *The Spanish Tradition in America* (New York: Harper & Row, 1968), p. 60.

Suggested for Further Reading

Bankes, George. *Peru Before Pizarro.* Oxford, England: Phaidon Press, 1977.

Bernal, Ignacio. *Mexico Before Cortez: Art, History and Legend.* Translated by Willis Barnstone. Garden City, N.Y.: Doubleday, 1975.

Boxer, Charles R. *The Portuguese Seaborne Empire, 1415–1825.* New York: Knopf, 1969.

Cobo, Bernabe. *History of the Inca Empire.* Translated and edited by Roland Hamilton. Austin: University of Texas Press, 1979.

Coe, Michael. *The Maya.* New York: Praeger, 1956.

Conrad, Geoffrey W., and Arthur A. Demarest. *Religion and Empire: The Dynamics of Aztec and Inca Expansionism.* Cambridge, England: Cambridge University Press, 1984.

Elliott, J. H. *Imperial Spain, 1469–1716.* New York: New American Library, 1964.

Hardoy, Jorge. *Precolumbian Cities.* New York: Walker, 1973.

Hassig, Ross. *Aztec Warfare: Imperial Expansion and Political Control.* Norman: University of Oklahoma Press, 1988.

Hassig, Ross. *Trade, Tribute, and Transportation. The Sixteenth Century Political Economy of the Valley of Mexico.* Norman: University of Oklahoma Press, 1985.

Kamen, Henry. *Spain 1469–1714: A Society of Conflict.* London: Longman Group, 1983.

Katz, Friedrich. *The Ancient American Civilizations.* New York: Praeger, 1974.

Kubler, George. *The Art and Architecture of Ancient America: The Mexican, Maya, and Andean Peoples.* Baltimore: Penguin, 1962.

Lomax, Derek W. *The Reconquest of Spain.* New York: Longman Group, 1978.

Lynch, John. *Spain Under the Habsburgs,* 2 volumes, revised edition. New York: New York University Press, 1984.

MacKay, Angus. *Spain in the Middle Ages: From Frontier to Empire, 1000–1500.* London: Macmillan, 1977.

Metraux, Alfred. *The History of the Incas.* New York: Pantheon, 1969.

Morely, Sylvanus G. *The Ancient Maya.* Revised by G. W. Brainerd. Stanford, Calif.: Stanford University Press, 1965.

Morison, Samuel E. *Admiral of the Ocean Sea: A Life of the Admiral Christopher Columbus.* 2 volumes. Boston: Little, Brown, 1942.

Morison, Samuel E. *The European Discovery of America: The Southern Voyages, 1492–1619.* New York: Oxford University Press, 1974.

Oliveira Marques, A. H. de. *History of Portugal.* 2 volumes. New York: Columbia University Press, 1972.

Parry, John H. *The Age of Reconnaissance.* New York: Mentor Books, 1964.

Payne, Stanley G. *A History of Spain and Portugal.* 2 volumes. Madison: University of Wisconsin Press, 1973.

Pike, Ruth. *Enterprise and Adventure. The Genoese in Seville and the Opening of the New World.* Ithaca, N.Y.: Cornell University Press, 1966.

Sauer, Carl Ortwin. *The Early Spanish Main.* Berkeley and Los Angeles: University of California Press, 1966.

Soustelle, Jacques. *Daily Life of the Aztecs.* Stanford, Calif.: Stanford University Press, 1970.

Soustelle, Jacques. *Mexico.* Translated by James Hogarth. Cleveland: World, 1967.

Vaillant, George. *The Aztecs of Mexico: Origin, Rise and Fall of the Aztec Nation.* Garden City, N.Y.: Doubleday, 1962.

Webb, Kempton E. *Geography of Latin America: A Regional Analysis.* Englewood Cliffs, N.J.: Prentice-Hall, 1972.

Wolf, Eric. *Sons of the Shaking Earth: The People of Mexico and Guatemala—Their Land, History, and Culture.* Chicago: University of Chicago Press, 1974.

TWO

THE AGE OF CONQUEST

The Conquest of Mexico

The conquest of Mexico gave substance to the Spaniards' dreams of find-ing great wealth in the New World and initiated a frenzy of later expedi-tions anxious to emulate the remarkable success. For the daring and imag-inative Fernando Cortés, the conquest brought riches, a title of nobility, and fame, and the Castilian Crown secured new lands, vassals, and reve-nue. For the native population, in contrast, the conquest ushered in epi-demic diseases, depopulation, and centuries of subservience to foreign masters.

Organizing the Expedition

Bored by the study of law and fortunate to have escaped death at the hands of a jealous husband, Cortés chose to leave Spain and seek his fortune in the New World. Reaching Española in 1504 at the age of nineteen, the young Extremaduran benefited from personal connections and received an *encomienda*. He impressed Diego Velázquez and served as his clerk dur-ing the expedition to conquer and settle Cuba. Rewarded for his bravery and service with a second *encomienda,* Cortés devoted himself to trade and exploitation of his Indians once the island was pacified. News from the west, however, disrupted this placid existence.

The remnants of a coasting and trading expedition that had reached Yucatán in 1517 returned to Cuba with word of a wealthy and populous Indian civilization different from the indigenous cultures of the Carib-bean. Governor Velázquez immediately placed a larger and better-equipped force under the command of his cousin Juan de Grijalva and ordered it back to the land of the Maya. Although the expedition suffered some military losses as the four ships and two hundred men made landings along the Gulf coast to Tabasco, it managed to trade for enough gold to demonstrate the region's richness. At the same time, an emissary of Moc-

tezuma made contact with the expedition. Long before Grijalva returned
to Cuba, the Aztec elite was studying drawings of these strange men and
their great ships. In the following months Moctezuma consulted with the
priests and soothsayers of Tenochtitlán to determine whether the long-
awaited return of Quetzalcóatl was imminent.

Discouraged by his cousin's lack of audacity, Velázquez appointed Cortés, his former secretary, to lead a third expedition. Cortés at once demonstrated his energy and leadership. Aided by the well-known stories of
the earlier expeditions and his own personal magnetism, he attracted more
than five hundred men, one of whom, Bernal Díaz del Castillo, later wrote
a richly detailed and beautifully told history of the conquest. As the date
of departure approached, Velázquez correctly sensed that Cortés was too
ambitious and headstrong to remain loyal. Warned that the governor
wanted to remove him from command, Cortés cut short his preparations
and set sail on February 18, 1519, with over five hundred men, eleven
ships, sixteen horses, and some artillery.

First Contacts

Within weeks of landfall, Cortés had the good fortune to secure two translators. Jerónimo Aguilar, the victim of a 1511 shipwreck, had learned Maya
during his unplanned residence in Yucatán. An Indian woman, Malitzin,
who spoke both Maya and Nahuatl was offered to the Spaniards as a gift.
Later known as Doña Marina, she became Cortés's mistress and bore him
a son. Translating in tandem with Aguilar, she provided Cortés with a tremendous political advantage over the Aztec emissaries forced to rely on
the Spaniards' translators. In addition, she gave Cortés crucial information
about the Aztec state and intentions, in some cases saving the Spaniards
from military disaster.

In battles along the coast of Yucatán and again on his march into the
interior, Cortés used his military assets with devastating effect. The natives
of Mesoamerica fought in massed ranks with slings, spears, two-handed
swords edged with flint, and bows and arrows. But the mounted Spaniards
could quickly flank these native formations or charge directly and break
them up. Even when unfavorable terrain limited the cavalry's mobility, the
firepower of artillery, steel swords, and armor gave the invaders an advantage. With each victory, moreover, Cortés incorporated into his force the
defeated warriors of the Aztec subject states. By the final stage of his campaign, Indian auxiliaries vastly outnumbered the Spanish conquistadors
and contributed immeasurably to Cortés's success.

The Spaniards also had the great advantage of realizing the political consequences of their arrival. Cortés and many of his men had participated in
earlier conquests in the Caribbean, an experience that gave them the confidence to compromise and temporize with native leaders until the opportunity arose to impose their will. In addition, the Spaniards believed they

were inherently superior to the natives and that their Christian God would lead them to victory. The Indian leaders, not perceiving the general threat to their indigenous culture, decided either to resist or ally themselves with the invaders in response to traditional, local concerns.

Moctezuma and the Aztec elite interpreted the Spaniards' arrival according to the Mesoamerican tradition that viewed history as an ongoing cycle of creation and destruction, invasion and assimilation. The myth-history of the god Quetzalcóatl reinforced this historical view and thus virtually paralyzed Moctezuma. Moctezuma shared the belief that Quetzalcóatl had left central Mexico for Yucatán in the tenth century but would ultimately return from the east to reclaim his authority. In fact, when the Aztec ruler met Cortés he affirmed, "We have always held that those who descended from him [Quetzalcóatl] would come and conquer this land and take us as his vassals . . . we believe and are certain that he [the king of Spain] is our natural lord. . . ."[1] Cortés, a political genius, used the natives' myths and beliefs whenever possible to promote a supernatural interpretation of Spanish military prowess and invincibility.

Two incidents shortly after the Spaniards reached the Gulf coast illustrate Cortés's political skill. Because he had left Cuba in rebellion against Velázquez, Cortés needed to legitimize his command and neutralize the disgruntled men still loyal to the governor. He solved this problem by founding a city, Villa Rica de la Vera Cruz (today Veracruz), whose newly elected town council then selected him its chief military and judicial officer. Having legitimized his independence from Velázquez's authority, Cortés further solidified his power by ordering his small fleet destroyed. Cut off from Cuba and facing Cortés's newly created local authority, Velázquez's supporters accepted their defeat and joined the march inland.

Indian Allies

Upon reaching Cempoala, the Spaniards were greeted by a friendly and generous *cacique* who provided them with firsthand information about Tenochtitlán. Cortés thereupon began to realize the antipathy that their subject peoples felt toward the Aztecs and resolved to turn some of these satellites into allies. When the Aztec tribute collectors arrived, Cortés convinced the Cempoalans to arrest them. Terrified by the possible repercussions of this treason but reassured by demonstrated Spanish military strength, the Cempoalans complied. Cortés had gained his first native ally. Yet he sought also to avoid a direct confrontation with the Aztecs. Playing a subtle strategy, he released the prisoners and sent them to Moctezuma with protestations of friendship.

Joined by their new ally, the Spaniards continued to march toward the Valley of Mexico via the territory of the fiercely independent Tlaxcalans. Seeing the Cempoalans, the Tlaxcalans presumed that the Spaniards were also allies of the hated rulers of Tenochtitlán and fought them ferociously.

For the first time the Spaniards lost valuable horses, of which they had brought only sixteen, and suffered numerous casualties. As related by Bernal Díaz, the major battle was reminiscent of a medieval romance:

> We were four hundred, of whom many were sick and wounded, and we stood in the middle of a plain six miles long, and perhaps as broad, swarming with Indian warriors. Moreover we knew that they had come determined to leave none of us alive except those who were to be sacrificed to their idols. When they began to charge the stones sped like hail from their slings, and their barbed and fire-hardened darts fell like corn on the threshing-floor, each one capable of piercing any armour or penetrating the unprotected vitals. Their swordsmen and spearmen pressed us hard, and closed with us bravely, shouting and yelling as they came.[2]

The intense pressure almost broke the Spanish formation, but in the end Spanish weapons forced the Tlaxcalans to retire. After further days of fierce fighting, the Tlaxcalans at last sought peace and swore fealty to Charles I. Their loyalty to Spain and military assistance to Cortés proved as impressive as their initial resistance.

Entering the Tlaxcalan capital Cortés saw for the first time the urban development of the Mesoamerican heartland:

> This city is so big and so remarkable [as to be] . . . almost unbelievable, for the city is much larger than Granada and very much stronger, with as good buildings and many more people than Granada had when it was taken, and very much better supplied with the produce of the land, namely, bread, fowl and game and fresh-water fish and vegetables and other things they eat which are very good. There is in this city a market where each and every day upward of thirty thousand people come to buy and sell, without counting the other trade which goes on elsewhere in the city.[3]

Both the indigenous tribute system and the urban-based political order suited perfectly the needs and resources of the conquistadors. A small number of Spaniards could control an enormous area and draw off huge amounts of wealth by usurping the traditional prerogatives of the native urban elite and rulers. Because Spanish colonial development would take on this urban character, it was fitting that the military campaigns for control of Tenochtitlán, the region's preeminent urban center, dominated the remainder of the conquest.

Moctezuma's agents arrived soon after Tlaxcala's submission and attempted to convince Cortés that the Tlaxcalans would betray him. Now appreciating how serious the Spanish threat was, they presented Moctezuma's offer to become a tributary of Charles I in return for Cortés's abandoning his march. Cortés cleverly played off these traditional rivals. He replied politely to Moctezuma's offer but informed the ambassadors that he would greet their lord in Tenochtitlán. As the Spaniards marched toward the Mexicas' capital, they were reinforced by thousands of Tlaxcalan warriors.

En route to Tenochtitlán, the Spaniards entered Cholula, an Aztec tributary. When informed of a rumored surprise attack, the Spaniards and their native allies responded by massacring some six thousand residents. Convinced by this action that the invaders and their allies were militarily invincible, Moctezuma henceforth made only halfhearted efforts to dissuade them from reaching the capital.

The Aztec Capital

Cortés led his force across the volcanic mountain chain that forms the southern boundary of the Valley of Mexico and stood looking down on the splendid complex of cities, lakes, and canals that served as the metropolis of Mesoamerican civilization. Bernal Díaz wrote years later:

> And when we saw all those cities and villages built in the water, and other great towns on dry land, and that straight and level causeway leading to Mexico, we were astounded. These great towns and *cues* [temples], and buildings rising from the water, all made of stone, seemed like an enchanted vision from the tale of Amadis. Indeed some of our soldiers asked whether it was all not a dream. . . . It was all so wonderful that I do not know how to describe this first glimpse of things never heard of, seen or dreamed of before.[4]

For the first time Cortés and his followers fully appreciated their momentous undertaking.

Members of the royal court and finally Moctezuma himself met the Spaniards as they crossed the broad causeway into the capital. After an exchange of ritual gifts in which the ruler stirred the invader's cupidity by providing items of gold, the gifts he knew the Spaniards valued most, he personally led Cortés and his men to quarters in the palace of his father, Axayácatl.

The splendors of Moctezuma's court with its elaborate rituals and opulence impressed the Spaniards. Yet their precarious position in the heart of the Aztec capital was frightening. In a characteristically audacious move, Cortés sought to strengthen his position by forcing Moctezuma under the threat of death to move to rooms in Axayácatl's palace.

The seizure of their ruler provoked a deep crisis among the highest levels of Aztec society. Moctezuma's failure to resist the invaders militarily had already angered many of his closest advisers and kinsmen. Once the undisputed ruler of Mesoamerica's greatest empire, the hostage was now merely a pawn of the foreigners. But despite public signs of submission, Cortés could not be certain that the traditional political discipline of this authoritarian and hierarchical state would hold firm. Popular resistance might still erupt.

From his first contacts with urban centers of coastal Mesoamerica, Cortés encouraged proselytization among the Indian population and sought to demonstrate the impotence and futility of the native religious beliefs. Repeatedly he overrode the advice of Spanish clerics to proceed slowly in order to avoid inflaming religious passions among the natives. Military victory whetted his efforts to promote Christianity, and the subsequent assaults on indigenous beliefs were often unrestrained. Exuberant Spaniards drove native priests from temple precincts and threw down and defaced religious ornaments. After cleaning the temples of the stains and stench left from human sacrifices and whitewashing their interiors, the Spaniards replaced the stone image of Huitzilopochtli or another native god with a cross and the image of the Virgin Mary. The political significance of symbols of the conquerors' religion replacing those of the Mesoamerican gods was apparent to both the invaders and the vanquished.

Threats to Cortés

News that a large Spanish expedition loyal to the governor of Cuba had arrived on the Gulf coast complicated Cortés's plans. Yet with his usual determination he turned the threat to his advantage. Leaving a garrison in Tenochtitlán under Pedro de Alvarado, Cortés marched rapidly to the coast and in a night attack smashed the larger force of Pánfilo de Narváez. Then, by treating the defeated men generously and promising great riches, he succeeded in winning most of them to his side. Quickly beginning the trek back to Tenochtitlán, the enlarged force soon received the distressing news that the Aztecs had attacked the Spanish garrison. What had happened was this:

During a major religious celebration, Alvarado ordered his troops to attack the unarmed crowd gathered in Tenochtitlán's central square. The assault cost many Aztec nobles their lives, enraged the city's populace, and provoked a massive popular uprising. Alvarado later claimed that the natives had planned to use the celebration as cover for an attack on the weakened garrison, but his attack, like the massacre that Cortés had ordered at Cholula, remains one of the most controversial events of the conquest.

The Aztecs made no effort to hinder the Spaniards' reentry into the capital, thus trapping them where their horses and weapons were less effective. Cortés and his reinforced column soon felt the full brunt of the Aztecs' rage. Although the Spaniards' harquebuses and small cannon claimed many victims, the Indians nearly succeeded in forcing the palace walls defended by the Spanish. Finally the Spaniards led Moctezuma onto the walls, hoping his people would end the attack at the sight of their once-mighty ruler. However, the storm of stones, spears, and arrows continued unabated. According to the most widely accepted account, a stone struck Moctezuma on the head and led to his death three days later.

Convinced that his defeat was imminent, Cortés decided to flee under cover of darkness. His men made careful preparations to avoid detection, covering the horses' hooves with cloth and constructing portable bridges to span gaps cut in the causeway. Finally, they divided the loot they had collected from Moctezuma and other natives since reaching Mexico. Many of the most recent arrivals loaded themselves down with gold and silver, sacrificing physical mobility in flight for the promise of social mobility later. For hundreds their greed proved a deadly mistake.

Despite the Spaniards' efforts to escape undetected, the Aztecs attacked them from all sides before they had cleared the first causeway gap. All pretense of discipline and military order collapsed under the onslaught. Cortés lost more than 400 Spaniards, 4,000 native allies, and many horses before the fleeing Spanish force reached the mainland. June 30–July 1, 1520, truly had been La Noche Triste (the sorrowful night) for the Spaniards. Confident of total victory, Aztec warriors boasted to the hard-pressed Spaniards that they would soon sacrifice them. The Spaniards could, in fact, look back across the causeway and see their captured compatriots being marched up the steps of Huitzilopochtli's temple for sacrifice by the waiting priests. Bernal Díaz later related that over 860 Spaniards, over half the number present in Mexico before Cortés reached a sanctuary in Tlaxcala, had been killed as a result of the flight.

Yet even this terrible defeat proved to be only a temporary setback for Cortés. The Tlaxcalans remained allies and provided a safe haven while he rested and resupplied his forces. Native armies recruited from Tlaxcala and other allied Indian states joined the Spaniards for a final assault on the hated Aztec capital. After La Noche Triste, Cortés realized that he must turn Tenochtitlán's island location to his advantage. He ordered a fleet constructed that would allow him to cut off the capital from its mainland supplies of food and water. Thirteen small brigantines were built and then disassembled. Once the Spaniards and their allies reached the shore of Lake Texcoco, they quickly reassembled and launched these small vessels armed with three-quarters of their valuable artillery.

Final Conquest

Cortés divided his force into three columns and began to move up the broad causeways that linked the capital to the mainland. His brigantines immediately proved their value by defeating a large force of Aztec warriors in canoes. Despite the heroic resistance of the city's garrison and the stoic suffering of a population denied adequate food and water by the blockade, the Spaniards slowly pushed toward the city center. At first they found it difficult to consolidate their gains, for each night the defenders retook the buildings that the Spaniards had occupied during the day. Accordingly, Cortés ordered his Indian auxiliaries to pull down the city's buildings to prevent their reoccupation.

The Spaniards also had an unexpected and valuable ally: Smallpox was introduced by one of Narváez's soldiers who had joined Cortés. Previously unknown to the Mesoamerican population, smallpox devastated it. In the confined space of the besieged city, the disease killed many of the people, already weakened by starvation. According to the Indian account of the conquest: "We were covered with agonizing sores from head to foot. The illness was so dreadful that no one could walk or move."[5] Probably many more Indians died in the epidemic than from wounds received in battle. Moctezuma's successor, Cuitláhuac, was among the first victims. Following his death, authority passed to his eighteen-year-old brother Cuauhtémoc. Because the Spaniards suffered no apparent effects from the disease, the epidemic served to confirm the most pessimistic assessments of Spanish invincibility and the impotence of native gods.

Finally, on August 21, 1521, the Spaniards breached the capital's last defenses, and the remaining warriors surrendered. Cuauhtémoc attempted to flee by canoe, but a brigantine captured him. Tenochtitlán, one of the grandest achievements of the Mesoamerican world, was little more than a pile of rubble. Bernal Díaz remembered that "we found the houses full of corpses, and some poor Mexicans still in them who could not move away. . . . The city looked as if it had been ploughed up. The roots of any edible greenery had been dug out, boiled and eaten, and they had even cooked the bark of some of the trees."[6]

Although Cortés emerged victorious, the spoils were far less than anticipated. During the debacle of La Noche Triste the Spaniards had lost much of the treasure accumulated since their arrival in Mexico. Although valuable booty was found in Tenochtitlán's ruins, few of the Spaniards received the immediate gold, silver, and rich *encomiendas* they had expected. Their disappointment produced some ugly confrontations among the victors, and Cortés was able to quiet his followers only with difficulty. In order to still these passions and provide a controlled outlet for his men's destructive energies, he encouraged and helped finance new expeditions to the south and west.

The execution of Cuauhtémoc in 1524 ended the line of Mexica rulers. Although the Spaniards continued to recognize the "natural rulers" of Mexico in the short term and the Tlaxcalans and other allies maintained some autonomy, the conquistadors and more recent arrivals from Spain and from the older colonies of the Caribbean soon became the indisputable lords of the land. Many of these conquistadors and first settlers took Indian mistresses, and a few married Indian women. Doña Marina, Cortés's mistress, for example, became a respected member of early colonial society and married one of his followers. The *mestizo* children that resulted from the longer-lived unions often identified with the culture and religion of their fathers and became an important bulwark of Spanish rule during the Indian rebellions of the following decades. By the 1550s, Spanish authority was firmly established in the densely populated regions of New Spain, as the conquered territory was known.

The Conquest of Peru

The fall of the Inca Empire climaxed the initial era of Spanish expansion in the Americas. Later expeditions continued to pursue rumored El Dorados, and Spaniards and their *mestizo* offspring settled vast new regions. Yet the participants, their financial backers, and the Castilian Crown considered each of these new achievements, often won at an exorbitant human cost, a failure when compared with Francisco Pizarro's spectacular success in Peru.

Early Expeditions

The illegitimate and poorly educated son of a modest Extremaduran noble, Pizarro emigrated to the New World as a young man. After a brief and unexceptional stay in Hispaniola, he joined an expedition to the isthmus of Panama. There he participated in Indian wars and slave raids. As an *encomendero* and one of the founders of the city of Panama, Pizarro was by his mid-life a fairly prosperous citizen of a small and obscure city on Spain's expanding American frontier.

In 1522 Captain Pascual de Andagoya sailed in an exploratory expedition south from Panama, hugging the Pacific coast and fighting the head winds. The voyage produced only rumors of a rich and powerful kingdom to the south but spurred interest among some colonists in pursuing them. Governor Pedrarias agreed to let Pizarro and two partners, Diego de Almagro and the priest Hernando de Luque, explore the region. Luque, probably as an agent for wealthier and more prominent men, provided the necessary capital. Pizarro led a small expedition south in 1524 but soon returned to Panama after hardship, famine, and battles with hostile Indians yielded no tangible gain.

A second effort began even more disastrously, and Pizarro was forced to seek shelter on the island of Gallo while Almagro returned to Panama. Refusing a later opportunity to turn back, Pizarro and thirteen men remained. When Almagro appeared with reinforcements and supplies seven months later, the expeditions' fortune improved. One of its ships captured a large oceangoing raft laden with gold and silver jewelry, finely woven textiles, and precious stones. Their greed aroused by this irrefutable proof that the rumored civilization existed, the adventurers pushed further south and discovered Tumbez, a northern outpost of the Inca Empire.

Despite their evidence of a rich civilization, Pizarro and Almagro failed to interest the new governor of Panama in supporting further exploration. After borrowing more capital, the partners sent Pizarro to Spain to seek a royal license for their next venture. There he secured a contract (*capitulación*) naming him governor of Peru, and the thirteen men who had persevered with him on the island of Gallo were ennobled. Significantly, Almagro received only the minor title of governor of Tumbez. Before returning to Panama, Pizarro stopped in his birthplace, Trujillo, where he recruited four brothers and a cousin, other kinsmen, and neighbors for his expedition.

The unequal rewards spelled out in the royal contract strained Pizarro's relations with Almagro. Finally, however, the partners resolved their differences and in late December 1530, Pizarro set sail from Panama with fewer than two hundred men. Almagro agreed to follow this vanguard with reinforcements and supplies. After advancing slowly down the coast, Pizarro reached Tumbez. Here evidence of destruction and depopulation revealed that the Incas were engaged in civil war. Joined by a small force led by Hernando de Soto, the expedition proceeded about a hundred miles to the south. There Pizarro founded the city of San Miguel de Piura and awarded *encomiendas* to the Spaniards he would leave behind as a garrison to protect communication with Panama.

Although Pizarro and his lieutenants did not immediately realize it, they were challenging the Incas at a particularly propitious moment. In the late 1520s an epidemic had swept along trade routes from the isthmus of Panama through the northern reaches of the empire. Probably the first smallpox to reach the region, the epidemic claimed countless victims, including the extremely vigorous and effective Huayna Capac, the *sapa* Inca, and his heir apparent. As in Mexico, disease proved to be a powerful ally to the Spaniards.

The deaths of Huayna Capac and his heir provoked a deep political crisis among the Incas: As he pushed the empire's frontier northward into modern Colombia in a long and bitter conflict, Huayna Capac had depended increasingly on professional troops and military advisers rather than the traditional Inca bureaucracy. As a result, the capital, Cuzco, had lost both prestige and power. Thus when news of the *sapa* Inca's death reached Cuzco, the court elite immediately selected his son Huascar as successor. In Quito another son, Atahualpa, controlled the professional army and retained political control over the newly conquered regions of Ecuador and Colombia. A strained peace between the brothers held for nearly two years before Atahualpa rebelled. Disputed successions were not unusual among the Incas, and nearly every *sapa* Inca had had to prove his authority militarily. The appearance of Pizarro's tiny expedition, however, transformed this internecine struggle and threatened the survival of the Inca state.

Huascar seized the initial advantage and briefly made Atahualpa his prisoner. However, the large, well-disciplined, and experienced armies that Atahualpa had inherited from his father soon overwhelmed the untried levies organized from Cuzco. His troops took the Incan capital, captured Huascar, and launched a brutal campaign against members of the royal family and nobility who had supported him. Recruited largely from the empire's northern frontier, the victors acted like an occupying army, singling out for particularly harsh treatment the Cañari ethnic group that had provided much of Huascar's experienced military support.

Pizarro's route south brought him close to a large military force escorting Atahualpa to Cuzco. Informed of the Spanish landing earlier, the Inca had sent a trusted adviser into the invader's camp to collect intelligence. Unfortunately for Atahualpa, his ambassador dismissed the Spaniards as an insignificant fighting force and arrogantly claimed that he could take them prisoner with a few hundred men. Pizarro, on the other hand, received remarkably good information about the Incas. He not only knew about the civil war but also managed to communicate with both camps through Indian youths he had captured on an earlier expedition and who now served him as interpreters and spies.

Cajamarca

As the Spanish and Inca forces approached the valley of Cajamarca, Pizarro sent a detachment of cavalry under Hernando de Soto's command to invite Atahualpa to meet. The Inca at last agreed, and that night Pizarro and his captains met to discuss how they would apply the well-tried model of capturing the enemy leader. With a victorious Incan army at least forty thousand strong camped across the valley, their situation was precarious.

Having determined to seize Atahualpa when he entered Cajamarca, the Spaniards carefully placed men to strike swiftly. Not suspecting his fate, Atahualpa left most of his armed soldiers on the plain in front of Cajamarca and entered the city's central plaza accompanied by five thousand to six thousand lightly armed retainers and servants.

At a prearranged signal, the Spaniards, who had been hidden from view, fired arquebuses and two cannons into the crowded square. Their cavalry then charged into the massed, defenseless Indian formations, cutting down men by the score. The terrified natives attempted to flee but found the city's adobe walls blocked their way. Many were crushed to death as they struggled to escape. As the walls collapsed and the terrified survivors fled onto the plain, the waiting troops panicked as well, and the Spanish cavalry, in pursuit, sealed this initial victory. In the square, Pizarro and his companions reached Atahualpa with difficulty and took him captive.

The results of this day, November 16, 1532, were remarkable even to the participants. Although not a single Spaniard was killed, and only a few suffered superficial wounds, probably at least 1,500 Indians, and by some accounts many more, perished and thousands more were wounded. Surrounded by his victorious army and misinformed about Spanish weapons, the Inca had underestimated the invaders' fighting potential and stumbled into a well-sprung trap. Without pikes or other means to stop the charging horses, the Incan foot soldiers were nearly defenseless. Their long-distance weapons—stones, arrows, and light spears—had little effect against the Europeans' metal and cotton armor.

The capture of Atahualpa and the unexpected military disaster paralyzed a state already shaken by the recent civil war. Without orders from their monarch, Atahualpa's generals hesitated to act, as they feared that a direct attack would cost his life. The defeated supporters of Huascar, on the other hand, now perceived the Spaniards as allies against their hated usurper.

Housed in the building in which Pizarro resided, Atahualpa shared his meals with the Spanish leaders and tried to determine their plans. Again the Spaniards proved more astute. Pizarro guessed correctly that he could compel Atahualpa to serve Spanish interests. Atahualpa, having observed the plundering of Cajamarca and his abandoned military camp, mistakenly believed that the invaders would leave Peru after seizing whatever treasure they could find. This erroneous belief prompted his boastful offer to ransom himself by filling a large room with gold and another twice over with silver. Pizarro quickly accepted and promised to free the Inca and establish him in his former capital of Quito once the terms were fulfilled. Atahualpa then sent agents throughout the empire to collect and transport gold and silver to Cajamarca.

In retrospect it is clear that in a futile effort to protect himself, Atahualpa squandered any opportunity to save the Andean peoples from Spanish domination. For despite the events at Cajamarca, his generals still commanded several undefeated armies, whereas the Spaniards were isolated geographically and months away from reinforcements and supplies. But Atahualpa, an absolute monarch even while a prisoner, used his authority to organize the collection and delivery of his ransom rather than to order an attack on his captors.

Atahualpa's rule, however, was recent and fragile, the result of his crushing military defeat of Huascar. Once Pizarro discovered that one of the Inca's generals held Huascar captive, he ordered his prisoner to deliver his brother safely to the Spanish camp. Instead, Atahualpa, who still thought Huascar and his supporters were the primary threat to his authority, ordered his brother's execution. This political murder was not, however, an isolated incident but only the latest royal murder that Atahualpa had ordered.

Hoping to gain his freedom, Atahualpa encouraged Pizarro to send some Spaniards to help organize the collection and delivery of his ransom. He identified temples at Cuzco and the ancient pre-Inca temple of Pachacamac as particularly valuable. By targeting certain southern shrines located in areas that had supported Huascar, Atahualpa sought further retribution for political disloyalty; the recent civil war still colored his actions. Pizarro duly dispatched small groups of Spaniards to various parts of the empire, and gold and silver flowed back to Cajamarca.

Although the specified amount was not collected, Atahualpa's ransom was indeed worthy of a great king. The Spaniards melted down 11 tons of worked gold to produce 13,420 pounds of 22-carat gold and obtained another 26,000 pounds of pure silver. Each infantryman present at Cajamarca received as his share the incredible sum of 45 pounds of gold and 90 pounds of silver. As was common in all Spanish expeditions, a cavalryman received double the foot soldier's share and the captains even more. Francisco Pizarro received 630 pounds of gold and 1,260 pounds of silver, seven times the share of a cavalryman. Shortly after the ransom's division, Diego de Almagro arrived with 150 reinforcements. The niggardly shares he and his men got from the spoils fueled deep resentment and gave rise to lasting factionalism.

With the ransom distributed, the Spaniards had no reason to remain in

Cajamarca. Cuzco beckoned with its great wealth and large population. But Atahualpa posed a problem. Almagro and the most recent arrivals wanted him executed as a traitor. They traced to him rumors of massing Incan armies, and some local Incan officials appeared to corroborate their ruler's guilt and thus to feed the Spaniards' fear of attack. Pizarro at first hesitated to execute a reigning monarch but then yielded to the pressure. There was neither a trial nor an opportunity for a defense. Provoked largely by fear and greed, Pizarro and his captains simply sentenced the Inca to death by burning in July 1533. But because the priest Valverde had convinced Atahualpa to accept Christian baptism, he was executed by garroting.

Consolidation of Spanish Power

Despite executing Atahualpa, Pizarro realized the usefulness of his office and quickly appointed a compliant successor, Tupac Huallpa. When this willing puppet died on the march to Cuzco, his brother Manco Inca replaced him. In addition to these political actions, the march to Cuzco produced the conquest's first large-scale pitched battles. Spanish mounted units of fewer than one hundred men defeated the same army that had easily crushed the forces of Huascar and taken Cuzco. In this conflict, Pizarro, like Cortés, had the support of native allies. The Cañari and other ethnic groups that supported Huascar in the civil war seized the opportunity to take revenge on Atahualpa's generals. By the time Pizarro reached the Incan capital, Atahualpa's military leadership was demoralized. Unable to withstand the onslaught, the remnants of the Inca's once-proud army fled north toward Quito.

Cuzco yielded an even greater treasure than Atahualpa's ransom. In its division Almagro and his men received a substantial share, but the greater number of participants reduced the reward of each. Consequently some bitterness remained between the Almagro and Pizarro factions. In order to defuse tensions, it was decided to mount a new expedition to probe the southern frontier of the Incan realm. Pizarro supplied much of the necessary capital and placed Almagro in command. Manco Inca organized a large force of Indian auxiliaries. Shortly after Almagro departed, Francisco Pizarro also left Cuzco. Correctly believing that the highland city was too distant from other Spanish colonial centers and would remain politically and militarily isolated and vulnerable, he founded a new capital near the coast on January 5, 1535. Named Ciudad de los Reyes because it was founded on Epiphany Day, by the latter part of the century it was known as Lima, a corruption of its native name.

The extraordinary riches that the Spaniards seized in Peru immediately lured their compatriots away from more-established colonies. One of the most famous adventurers thus attracted was the veteran captain Pedro de Alvarado. Not satisfied with the wealth he had already won in Mexico and the results of his conquest of Guatemala, he led a force south to conquer the northern reaches of the Inca Empire. News of this alarming threat to the interests of the Pizarro–Almagro partnership reached their lieutenant Sebastián de Benalcázar, who quickly organized a mixed force of Spaniards and Indians loyal to Huascar and marched on Quito. While Alvarado struggled through the coastal jungles, Benalcázar moved directly into the Andes and engaged the largest of Atahualpa's remaining armies. Once again the Spaniards and their Indian allies demonstrated battlefield superiority. The defeated Incan army burned and abandoned Quito, but Rumiñavi, the leader of the resistance, was finally captured and then burned alive. Alvarado, having reached the highland after Benalcázar's destruction of Inca military power, accepted a bribe of 100,000 gold pesos to return to Guatemala. Many of his followers, however, remained in Peru.

Inca Rebellion

In Cuzco Manco Inca ruled only a shadow kingdom. Both Almagro and Francisco Pizarro had treated him with great courtesy and had sought to protect the useful fiction of his independent authority. But even though Manco enjoyed immense prestige among the indigenous population, the lowliest Spaniard considered himself the Inca's superior. Spanish exactions and mistreatment finally pushed the natives too far; the factions of the civil war were ready to unite and rebel under Manco's leadership. Although the Inca's first effort to flee miscarried, he eventually escaped Cuzco and joined his troops. In early 1536, supported by an army of perhaps 100,000, Manco began to besiege Cuzco while subordinate commanders moved to attack other Spanish settlements.

During the three years since the Spanish surprise attack at Cajamarca, Incan commanders had learned how to neutralize some of the invaders' military advantages. By waiting patiently until the Spaniards were deployed in steep terrain where their horses could not charge, the Incas could maintain their positions and crush them under a rain of rocks, arrows, and spears. Using this approach, Inca troops annihilated large expeditions sent from Lima to relieve the siege at Cuzco. Indeed, the number of Spanish casualties exceeded the number of Spaniards who had been present with Pizarro at Cajamarca.

Despite winning several battles, however, Manco's troops failed to dislodge the Spaniards from Peru. The inability of a native army of more than 60,000 to force fewer than two hundred Spaniards to surrender in Cuzco demonstrated definitively the permanence of Pizarro's victory: An attack on Lima by the Incan army that had defeated the relief columns ended in the near massacre of some of Manco's finest troops by a Spanish force led by Francisco Pizarro himself. As his main force melted away for the planting season, Manco lifted the siege and retreated toward Vilcabamba where an independent Inca kingdom was maintained until 1572. Frustrated by Manco's continued resistance, Pizarro took revenge on the Inca's wife Cura Ocllo. She was stripped, beaten, and shot to death by arrows, and later the Spaniards floated her body down the Yucay River so that Manco's forces would find it.

Civil War

Internal divisions, however, prevented the victorious Spaniards from immediately following up their advantage. During the last stage of the siege of Cuzco in 1537, the disillusioned survivors of Almagro's expedition returned from Chile. After a long and difficult march, they had little to show for their hardships. Almost all of the Indian porters and scores of Spaniards had died during the difficult Andean crossings. Back in Cuzco Almagro sought to assert his claim to govern this important city. Having just defeated Manco's warriors, however, the Pizarro family was in no mood to compromise with an ally turned rival.

Negotiations failed to end this impasse, and so Almagro used his superior force to enter Cuzco and arrest Francisco's brothers Gonzalo and Hernando. Although his closest advisers urged him to execute these dangerous prisoners, Almagro instead attempted to force Francisco Pizarro to accept the loss of the old Incan capital. Gonzalo's escape substantially weakened Almagro's position, but Francisco agreed nonetheless to the rebel's demand to govern Cuzco and secured Hernando's freedom. But the peace was short-lived. Within days the Pizarros declared the agreement null and void, and both sides began preparing for war. When the contending armies finally met on the plain of Las Salinas near Cuzco in 1538, Pizarro's forces defeated Almagro's army and captured the old conquistador. Hernando Pizarro ordered the execution of his brother's former partner, but when he returned to Spain months later, Hernando was imprisoned for his action.

The execution of Almagro appeared to end the long rivalry between his faction and that of the Pizarros. Yet peace proved an illusion. Almagro's young *mestizo* son, also named Diego de Almagro, inherited the leadership of his father's supporters and rejected Francisco Pizarro's efforts to mollify him. The faction's continued frustration ultimately erupted in violence. In 1541 a group of twenty heavily armed supporters of young Almagro stormed Pizarro's palace, assassinated him, and then forced the terrified city council to appoint the young Almagro as the new governor of Peru.

The Almagro faction's rebellion was doomed from the outset. Upon hearing of the civil war, Charles I sent Cristóbal Vaca de Castro to be governor of Peru, with the authority to settle the political chaos. Reaching the colony soon after Pizarro's assassination, Vaca de Castro quickly organized the Pizarro loyalists and in September 1542 defeated the young Almagro's forces. Although the unfortunate youth may have been only a figurehead for the unhappy partisans of his father, he paid with his life for Pizarro's murder.

Vaca de Castro and the supporters of the Pizarros had little time to savor their triumph, however. In November 1542, Charles I issued the famous New Laws in an effort to improve conditions for the Indians and to prevent the *encomenderos* from becoming a true nobility. The New Laws threatened *encomenderos* throughout the Indies, for they ordered that their *encomiendas* revert to the Crown after their death. For the *encomenderos* in Peru, one provision was even more ominous, stating that "Indians are to be taken away from the persons responsible for the disturbances between Pizarro and Almagro." As the chronicler Agustín de Zárate later noted, "It is clear that no one in Peru could retain his Indians."[7]

Brought to Peru by the colony's first viceroy, Blasco Núñez de la Vela, the New Laws and the ill-advised efforts to enforce them played into the hands of the ambitious Gonzalo Pizarro. In the 1540s the *encomienda* provided the economic base for the social and political power of the conquistadors and first settlers. Men who had survived the Indian wars and civil conflicts of Peru's early years would not voluntarily surrender their hard-won financial welfare and place at the apex of the social order. Núñez de la Vela's intemperate actions and ill-conceived efforts to enforce the New Laws, however, finally convinced the colonial elite that revolt might be necessary to preserve their power. Slowly, an armed opposition to the viceroy began to form around Gonzalo Pizarro. The climax was reached when Núñez de la Vela stabbed to death in the viceregal palace a royal official whom he suspected of disloyalty.

The *audiencia,* or high court of Lima, already opposed to the viceroy, arrested Núñez de la Vela in 1544, but he escaped and tried to organize an army in Quito the following year. The forces of Gonzalo Pizarro quickly hunted him down and killed him. Following the ex-viceroy's death in 1546, Gonzalo Pizarro remained the effective ruler of Peru. Rejecting advice to declare the colony independent from Spain, he unleased a reign of terror against Spaniards suspected of disloyalty to him. He executed 340, many more than had died during the conquest.

Gonzalo Pizarro's brutality and the patent illegality of his authority worked to produce an armed opposition. When a new representative of royal authority, the priest Pedro de la Gasca, arrived, Gonzalo's military support melted away. By the time royalist forces cornered his army on the plain in front of Cuzco in 1549, there was no longer a will to fight. Without a test of strength, his men simply crossed the plain to join the royalists and accept pardons. Gonzalo Pizarro was tried for treason and beheaded.

Pedro de la Gasca thus succeeded politically where the violent men of the conquest had failed. He ended an era of civil war that had repeatedly endangered Spanish control of Peru, although there continued to be brief challenges to royal authority in the 1550s. Soon the colony moved dramatically away from the direct expropriation of Indian wealth and production through the *encomienda* and pushed forward to an economy based heavily on mining. The discovery of silver at Potosí in 1545 and mercury at Huancavelica in 1563 enabled an economic direction to be established by the 1570s that persisted until the end of the colonial era.

The much-diminished Incan kingdom in Vilcabamba that Manco Inca had established after his flight from Cuzco survived his murder and the rule of two successors. Viceroy Francisco de Toledo, however, finally overwhelmed the last Incan emperor, Tupac Amaru, by military force in 1572. After a trial, the royal prisoner was executed in the central square of the ancient Incan capital. His death ended the saga begun forty years earlier at Cajamarca.

With the conquest of the Incas, the Spaniards gained dominion over a populous and wealthy region extending from Colombia to Chile. The ransom of Atahualpa and the riches subsequently seized in Cuzco far exceeded the precious metals that Cortés and his men had secured in Mexico. The number of immediate beneficiaries in both conquests, however, soon paled in comparison with the thousands of Spaniards who arrived in their wake. Eager to emulate the early conquistadors, these later arrivals joined expeditions that in a few years had combed much of the Western Hemisphere in a vain search for other wealthy native civilizations.

The Ebbtide of Conquest

The Spanish and Portuguese exploration and occupation of Latin America followed no coherent plan devised in Europe. Rather, individual ambition, the desire for personal wealth, and family fame and fortune propelled this unprecedented territorial expansion. Frequently leaders organized expeditions and determined objectives in response to rumors of riches or minimal prior contact with a native culture. The funds, people, and leadership expended in new explorations dangerously reduced the scarce human and material resources of existing settlements. Indian societies were the primary victims of these expeditions. They suffered attacks, often for no other reason than they were along the route of march, and depletion of their populations by death and slavery. In most cases, the indigenous peoples fought to defend their territories. When further resistance proved impossible, many natives fled their traditional lands to escape further depredations.

A handful of large, well-funded expeditions sailed directly from Spain, but small groups of lightly armed Europeans organized in the New World explored most of the Indies and conquered its indigenous populations. Cortés's military force, one of the largest and best armed, numbered fewer than two thousand Spaniards when Tenochtitlán fell. Because most expeditions had few men and limited resources, their success, even survival, often depended on individual leaders' ability and determination. The conquistadors cannot be reduced to a type, but clearly endurance, physical courage, audacity, and cunning, rather than high birth or formal military training, were among the important characteristics of the leaders of this era. Only prior experience in campaigns against the Indians consistently paid dividends.

In addition to the challenges posed by geography and climate and the nearly constant threats of hunger, thirst, and illness, the conquistadors confronted vast populations of often hostile natives. Their weakness and vulnerability in an environment of nearly constant danger increased the likelihood that both the Spanish and Portuguese would seize on exemplary violence as a useful political tool for breaking the independence of native peoples.

Central America

After the destruction of Tenochtitlán, Cortés organized new expeditions under the command of his most trusted lieutenants. They were to subjugate former tributaries of the Aztec confederation and to follow up reports of rich civilizations that remained independent. Cortés himself led a small expedition to impose Spanish rule on Pánuco, located on the coast of the Gulf of Mexico. The arrival of an undisciplined military force sent by the governor of Jamaica, however, soon undid Cortés's pacification of this region. The newcomers' greed and cruelty provoked a violent Indian uprising. The seasoned veteran leaders Pedro de Alvarado and Gonzalo de Sandoval subdued the new arrivals and then mercilessly crushed the Indian rebellion. The two groups of rebels received strikingly different treatment. Alvarado and Sandoval forgave the Spanish intruders who had caused the uprising but burned to death four hundred captured Indians.

Looking toward southern Mexico, Cortés ordered Cristóbal de Olid to sail to the coast of modern Honduras to follow up rumors of rich kingdoms. Once on his own, Olid imitated Cortés's earlier action at Vera Cruz and declared himself governor. When news of this mutiny reached Cortés, he organized a punitive expedition and set off for Central America.

Cortés took with him the captured Aztec monarch Cuauhtémoc and his kinsman, the king of Tacuba, as hostages to prevent a native uprising in the Valley of Mexico during his absence. As the expedition struggled forward through nearly impassable terrain, Cortés faced a near mutiny. The Spaniards believed that Cuauhtémoc knew where treasure was secretly hidden before the Aztec's surrender. Tortured before the expedition, the defeated monarch had directed the Spaniards to a rich cache. Frustrated by the futility of their expedition and, in many cases, embittered by the uneven distribution of booty following the surrender of Tenochtitlán, Cortés's followers demanded that Cuauhtémoc and his kinsman divulge the location of additional treasure. When torture failed to produce the desired results, both native rulers were executed. Cortés's expedition did not lead to the establishment of Spanish political authority or permanent settlements. It did mark, however, the beginning of the military conquest of Central America.

With the blessing of Cortés, Alvarado undertook a separate expedition to Central America, which proved more successful than his mentor's. In hard fighting, Alvarado's men defeated the Quiches of Guatemala.

Although materially poorer and militarily weaker than the Aztecs, the Quiches were formidable foes. With a population of forty thousand, their capital of Utatlán impressed the veterans of the Aztec campaign. Built from cut stone and well fortified, the city nonetheless proved unable to resist a determined Spanish attack. In Central America, as in the Valley of Mexico, the conquistadors exploited bitter tribal rivalries that divided the indigenous peoples. The Quiches' traditional enemies, the Cakchiquels, remained on the sidelines watching Alvarado destroy the rival capital. Their turn came next.

The guerrilla tactics and determined resistance of the Cakchiquels so angered Alvarado that he ordered the captured chiefs burned to death, an action he eventually had to defend in a Spanish court. As the resistance crumbled, the Spanish branded and sold as slaves thousands of captured Quiches and Cakchiquels. The king's treasury received the yield from one-fifth of all slaves sold. This merciless exploitation provoked Indian uprisings in 1524 and 1526 that the Spaniards crushed cruelly and ended by taking a new harvest of slaves.

The Mayas of the Yucatán resisted Spanish domination for more than a decade. Because the Mayas were not organized in a unified political state, they proved more resistant to Spanish conquest. In the Yucatán the Spaniards faced the difficult task of imposing centralized government on a divided and contentious people. Francisco de Montejo undertook their conquest in 1527, but as late as 1535 the Spaniards found themselves able to control little more than the ground on which they stood. The effectiveness of Mayas' hit-and-run tactics slowed, but could not stop, the imposition of Spanish authority. They established effective political control only in 1545 and did not defeat the last independent Mayan group until 1697.

The Northern Frontier

Throughout the Americas, indigenous peoples with decentralized political structures and little agriculture or urbanization resisted Spanish domination more effectively than did the rigid and disciplined Aztec and Incan states. Much of this success came from employing guerrilla tactics that dispersed Spanish resources and neutralized the advantages of superior armaments. On the northern frontier of New Spain such tactics made pacification difficult. Cortés's enemy, Nuño de Guzmán, president of the first *audiencia* of Mexico, carved out between 1529 and 1536 a new province, Nueva Galicia, north and west of Mexico City. With the center at Guadalajara, the region was initially renowned for the fierce resistance of its Chichimec inhabitants.

Spanish interest in Nueva Galicia increased dramatically when Indians showed a small group of missionaries and soldiers a rich silver deposit in 1546. Within four years, thirty-four mines were operating. The Chichimecas, however, struggled desperately to hold back this flow of Europeans, just as their ancestors had resisted the Toltecs and Aztecs. It took a combination of mission settlements peopled by pacified Indians from the south, frontier forts *(presidios)*, and an extensive system of bribes paid to the unpacified Chichimecas finally to establish peace in the 1590s.

Exploration of the far northern frontier began in 1540. The reports of Alvar Núñez Cabeza de Vaca, who with four other men had survived an incredible eight-year odyssey walking from the Gulf coast of Texas to Mexico, seemed to confirm Indian tales of great civilizations located in the north. Viceroy Antonio de Mendoza selected his well-born favorite, Francisco Vásquez de Coronado, to lead more than two hundred horsemen, sixty infantry, and over a thousand Indian warriors to the far north. Passing through Arizona, New Mexico, Texas, Oklahoma, and Kansas, Coronado failed to fulfill the expectations that had launched the expedition. Nonetheless, his effort initiated the systematic exploration of the American Southwest and brought the settled agriculturalists of the region, primarily Zuñi, into the Spanish orbit.

Chile and the Pampean Region

The vast, sparsely settled Pampean region contained a variety of indigenous peoples dispersed in small groups. These cultures were based on hunting and some agriculture and lacked significant cities, a complex political organization, and a social hierarchy. This physical dispersal and the absence of an integrated political system proved to be assets when the Spaniards invaded.

To reward Pedro de Valdivia for his service in the crucial battle of Las Salinas, Pizarro gave him a license to pacify Chile. The stories told by participants of Almagro's earlier unsuccessful expedition, however, hindered efforts to recruit men and raise capital to purchase equipment. Borrowing heavily, Valdivia assembled a force less than half the size of its predecessor. Leaving Peru in early 1540, the Spanish reached Chile via the less arduous coastal route.

Shortly after his arrival, Valdivia founded Santiago, but the hostility of the indigenous population placed in doubt the settlement's very survival. An Indian attack while Valdivia was away nearly overwhelmed the settlers. Only the heroic, though brutal, actions of a priest and Inés Suárez, Valdivia's mistress, prevented their annihilation: Following the common practice of terrorizing the natives through violence, they ordered seven hostage *caciques* executed and their severed heads thrown among the attackers.

The discovery of gold in 1552 attracted a new wave of Spanish settlers to Chile, and within a year Chile had hosted more than a thousand colonists in a series of towns founded along the southern frontier. Fertile soil and a temperate climate contributed to the rapid expansion of agriculture and ranching in the region.

Yet this period of expansion masked Chile's continued military vulnerability. Harsh exploitation by *encomenderos* and the common receipt of brutal punishments embittered the pacified population of the central valley. In the south a large unconquered population with an increasingly effective military capacity still exercised control. In an attempt to secure the small frontier forts, Valdivia put together a force of veteran Indian fighters. The speed, maneuverability, and bulk of mounted Spaniards broke every Indian formation and reduced native heroism to futility.

Everywhere in the Indies the natives adapted—though seldom quickly enough—to the horse and to Spanish weapons. The Aztecs dug pits to trap mounted Spaniards. Manco Inca learned to ride and use Spanish weapons. In Chile a former groom in Valdivia's stables, Lautaro, developed a devastatingly successful tactic to use against his former master. By dividing the Indian forces into separate units that would attack and then fall back and regroup while others moved forward, he was able to tire the horses and reduce the Spaniards' maneuverability. Brilliantly employing his theory, Lautaro handed Valdivia his first defeat and captured and executed the governor. Not until 1557 did an army sent from Peru finally pacify Chile as far south as the border that Valdivia had established in 1552.

Spanish exploration of the Río de la Plata region began with Juan de Solis in 1516. Ten years later Sebastian Cabot began a remarkable investigation of the estuary and inland river system. As a result of trading for a small amount of silver, or *plata,* that was probably Peruvian in origin, he gave the river the inappropriate name of Río de la Plata. After three years and the loss of nearly half of his men, Cabot returned to Spain. For nearly a decade, no effort was made to follow up his voyage.

Fearful of the growing Portuguese presence along the Brazilian coast, the Spanish Crown organized, but did not invest in, one of the largest military forces ever sent directly from the Old World. Pedro de Mendoza arrived in the estuary with ten ships and more than a thousand men. He established a settlement on the low flat south bank of the river in 1536 and was at first welcomed by the Indians of the region. Violence broke out, however, when Spanish demands for food and labor outstripped the natives' hospitality. In the resulting struggle, the fortified mud-and-straw village of Buenos Aires barely escaped destruction. In 1537 Mendoza loaded most of the survivors on ships and sailed for Spain but died before arriving.

Buenos Aires and its few settlers remained under the command of the energetic Juan de Ayolas. After securing the town's immediate safety, Ayolas explored the interior. In 1537, he founded Asunción, Paraguay, near a large population of sedentary agriculturalists, the Guaraní. The native culture permitted the Spaniards to develop an *encomienda*-based economy not unlike those found in Oaxaca, Central America, and central Mexico. Reinforced by refugees from Buenos Aires, Paraguay became a permanent Spanish colony.

During this same period, Spaniards from Peru and Chile entered western Argentina, competing for political preeminence with one another and with the settlers from Asunción. In 1553 the Peruvians founded Santiago del Estero, the oldest permanent settlement in Argentina, and in 1580 Juan de Garay refounded Buenos Aires with settlers from Asunción. This second settlement of Buenos Aires overwhelmingly depended on creoles, the offspring of Spanish couples, and *mestizos,* the children of Spanish and Indian unions. It represented both the culmination of the Spanish colonization effort in South America and the effective coming of age of the native-born Hispanic population.

Northern South America

Early coastal reconnaissance and exploration of the northern South American mainland largely occurred as a result of the Spanish slave raids. As late as 1530 only a handful of permanent settlements existed between the mouth of the Orinoco River and the isthmus of Panama. This comparative isolation ended when Diego de Ordas, one of Cortés's captains, used his influence at court to gain a license in 1530 to explore the Orinoco basin. Like many of his contemporaries, Ordas believed that gold "grew" better near the equator. With more than six hundred Spaniards, he sailed up the Orinoco only to have to endure nearly constant battle and incredible privation. His force broken, the unfortunate Ordas gave up. He died while returning to Spain.

The level of activity altered dramatically after Charles I granted the administration of Venezuela to the German banking house of Welser. The king made this unique arrangement in exchange for the Welser's considerable financial support during his successful campaign to become Holy Roman Emperor. Governor Ambrosius Dalfinger and Nicolaus Federmann led the first expeditions, which were largely filled with Spanish recruits. Both failed to find advanced civilizations, despite overcoming great hardships. As Dalfinger's expedition moved along the eastern flank of the mountains, the invaders found beautifully finished gold ornaments that the forest Indians indicated had come from the Muiscas or Chibchas. Most of the gold that Dalfinger had collected disappeared when the men escorting it to the coast became lost and perished. Dalfinger himself died as a result of being wounded by a poisoned arrow.

The end for the Muisca, the last high civilization conquered by the Spanish, came quickly once the Andes was penetrated. Three separate expeditions ultimately entered their territory, but the glory and most of the treasure fell into the hands of the lawyer Gonzalo Jiménez de Quesada. Selected to lead the expedition by the governor of Santa Marta on the Colombian coast, Quesada began with more than 500 Spaniards. But by the time he reached the Muiscas' realm, only 170 men were left, nearly the same number as were present with Pizarro at Cajamarca.

Approximately one million Muiscas were organized in an integrated and well-ordered village system located in rich mountain valleys near the present city of Bogotá. Although sharing the same basic culture and technology, two large political confederations headed by rival rulers, the *zipa* of Bogotá and the *zaque* of Tunja, had evolved.

The Muiscas enjoyed material prosperity and relative peace but were politically and technologically less advanced than were the Aztecs and Incas. They had no large cities, and even the nobles' palaces were built of decorated wood rather than cut stone. Their textiles had painted rather than woven or embroidered designs, and their tools and weapons were made of stone or wood. Unlike the forest and plains Indians to the east, the Muiscas did not use poisons and rarely used bows and arrows.

The Muiscas cultivated potatoes, quinoa, sweet potatoes, tomatoes, squash, beans, and a great variety of fruits. Along with salt, cotton, emeralds, and metals, they traded these agricultural products through a well-developed market system. Their most famous product, beautiful gold work, depended on this market system to secure a flow of gold ore from neighboring regions.

In March 1537, when Quesada's men looked out on the broad valleys and prosperous villages of the Muiscas' domain, they recognized immediately that the terrain was ideal for cavalry. The Muiscas, however, struck first. They began their futile struggle with a surprise attack against Quesada's rear guard. The Muiscas' initial advantage faded quickly, however, as the Spanish cavalry rapidly advanced over the flat ground and turned the contest into a bloody rout. Although the conquest took a year to complete, the outcome was never in doubt.

The elusiveness of the *zipa*—more than the military competence of his armies—delayed the defeat. Quesada's men, however, moved quickly to capture the other Chibcha leader. The *zaque*'s palace yielded 135,500 pesos of fine gold, 14,000 pesos of base gold, and 280 emeralds. Under torture Muiscan leaders led the Spaniards to tombs that provided additional booty.

When the *zipa*'s hideout was finally discovered, Quesada launched a successful night attack. Once victorious, he selected a new ruler who foolishly offered to duplicate Atahualpa's ransom to escape further torment. His failure to deliver the promised treasure, however, caused the Spaniards to burn off his feet. The *zipa* died in great agony, but without providing additional booty. Quesada ordered the division of all spoils in June 1538. The governor of Santa Marta received ten shares, Quesada nine, the other captains four, each cavalryman two, and each soldier one. Each share was calculated at 510 pesos of fine gold, 57 pesos of base gold, and five emeralds.

Two other expeditions arrived in the Muisca region as Quesada brought his military campaign to a close. Benalcázar, Pizarro's lieutenant who had conquered Quito, was attempting to carve out an independent territory to the north of Peru. The Welser captain Federmann arrived after having found a pass though the Andes. Avoiding a military confrontation, the three leaders agreed to sail to Spain to allow the Crown to determine the merits of their competing claims for the governorship of New Granada. All were disappointed when Charles V named another man.

El Dorado

Rumors of a wealthy Indian civilization located in the interior of northern South America fueled a last wave of exploration. These tales commonly featured a native prince who covered himself in gold dust, El Dorado. Separate efforts to find this astonishing ruler were undertaken in 1541 by Gonzalo Pizarro; Hernán Pérez de Quesada, the brother of the conqueror of the Chibcha; and Philip von Hutten, the last of the Welser explorers. The indomitable Benalcázar pursued this same mirage in 1543. The most important result of this succession of failed expeditions was the navigation of the length of the Amazon by Francisco de Orellana, one of Gonzalo Pizarro's captains.

The remarkable and terrifying story of Lope de Aguirre brings to an end the violent exploration and conquest of this region. In 1559 the nobleman Pedro de Ursúa received a royal license to undertake a new search for the elusive El Dorado. A year later 370 Spaniards and thousands of highland Indians began to march to the east. Ursúa proved to be an inept and ineffective leader more interested in the charms of his mistress than in managing an expedition. As losses to disease and hostile action by forest Indians mounted, mutinous soldiers murdered Ursúa and named the Spanish nobleman Fernando de Guzmán their leader. The real power, however, rested with an embittered commoner, Lope de Aguirre, who, along with his supporters, believed that he had not received fair treatment in Peru.

Aguirre forced his puppet Guzmán to proclaim himself in rebellion against royal authority and to assume the title lord and prince of Peru, the Main, and Chile. Aguirre planned to sail the length of the Amazon and then seize Panama as a base for attacking Peru. He soon tired of Guzmán and had him and Ursua's mistress butchered; indeed, before reaching the Brazilian coast, this dangerous psychopath had executed all the *hidalgos* in the expedition. The 170 Indian porters who survived the voyage down the Amazon were abandoned to their fate on the banks of the river. On reaching the coast of Venezuela, Aguirre seized the island of Margarita and ordered the governor executed.

Although Aguirre's arrival threw the colonial authorities into a panic, he had only a small force left. Desertions sealed his fate. In a final act of rebellion against conventional moral and legal constraints, Aguirre murdered his own daughter, Elvira, rather than have her captured by royal officers. Outraged by this awful act, Aguirre's own men then killed him. His body was quartered, and pieces of it were displayed in marketplaces throughout the colony.

Brazil

The Portuguese occupation of Brazil shared many characteristics with the Spanish experience in the Río de la Plata region. Brazil had no wealthy, urbanized native societies, and the early exploration and settlement of this vast colony lacked the great drama of Cortés's conquest of the Aztecs or Pizarro's triumph in Peru. There were approximately 2.4 million Indians divided among a large number of nonsedentary and semisedentary cultures. Along the coast where the first contacts were made, the Portuguese encountered many large settlements. Language differences and a tradition of armed conflict often permitted the Portuguese, and later the French, to establish alliances and gain a foothold.

Following Cabral's landing in 1500, initial contacts between Indians and Europeans were generally peaceful. At the time, Portugal was using its limited resources for the exploitation of the Far East whose spices and silks found eager buyers in Europe. The Brazilian product that found the largest market was a red dyewood, brazilwood, although tropical birds, animals, and some Indian captives were also sold in Europe. Portuguese and soon French ships anchored along the coast and traded iron tools, weapons, and other European goods to the Indians, who cut and transported the heavy logs. Initially Indians eagerly cut and hauled the brazilwood to the waiting ships. But competition between the Portuguese and French for dyewood placed unacceptable pressure on the Indians and undermined the early barter economy. The attractiveness of European trade goods was limited, and the Indians resisted labor demands that would fundamentally alter their culture. As a result, the Portuguese turned to forced labor to break this cultural constraint on the profitable harvesting of brazilwood.

The creation of more permanent settlements and the introduction of sugar cultivation led to a rapid expansion of Indian slavery. Sugar was produced in Pernambuco in 1526 and was introduced successfully in São Vicente and Espirito Santo in the 1530s. Nearly constant war among the indigenous peoples provided the invaders with a ready opportunity to organize the supply of slaves. With the exception of a few captives kept for sacrifice and cannibalism, native warriors had slain their enemies on the battlefield. Now the labor needs of expanding European agriculture transformed these practices by turning the captives into a commodity. The advent of new weapons and a new objective, procuring captives for market exchange, promoted an increase in native violence.

Divided by ancient rivalries and vendettas, the Indians were incapable of uniting to resist European settlement. The integration into the native elite of Tupí-speaking Portuguese who married Indian women in indigenous rites or lived with them in concubinage further reduced the potential for native resistance. These Portuguese males often gained leadership positions in tribal affairs. Their *mameluco* children, especially in Bahia and São Paulo, later created a political and cultural bridge between a temporarily independent Indian culture and its future subordination in the context of a colonial society.

By the time that some indigenous groups tried to overthrow the encroaching colonial order in the 1550s, the European population, reinforced by *mameluco* kinsmen and a Crown finally willing to commit resources to Brazil, proved too strong. The Indians had their victories, including killing the colony's first bishop and nearly destroying Ilhéus, Espirito Santo, and Bahia, but the action of Governor Mem de Sá (1558–72) turned the tide. Horses, firearms, and metal weapons and armor provided an advantage that no amount of native heroism or military competence could overcome. Eventually the Tupinambas, the Caetes, and the Tupinkins were defeated by the Portuguese, and by the end of the sixteenth century nearly all of the coast between Rio Grande and São Vicente was pacified. After a ten-year occupation of land near present-day Rio de Janeiro, a small colony of French settlers was expelled by Mem de Sá in 1565.

By the late sixteenth century, explorers reached what became the effective territorial limits of Spain's and Portugal's American empires. The conquerors had defeated militarily or subordinated in the new colonial order nearly all the native peoples they had encountered. They had accomplished this enormous undertaking, moreover, with few resources and little government control. As each region fell to conquest and settlement, the Iberian crowns turned to the task of imposing order and elaborating the institutions of government, church, and economy.

Conundrums and the Columbian Exchange

The exploration, conquest, and settlement of the New World produced numerous problems for intellectuals to ponder as well as exchanges between the conquering and vanquished cultures. The addition of the Western Hemisphere to the Old World's geographical knowledge necessitated the redrawing of world maps. The Iberians' right to conquest, the nature of the Amerindians and the treatment they should receive, and the best means to convert the natives to Christianity were topics debated by Spanish jurists and theologians in particular. On a more prosaic level, plants, animals, and diseases crossed the Atlantic both to and from the Americas and initiated a blending of cultures that continues today.

Cosmography showed the first and most noticeable changes resulting from the exploration of the Americas. Whereas Columbus died convinced he had reached Asia, other early explorers presented evidence that the land reached was a "new world," a territory unknown to the ancients and separate from the "Island of Earth"—the landmass comprising Europe, Asia, Africa, and adjacent islands—that fifteenth-century thinkers considered the only place in the universe where humans could live. The Florentine navigator Amerigo Vespucci's *Mundus Novus* (1503) was the first published description of a major landmass absent from Ptolemy's geography, although the author mistakenly related it to Asia. Cartographers soon had to come to grips with these newly discovered lands. The first map incorporating the Western Hemisphere appeared in Florence in 1506. The publication in the following year of a map by Martin Waldseemüller provided a better representation, showing the continent as an independent entity labeled "America" in honor of Vespucci. After the first circumnavigation of the globe, in the late 1520s mapmakers were able to start doing some justice to the Pacific Ocean and the west coast of the Americas. Gerardus Mercator's map in 1569 ended dependence on the ancients, notably Ptolemy, and opened a new era for cartography. Better detail, of both of the coasts and the interiors of the continents, followed the later coasting expeditions and exploration. Already by 1569, however, voyages to the Americas from Europe were routine, and considerable attention had been given to their inhabitants.

Even as exploration revealed a separate hemisphere unattached to the previously known world, questions about the nature of its inhabitants began to attract attention. The first reports made clear that the natives behaved very differently from the Europeans. Their nudity, for example, immediately caught the Iberians' attention. Columbus related in a letter published more than twenty times by 1500 that with rare exceptions the people of the islands went about unclad. The chronicler of Cabral's landfall in Brazil was particularly enchanted by the women there, "just as naked [as the men and] . . . not displeasing to the eye."[8] Equally impressive to Iberian males was the natives' generosity and less inhibited sexuality; they especially appreciated hospitality that at times included an attrative woman as well as food and lodging.

There were other customs that the explorers found astonishing and even revolting. The Brazilian women's practice of bathing frequently astounded men who rarely washed. Worse in the Iberians' perception was the cannibalism they noted in Brazil, some Caribbean islands, and on the Spanish Main. The human sacrifices and cannibalism later witnessed in central Mexico simply confirmed for them their belief in the Amerindians' inferiority. For some observers, certain aspects of indigenous culture raised doubts about their humanity; a slightly more generous interpretation elevated them to the category of "natural slaves"; yet some contemporaries considered them simple, beautiful, innocent people living according to their instincts. Were the natives truly part of humanity? Did they possess souls and thus the potential for conversion to Christianity? Was conquest just? The answers to these questions largely underlay the Spanish Crown's effort to protect the Amerindians and the clergy's efforts to convert them.

The papal donation of 1493 gave the Crown of Castile both title to the Indies and the initial justification for war against the natives, but other arguments soon supplemented it as reasons for the Spaniards' actions. According to one school of medieval thought, a Christian ruler serving the pope could legitimately declare war on infidels who refused to acknowledge papal authority. Spanish critics of this far-reaching claim denied that such a refusal was adequate to justify war and the seizure of the natives' property. The Dominican Francisco de Vitoria, one of the founders of international law, outlined in the 1530s other reasons justifying Spanish conquest and rule. Although Vitoria opposed war for war's sake, he considered it just if the natives sought to prevent the Spaniards from living among them in peace, opposed the preaching of the gospel, or tried to return converts to idolatry. In addition, the Spaniards could intervene to save innocent people from cannibalism or other "unjust death" or to aid native friends and allies. The eminent humanist and translator of Aristotle, Dr. Juan Ginés de Sepúlveda, was more direct. Employing Aristotle's theory of natural slavery, Sepúlveda argued that the natives' natural inferiority, idolatries, and other sins justified war to civilize them. That is, the barbarity that constituted the natives' very nature vindicated their conquest and even enslavement. Moreover, war would facilitate their conversion to Christianity. By the mid-sixteenth century, these and other related arguments effectively supplemented and even supplanted reliance on the papal donation as a justification for Spanish conquest and rule in the Indies.

In 1537 Pope Paul III stated the Church's official position on the natives' nature. His bull *Sublimis Deus* declared the Indians "truly men" and thus capable of Christianization. More importantly, the bull confirmed the Indians' right to possess property and prohibited their enslavement and the seizure of their property. But this pronouncement failed to terminate Indian slavery in either Spanish America or Brazil.

A broader debate took place in Spain over the conquest and forced conversion of the natives. The principal protagonists were Sepúlveda and the Dominican Bartolomé de las Casas. A former conquistador and *encomendero,* Las Casas's earlier denunciations of the Spanish mistreatment of Indians had influenced the Crown's decision to promulgate the New Laws of 1542. A vehement opponent of conquest and forced conversion, he maintained that the natives had sufficient "capacity" to become Christianized peacefully and live like Spaniards. Sepúlveda, on the other hand, relied on the papal donation and Aristotle's doctrine of natural slavery to justify both Spain's conquest and the use of forceful conversion. The consequence, he argued, was to end barbarous customs such as idolatry, cannibalism, and human sacrifice.

In 1550 Charles I entered the controversy. He convened a panel of theologians and jurists in Valladolid to resolve the debate and ordered an end to conquest until the issue was settled. To the dismay of the combatants, no resolution followed, although Philip II's subsequent ordinance of 1573 using "pacification" rather than "conquest" in outlining the Spanish settlement of the Philippine Islands demonstrated how seriously he considered the questions raised. This well-intentioned distinction would have been more effective if the age of the greatest conquests had not already ended.

The most important long-term consequence of the controversy was the use that Spain's enemies made of some of its assertions. The English and Dutch in particular gleefully seized upon Las Casas's allegations of the conquistadors' cruelty. Adding to the anti-Spanish sentiment that had developed earlier in Italy, foreign publicists elaborated the so-called Black Legend focusing on allegedly unusual and unique Spanish cruelty. So effective was this propaganda campaign that a continuous thread of anti-Hispanic prejudice can be traced to the present day in the English-speaking world. In contrast, there was no similar Black Legend about the Portuguese. The reasons were not that they were less cruel that the Spaniards but, rather, that the Portuguese were not involved in the Revolt of the Netherlands, that there was no equivalent Portuguese conflict with the English, and that there was no Portuguese counterpart to Las Casas whose writings the Protestant propagandists could cite.

The Diffusion of Plants and Animals

The New World provided the Old with more mundane items than topics for theological and juridical discourse and royal soul-searching. In their long-term impact, these items certainly affected far more people. Maize, potatoes, sweet potatoes, beans, and manioc or cassava were the five New World plants that had the greatest influence on diet elsewhere. Squashes, peanuts, tomatoes, a variety of peppers, avocados, cacao, cherimoyas, and scores of other plants have further enriched tables in many parts of the world. Tobacco, too, became internationally popular.

Maize was present throughout much of the Americas when the Iberians arrived. Returning travelers soon carried it to Spain, and its presence in Castile was noted in 1530. Used as a food for animals, maize cultivation generally expanded after that date, and by the late eighteenth century it was a common crop in northern Spain and the provinces of Granada and Valencia. The Portuguese began to grow maize by 1525, and the area devoted to its planting increased substantially in the following years. Only late in the seventeenth century, however, did maize become an important staple on other European tables.

Returning Spaniards introduced potatoes not long after the conquest of Peru. By the mid-1570s a hospital in Seville was feeding patients potatoes. It was well after that date, however, before potatoes became an important part of Europeans' daily fare. Peasants and laborers were the primary consumers of this easily grown tuber. The Irish became heavily dependent on potatoes for sustenance before 1700, and many workers of eighteenth-century Europe found the inexpensive starch a valuable addition to their diet.

No other American plants matched maize and potatoes for their importance in the European diet, but a number of others found their way to Old World tables. Lima, butter, kidney, navy, string, and innumerable other varieties of beans were grown in the New World. These protein-rich forms of "poor man's meat" soon spread to the remainder of the known world. Their frequent cultivation in private gardens rather than fields prevents quantifying their importance, but they are a common addition to meals in many places. Manioc, the staple food crop of Brazil, is now an important crop in the tropics, although rarely found in North America or Europe except as the dessert tapioca. Sweet potatoes and yams are now important secondary crops in many areas of the world but have not impressed many European diners.

Amerindians ate wild game, fowl, and fish but had few and modest sources of domesticated animal protein to share with their invaders. Turkeys found some favor with European palates, and Muscovy ducks were imported for raising in the Old World as well. Guinea pigs, raised by the Incas for food, entered Europe in the sixteenth century but did not become popular there.

The Old World provided a wider range of plants and animals than the New did, which transformed the use of extensive regions of Latin America and affected diets and economies as well. Beginning with Columbus's second voyage in 1493, Spaniards began to import plants and animals that would enable them to maintain the customary Andalusian diet. Wheat, olive oil, wine, domestic meat, and cheese were essential foodstuffs without which they could not have the "good life" they sought in the Indies. The early settlers also imported familiar vegetables and fruits to complement their dietary staples. The Caribbean islands were not well suited for many plants the settlers introduced. For example, the sources of Mediterranean sustenance—wheat, olive trees, and grapevines—did not prosper. On the other hand, garden vegetables such as cabbage, radishes, and lettuce did well. Melons and a variety of other fruits also flourished. Sugarcane, introduced by Columbus in 1493, immediately took hold and became a staple of Hispaniola's economy for much of the sixteenth century. In the appropriate soil and climate, sugarcane could be grown from the Gulf of Mexico to Argentina. Brazil, in particular, began producing sugar soon after its first settlers arrived, and by 1580 it was the leading producer in the world. Bananas also prospered in the Antilles. Introduced in 1516, they quickly spread to the other Caribbean islands and Tierra Firme.

Compared with the mixed results of early horticulture in the Antilles, the initial efforts at raising livestock were spectacular. Horses, cattle, pigs, sheep, goats, and chickens reached Hispaniola in 1493. Ample forage and a growing amount of open land as a result of rapid decline in the Indian population provided an excellent environment. Pigs and cattle thrived; their encroachment on native agriculture, however, further exacerbated the drop in native population. As the Spaniards advanced from one island to another, they routinely took with them domestic animals, whose continued expansion in number diminished the effects of decreases in native agricultural products. The Spaniards' ability to travel with a mobile food supply, most notably swine, facilitated their subsequent exploration and conquest beyond the Caribbean.

The American mainlands, unlike the Antilles, provided the proper conditions for the full development of European crops and animals. Although they introduced many European plants, the Spanish colonists were especially anxious to grow wheat, grapes, and olives. Central Mexico by the mid-1530s produced enough wheat that exporters were sending it to the Caribbean islands and Tierra Firme. A decade later, agriculturists in parts of highland Peru also were producing substantial quantities of wheat. Indeed, the Spaniards planted wheat wherever they settled if the climate and topography were right. Growing grapes for good wine was more difficult, however. The first success was recorded in Peru, although one suspects that the 1551 vintage was best remembered for being pressed at all. The region around Arequipa was soon producing wine for resale in a number of markets in the viceroyalty. Tucumán and other parts of the Río de la Plata also supplied eager drinkers with the fruit of the vine. Chile, too, developed major vineyards. In contrast with wheat and grapes, success with olive trees came more slowly. An early settler in Lima, Antonio de Rivera, planted the first seedlings in 1560. Despite his efforts to guard them with slaves and dogs, a plant was stolen and whisked to Chile. Over time a substantial olive oil industry developed in a number of valleys along the Pacific coast of South America.

Most colonists in Brazil relied on manioc made into a flour for a staple food and consumed far less wheat than did their counterparts in Spanish America. The wealthy imported wheat, olive oil, cod, and wine from Portugal. Wheat grown in São Paulo and later in Rio Grande do Sul was for local consumption. The importance of sugar for exportation in Bahia and Pernambuco meant that planters there invariably devoted the best lands to sugarcane. Some colonists also grew tobacco and, for a time, ginger for export. Vegetables and manioc were grown on less fertile land.

Although the plants the Iberians brought from the peninsula and the Atlantic islands considerably changed the New World's arable landscape, the introduction of domesticated animals altered it even more. Pigs were the most important source of meat for the conquistadors, but their significance declined with more settled conditions and the expansion of cattle and sheep herds. Cattle and sheep provided not only meat but also other products—hides, tallow, and wool—for domestic markets. Hides also were exported from New Spain and later from Venezuela, the Río de la Plata, and Brazil. The fleet of 1587 carried nearly 100,000 hides to Seville, most of them from New Spain. Oxen in Brazil were indispensable in many phases of the production of sugar, and their number increased rapidly. Planters used them in hauling firewood, planting fields, and grinding cane. Horses also expanded in number after the Iberians settled in New Spain, in the highland pasture areas of Peru and Ecuador, and in Brazil. Chile and especially the Río de la Plata became sources of quality mounts too. With horses and cattle, a distinctive social type emerged in several frontier regions. Called *gauchos* in the Río de la Plata, *llaneros* on the plains of Venezuela, and *vaqueiros* in the *sertão* of Brazil, these cowboys of mixed ancestry played an important role in pushing back the frontier and providing cattle and their by-products to urban centers and for exportation.

The introduction of European plants and animals enabled the Iberians to emulate and in some ways to surpass the living standards of their peers on the peninsula. Meat became plentiful quickly, and the quality of the colonists' diets was well above that of most Iberians. The consequences for the Indians of Old World flora and fauna, on the other hand, were quite different.

Beginning with their settlement in the Caribbean, the Spaniards required the natives to grow and provide as tribute these new European foodstuffs. Forced to grow new plants with new methods, the natives complied reluctantly. They did not have to eat the new foods, however, and few incorporated wheat or other European crops into their diet. The native response to imported animals, in contrast, was markedly more favorable.

Indians quickly integrated small domestic animals into their lives. Dogs, cats, chickens, and pigs did not require the living space of cattle or sheep. Consequently, many natives kept the smaller animals, but relatively few in densely settled regions maintained herds of cattle or sheep. Indeed, the Spaniards' herds caused the natives no end of trouble as they trod through fields and villages, destroying crops. On the frontiers the story was different. In the interior of Brazil the Indians found it difficult to refrain from hunting cattle as large and easy prey. Natives in the frontier regions of New Spain and Chile, on the other hand, herded the larger domestic animals with the aid of horses. Horsemanship became prized in a number of frontier cultures, and the Araucanians of Chile and Guaicurú of Brazil and the Chaco, for example, expertly rode horses in battle against other natives and the Iberians.

Disease

Diseases joined plants and animals in the passage back and forth across the Atlantic. The Indians' millennia of isolation had prevented them from developing immunities against a series of devastating diseases imported from Europe and Africa. Smallpox reached Hispaniola by January 1519, was carried to New Spain in the following year, and then passed through Central America and, no later than 1527, to Peru. Wherever it passed, the epidemic facilitated the Spanish conquest, as it left an astronomical death toll in its wake. Frequently villages lost half or more of their population; cases of villages' losing 90 percent were even reported. Measles struck México and Peru in 1530–31. An epidemic that was probably typhus arrived fifteen years later. A virulent form of influenza followed, after killing perhaps 20 percent of the population in parts of Europe. Yellow fever and malaria came from Africa in the mid-seventeenth century. These and other diseases, which included diphtheria and possibly bubonic plague, further afflicted an already-weakened population. By the mid-seventeenth century, the native population of Spanish America was a small fraction— probably less than 10 percent and perhaps not even 5 percent—of its size in 1500.

The timing was different, but the pattern of destruction in Brazil was similar. The first wave of epidemics struck near Bahia in 1562 and a broader area the following year. Probably a variety of hemorrhagic dysentary was the biggest killer. As a contemporary described its painful course, "the disease began with serious pains inside the intestines which made the liver and the lungs rot. It then turned into pox that were so rotton and poisonous that the flesh fell off them in pieces full of evil-smelling beasties."[9] Perhaps one-third to one-half of the native population perished in this initial onslaught. Another wave of diseases, including smallpox and measles, killed thousands in northeastern Brazil in the 1620s. By 1800 the native population of Brazil was probably no more than a quarter of its size in 1500.

Although the consequences of new diseases were far more calamitous in the New World than in the Old, the Europeans did not escape unscathed. At least some of the men who had accompanied Columbus on his first voyage returned to Barcelona with symptoms of venereal disease. Carried to Italy and spread among Italians and Frenchmen in the military campaigns of 1495, the disease quickly passed throughout the continent. Regardless of what they told their wives and lovers, Columbus's sailors had indeed contracted what physicians know as syphilis and yaws. Although the diseases' origins have now been traced to Africa, from whence they passed through Asia to America, the sailors' contact with native women was initially responsible for the spread of syphilis in Europe.

Whatever the qualms raised about the justice and legitimacy of the Iberian presence in the Western Hemisphere, it was clear in the Caribbean from the time of Ovando and in Brazil from the 1530s that the invaders were going to stay. To the extent that local conditions permitted, they introduced the plants, animals, and tools that they took for granted at home. Tragically they also brought a variety of epidemic diseases to which the Amerindians had no immunity. Those Iberians who returned to the peninsula carried with them New World plants, animals, an occasional native, and often venereal disease. Over time this "Columbian exchange" indelibly altered the demographic and economic landscapes of both the Old World and the New.

Notes

1. Hernán Cortés, *Hernan Cortés: Letters from Mexico*, trans. and ed. A. R. Pagden (New York: Orion Press, 1971), pp. 85–86.

2. Bernal Díaz, *The Conquest of New Spain*, trans. J. M. Cohen (New York: Penguin Books, 1963), pp. 148–49.

3. Cortés, *Letters*, p. 67.

4. Díaz, *The Conquest*, p. 214.

5. Miguel León-Portilla (ed.), *The Broken Spears: The Aztec Account of the Conquest of Mexico*, trans. Lysander Kemp (Boston: Beacon Press, 1961), p. 93.

6. Díaz, *The Conquest*, p. 406.

7. Agustín de Zárate, *The Discovery and Conquest of Peru*, trans. J. M. Cohen (Baltimore: Penguin Books, 1968), p. 236.

8. John H. Parry and Robert G. Keith (eds.), *New Iberian World*, 5 vols. (New York: Times Books, 1984), V, p. 10.

9. John Hemming, *Red Gold. The Conquest of the Brazilian Indians* (Cambridge, Mass.: Harvard University Press, 1978), p. 142.

Suggested for Further Reading

Clendinnen, Inga. *Ambivalent Conquests. Maya and Spaniard in Yucatán, 1517–1570.* Cambridge, England: Cambridge University Press, 1987.

Cortés, Hernan. *Hernan Cortés: Letters from Mexico.* Translated and edited by A. R. Pagden, with an introduction by J. H. Elliott. New York: Orion Press, 1971.

Crosby, Alfred W. *The Columbian Exchange. Biological and Cultural Consequences of 1492.* Westport, Conn.: Greenwood Press, 1972.

Day, A. Grove. *Coronado's Quest.* Berkeley and Los Angeles: University of California Press, 1940.

Díaz del Castillo, Bernal. *The True History of the Conquest of New Spain, 1517–1521.* Translated by A. P. Maudslay. New York: Farrar, Straus & Giroux, 1966.

Gardiner, C. Harvery. *Naval Power in the Conquest of Mexico.* Austin: Univeristy of Texas Press, 1956.

Hanke, Lewis. *The Spanish Struggle for Justice in the Conquest of America.* Philadelphia: University of Pennsylvania Press, 1949.

Hemming, John. *The Conquest of the Incas.* New York: Harcourt Brace Jovanovich, 1970.

Hemming, John. *Red Gold. The Conquest of the Brazilian Indians.* Cambridge, Mass.: Harvard University Press, 1978.

Hemming, John. *The Search for El Dorado.* London: Michael Joseph, 1978.

Henschen, Folke. *The History and Geography of Diseases.* Translated by Joan Tate. New York: Delacorte, 1966.

Huddleston, Lee Eldridge. *Origins of the American Indians: European Concepts, 1492– 1729.* Austin: University of Texas Press, 1967.

Kelly, John E. *Pedro de Alvarado, Conquistador.* Princeton, N.J.: Princeton University Press, 1932.

Kirkpatrick, F. A. *The Spanish Conquistadores.* London: A. & C. Black, 1946.

Lanning, John Tate. *Pedro de la Torre. Doctor to Conquerors.* Baton Rouge: Louisiana State University Press, 1974.

León-Portilla, Miguel, editor. *The Broken Spears: The Aztec Account of the Conquest of Mexico.* Translated by Lysander Kemp. Boston: Beacon Press, 1961.

Lockhart, James. *The Men of Cajamarca: A Social and Biographical Study of the First Conquerors of Peru.* Austin: University of Texas Press, 1972.

Lopez de Gomara, Francisco. *Cortés: The Life of the Conqueror by His Secretary.* Translated and edited by Lesley B. Simpson. Berkeley and Los Angeles: University of California Press, 1964.

Markham, Sir Clements. *The Conquest of New Granada.* Port Washington, N.Y.: Kennikat Press, 1971.

McNeill, William H. *Plagues and People.* Garden City, N.Y.: Anchor/Doubleday, 1976.

Padden, R. C. *The Hummingbird and the Hawk: Conquest and Sovereignty in the Valley of Mexico, 1503–1541.* Columbus: Ohio State University Press, 1967.

Pagden, Anthony. *The Fall of Natural Man. The American Indian and the Origins of Comparative Ethnology.* Cambridge, England: Cambridge University Press, 1982.

Romoli, Kathleen. *Balboa of Darien. Discoverer of the Pacific.* Garden City, N.Y.: Doubleday, 1953.

Sauer, Carl Ortwin. *Agricultural Origins and Dispersals.* New York: American Geographical Society, 1952.

Super, John C. *Food, Conquest and Colonization in Sixteenth-Century Spanish America.* Albuquerque: University of New Mexico Press, 1988.

Wachtel, Nathan. *The Vision of the Vanquished: The Spanish Conquest of Peru Through Indian Eyes, 1530–1570.* New York: Barnes & Noble, 1977.

THREE

RULING NEW WORLD EMPIRES

Imperial Organization and Administration

The New World's huge size and distance from Iberia formed an immutable background against which the Castilian and Portuguese crowns sought to establish and maintain their authority. Ambitious conquistadors in the Spanish colonies and early settlers there and in Brazil sought to become genuine aristocrats with all the seigneurial rights such status implied. Spanish and Portuguese rulers, in turn, opposed the emergence of a powerful, hereditary nobility located beyond their direct control. In addition, they expected the colonies to contribute to royal revenue. To address these problems, the Crowns relied on bureaucrats located both on the peninsula and in the Americas. The expansion of New World settlement invariably brought a complement of officials to the capital of each new colonial territory. For nearly three centuries the presence of royal bureaucrats contributed significantly to the colonies' overall political stability.

Problems of Time and Distance

The distance and resulting length of time for communication between the New World and Iberia affected both the offices established in the Americas and the authority their incumbents enjoyed. Winds and currents normally made the trip from Iberia to the Indies shorter than the return voyage. The following table indicates approximate convoy sailing times in the sixteenth and early seventeenth centuries to and from Cádiz, Sanlúcar, or Seville and selected ports. Many voyages, however, were shorter or longer, sometimes by several weeks. Sailing from Lisbon to Bahia took seventy to nearly one hundred days; voyages to Recife were a little shorter and to Rio de Janeiro slightly longer. The combination of winds and currents made the travel from Belém, near the mouth of the Amazon, and other northern Brazilian ports to Lisbon easier than to Bahia, thus making communication with officials in the metropolis more convenient than with those in the

Days from Andalusian Port to		Days to Andalusian Port from	
Canary Islands	13	Azores	31
Hispaniola	51	Florida	65
Havana	64	Havana	67
Cartagena	51	Cartagena	110
Vera Cruz	75	Vera Cruz	128
Isthmus of Panama	75	Isthmus of Panama	137

colonial capital. Slave ships from Angola could reach any Brazilian port in the comparatively brief time of thirty-five to sixty days.

A fleet sent from Spain to the Indies usually returned fourteen to fifteen months later. Annual fleets in the late sixteenth and early seventeenth centuries helped maintain orderly commerce and communication by reducing the time between departures. Small mail boats provided supplemental service, but their sailings were intermittent in the sixteenth century and often only two to four times a year in the seventeenth century, despite the growing irregularity of the fleet's sailings.

The coastal location of all of Brazil's major cities until the establishment of São Paulo facilitated their communication with Lisbon. The inland location of Mexico City and Bogotá, in contrast, added the extra time of land travel. Maintaining speedy communication with cities on the Pacific coast side of the Andes was even more difficult. Travel time from the mining center of Potosí to the Panamanian port of Portobelo, for example, was often seven weeks or more.

The constraints on the speed of communication between any location in the New World and Lisbon or Madrid gave officials resident in the New World greater authority than their counterparts on the peninsula had. At the same time, the distance separating the colonies from their metropolises exacerbated the problem of overseeing the officials themselves. The consequence was substantial flexibility when officials far from the source of their authority responded to local pressures.

Overview of Administration for the Spanish Colonies

The immense physical extent, the presence of densely populated and advanced sedentary civilizations, and scattered rich mineral deposits in the New World led the Crown of Castile to move quickly to gain control over conquistadors, settlers, and natives as successive regions were added to its domain. Most of the major administrative offices used to oversee its political and financial interests, provide justice to colonists and natives, and supervise the allocation of resources—primarily land, native labor, and offices—in the Indies were operating by 1535, although their number increased with later settlement. Fully developed by 1570, the administrative organization underwent little structural modification until the eighteenth century.

The Castilian Crown transplanted a number of institutions proven in Spain and the Canary Islands. General oversight of the colonies and administration of their largest territorial divisions followed the Aragonese model, in which a council resident at court provided the overall supervision and viceroys administered the largest territorial units—Aragon, Catalonia, and Valencia. Below the office of viceroy, the Crown turned to Castilian precedents and introduced regional courts, provincial administrators, and treasury officials. It also allowed the municipality and its local officials to exercise a variety of responsibilities. The one institution the Crown refused to introduce into the colonies was the *cortes,* an assembly attended by representatives from major towns and a potential brake on its authority.

The size of the New World possessions made imperative their division into more manageable administrative units. Accordingly, in 1535 Charles I created the viceroyalty of New Spain for land running from Panama's northern border into the present United States as well as the Caribbean islands and part of Venezuela. The Philippine Islands also were included in this viceroyalty after their settlement in the 1570s. In the early 1540s, Charles created the viceroyalty of Peru, which included Panama and all Spanish possessions in the Southern Hemisphere except for a strip of Venezuela. Then not until the eighteenth century were additional viceroyalties created.

Soon recognizing that the viceroyalties were too large for many administrative purposes, the Crown divided them into units called *audiencias.* These territories increased in number as the lands and non-Indian population of the empire expanded. The *audiencias* were themselves subdivided into districts variously called *corregimientos, alcaldías mayores,* and *gobernaciones.* The smallest territorial unit, the municipality, included a city or town and its adjoining hinterland.

Listing the territorial units from smaller to larger—municipalities, provinces, *audiencias,* viceroyalties, and empire—suggests a pyramidal structure culminating in centralized authority held by the king and his advisers in Spain. A more accurate image, however, is that of a group of wheels with their hubs in the *audiencia* capitals and their spokes extending to the provinces. The Spanish court, in turn, formed the hub of a wheel whose spokes were each *audiencia.* From this perspective, the imperial administration was characterized by decentralization.

The Council of the Indies

The Council of the Indies was responsible for overseeing colonial affairs from its foundation in 1524 as a "royal and supreme council" until the early eighteenth century. It ranked below the Council of Castile or Royal Council but above all other councils in Spain. Like the older Royal Council for Castile, the Council of the Indies oversaw every kind of government

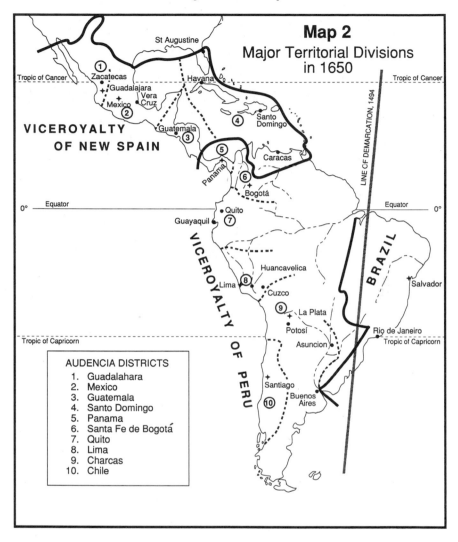

Map 2

Major Territorial Divisions in 1650

LINE OF DEMARCATION, 1494

VICEROYALTY OF NEW SPAIN

VICEROYALTY OF PERU

BRAZIL

Tropic of Cancer

Tropic of Capricorn

Equator 0°

St Augustine

Zacatecas
Guadalajara
Vera Cruz
Mexico
Havana
Guatemala
Santo Domingo
Caracas
Panama
Bogotá
Quito
Guayaquil
Huancavelica
Lima
Cuzco
La Plata
Potosí
Rio de Janeiro
Asuncion
Santiago
Buenos Aires
Salvador

AUDENCIA DISTRICTS
1. Guadalahara
2. Mexico
3. Guatemala
4. Santo Domingo
5. Panama
6. Santa Fe de Bogotá
7. Quito
8. Lima
9. Charcas
10. Chile

activity in colonies. Legislative, judicial, financial, commercial, military, and ecclesiastical matters fell under its purview in the blending of authority characteristic of Spanish administrative offices. The council issued laws, made recommendations to the monarch, approved major expenditures in the colonies, and heard cases appealed from the American *audiencias* and the House of Trade. It also made arrangements for *residencias,* the judicial reviews conducted at the conclusion of officials' terms of office, and occasional general inspections, or *visitas.* In addition, it exercised royal patronage over the Church in the American realms and recommended candidates for most of the high-ranking positions in the New World.

The council employed a variety of senior officials and support staff, with councilors assisted by crown attorneys forming its core. The first councilors were men with university training in civil or canon law, or *ministros togados* (robed ministers), who had previously served on a lower court. In 1604, however, Philip II began naming men with neither credentials in jurisprudence nor a common professional experience. The absence of professional criteria for the appointment of these ministers *de capa y espada* (cape and sword) opened the door to favoritism and abuse.

Only a dozen *ministros togados* named before 1700 had prior New World experience. Moreover, those who were familiar with American affairs usually advanced to the Council of Castile. The Crown's failure to come to grips with basic personnel issues thus weakened the Council of the Indies' ability to provide high-quality oversight and administration. The delays inherent in administration by committee, coupled with the ongoing problem of slow communication with officials in the New World, also reduced the tribunal's effectiveness.

Illustrative of the *togados'* careers during the Habsburg rule was that of Asturian Alonso de Llano y Valdés. After study at the University of Salamanca, Llano entered the prestigious senior residential college at the University of Valladolid. He earned a baccalaureate in civil law in 1645 and soon held chairs in law. After service in the Chancellory of Granada that began in 1653, he briefly was regent of the Council of Navarre. Named a minister *togado* of the Council of the Indies in 1664, he advanced to the Council of Castile in less than four years. Although his well-established bureaucratic family origins undoubtedly hastened Llano's progress, the kinds of positions he received before advancing to the Council of the Indies were typical, as was the absence of service in the New World.

Viceroys

When Charles I sent Antonio de Mendoza to New Spain as its first viceroy, he was acknowledging that despite having taken political power from Cortés, his earlier efforts to establish order and stability in the region had failed. Mendoza, the scion of one of Castile's most illustrious noble families, introduced the requisite aura of proximity to the monarch and display of authority. As Charles's personal representative, he lived in a palace with sixty Indians in constant attendance and a personal escort of gentlemen.

The festivities that welcomed Mendoza in 1535 initiated a tradition of viceregal receptions that over time became truly lavish. Colonial society loved fiestas, and the arrival of a new viceroy provided a wonderful excuse to celebrate. Ceremonies lasted for days as different corporate bodies vied to impress the new executive. For example, the arrival of Viceroy Conde de Salvatierra in Lima in 1648 elicited repeated artillery salutes and a procession that passed under an arch rising above a portion of street paved for the event with nearly three hundred bars of silver. Jousting games and bullfights took place later in the plaza in front of the viceregal palace.

As the foremost executives in the colonies, the viceroys were responsible for general administration; the imposition, collection, and disbursement of taxes and the remittance of surplus revenue to Spain; the construction and maintenance of public works; the maintenance of public order; defense against both internal rebellions and foreign enemies; support of the Church; protection of the Indians; and the exercise of patronage. At the same time, other high-ranking officials, ecclesiastical hierarchies, *audiencias,* treasury officials, and corporate bodies constrained the viceroys' ability to act independently. The Council of the Indies received from these political rivals correspondence regarding the viceroy's activities and issued an endless stream of orders for implementation. Although the viceroy could delay them and contribute to a revision of directives through the formula *obedezco pero no cumplo* ("I obey but I do not execute"), repeated failure to carry out royal mandates invited conflict and judicial scrutiny after the *residencia.*

Mendoza was the first of ninety-two viceroys in the Indies. Although he and several other viceroys in the sixteenth century served for a decade or more, the average tenure in office for viceroys in the seventeenth and eighteenth centuries was between six and seven years. With few exceptions, viceroys were born and reared in Spain; for them the New World was a place to serve but not their home. Especially with its earliest appointments, the Crown exercised special care to name men of impeccable social standing and demonstrated ability. Most bore titles of nobility. Viceroys expected and, despite legal prohibitions, often sought to use their office to benefit both themselves and the large retinues of family, friends, and retainers who accompanied them to their post. By naming retainers to lucrative commissions and positions and smiling beneficently when their minions married well-placed local women or their wives' ladies-in-waiting made favorable matches, the viceroys set an example that other bureaucrats tried to emulate.

Each *audiencia* district had an executive head. The viceroys themselves exercised direct authority over the *audiencia* in which their capital was located. By the late sixteenth century in the subordinate *audiencia* districts, each court had a president-governor who held executive authority. In most cases this official also was in charge of defense for the district and held the title captain-general. Raids by corsairs, Sir Francis Drake, and other English sea captains led the Crown to replace university-trained jurists with experienced military officers as presidents and captains-general of most *audiencias.* Like viceroys, these men were political appointees, served term appointments, and often considered the Americas a place for a tour of duty rather than a permanent residence. Although some entered into illegal commercial activities with local entrepreneurs for private financial gain, their usual intention was to return to Spain with their earnings rather than to invest permanently in local production. This sentiment helps distinguish these term appointees from those men named to lifetime positions: *audiencia* ministers, treasury officials, and numerous municipal officeholders.

Native Sons, Radicados, *and Outsiders*

Most officials became enmeshed in the local society of the city to which they were posted. Some were "native sons," men with positions in the region of their birth. Others were *radicados,* men born elsewhere who had become "rooted" in local society. Although "outsiders," or newcomers to the region of service, regularly received bureaucratic positions, those with lifetime appointments tended to become *radicados* within a few years. Thus most officeholders were fully integrated into local society and were joined to nonofficeholders in a myriad of social and economic ways. Keenly sensitive to local needs, on occasion they could frustrate the implementation of unpopular royal legislation.

For high-ranking positions in the colonies, the Castilian Crown preferred to name outsiders. The sale of appointments in the seventeenth and early eighteenth centuries, however, compromised this principle. Native sons and *radicados* increased in number and prominence while royal control over colonial government fell to its nadir around 1750. Conversely, local elites enjoyed an unprecedented access to power, both directly through securing offices and indirectly through family and economic ties to officeholders.

The Sale of Offices and Appointments in Spanish America

Following the Crown's bankruptcy in 1557, Philip II extended the practice of selling offices from Castile to the Indies. Municipal offices were among the first to be affected, as the Crown not only put them up for sale but also increased their number in its search for additional revenue. By 1606 the list of posts for sale included the full range of fee-collecting, honorific, and municipal offices. A decree in that year provided that present and future purchasers could hold their posts in full propriety and could pass them on to heirs upon payment of specified taxes. The solid entrenchment of local families in local office for generations, in short, was blessed by law.

The municipality was the cornerstone of Spanish rule and settlement. Wherever colonists settled, they created a town council *(cabildo)* to oversee the development and administration of the new community. Originally they elected aldermen to administer town affairs and magistrates to provide local justice. Additional officials included a clerk, a sheriff, a standard bearer, and an inspector of weights and measures. The *cabildo* distributed town lots and nearby garden plots, supervised the construction and maintenance of roads and public works, provided protection against fraud in the markets and against criminal activities in general, regulated holidays and processions, and performed a variety of other duties essential to a settled, civilized existence. For revenue the *cabildos* relied on the rent or lease of town property, local judicial fines, and other modest sources.

An examination of Lima's city council illustrates the expansion of locally born aldermen after three *limeños* purchased their offices in 1561. By 1575 native sons began to outnumber their peninsular counterparts. With rare exceptions, *limeños* henceforth enjoyed numerical preponderance. Similar extensive local representation was present in the elected office of magistrate. Native sons also dominated in Mexico City and numerous other locations. Although the power of the Spanish American city councils declined in the seventeenth and eighteenth centuries, municipal office positions still enhanced the social status of incumbents.

Excluded from the category of salable offices were positions that the Crown correctly considered most central to its maintenance of authority, revenue, and security—those held by the political administrators and professional bureaucrats. Under unrelenting financial pressure, however, the Crown gradually turned appointments to these offices as well into a source of revenue, although never alienating the posts in perpetuity.

When Spain's repeated involvement in European wars exhausted the Crown's finances, it started selling appointments to treasury posts and the tribunals of accounts in 1633. Provincial administrative positions went on the block in 1677. A decade later the systematic sale of *audiencia* appointments began, and by 1700 a desperate Crown had even sold appointments to the office of viceroy.

The importance of the sale of offices and appointments to the composition of the bureaucracy and its activities cannot be overestimated. First, sales altered the character of bureaucratic recruitment. Service at home, if an appropriate position were available, was far more attractive for both peninsulars and creoles than was service in another district on either side of the Atlantic. Thus an immediate result of such sales was to raise the proportion of native sons and *radicados* in bureaucratic offices. The necessary corollary to this changed recruitment was diminished royal authority over colonial officeholders. In addition, the purchase of an office increased the pressure on the incumbent to secure not only a reliable income but also a profit on his investment. Given the modest salaries associated with most non-fee-earning positions, the temptation to resort to extralegal sources of income was irresistible for many bureaucrats. This, too, worked against the Crown's interest.

Treasury officials throughout the Indies and auditors on the tribunals of accounts established in Lima, Mexico City, and Santa Fe de Bogotá in 1605 received lifetime appointments. Even though these officials usually earned substantially lower salaries than did the *audiencia* ministers, their compensation was well above that earned by the average government employee. Because of the salary, the rank, the security, and, in some cases at least, the financial opportunites available for a person with access to government funds, there was considerable demand for appointments.

When in 1633 the Crown finally turned to systematically selling appointments to treasury positions, it found that the purchasers were often young and inexperienced. Their youth ensured both limited maturity and knowledge and, barring premature death, decades of service. In addition, as money replaced merit as the primary criterion for appointment, would-be purchasers sought the most coveted posts, those in the viceregal capitals. Native sons were especially anxious to secure these offices and, once in place, showed no desire to leave. This limited the potential for advancement from regional subtreasuries and undoubtedly intensified the social, political, and economical ties that the officials shared with the leading local families.

The *audiencias* also had little turnover. The tribunals were the supreme courts of their districts and subject to appeal to the Council of the Indies only in cases involving very large sums of money. In addition, they had administrative and legislative responsibilities. Named for life or the pleasure of the king, *audiencia* ministers commonly resided many years in a single location. Once in Mexico City or Lima, ministers most commonly left the court only when they died. The combination of major responsibilities and protracted service by their ministers made the *audiencias* the most important single civil institution in the Spanish colonies.

Before 1687, few men began their *audiencia* careers in their home district. Nonetheless, the Crown named Americans in every decade from the 1580s onward: Nearly a quarter of all *audiencia* appointees from 1610 to 1687 were creoles. The initiation of systematic sales of *audiencia* appointments in late 1687 not only enabled more Americans to reach the courts but also increased the number of native sons. By resorting to the sale of supernumerary or extra appointments, moreover, the Crown clogged the normal chain of advancement from the smaller regional courts to the viceregal courts and greatly expanded the number of *radicados* throughout the system. The sales, which continued during each time of war until 1750, brought unprecedented local direct and indirect access to the tribunals, thus enabling local elite families to influence judicial and political decisions.

Unlike purchased municipal, treasury, and *audiencia* positions, the post of provincial administrator—variously called *alcalde mayor, corregidor,* and *gobernador*—was for a term appointment. In the sixteenth century the Crown had introduced provincial administrators both to provide sustenance for non-*encomenderos* and poor *encomenderos* and to expand the royal authority from the urban areas into the countryside and over the indigenous population. The posts were numerous—eighty-eight in Peru and about two hundred in New Spain in the early seventeenth century. Most provincial administrators held only a single appointment, and service of five years or less was common. Unlike in Castile, where lawyers were named to many *corregimientos,* in the New World the Crown preferred men with military or at least militia backgrounds.

During the century after the stabilization of these provincial positions between 1570 and 1580, the notorious system of *repartimiento* took root.

Although located varying distances from the viceregal capitals, the provincial administrators were regularly closely linked to them economically. Using goods provided on credit by merchants in Mexico City and Lima, the officials participated in the profitable *repartimiento* of merchandise by which Indians were forced to purchase mules, clothing, food, and other items, whether needed or not. In some regions at least, avaricious officials subjected their production to monopolistic control as well.

By 1677 an even more financially desperate Crown began to sell appointments to provincial positions. Soon nearly all of these positions had passed from viceregal to royal provision. As with treasury posts, the Crown sold appointments of *corregidor* and *alcalde mayor* on an individual basis, with the amount and terms of the agreements varying. Unlike the situation for municipal, treasury, and *audiencia* posts, however, creoles seem to have secured fewer, rather than more, provincial offices after the sales began. This may have been because wealthy and well-educated creoles, especially those who went to Spain, devoted their attention to securing either the more prestigious *audiencia* and treasury positions or hereditary offices. In addition, the close link between the *repartimiento* of merchandise and the provincial officials made it particularly advantageous for monopolistic merchants in Spain to lend the purchase price and travel expenses to men whom they knew personally and whom they could trust to distribute their goods, that is, usually men born in Spain. Ties with merchants in Lima and Mexico City persisted as well, however, and provincial officials, whether native sons, *radicados*, or outsiders, formed an important part of the colonial economic world.

The anticipated expenses for a five-year term of the *corregidor* of the Peruvian province of Chancay in the mid-eighteenth century offer a glimpse of the financial requirements of provincial administration: Manuel de Elcorrobarrutia paid 16,000 pesos for his appointment plus an additional 4,000 pesos for fees and taxes. Paying an assistant and an agent and a lawyer in Lima consumed another 7,000 pesos. Personal living expenses he estimated at 15,000 pesos. Gratuities to officials in Lima, entertainment for the viceroy when he visited Chancay, and expenses for the *residencia* and audit cost 9,000 pesos. Interest on this total was 8,700 pesos. To distribute through *repartimiento* 1,900 mules, the *corregidor* anticipated paying 67,004 pesos. This amount purchased the mules and paid for their feed and distribution, tax, salary for collection agents and interest. But he expected to receive only 80,000 pesos from selling the mules and thus had to sell other items for 46,724 pesos to cover his investment. With only 1,125 able-bodied adult males in the province in 1754, each household had to contribute an average of 112 pesos for this *corregidor* to break even. In the final analysis, the money paid to the Crown to secure this office, the commercial profits of the merchant speculator who advanced the funds to purchase the appointment, and the "profits" earned by the *corregidor* himself all were paid out of the collective earnings of this Indian community.

One unplanned result of the sale of appointments and offices and the evolution of a bureaucracy drawn largely from the native born and *radicados* was an increasing compatibility between colonial administration and the requirements of local elites. Bureaucrats who borrowed money from merchants and other affluent colonials were not likely to enforce vigorously laws that harmed them. Although the venal antecedents for this sensitivity to local interests are clear, the practical result was to reduce the potential for dangerous conflicts between powerful interest groups in the New World and the distant metropolis.

Brazilian Counterpoint

Portuguese administration in Brazil developed more slowly and modestly in scale than did its Spanish American counterpart. The early concentration of the small colonial population in several coastal locations, the difficulty of intracolonial communication between northern and southern settlements, and the absence of a powerful and ambitious group of conquistadors contributed to a more regionally decentralized and smaller administrative system than that found in the Spanish colonies.

Administrative responsibility for Brazil was divided among various agencies and offices in Portugal. There was no Portuguese equivalent to Spain's Council of the Indies until a decade-long experiment in the early seventeenth century. Then in 1642 the Braganza dynasty created the Overseas Council which exercised many functions for Portugal's empire similar to those of the Council of the Indies. The Desembargo do Paço located in Lisbon oversaw judicial matters for Portugal and the empire, appointing, promoting, and reviewing the conduct of royal magistrates.

Initially the Portuguese Crown sought to treat Brazil as part of the royal factory system used in Africa and Asia. When French merchants began trading for dyewood directly with the natives, however, John III (1521–57) decided that a permanent colony was necessary. In the 1530s he granted to twelve men with good court connections hereditary captaincies extending inland from the Atlantic coast to the Line of Tordesillas. These "donatary captains" received rights similar to those granted in Portugal and the Atlantic islands earlier. Each recipient was to colonize and defend his captaincy in return for a number of revenues, the right to grant land and name numerous officials, and jurisdiction in most criminal and civil matters. The Crown retained several royal taxes and its monopoly over the dyewood trade. But with the exception of São Vicente and Pernambuco, the private enterprise donatary system was not successful. Continued French pressure, moreover, convinced John III to regain some of the authority bestowed in a manner analogous to that employed by the Castilian Crown.

In 1549 John purchased the captaincy of Bahia from its owners and named a governor-general to administer it. Following this political reorganization, exploration, Indian campaigns, and colonization proceeded in the north, beginning in the 1570s. Paraíba was settled in the 1580s, Rio

Grande do Norte in 1598, Ceara in 1610, Maranhão in 1612–14, and Belém and the lower Amazon from 1616 to 1630.

As the chief executive in Brazil, the governor-general had responsibilities and restrictions similar to those of the Spanish American viceroys. He exercised general oversight of administration, defense, Luso-Indian relations, the treasury, the secular clergy, trade, and land grants. Legislation circumscribed his activities in many ways, however. The governor-general was prohibited from investing in trade or agriculture and could travel outside Bahia only with royal permission. He was subject, moreover, to a special investigation *(devassa)* during his term in office and a review *(residencia)* at its conclusion, checks similar to the Spanish *visita* and *residencia*. Named to a three-year term, many governors-general served longer, some more than two decades. Most came from Portugal's upper nobility and had been professional soldiers; none had been high-ranking clerics. Usually they reached Brazil accompanied by kin and retainers eager to benefit from their patron's largesse.

Governors served as the commanders in chief of their captaincies and were responsible for overseeing treasury and judicial offices and protecting the natives. Like the governor-generals, they were to act under standing instructions and directives sent from Lisbon and were subject to the *devassa* and *residencia*. The importance of military security on the exposed Atlantic coast led the Crown to name seasoned military veterans with administrative experience as governors. In the seventeenth century the governors of Pernambuco, Maranhão, and Rio de Janeiro were *fidalgos* and/or in a military order, but rarely titled nobles. Professional soldiers of commoner origins sometimes held the governorship of a less important captaincy. Nearly every governor was born in Portugal; among the few Brazilians named, almost none served in their native province. In striking contrast with Spanish America, there is no evidence that governorships were sold.

In 1621 the northern captaincies of Ceara, Maranhão, and Pará were united as the state of Maranhão, whose separate administration continued until 1772. The remaining captaincies were included in a single unit called the state of Brazil. In subsequent territorial reorganizations, the Crown generally added jurisdiction to the governors in Pernambuco and Rio de Janeiro at the expense of the governor-general. It also enhanced the governors' titles; by 1715 both were "governor and captain-general." By 1772 Brazil had nine captaincies-general. Although the office of viceroy replaced that of governor-general in 1720, this change in title was window dressing for a post whose effective authority had been reduced in favor of the governors and captains-general who communicated directly with the authorities in Lisbon.

Although since the late Middle Ages, the Portuguese monarchs had relied on royal magistrates to extend their authority at home, they gave the donataries the right to name magistrates in their captaincies if they did not personally oversee the administration of justice. With the decision to assert royal control in 1549, however, John III superimposed a superior royal magistrate to handle appeals from municipal and donatary-named judges and to serve as the royal judge for the captaincy of Bahia. Not until 1609, nearly a century after the first Spanish American *audiencia* was created, did the Portuguese Crown establish a high court of appeals *(relaçao)* for Brazil in the city of Salvador. Suppressed in 1626 after the Dutch seized Salvador, the court was reestablished in 1652 and remained the sole high court in Brazil until the creation of another in Rio de Janeiro in 1751. As in Spanish America, the judges had administrative and advisory responsibility in addition to judicial service. Their frequent use in assignments outside the court adversely affected its administration of justice and led to repeated complaints about its dilatory conduct.

The most professional bureaucrats in Brazil, members of the high court of Bahia came primarily from modest families neither peasant nor noble. All had a university degree in law, almost invariably earned at the University of Coimbra in Portugal, the only university in the Portuguese world empowered to confer degrees in civil and canon law. Magistrates received appointments for a term of six years, but some stayed longer, occasionally over two decades. Their protracted service routinely brought closer ties to the region they served. Frequent promotions to a court in Portugal, usually the High Court of Oporto, and the paucity of Brazilians named to the Bahia tribunal, however, meant that the judges' social and economic bonds to the region were less common and intense than those of their counterparts in Spanish America. Corruption, nonetheless, was typical, and magistrates in Brazil repeatedly engaged in commercial affairs and often sought to become landowners. Because most magistrates reached Brazil in middle age, few married locally. The ten native-son magistrates, not surprisingly, were most involved in the local society and economy.

Except for the high executive and judicial posts and municipal council positions, virtually every office in Brazil could be obtained by purchase or royal concession. The key fiscal offices, for example, were proprietary, and the problems of graft and embezzlement noted in Spanish America were present in Brazil as well. The practice of farming out almost all tax collection, of which the tithe and customs duties were the most important, compounded the financial mismanagement.

As in Spanish America, the municipal council was the fundamental institution for the administration of the towns and their surrounding jurisdictions. The councils were important, among other reasons, because they distributed and leased municipal and common land, fixed the prices on numerous commodities, maintained roads and other public works, helped control slaves, policed the town, and oversaw public health and sanitation. Councils collected taxes and fines, licensed vendors, and leased municipal property for their income. In Bahia the council had three aldermen, two local magistrates, and a municipal attorney selected annually from a list of eligible candidates in a complicated indirect electoral process. Although after 1696 a royal magistrate presided over the council and the governors named the aldermen from eligible citizens, the councils remained important spokesmen for local concerns. The fact that the aldermen were elected prevented the councils from becoming the closed and self-perpetuating corporations that emerged from the sale of the position of *regidor* in Spanish America. But in both Brazil and Spanish America, citizens valued council seats for their prestige as well as for the personal economic benefits available through participation in government.

Although the Portuguese Crown employed *corregedores* as royal agents in the districts in Portugal, it did not extend this middle level of administration to Brazil. Instead, it relied on governors and city councils to administer the reasonably compact zones of settlement along the coast and sent circuit magistrates into less populous regions. Not until the economic boom that began with the discovery of gold in Minas Gerais in the 1690s did the Crown devote much attention to providing administration in the vast Brazilian interior.

The single most impressive feature of bureaucrats in the Iberian empires was the extent to which they were rooted to the region in which they served. Time after time the Crowns turned to newly appointed outsiders when they wanted to effect changes. Thus they employed visitors to investigate abuses or the failure to implement specific legislation. The extent of innovation, however, was often modest. Deeply rooted local elites, of which high-ranked officials formed a part, proved resilient to challenge. When examined closely, so-called change and reform often turned out to be the old politics with a few new players. Yet it was precisely the flexibility and resilience produced by the fusion of individual bureaucrats' interests and those of other members of the elite in their district that reduced pressure within a system of bureaucratic rule.

The Colonial Church

The Church joined the colonial bureaucracy as a major institutional buttress of European power in the New World. Nurtured by the Crown financially and legislatively, the Church in Spanish America prospered under a degree of royal control greater than that exercised in Spain itself. Conversion of the Indians, the theoretical justification for the Iberian presence in the Indies, was the Church's initial priority.

The primary vehicle of acculturation, conversion drew the indigenous peoples into the cultural orbit of the Spanish and Portuguese settlers. The missionaries simultaneously tried to shield the Indians from the corruption and immorality of the European settlers and the labor demands of an encroaching colonial economy. In addition, they imposed Christian beliefs, social practices such as monogamy, and political organization through a mission system that undermined the Indians' potential for resistance and rebellion. These changes helped prepare the indigenous communities for integration into the emerging colonial order.

The Church in Spanish America also ministered to the Spaniards there, dominated their education, and provided social services for which the Crown was unwilling to assume direct responsibility. By the 1570s, the initial evangelical commitment was noticeably diminished. A royal policy favoring the secular clergy over the orders contributed to the malaise. In subsequent years, the Church consolidated its gains, participated in nearly every dimension of colonial life, and accumulated and displayed its wealth. Spiritual enthusiasm and utopian vision declined, and an era of ecclesiastical routine began, although individual examples of clerical activism remained. The composition of the clergy, moreover, began to change noticeably. By the early seventeenth century, creoles far surpassed peninsulars numerically and firmly anchored the Church in the fabric of colonial society.

Royal Patronage

The Spanish kings' control over the Church rested on their *patronato real,* or royal patronage. Papal bulls in 1501 and 1508 formalized a degree of oversight implicit in the papal donation of 1493, and subsequent legislation spelled out the extent of supervision exercised by the Council of the Indies. Through their royal patronage Spanish monarchs assumed responsibility to promote the conversion of the Amerindians and to support the colonial Church. The Crown received control of tithe income, the tax levied on agricultural production and livestock, to sustain the ecclesiastical hierarchy, its physical facilities, and its activities. It also controlled the founding of churches, convents, and hospitals and the appointment of and payment to ecclesiastics. Clerics needed royal licenses to sail to the Indies, and their movement upon arrival was inhibited. The Council of the Indies examined all papal documents for statements that infringed on the Crown's patronage. Only after the council's approval could these materials be sent to the New World.

The Portuguese Crown also exercised a supervisory control over the Church. The *padroado,* patronage, derived from a series of papal bulls issued between 1456 and 1514. The king controlled the creation of colonial bishoprics, the appointment of bishops, the movement of missionaries, and the evangelical efforts among the Indians. The Portuguese Church, however, lacked the wealth and political power of the Spanish Church. The end of Muslim rule in Portugal in the thirteenth century gave the Church a history different from that of its Spanish counterpart. Still, Portugal's later expansion into North Africa and especially India gave the Portuguese Church some of the crusading zeal and material rewards gained in Spain during the long Reconquest.

The Evangelical Effort

The conquests of Mexico and Peru opened the most populous regions of the American mainlands to clerics anxious to convert the natives to Christianity. Although clerics accompanied Cortés on his march to Tenochti-tlán, systematic efforts to convert the indigenous population awaited the arrival of the regulars, as members of the religious orders were known. Cortés repeatedly urged Charles I to send friars, preferring them to the more worldly secular clergy. Twelve Franciscans arrived in May 1524, the first contingent of an order that would lead conversion efforts in New Spain. In the following decade Dominicans, already active in the Carib-bean colonies, and Augustinians joined in the "spiritual conquest." Although all of the orders emphasized conversion, the Franciscans approached the effort with a millenarian hope that their evangelization and the creation of a primitive apostolic church would be followed by the second coming of Christ.

The friars faced numerous obstacles to their conversion campaign. The many native languages posed a special problem, and the dispersed residen-tial patterns of natives outside the urban centers hindered rapid evangel-ization. Superficial resemblances between native and Christian religious practices increased the difficulty of presenting Christianity as new and dis-tinct. Yet the friars enjoyed some advantages as well.

The conquest transferred political power to the Spanish and gave great prestige to the Christian religion, for the gods of the Aztecs and Incas had proved inferior. Unlike the native conquerors in central Mexico, the Span-iards refused to respect the gods of the vanquished; the Christian God was to stand alone. The destruction of indigenous religion was systematic and persistent. Priests in particular were singled out for persecution; prudence thus dictated that the natives, whatever their private beliefs, publicly com-ply with their conquerors' religion.

About eight hundred friars were residing in Mexico by 1559. At first they directed much of their attention to converting the native chieftains *(caciques)* and nobles who, they anticipated correctly, would bring their peoples with them into the Church. Although the Crown wanted the natives to learn Spanish, many religious quickly began to study and preach in the languages of the peoples they were evangelizing. One prodigiously learned cleric, Andrés de Olmos, preached and wrote in more than ten Indian languages. The Aztec language, Nahuatl, received the most atten-tion, for many native peoples were able to comprehend instruction in that tongue in addition to their own. Friars also taught Nahuatl where it had not previously been used, in order to establish a common language in New Spain, while keeping the natives separated from other Europeans who, they feared, would corrupt them. In Peru the friars promoted Quechua and Aymara over the other indigenous languages.

To segregate the natives from Europeans and to streamline their own activities, the friars founded villages to bring together Indians scattered throughout a region. The Indians' declining population further stimulated this process. The Augustinians were particularly effective at founding new villages. In Michoacán, for example, they gathered together natives who had been dispersed around Tiripitío and built, using Indian labor, a town complete with plaza, convent, hospital, water supply, and well-constructed houses. In towns such as this the friars oversaw political and economic activities as well as religious affairs.

By baptizing the natives, the friars obliged the Church to provide the sacraments of marriage, confession, communion, and confirmation that would enable the new converts to live as Christians. Christian insistence on monogamous marriage immediately ran up against the polygyny common among the Indian elite, especially in Mexico. Even after two generations of natives baptized during their youth and educated in Christian precepts, some Indians still married one wife in the Church and kept other women as concubines, although this custom faded away over time.

Many Indians responded enthusiastically to evangelization. Religion was a central feature of native life before the conquest, and the vanquished could not imagine existence without belief in the supernatural. In addition, they at once recognized the Spaniards' veneration of images of the Virgin, the Cross, and clerics. The customary Spanish practice of building churches or at least placing crosses on preexisting religious sites reaffirmed the sacredness of the locations and promoted syncretism, the fusion of Christian and indigenous beliefs. The natives' veneration of Our Lady of Guadalupe, the most celebrated image of the Virgin Mary in New Spain, was associated with the persistence of their earlier devotion to the native goddess Tonantzin. The Indians perceived Guadalupe-Tonantzin as "God," much to the dismay of the Franciscans, who opposed the syncretic religious beliefs and practices that came to characterize "Christianity" among the natives. Crediting Our Lady of Guadalupe with miraculous healings, Indians flocked throughout the colonial era to her sanctuary on a hill just north of Mexico City.

In 1526 the Franciscans opened the College of Santiago Tlatelolco near Mexico City to train for the priesthood the sons of the native nobility. The students were taught reading, writing, music, Latin, and philosophy, among other subjects. Some mastered Latin and could translate it into Spanish and Nahuatl. Yet the college and the effort to train a native clergy ultimately failed. Antinative sentiment among many non-Franciscan clergy fueled opposition to the ordination of natives. No alumni entered the clergy, and with its principal reason for existence negated, the Tlatelolco experiment ended. The synod of 1555 formally prohibited the ordination of Indians, thus ensuring perpetual inferiority for Indians in the Mexican Church.

Vasco de Quiroga entered the Franciscan order after serving as *oidor* on the second *audiencia* of Mexico. In Michoacán he invested most of his own wealth in the creation of mission communities modeled on Sir Thomas More's *Utopia*. All land was held communally. New skills based on European technology were taught, but labor was closely regulated so as to prevent abuse. In addition to a church, the settlements provided hospitals and a wide array of social welfare benefits. After his appointment as bishop of Michoacán in 1537, Vasco de Quiroga continued to promote the use of mission settlements, a strategy later used successfully by the Jesuits and other regulars as the Christian frontier was pushed north to Texas and California and south to the Río de la Plata region.

The Dominican Vicente de Valverde and several other clerics accompanied Pizarro to Cajamarca. Franciscans and Mercedarians had arrived before Atahualpa's execution, and Augustinians appeared in 1551. However, the intensive evangelization of New Spain's "spiritual conquest" was not duplicated in Peru. Although the disruption of civil war undoubtedly hindered efforts at conversion, it appears that the quality of the early clerics in Peru was inferior to that of the friars in Mexico. Not until the first Conciliar Council of Lima in 1551 did the Church launch a full-scale attack on surviving Incan religious activities. Declaring all Andean people who had died before the conquest to be in Hell, the council vigorously attacked the worship of *huacas* and ancestors. Priests and government officials henceforth destroyed *huacas* and burned mummies whenever possible. The response in the central Andes was a millenarian movement in the 1560s that believed that the *huacas,* angry at being deserted for Catholicism, had brought epidemics, from which the only escape was a return to traditional religious beliefs. Considering the movement heretical and thus treasonous, the state was able to eliminate the threat by the 1570s.

Religious orders spread throughout the Spanish empire, often advancing its boundary of effective settlement. Nearly twenty years after reaching Brazil, the Society of Jesus arrived in Peru in 1568 and New Spain in 1572. Quickly the Jesuits came to dominate elite education in the cities. In addition, the Society soon began to establish missions in numerous locations, from the northern frontier of Mexico to Paraguay. The first of the famous Guaraní mission villages in Paraguay was founded in 1610. By 1707 there were thirty villages with nearly 100,000 Indians.

The Society of Jesus dominated the evangelical effort in Brazil after the arrival in 1549 of Manoel da Nobrega and five other Jesuits in Bahia; the few Franciscans who had been living in Brazil had shown little interest in converting the Indians. Defeated Indians near Bahia provided the Jesuits' first converts. As in New Spain and Peru, European military successes enhanced the prestige of the new religion and enabled superficial conversion. The Jesuits concentrated the Indians in villages *(aldeias)* in order to maximize the evangelical potential of their small numbers. After 1557, when voluntary concentration failed, the Jesuits supported Governor Mem de Sá in crushing the remaining armed resistance. By 1560 more than 40,000 Indians were in the Jesuit *aldeias* of Bahia alone, and by the end of the century the colony's 169 Jesuits controlled nearly the entire pacified Indian population.

In Brazil the missionaries promoted the use of Tupí as a common language. In the *aldeias* they taught crafts, introduced new crops, and enforced European work habits and social practices—monogamy and an abhorrence of nudity, in particular. They also fostered European culture, especially music.

After the early achievements—mass baptisms and the creation of the first *aldeias*—the Jesuits realized the shallowness of the conversion experience. Old beliefs persisted, intermingled with Christian doctrine. By the 1560s this frustration was clearly revealed in their reports and letters. As they recognized the difficulty of converting adults, the Jesuits began to emphasize more the close supervision and education of young males. When some of these young converts denounced their own elders for continuing ancient customs, the missionaries happily noted their achievement.

The development of mission settlements as a conversion tool led necessarily to a conflict between the Church and the settlers. The colonial economies of Latin America depended on Indian labor. Miners, planters, and *obraje* owners coveted control over converted Indians already accustomed to the discipline and organization of the missionaries and familiar with rudimentary European technology. Because the missionaries, especially the Dominicans and the Jesuits, tried to defend the Indians from what they saw as exploitation and abuse, they continually found themselves in political and judicial conflict with the settlers. When epidemics drastically reduced the Indian population, these pressures grew. In Brazil, for example, the Jesuit Antônio Vieira's efforts to protect the Indians led to a revolt and the temporary expulsion of the Society from Maranhão and Pará in 1661. Earlier, Jesuits working with the Guaraní in disputed borderlands that separated Brazil and Paraguay had armed their Indians against slave raiders from São Paulo. Forced to choose between the claims of the missionaries and those of the wealthy colonial elites, the monarchs of both Spain and Portugal moved to restrict the Church's control over pacified Indian communities.

The Mature Church

The secular clergy made up the ecclesiastical hierarchy that extended from parish priests upward to cathedral chapters, bishops, and archbishops. Unlike the regulars—many of whom took vows of poverty and whose subsistence was provided by their orders—secular priests were primarily responsible for their own financial security, which led them into a variety of economic activities. Although they were supposed to refrain from wholesale or retail trade, crafts, and direct employment outside the Church, not all seculars observed these restrictions.

Secular clergy were present in Brazil from the first decades but had little influence. Indeed the Jesuit Nobrega characterized the secular priests of Bahia as "irregular, apostates and excommunicates." When the first bishop of Bahia arrived in 1552, he had little interest in converting the natives. In 1676 the Bishop of Bahia was elevated to archbishop, and by the late eighteenth century six bishoprics were subject to Bahia. Although the development of the episcopal structure coincided with an expansion in the secular clergy, approximately half of the bishops appointed before 1800 were regulars.

The establishment of bishoprics and then archbishoprics in Spanish

America and an increase in the number of secular clergy led to conflict with the regulars. At issue was the control of the native population and its labor and income. The regulars, moreover, were justly proud of their accomplishments and loath to share the benefits with seculars whom they considered inferior in ability and commitment. Their antagonism was not limited to words. On one occasion in 1559, seculars raided the Dominican convent in Puebla, Mexico, sacked it, broke the prior's teeth, and departed with every item of value. In a similarly uncharitable spirit, on another occasion Franciscans armed six hundred Indians in the Toluca region of Mexico with bows and arrows and shields and led them in the destruction of a church under the care of secular clergy.

In 1568 Philip II named a committee to investigate the relations between seculars and regulars. The resulting Ordenanza del Patronazgo of 1574 increased the power of the secular clergy and limited the regulars' activities. Eventually, secular priests took over many Indian parishes, or *doctrinas.* Henceforth the regulars' mission activities, when they took place, were in isolated frontier areas.

By 1600 the Church was beginning the financial ascent that would make its economic base second to none in the colonies. The growth of commercial agriculture in New Spain, Peru, Central America, and Brazil brought unprecedented revenues from the tithe in the 1590s. With the Jesuits leading the way, the regular orders—save perhaps the Franciscans—became active and successful landowners. In New Spain and Peru, the expansion of mining and commerce after the conquest era also created excess capital that its owners used, in part, to endow pious works.

Pious works included chantries, the foundation of convents and colleges, and the provision of dowries and burial funds. Frequently an individual established a chantry to celebrate in perpetuity privately administered memorial masses for his soul. The founder and his heir typically designated a family member as chaplain. This strategy had the great advantage of retaining in the family the income of the endowment, whether it had been established with cash, a gift of property, or through encumbering real property as though it were mortgaged by pledging specified annual payments.

The Church was the most important source of mortgages, normally receiving a return of about 7 percent in the sixteenth century. The conditions of the loan, however, had to be such that the recipient was buying capital rather than simply borrowing money at interest, a transaction that canon law forbade as the sin of usury. Not only was the Church the major source of investment capital, it also became the major colonial property owner.

As time went on, tithes; fees that clerics received for marriages, burials, and other services; gifts; and pious works enabled the Church and individual clerics to become extremely wealthy. The Church acquired both urban and rural property. The Jesuits, other regular orders, and individual secular priests actively operated in the colonial marketplace, producing sugar, wine, textiles, pottery, and other products. In Mexico City and other large cities, the Church was the largest landlord, renting its property to both residential and commercial users. By employing part of its wealth and income to sustain cultural activities and welfare functions for the poor, the Church added substantially to the well-being of colonial society.

Some orders routinely opened schools in conjunction with their convents in order to educate later generations to enter the orders or assume other responsibilities in society. The Jesuits in Lima began organizing schools from the time they reached the City of Kings in 1568. The Jesuit college in Bahia had 215 students by 1589 and offered a curriculum that extended from the elementary grades to the study of theology. Together with the Dominicans, the Jesuits dominated education until expelled from Portugal, Spain, and their colonies after 1750. The Dominicans were influential in the founding of Lima's University of San Marcos which was established in 1551 but functioned as a convent school until the 1570s. The University of Mexico, also established in 1551, held its first classes in 1553, in part as a result of efforts by Archbishop Juan de Zumárraga. Eventually universities were created in nearly every major city in Spanish America.

The immediate result of establishing universities in Spanish America was a greater number of educated creoles for vocations in the Church and the royal bureaucracy. In consequence, the composition of the clergy began to change noticeably. By the early seventeenth century, creoles had gained prominence in both the secular clergy and at least several of the regular orders. Although a few well-placed *castas* and Indians initially enjoyed limited educational opportunities, they were later excluded from the universities, colleges, and even primary schools. This restriction was imposed in Lima in the 1640s, despite the Jesuits' resistance. Brazilians also entered the Church, although the absence of a university during the colonial period retarded this development.

The presence of Europeans and American-born clerics in both the secular and regular clergy added a further rift to the already-divided Church. Conflict focused on the highest positions, especially in the orders, save for the Jesuits whose provincials and supervisors were named in Europe. Europeans believed themselves superior to their American rivals by virtue of their birth in the Old World. This became a grave problem in Spanish America, for the growing creole majority threatened the peninsulars' dominance in provincial elections. The peninsulars responded by obtaining decrees that authorized the mandatory alternation of offices between themselves and creoles. In mid-seventeenth-century Peru, only the Franciscans and Jesuits were not bound by this forced rotation in office. Beginning in the 1660s the peninsular Franciscans sought, and in 1683 received, final approval for rotation in office. Eventually the Franciscans in Brazil also instituted alternation in office.

There was less conflict among the secular clergy of Spanish America. The American-born religious repeatedly sought and at times secured high ecclesiastical offices. By 1640 five men born in the viceroyalty of Peru had

Juan de Zumárraga (1468–1548). Franciscan priest who served
as the first Bishop and later Archbishop of Mexico

been named archbishops, and another twenty-three had been named bishops in the New World. Nonetheless, peninsulars secured most of the
appointments at these levels. The five high-ranking positions that constituted the cathedral chapters, in contrast, routinely had heavy creole representation from at least the early seventeenth century. Creoles also predominated at the parish level, although by 1700 there were visible
numbers of *mestizo* priests and even a few Indians. European immigrants
were noticeable in some of the wealthiest parishes.

The increase in number of American-born clerics in the seventeenth
century and the Church's growing economic influence bound it to American soil in a way that the early focus on missionary activity had not. Nearly

every colonial family of the middle and upper sectors had relatives in one or more of the Church's branches. Leaving aside the pervasiveness of religion in colonial society, the clergy themselves were pervasive in creole society at its most fundamental level, that of the family.

The León Garavito y Illescas family illustrates this pattern. Francisco de León Garavito emigrated to Lima where he prospered as a merchant, property owner, law professor, government attorney, and alderman. About 1574 he married Isabel de Illescas. The wealthy couple's sons included an *oidor* of the *audiencia* of Panama, three Dominicans, a Jesuit, and a priest in Lima. Isabel's four sisters entered Lima's prestigous convent of La Encarnación early in the seventeenth century, and three of her daughters followed them. All became nuns of the black veil, that is, full voting members of the house, and one was elected abbess.

The seven nuns of the Illescas and León Garavito families underscore the presence of women in ecclesiastical vocations. Convents enabled women to pursue a religious life, control their own affairs, obtain and provide education, and, in many cases, live a very comfortable existence. Protected from the demands of husbands and families, many nuns cultivated the arts and literature, providing a venue for the transfer of European culture. The majority of convents date after 1570 and reached their numerical apogee in the seventeenth century. At their height, the thirteen convents in Lima housed more than 20 percent of the city's women. Far fewer were founded after 1700 than earlier, and in Peru, at least, the number of nuns fell sharply beginning in the early eighteenth century.

The first convent in Brazil was founded in Salvador in 1677. Before then, small numbers of Brazilian women seeking this contemplative life entered convents in Portugal or the Azores. By the end of the eighteenth century three more convents were added. But Mexico City still had proportionately twice as many nuns as did the capital of colonial Brazil.

The many religious orders for women in the colonies were founded locally and maintained only loose ties to metropolitan establishments. Franciscan, Carmelite, Augustinian, and all other orders before the 1750s were devoted to contemplative routines and played no substantial educational or charitable roles. The elite within these orders were nuns of the black veil, the most educated group of women in the colonies. Almost exclusively colonial born, they brought with them sizable dowries, and they alone could vote and serve in offices in the convent and sing the canonical hours in the choir. The Convent of N. S. da Mercedes was founded in 1735 in Bahia by the wealthy heiress Ursula Luisa de Monserrat, who also became its first abbess. Rich families commonly purchased or built the quarters or cells for their daughters and made specified donations to the houses. Although convents occasionally waived the required dowry—most frequently for women of unusual musical ability—they did enforce the social prerequisites. In the convents in Lima, for example, nuns of the black veil were daughters of socially prominent families and accordingly were addressed as "Doña."

Other women in colonial convents lacked family ties to the local social and economic elite. Nuns of the white veil served as housekeepers and in other activities considered inappropriate for the nuns of the black veil with whom they lived. Born into modest white and mixed-race families, their limited opportunities in the convents reflected their social and economic inferiority. Still lower were the poor, mixed-race women who served the nuns of the white veil and were allowed to wear nuns' habits. With servants and black slaves present as well, the convent in many ways mirrored the society outside their walls.

The convents participated actively in the colonies' economic life. Not only did their residences, some occupying several city blocks, require constant attention, but the nuns and their servants, who totaled nearly a thousand persons in some of Lima's larger convents in the seventeenth century, were important consumers as well. In addition, the convents owned urban property both for their own residences and schools and as sources of income. As did other bodies within the Church, the wealthy convents earned capital by providing mortgages, mainly on urban properties. Unlike many male orders, however, the female orders normally did not engage in agricultural production.

The early presence and importance of the convents, the vigor of the male religious orders, the size of the secular clergy, and the continued support of both the colonists and the Crown combined to make the Church in Latin America a powerful, wealthy institution whose influence permeated colonial life. Although examples of individual clerics failing to observe their vows and conniving with colonists to exploit the Indians certainly can be found, their number pales in comparison with the many clergymen who sought to establish and maintain Christianity among the native peoples. A bastion of European culture and civilization, the Church in Latin America retained its strength throughout the colonial era.

The Inquisition

In 1569 the Spanish Crown replaced the earlier and unsatisfactory episcopal inquisitions in its colonies by authorizing the establishment of Tribunals of the Inquisition in Mexico City and Lima. A third tribunal was approved for Cartagena in 1610. Unlike the fear of converted Jews *(conversos)* that had prompted the tribunal's creation in Spain in 1480, the tribunals in the New World were founded out of the Crown's desire to maintain the purity of the Catholic faith against the spread of heretical Protestant beliefs brought to the Indies by foreign interlopers. Once created in the colonies, the Inquisitions of Peru and New Spain periodically persecuted New Christians who persisted in the faith of their ancestors. Within their districts the tribunals held jurisdiction over all non-Indians who had received Christian baptism. Protestants, by virtue of their baptism, were subject to the Inquisition.

The colonial tribunals were similar to their peninsular predecessors in organization and procedure. Normally a tribunal had two inquisitors, an expert who examined evidence for heresy, a prosecutor, a constable, and a notary. Other officials were added as necessary. In addition, tribunals had in each province of their jurisdiction investigators or commissaries, who could be lay or clerics, and lay police, or *familiares,* to arrest suspects and enforce the bodies' decrees. Although the first inquisitors were born and educated in Spain, by 1640 the tribunals in Mexico City and Lima had each received at least one creole inquisitor. A sprinkling of Americans continued to secure appointments as long as the Holy Office existed.

Because it was a powerful body independent of civil and ecclesiastical hierarchies, the Inquisition unavoidably conflicted with both. Its authority, moreover, made it an attractive ally for persons who found the other hierarchies unable or unwilling to support their ambitions. The judicial privileges enjoyed by the tribunal's agents further enhanced the advantages of cooperation and encouraged the participation of wealthy citizens. The tribunal also sought *familiares* who were well placed in local society, an approach that guaranteed prominent support.

The Inquisition initiated a case only after receiving a denunciation. Although self-denunciation was possible, usually by an individual who anticipated lighter penance as a result, generally a third party levied the charge. The accepted procedure was for the inquisitors to gather corroborating evidence before taking further action, a process that could drag on for years. When the evidence seemed conclusive, the tribunal's agents arrested and jailed the accused and sequestered his or her property for later auction as necessary to pay the costs of imprisonment.

The most important feature that distinguished the Inquisition's procedure from that of other tribunals was secrecy. The accused was totally cut off from the outside world while the case proceeded; in some cases this isolation lasted years and terminated only with death. Moreover, the victim was ordered to confess an offense so that he or she could receive absolution from and reconciliation with the Church. The victim, however, was not informed of the charge or the accuser. In a majority of cases, probably most, these omissions were not a major problem, for the accused was indeed guilty. For an innocent party, however, the problems of demonstrating innocence through such means as naming personal enemies were formidable.

The Inquisition prescribed punishment or penance at an *auto da fé,* or, literally, an "act of faith." An *auto da fé* could be private or public. Here the condemned revealed remorse for their sins and professed their hatred of heresy. Public *autos* were great spectacles that public officials, clerics, nobles, and the general populace attended. Throughout its existence in Spanish America, the Inquisition ordered death, a penalty given only to heretics who would not recant, in no more than a hundred cases, perhaps 1 percent of the total considered. Bigamy, blasphemy, and other offenses against public morality were the Inquisition's primary concerns. For such offenses, fines, flogging, confiscation of property, gagging, exile, and service on the galleys were the principal punishments. Punishments were more severe in the early years of the Holy Office than later. After the middle of the seventeenth century the greatest *autos de fé* had taken place, and the importance of the tribunals had begun to dwindle.

A major part of the Inquisition's efforts to protect the colonists from heresy and unorthodox ideas involved censorship. This included both searching ships that arrived at colonial ports for prohibited literature, works listed on the Spanish *Index* of forbidden publications, and censoring manuscripts before they were published in the New World. Although these activities certainly limited the amount of protest literature that entered the colonies and slowed the publication of locally written works, the censors were most interested in ecclesiastical materials.

The Spanish population as a whole supported the Inquisition in the colonies. Most Spaniards did not feel personally threatened by the tribunal. They considered protection from heresy a worthy objective and actively participated in prosecuting those persons who strayed too far from the accepted morality. In an era in which formal political representation was absent, moreover, the Inquisition provided, during its first century of existence in particular, an alternative institution from which the colonists could seek support for their own purposes. The political dimension of the Inquisition gave added importance to the repeated conflicts, often over seemingly trivial matters, that the inquisitors had with civil and ecclesiastical authorities.

Portugal established an effective Inquisition only in 1547. Although there were several tribunals in Portugal and one in Goa, a separate tribunal for Brazil was not created. Bishops, familiars, or other agents that the Portuguese Holy Office employed in the colony investigated persons accused of heresy or other offenses. Those persons considered guilty were shipped to Portugal for trial. The procedures employed were similar to those in Spain and Spanish America except that the Portuguese Inquisition may have been even more harsh in its early years.

On three occasions the Portuguese Inquisition sent special agents to Brazil. The first reached Bahia in 1591 and spent four years investigating the numerous "New Christians"—converted Jews and their descendants—residing in the colony. Two other inquisitorial visits took place in 1618 and 1763–69. As in the Spanish colonies, local agents rather than special investigators usually filed charges of bigamy, blasphemy, reading prohibited literature, and other infractions. Such offenses led to investigations far more often than did allegations of heresy.

The Church provided for the spiritual life of a diverse and complex population and was one of the principal buttresses of social stability and public order in both Spanish America and Brazil. It organized much of colonial society's communal life through public celebrations associated with the religious calendar. By converting Indians and blacks to Christianity, it extended European cultural values; and its role in education and public charity further emphasized its centrality in the lives of rich and poor alike.

Suggested for Further Reading

Aiton, A. S. *Antonio de Mendoza, First Viceroy of New Spain.* Durham, N.C.: Duke University Press, 1927.

Andrien, Kenneth J. *Crisis and Decline: The Viceroyalty of Peru in the Seventeenth Century.* Albuquerque: University of New Mexico Press, 1985.

Bolton, Herbert E. *Rim of Christendom: A Biography of Eusebio Francisco Kino, Pacific Coast Pioneer.* New York: Macmillan, 1936.

Borah, Woodrow W. *Justice by Insurance: The General Indian Court of Colonial Mexico and the Legal Aides of the Half-Real.* Berkeley and Los Angeles: University of California Press, 1983.

Bushnell, Amy. *The King's Coffer: Proprietors of the Spanish Florida Treasury, 1565–1702.* Gainesville: University Presses of Florida, 1981.

Farriss, N. M. *Crown and Clergy in Colonial Mexico, 1759–1821: The Crisis of Ecclesiastical Privilege.* London: Athlone, 1968.

Greenleaf, Richard. *The Mexican Inquisition in the Seventeenth Century.* Albuquerque: University of New Mexico Press, 1969.

Greenleaf, Richard E., editor. *The Roman Catholic Church in Colonial Latin America.* New York: Knopf, 1971.

Greenleaf, Richard E. *Zumárraga and the Mexican Inquisition, 1536–1543.* Washington, D.C.: Academy of American Franciscan History, 1961.

Haring, C. H. *The Spanish Empire in America.* New York: Oxford University Press, 1947.

Israel, J. I. *Race, Class and Politics in Colonial Mexico 1610–1670.* New York: Oxford University Press, 1975.

Kiemen, Mathias C. *The Indian Policy of Portugal in the Amazon Region, 1614–1693.* Washington, D.C.: Catholic University of America Press, 1954.

Korth, Eugene H., S. J. *Spanish Policy in Colonial Chile: The Struggle for Social Justice, 1535–1700.* Stanford, Calif: Stanford University Press, 1968.

Lafaye, Jacques. *Quetzalcóatl and Guadalupe. The Formation of Mexican National Consciousness 1531–1813.* Translated by Benjamin Keen. Chicago: University of Chicago Press, 1976.

Lea, Henry Charles. *The Inquisition in the Spanish Dependencies.* New York: Macmillan, 1908.

MacLachlan, Colin M. *Spain's Empire in the New World: The Role of Ideas in Institutional and Special Change.* Berkeley and Los Angeles: University of California Press, 1988.

Marzahl, Peter. *Town in the Empire: Government, Politics, and Society in Seventeenth-Century Popayán.* Austin, Tex.: Institute of Latin American Studies, 1978.

Moore, John Preston. *The Cabildo in Peru Under the Hapsburgs.* Durham, N.C.: Duke University Press, 1954.

Mörner, Magnus. *The Political and Economic Activities of the Jesuits in the La Plata Region: The Hapsburg Era.* Stockholm: Library and Institute of Ibero-American Studies, 1953.

Parry, J. H. *The Audiencia of New Galicia in the Sixteenth Century.* Cambridge, England: Cambridge University Press, 1948.

Parry, J. H. *The Sale of Public Office in the Spanish Indies Under the Hapsburgs.* Berkeley and Los Angeles: University of California Press, 1953.

Phelan, John Leddy. *The Kingdom of Quito in the Seventeenth Century.* Madison: University of Wisconsin Press, 1967.

Phelan, John L. *The Millennial Kingdom of the Franciscans in the New World: A Study of the Writings of Gerónimo de Mendieta, 1525–1604.* Berkeley and Los Angeles: University of California Press, 1956.

Poole, Stafford. *Pedro Moya de Contreras: Catholic Reform and Royal Power in New Spain, 1571–1591.* Berkeley and Los Angeles: University of California Press, 1987.

Prado, Caio, Jr. *The Colonial Background of Modern Brazil.* Translated by Suzette Macedo. Berkeley and Los Angeles: University of California Press, 1967.

Ricard, Robert. *The Spiritual Conquest of Mexico.* Translated by Lesley B. Simpson. Berkeley and Los Angeles: University of California Press, 1966.

Schwaller, John Frederick. *Church and Clergy in Sixteenth Century Mexico.* Albuquerque: University of New Mexico Press, 1987.

Schwaller, John Frederick. *Origins of Church Wealth in Mexico.* Albuquerque: University of New Mexico Press, 1985.

Schwartz, Stuart B. *Sovereignty and Society in Colonial Brazil: The High Court of Bahia and Its Judges, 1609–1751.* Berkeley and Los Angeles: University of California Press, 1981.

Tibesar, Antonine. *Franciscan Beginnings in Colonial Peru.* Washington, D.C.: Academy of American Franciscan History, 1953.

Van Oss, C. Adriaan. *Colonial Catholicism: A Parish History of Guatemala, 1524–1821.* Cambridge, England: Cambridge University Press, 1986.

Zimmerman, Arthur Franklin. *Francisco de Toledo, Fifth Viceroy of Peru, 1569–1581.* Caldwell, Idaho: Caxton Printers, 1938.

FOUR

POPULATION AND LABOR

Changes in the Colonial Population

The Iberians' arrival caused major changes in the population of the Americas. The most dramatic was the immediate decline in the indigenous population. European conquest and settlement opened a sorrowful tale of demographic disaster. In contrast, the scant number of Iberians who conquered and settled the New World grew steadily and rapidly as immigration and, within a few years, natural reproduction swelled their ranks. The forced migration of Africans added a third racial group to the colonial gene pool. Their number also increased, in large part because of the continuing slave trade. Finally, the forced and free sexual unions among Iberians, Indians, and blacks introduced into Latin America new racial groups whose importance increased throughout the colonial era.

Changes in population totals and race mixture, however, are only two dimensions of the demographic alterations that marked colonial Latin America. In addition, there were significant regional variations in the timing of these population changes as well as in their racial composition. Urban and rural areas also exhibited substantially different racial compositions and rates of population growth and decline. Finally, internal resettlement and migration affected the dispersion of population within specific geographic areas.

The Indian Population

Scholars disagree widely about the size of the indigenous population at the time the Iberians reached the American mainland. Overall estimates range from about 8 million to over 100 million. Substantial differences also appear in the estimates for each major region. Did central Mexico have fewer than 5 million inhabitants or over 25 million? Did the Andes region have 3 million or 30 million or more? Did Central America have fewer than

1 million or over 10 million? Did Brazil have 1 million or more than 6 million? There is no consensus, although a total for the Americas as a whole between 35 million and 45 million seems most plausible. Certainly the Americas had a population of over 13 million before the Iberians arrived. On the other hand, most scholars agree that soon after Iberians arrived the indigenous population plummeted.

Answers to the question of population size must rest on a limited number of sources, for example, counts of natives for labor and tribute assessments, contemporary estimates, censuses, and parish records, and consideration of such things as physical resources, land use, social structure, technology, and settlement patterns. Whenever the original source provides an estimate, for example, the number of tributaries, it introduces a range of accuracy. Multiplying the variables, each more or less accurate, broadens the range of the final estimate. As this range expands, the estimate's utility decreases. The better the quality of the sources is, the smaller the disagreement over population size will be. Accordingly, the range of estimates for the population of the New World after the Spanish Crown began reforming tax collection in the mid-sixteenth century is much narrower than that for the preceding years.

The most extensive demographic research has focused on central Mexico, the region from the isthmus of Tehuantepec to the northern limits of the Aztec Empire. Woodrow W. Borah provided the following estimates of its population:

Year	Native Population
1518	25.2 million
1532	16.8
1548	6.3
1568	2.65
1585	1.9
1595	1.375
1605	1.075
1622	.75

Source: Woodrow W. Borah, *Justice by Insurance: The General Indian Court of Colonial Mexico and the Legal Aides of the Half-Real* (Berkeley and Los Angeles: University of California Press, 1983), p. 26.

The figures in the table are estimates, not exact counts. The figures before 1568 have provoked substantial dispute, and a number of scholars are more comfortable with an estimated population of 10 million to 12 million for 1518. There is widespread, although not universal, acceptance, however, that the native population began to decrease rapidly after Cortés's arrival, reaching its lowest point before 1650. By that date, the native population began a sustained growth that, with only brief interruptions caused by epidemics and famine, continued throughout the remainder of the colonial era.

Regional Population Changes

The overall decline of the native population in Mexico for a century does not apply to every region and locale. The population loss was greater and more rapid in the coastal regions, in part because of climatic differences and the more rapid transmission of the newly imported diseases in humid, tropical settings. Recovery began by the late sixteenth century and slow growth followed. In the Valley of Mexico, an estimated preconquest population of 1.5 million fell to about 325,000 by 1570 and reached a low of about 70,000 in the mid-seventeenth century. The population then rose to about 120,000 by the early 1740s and 275,000 by 1800.

Yucatán followed a chronology different from that of central Mexico. The native population of Yucatán had probably reached its apogee a century or more before the Spaniards arrived. The ensuing drop caused by wars and various other calamities accelerated, however, after the devastation of the conquest and the appearance of new diseases. The estimated population fell from perhaps 800,000 in 1528 to 240,000 by 1550 and 185,000 by 1605. A recovery until about 1645 gave way to a collapse that lasted until about 1740, bringing the population to a new low. A rapid increase followed for the remainder of the colonial era.

For Central America, the arrival of plague and smallpox reduced the highland population by as much as a third before the Spaniards physically entered the region. A conservative estimate places the original population at 2.225 million in 1520 and 500,000 in 1570. Later pandemics in 1576–77, 1600–1, and later further reduced the total.

Peru also lost much of its indigenous population after the Europeans reached the New World, both before and after Pizarro's arrival. Estimating a population of about 9 million in 1520, Noble David Cook reduced this figure to only 1.3 million natives in 1570 and 600,000 in 1630. The greatest and earliest collapse occurred in the densely settled narrow coastal valleys where many diseases thrived. The low-lying regions of the northern highlands also had extensive losses. The more dispersed highland populations proved more resistant to the demographic decline, although they suffered heavy losses as well. In contrast with the chronology for central Mexico, the native population of Peru did not reach bottom until after the epidemic of 1718–20. Recovery after that raised the population by mid-century to around 610,000, roughly equal to that in 1630.

Colombia's population followed a similar pattern. The proportion of natives in the province of Tunja in the eastern Andes fell about 80 percent from the mid-1530s to the mid-1630s. To the east, Venezuela dropped 50 to 75 percent, and Ecuador's early population decline was precipitous, but recovery came early, beginning by the end of the sixteenth century. Smallpox and measles epidemics in the late seventeenth century caused temporary setbacks.

Twentieth-century estimates of Brazil's Indian population in 1500 range from lows of 1 million to 1.5 million to highs of 5 million to 6 million. After identifying the various groups and then developing population estimates for each, John Hemming suggested a total population of about 2.4 million. As in Spanish America, a decline in the native population in Brazil followed the appearance of Europeans.

DISEASE

There are several reasons for the sharp reduction in the colonies' native populations. The devastation and disruption that accompanied military conflict, the mistreatment of the Indians through overwork and abuse, their starvation and malnutrition as a result of altered subsistence systems and natural disasters that destroyed entire crops, and the psychological trauma that weakened the Indians' will to live and reproduce all helped to reduce the population. Among other things, these conditions facilitated the horrific effects of epidemic diseases introduced by the Europeans and Africans. More than any other single reason, these new diseases to which the native populations had no immunity led to astronomical mortality rates. Smallpox devastated the population of Tenochtitlán and facilitated its conquest and then moved through southern Mexico into Central America, reaching the northern reaches of the Inca Empire by the mid-1520s. Measles first appeared in New Spain and Central America in the early 1530s. In the mid-1540s, a virulent pestilence accompanied by bleeding of the nose and eyes produced high mortality rates in central Mexico and Central America. Thirty years later, another outbreak afflicted the same areas, again killing tens of thousands, if not more. Five other pandemics had struck Central America by 1750. Apparently spared from the initial onslaught of smallpox until the mid-1540s, the Andean region then experienced repeated epidemics. With the epidemic of 1718–20, the population of the Andean area reached its low point. Smallpox raged throughout Brazil from 1562 to 1565. This first infection was brought to Salvador by a ship from Lisbon. Within three or four months, thirty thousand Indians had died in nearby Jesuit missions, and eventually the disease spread from Pernambuco to São Vicente. The later African slave trade then touched off a succession of epidemics in the seventeenth and eighteenth centuries.

Although the amount and timing of the native population decline varied throughout the New World, finally the downward trend was stemmed and growth followed. In New Spain, the Indian population increased from its low point in the first half of the seventeenth century to 3.7 million by the late eighteenth century. In Peru, where the low point was reached a century later, the native population had increased to about 700,000 in 1800. The primary reason for this widespread recovery was the increased immunity of the native populations to the diseases that accompanied European conquest and settlement.

FLIGHT AND FORCED MIGRATION

The appalling drop in the native population is only part of the story. The flight and forced migrations of Indians from their lands also altered Latin America's demographic map during the colonial era. To escape the military depredations of the conquest, tens of thousands relocated to safer regions, but the migration continued even after Spanish power was consolidated. The dispersion of natives in the countryside hindered the Spaniards' efforts both to convert them and to organize them for labor. Faced with the added organizational and economic difficulties posed by the rapid depopulation, both clerics and government officials saw advantages in gathering together the Indians in new or expanded and reorganized communities under more direct European supervision.

This congregation occurred in Central America in the 1540s, Yucatán in the 1550s, and in central Mexico in two stages, first in the 1550s and later from 1593 to 1605. The process in each area followed the same pattern: Smaller outlying towns were combined with larger native communities, or they both were joined into new communities and the old settlements were razed. Sometimes the larger communities were themselves moved into new towns structured according to the characteristic Spanish grid pattern. This also made additional land available to Spaniards, even if there was no immediate rush to secure it.

The initial efforts failed in the 1560s in Peru to consolidate the native population into new towns. Under the firm administration of Viceroy Francisco de Toledo, however, the resettlement or "reduction" of the Indians was accomplished, at least in southern Peru. Toledo sought to group the Indians into as few Spanish-style towns as possible. Over two hundred villages in one region, for example, were consolidated into thirty-nine towns. In some cases as many as eighteen villages were telescoped into one. In Huarochirí, repeated efforts to resettle natives who preferred to return to their traditional lands combined over one hundred small settlements into seventeen villages with about 1,000 to 1,700 persons each. Within twenty years, however, these populations had reasserted their traditional residential patterns.

In Brazil, the Jesuits actively promoted the resettlement of pacified Indian populations into mission communities, believing that this would facilitate their conversion and eliminate cultural practices such as cannibalism and polygyny. The inadvertent effect, however, was to increase the Indians' vulnerability to new diseases. After 1560 both bubonic plague and smallpox devastated Brazil. As a Jesuit leader put it, "The number of people who have died here in Bahia in the past twenty years seems unbelievable."[1] The loss was further aggravated by law and custom that permitted Portuguese governors to assign *aldeia* Indians as laborers, similar to the Spanish *repartimiento*.

The extent of voluntary migration also varied regionally. In Yucatán, for example, Indians seem to have moved more than in central Mexico, suggesting that the relative success of congregation in central Mexico resulted largely from the greater coercion of Spanish authorities there. Where Spanish power was weaker, as in Yucatán, the Indians were able to maintain elements of their social and economic structures. For example, over a third of the native population in Yucatán resided in locations other than their congregated towns. Some had fled into unpacified areas to escape colonial rule. Others had moved to different communities under Spanish control. And still others had left the congregated towns for new, outlying settlements in the same region. Such movement provided an escape, however temporary, of community pressures, for example, in regard to taxation and labor, exacerbated by the declining population.

Voluntary migration was also prevalent in Peru. Before the Spaniards' arrival, there was a small group known as the *yanaconas* in Inca society. Unattached to a community or *ayllu*, the *yanaconas* quickly joined the Spanish both during and after the conquest. They enjoyed freedom of movement and were exempt from the tribute demanded of the commoners who belonged to *ayllus*. Because of this exemption, the number of *yanaconas* increased as the *encomienda* Indians sought to better their lot by abandoning their homes. More quickly Hispanized than the *encomienda* Indians were, the *yanaconas* worked for Spanish employers and often moved far from their birthplace. In the 1550s and 1560s, many were in Potosí opening mines. Indeed, it was the large and growing number of *yanaconas* in Peru that led Viceroy Toledo in 1572 to remove their exemption from tribute and order them to remain in their current residence, a decision that turned the *yanaconas* into a stationary work force.

In the same decade, Toledo transformed the labor draft to provide a regular labor pool of over thirteen thousand men annually for Potosí. Both the indigenous and colonial drafts were called *mita*. Drawing on the provinces closest to the mines, the *mita* required one-seventh of the adult male population to work at Potosí for one year out of seven. By its nature the *mita* forced a substantial population movement in the southern highlands. Over the long run, however, its legacy was permanent migration, as wives and children accompanied their husbands, thereby undermining traditional residential and kinship patterns. Indians anxious to avoid *mita* service fled their homes, thereby surrendering access to land that membership in an *ayllu* provided. They took up residence near Spanish settlements or in other Indian communities as *forasteros* or foreigners, thus winning a statutory exemption from future *mita* labor. In addition, some Indians who performed *mita* service chose to remain at the mines as wage laborers and never returned to their homes. These population movements, coupled with recurrent epidemics, increased the pressure on those who remained in their villages. By the early 1680s, not only was the total Indian population of Upper Peru reduced to roughly half of its level in 1570, but also half of the population in the sixteen provinces subject to the Potosí *mita*

were *yanaconas* or *forasteros*. In the fourteen provinces exempt from providing *mita* labor, as many as three-quarters of the population were
forasteros.

The Iberian Population

Population growth, not loss, characterized demographic change in the Iberian population. Immigration accounted for the initial expansion, but the
increasing number of Iberian women in the colonies led to the natural
growth of the population.

The number of emigrants from Spain to the Indies is unknown. Given
the smaller number of ships sailing to the Indies beginning in the second
quarter of the seventeenth century, it is probable that emigration
decreased steadily from then until at least 1720. The number of European
Spaniards arriving then rose again, although never to that reached
between 1550 and 1650.

The following table is based on information regarding ships sailing from
Spain between 1506 and 1699:

	Passengers	Sailors Remaining in America	Total	Average per Year
1506–60	56,935	28,736	85,671	1558
1561–1600	104,910	52,272	157,182	3930
1601–25	74,400	35,912	111,312	4452
1626–50	54,640	28,864	88,504	3340
1651–99	29,348	10,853	40,201	820
Totals	320,233	156,637	476,870	

Sources: Magnus Mörner, "Spanish Migration to the New World Prior to 1810: A Report on the State of
Research," in Fredi Chiapelli, editor, *First Images of America* (Berkeley and Los Angeles: University of California Press, 1976), vol. 2, pp.766–7; and Lutgardo García Fuentes, *El Comercio Español con America
(1650–1700)* (Seville: Escuela de Estudios Hispano-Americanos de Sevilla, 1980), chap. 4.

Although a few foreigners, mainly Portuguese, entered the Spanish colonies, the Crown always tried to regulate immigration and limit it to its own
subjects. Protestants, descendants of Jews, *moriscos,* and gypsies were
excluded by law from the Spanish Indies, but small numbers entered
anyway.

Emigration

Little is known about the history of Portuguese emigration because the
Lisbon earthquake of 1755 destroyed many records. In 1584, the pacified
coastal region of Brazil had an estimated population of 57,000, of which

whites, a group that must have been largely immigrant, numbered 25,000. By 1600, the total population is believed to have been 150,000, of which 30,000 were white. A century later an estimated 100,000 whites made up a third of the population of Brazil's settled areas. These estimates of the white population included substantial numbers of American-born whites and white and Indian mixtures, who because of their high status were considered white. Fewer women left Portugal for Brazil than Spain for Spanish America.

The Portuguese emigrated to Brazil to take advantage of the sugar and mining booms. Both events caused an increase in the total number of arrivals and in the number of emigrants from the middle and upper classes. In the early eighteenth century, perhaps three thousand to four thousand people left Portugal each year, primarily from the populous northern provinces, for the new mining regions of Brazil. Worried by the size of the exodus, in 1720 the Portuguese Crown tried, with some success, to restrict it.

Most of the first emigrants to the Spanish colonies were young males who joined the early expeditions of exploration, conquest, and settlement. By the middle of the sixteenth century, however, such adventure-hungry and unskilled young men were not encouraged to go west. Instead, artisans and professional men, civil officials, clerics, servants and retainers, and women and children now swelled the ranks of emigrants. For the rest of the century the percentage of women almost doubled, with officials, clerics, their retinues, and skilled craftsmen also rising in number. Most of the emigrants came from Andalusia and Extremadura; by 1600 roughly one of every five males, two of every five females, and one of every two merchants hailed from the city of Seville alone.

Mexico attracted the largest number of settlers in the sixteenth century, over a third of the total. Peru and Bolivia together received about a quarter. The Antilles, New Granada, and Tierra Firme were destinations for another quarter of the emigrants, and the Río de la Plata and Central America accounted for just under a tenth. The remaining emigrants were spread throughout the other regions of the empire—Chile, Florida, Venezuela, and Ecuador.

The emigrants left Spain for a variety of reasons: Those who departed in the years of Columbus, Cortés, and Pizarro sought glory and fortune, but later emigrants had more mundane goals. Most hoped to escape the growing economic problems in Spain and Portugal. Many had relatives established in prosperous regions who wrote glowing accounts of life in the New World. Ties to family, in fact, was the main reason for emigration.

By 1600 the number of Spaniards born in the New World exceeded the number of recent arrivals. Between 1570 and 1620 the Spanish population roughly trebled, from perhaps 125,000 to 150,000, to 375,000 to 450,000. About half of the growth is attributed to natural increase. With every generation the creole population's proportion of the Spanish population in the Americas grew. The decline in Spanish emigration after

1625 meant that the number and proportion of peninsulars within the white population continued to fall.

The Spanish population was spread unevenly throughout the colonies. By the mid-seventeenth century, Mexico had the largest white population, with 200,000. The Antilles, Peru, Central America, Colombia, Argentina, and Bolivia together had about 350,000 whites. This population also moved around the New World, particularly in the sixteenth century. Settlers left Central America, for example, after the riches of Peru were discovered. The white population of Potosí exploded after the discovery of silver in 1545 and then dropped in the seventeenth century. The number of Spaniards there in 1557 is thought to be 12,000. By 1610, peninsulars reportedly numbered 3,000 and creoles 35,000. The falling silver production precipitated a general exodus, decreasing Potosí's total population to 8,000 by the close of the eighteenth century.

The Spanish population was most numerous in and near the urban centers: Mexico City had two thousand *vecinos* in the mid-sixteenth century and three thousand by 1570, a number that continued to rise until the end of the colonial era, at which time about seventy thousand Spaniards resided in the city. It is estimated that by the late eighteenth century just over half of the Spanish population of the Indies lived in urban areas.

Starting from a negligible number at the time of conquest, the Spanish population had grown to almost a quarter of the total population by the 1790s. By that time as well, the number of racially mixed people had become increasingly visible.

Racial Mixtures

The military success of European males in the New World, the initial paucity of European women, and the widespread availability of Indian women led to the birth of many racially mixed babies. Indeed, according to R. C. Padden, the Spanish "commonly left more pregnancies in their camps than they did casualties on the field of battle."[2]

Although some Europeans married Indian women, most of the early interracial children were illegitimate. When such children's parents were married or their fathers were upper-class Europeans, they were included in the white society and enjoyed their fathers' social status. Those children not acknowledged by their white fathers were raised in the Indian society. Some mixed-race persons experienced discrimination, but others were able to obtain positions of responsibility and leadership. Very quickly, however, the rapidly growing number of children of Spanish-Indian unions was given a separate racial identification, *mestizo*. In Portuguese America this mixed-race population—called *mamelucos*, *mestiços*, and *caboclos*—grew in the late sixteenth and seventeenth centuries, often playing a crucial role in enforcing Portuguese authority in the frontier zones and in protecting Brazil from French, and later Dutch, intervention.

The arrival of Africans introduced a third racial group into the Americas. They quickly added to the genetic pool and racial nomenclature through their unions with Indian women. Very few white males married black women, although casual contact was common. The consequence of such relationships was a rapidly growing nonwhite, non-Indian population. In Mexico and some other regions, the term *pardo* was sometimes merely a synonym for mulatto, and by the seventeenth century the term *casta* was widely, if loosely, applied to any nonwhite who was not clearly an Indian.

Slavery

Spurred by the early development of the sugar industry in the late sixteenth century and a mining boom after 1695, the slave trade to Brazil dwarfed the Spanish experience. During the sugar industry's expansion in the seventeenth century, the number of slaves imported averaged about 5,600 per year. By 1750 black slaves constituted approximately 70 percent of the plantation zone's population. Portugal's control of Angola and other West African slave ports encouraged this trade. By 1810 more than 2.5 million African captives had arrived in Brazil.

The resulting imbalance of two males to one female led to racial mixing on plantations using both Indian and African slaves and in plantation zones with contiguous indigenous populations. This same imbalance, however, also retarded any natural increase in the black population. The high mortality rates of the newly arrived Africans further contributed to a low population growth rate.

By the late eighteenth century, almost 45 percent of the Spanish empire's population of 14.1 million was non-Indian and over 20 percent of it was *mestizo* or *pardo*. The racially mixed population had grown much more rapidly than any other sector of the population.

Important demographic changes took place during the colonial era. Throughout the Hispanic world the Indian population declined by 90 percent or more from its precontact numbers before beginning, in the fortunate cases, a modest recovery at the end of the sixteenth century. Nowhere was the indigenous population as large in 1808 as it had been before the Europeans reached the New World. The white population grew because of high levels of reproduction and, at least until the mid-seventeenth century, immigration. In the Caribbean islands and adjacent lowlands and in the lowlands of the Pacific slope, African slaves largely replaced semisedentary native populations devastated by disease. Finally, the racially mixed population was expanding rapidly by the late sixteenth century and continued to increase its proportion of the total population of Latin America as the colonial era progressed.

Indian Labor

The domestic and export economies of colonial Latin America rested largely on forced labor. Although supplemented over time by African slaves and a growing *casta* population, Indians provided the labor power that overcame Spain's limited capital resources and technology in developing mining and agriculture for the export market, and in agriculture, grazing, and textiles for the domestic market. Brazil's sugar plantations were well established by the mid-sixteenth century with the help of Indian slaves. Then with the development of the African slave trade, they became less dependent on the Indians, and by the early seventeenth century, the sugar plantations of Pernambuco and Bahia were worked mainly by African slaves.

Because the Indians rarely volunteered to work for the colonial settlers, the administrators evolved various forms of compulsory labor and fiscal demands to mobilize them. Depopulation, the separation of labor from goods as tribute, the conversion of goods into cash as tribute, and the compulsory purchase of goods from Spanish officials all forced changes in the organization of labor and compelled the Indians to participate in the monetized colonial economy, an economy that overlapped but did not totally replace the indigenous one. The methods used to secure labor varied by region and over time. *Encomienda, repartimiento/mita,* free wage labor, *yanaconaje,* and slavery were the principal means employed in Spanish America. In Brazil, Indian slavery provided much of the agricultural labor from the 1550s until replaced by African slaves.

Encomienda

Both the Spanish Crown and individual Spaniards wanted to profit from their presence in the New World. With the exception of the Incan treasure, plunder produced only modest riches. But in Mesoamerica and the Andean region, urbanized, economically advanced societies were accustomed to providing agricultural surplus and labor as tribute to native overlords even before the conquest. The problem for the Crown and the conquistadors was how best to harness this labor power.

In the Caribbean, Spaniards employed an early form of *encomienda* as well as slavery to mobilize Indian labor. *Encomienda* Indians on Hispaniola were forcibly moved to the gold fields; subjected to outrageous demands for labor, food, and, in the case of women, sexual favors; and even sold. They were scarcely distinguishable from the enslaved natives imported from other islands and Tierra Firme. Faced with incontrovertible evidence of this excessive exploitation, Ferdinand issued the Laws of Burgos in 1512, the first systematic attempt to regulate the Spaniards' treatment of the Indians. Better work conditions, adequate food and living standards, and restrictions on punishment were among its many, though unenforced, provisions.

By the time the Spaniards reached Mexico, the allocation of Indians through *encomienda* was fixed in conquistadors' minds as an appropriate, if not indispensable, reward for their actions. Cortés, despite fearing a repetition of the demographic disaster he had witnessed in the islands, yielded to his followers' clamor and assigned them Indian *caciques* and their peoples. Grants of *encomienda,* often the most valuable spoil available, subsequently accompanied conquest in each region the Spaniards occupied.

The conquistadors and early settlers who received *encomiendas* constituted the colonial aristocracy for several decades. Their large households dominated city centers, and their rural enterprises tied the Indian communities to the marketplace. The *encomiendas* themselves varied enormously in size and value. The Crown confirmed Cortés in *encomiendas* totaling 115,000 natives, a statutory number probably far below those he actually held. Pizarro assigned himself 20,000 tributaries for his services in Peru. Thirty *encomiendas* in the Valley of Mexico in 1535 averaged 6,000 Indians, far above the legal maximum of 300. More common than large awards, however, was the presentation of a single *cacique* and his people.

Even in central New Spain and Peru, the number of *encomenderos* was never large. Soon after the conquest, New Spain briefly had over 930 *encomenderos,* but by 1560 the number had dropped to 480, after many of the grants reverted to the Crown. Peru never had more than about 500 *encomenderos,* and by 1555 only 5 percent of an estimated Spanish population of 8,000 held Indians in *encomienda.*

Initially the mainland *encomienda* supported essential elements of indigenous culture and economy. Except where precious metals were found, the *encomenderos'* demands were similar to those of the preconquest indigenous elites. The well-established patterns and the settled nature of the indigenous agricultural economies of central Mexico and Peru altered the labor practices of the Caribbean *encomienda*. In Hispaniola and Cuba, *encomenderos* routinely moved Indians to the gold mines, thus breaking the natives' ties to their lands. But even though Cortés, Pedro de Alvarado, and others forcibly enlisted Indians as military auxiliaries and porters, the *encomenderos* usually tried to profit from the existing indigenous economy. In comparison to the Caribbean experience, the *encomienda* in Mexico and Peru had a settled character.

The small number of conquistadors and the administrative problems inherent in the tribute system forced reliance on local native leaders to serve as middlemen. The *kurakas* in Peru organized and supervised the delivery of labor and goods for sale and exchange in the urban centers where the *encomenderos* resided. The *kurakas* also acted as intermediaries for the *encomenderos* in efforts to limit or transform the tribute requirement. Indeed, the Andean tradition of mutual service may have mitigated the abuses that marked the behavior of the first generation of *encomenderos* in New Spain.

In central Mexico, the early *encomenderos* appeared to have learned nothing from their predecessors in the Antilles. They overworked the Indians, forcing them to construct buildings, provide labor for farms and mines, and transport goods. They seized the Indians' property and women and beat, jailed, and killed those that resisted. Some *encomenderos* sold the Indians' labor, whereas others pushed them off their land in order to introduce cash crops and grazing animals. The *caciques* and Indian nobles who required taxes on top of the *encomenderos'* demands added to the commoners' burden.

The *encomenderos'* central concern was income, and they made every effort to extract tribute goods that could be sold at a profit. Tribute payments varied, depending on local resources and skills. They were paid in cash or in foodstuffs, raw materials, and finished goods. One Mexican *encomienda* in the 1540s provided daily two chickens, fodder for horses, wood, maize, and, every eighty days, shirts, petticoats, and blankets. Depending on the region, *encomiendas* supplied cotton mantles, cacao, cochineal, llamas, wheat, and coca. Regardless of the monetary benefits of selling tribute goods, most *encomenderos* also demanded labor for service in their homes, on their rural properties, or in their workshops.

When the *encomenderos* could use the Indians' labor to enter the profitable export business, they altered the traditional economy. Hence, the *encomenderos* in Central America demanded cacao as tribute and became, in effect, cacao wholesalers for the large Mexican market. And the *encomenderos* in Tucumán and Córdoba organized Indian men, women, and

Spanish judge punishing an Indian

children to produce textiles for the growing market at Potosí after the discovery of silver there in 1545.

The New Laws

The catastrophic native depopulation, the growing Spanish emigration, and the denunciation of the *encomenderos'* abuses came to a head in the 1540s. Correctly suspicious that the *encomenderos* wanted to became a New World version of the Castilian aristocracy, the Crown listened to colonists excluded from grants of *encomienda* and to a small, articulate group of clerics who condemned the *encomienda* as a major source of the ills suffered by the natives. The most effective lobbyist was the Dominican Bartolomé de las Casas, whose efforts led to the New Laws of 1542.

The New Laws authorized a viceroy for Peru and *audiencias* in Lima and Guatemala as part of their provisions to create a more effective administration and to improve the judicial system. But they are best known for prohibiting Indian slavery, attacking the *encomenderos* in general, and ordering in particular that individuals responsible for the civil war in Peru be stripped of their *encomiendas.* This last provision and one prohibiting new assignments of *encomiendas* and ordering the reversion of existing ones to the Crown upon the death of their incumbents angered the *encomenderos* and their supporters. The ensuing rebellion in Peru brought the death of the region's first viceroy, and in New Spain, a wiser viceroy, Antonio de Mendoza, refrained from the laws' enforcement rather than provoke rebellion.

Faced with the unexpectedly violent reaction, the Crown relented, and by allowing succession for a second "life," it enabled the *encomenderos* to pass on their grants for another generation. But ironically, as a result of the civil wars and the frequent lack of heirs, many of the *encomiendas* had already become part of the royal patrimony and provided tribute to the royal treasury, tribute whose collection was overseen by royally appointed *corregidores,* who were named for a short term rather than for life. The slow transfer of *encomiendas* from private to royal domain meant a shift in power away from the original colonial aristocracy in central Mexico and Peru. Before 1570 about three-quarters of the *encomienda* income in the Valley of Mexico had reverted to the Crown, and so extensions of *encomiendas* for third and fourth lives had little significance. *Encomiendas* and other types of labor services and tribute in kind did survive in Paraguay, the Yucatán, remote areas of Central America, New Granada, Chile, and northwestern Argentina until the late eighteenth century. Although essential to these areas' economies, their size and value were not important enough to the Crown to make their complete suppression necessary.

Repartimiento/Mita

As direct control of the *encomiendas* passed into the hands of colonial officials, the Indian communities increasingly were required to substitute cash tributes for the earlier payments in kind, although this transition was never completed. For tributaries to meet annual payments of up to eight pesos, they had to produce goods for the market and work for wages. In the areas near the major Spanish towns and the mining camps of New Spain and Peru, wage labor and market agriculture thus became a fixture of the Indians' life. Elsewhere, however, the natives participated less in the money economy. But by 1600, Indian communities throughout much of the empire had reorganized to meet the monetary requirements of the colonial state and the Church as well as to satisfy new needs associated with the assimilation of the European material culture.

Neither cash tribute nor the desire to work for wages to subsidize the purchase of nonsubsistence goods pushed enough Indians away from their traditional production to provide the amount of cheap labor demanded by Spanish landowners, miners, and textile manufacturers. In addition, the diminished Indian population that survived the early epidemics often lived far from the new economic centers, particularly the mining regions of Mexico and Peru. Thus large numbers of Indian laborers had to be relocated.

The solution to this problem was a system of rotational labor drafts, called *repartimiento* in New Spain and *mita* in Peru. Compulsory labor service had been common in both the Aztec and Inca empires, and Spaniards had used it from the beginning of the colonial period for the construction of roads, aqueducts, fortifications, churches, and public buildings and for some agricultural purposes. Formal *repartimiento/mita* drafts were established in New Spain in the 1550s, the central Andes in the 1570s, and the eastern highlands of Colombia in the 1590s. Under this system the Indian communities filled a quota of laborers for a prescribed time, usually two to four months of the year. The workers then could apply the minimal wages they received to their tribute and other required payments.

This labor system differed according to region. In New Spain the *repartimiento* supplied labor mainly for agriculture, although silver miners used it in central Mexico. The *mita* was the labor base for the early Peruvian mining industry, on coastal plantations, and for road repair and maintenance projects. In Quito and Tucumán, labor in textile factories *(obrajes)* was a common form of *repartimiento* service. In Central America, *repartimientos* provided labor for wheat farming and indigo production. Their use in the latter activity was illegal, but both the producers and royal administrators came to regard the small fines as part of the labor cost. In Oaxaca, where Indians were assigned primarily to Spanish wheat farmers, the *repartimiento* made up only about 4 percent of all tributaries.

In some regions the *repartimiento/mita* remained an important mechanism for mobilizing Indian labor until the end of the colonial era. The mining *mitas* in Peru, the *repartimiento* for *obraje* labor in Ecuador, and the agricultural *repartimiento* in Central America survived into the nineteenth century. In central New Spain, the *repartimiento* was important to agriculture for less than a century, but in New Galicia it supplemented free labor until the early eighteenth century.

Free Wage Labor

The continuing decline of the native population and the growth of the Spanish population rendered the *repartimiento* an inadequate source of labor for agricultural and mining production. Large estate owners *(hacendados)* and miners in central New Spain solved the need for a regular supply of labor by contracting directly with Indians and *castas,* often paying wages slightly higher than those for *repartimiento* labor. Originally a supplement to *repartimiento* labor, in time free wage labor replaced it. Indians who lost their lands through sale or usurpation and those who found the financial demands of their village unbearable formed a pool of labor available for hire and, in some cases, for permanent residence on the *haciendas.*

By 1630 free wage labor had largely supplanted *repartimiento* in New Spain, and the number of hacienda residents, often *castas,* was expanding. The forced labor draft remained in use in the Valley of Mexico only for the interminable project of draining Lake Texcoco. By the late sixteenth century in Peru and Bolivia, free wage labor was more prevalent than *mita* labor in the mining districts. In Chilean agriculture, free wage labor became important in the mid-seventeenth century, and a century later it was widespread in Ecuador and the eastern highlands of Colombia. Throughout Spanish America, powerful landowners and mine owners were able to control the cost of labor and keep wages at artificially low levels. Wage earners may have been free, but a true labor market seldom existed.

An outgrowth of free wage labor was debt peonage. *Hacendados,* miners, and owners of *obrajes* sought to hold workers in debt in order to prevent them from moving to another job. For their part, the laborers sometimes demanded credit before accepting employment. In many cases, neither creditor nor debter expected to settle the account.

Debt peonage associated with free wage labor varied greatly by region. It was common throughout New Spain, where the amount of debt ranged from averages of fewer than three weeks to eleven months of work. The extent of debt peonage varied over time as well, remaining generally constant in Morelos in the eighteenth century but eroding in Guadalajara owing to the workers' weakened bargaining power as a result of demographic expansion. Debt peonage seems to have been more widespread in Ecuador than in Mexico, less prevalent on the coastal estates of Peru, but on the Jesuit estate in Tucumán, its use to tie down workers was routine. In Chile, peonage eventually took the form of *inquilinaje,* or land loans.

Yanaconaje

The progression from *encomienda* to *repartimiento* to free wage labor and at times debt peonage—the classic pattern of labor institutions in Spanish America—appeared first and developed most fully in New Spain, but one or more stages could be found throughout the colonies. In some cases different labor systems coexisted during times of economic transition. Two other institutions, *yanaconaje* and Indian slavery, were also important, either in a particular region or for a brief period of time.

Individuals unattached to *ayllus* in the Inca Empire were, as mentioned, known as *yanacona*. Growing in number even before Atahualpa's capture, the disruption of the Spanish conquest and the demands of the mining *mita* augmented the population of uprooted natives even more. Spanish landowners willingly allowed them to settle on their estates in return for specified amounts of labor and produce. Although not sold individually, *yanacona* were included with the estate on which they resided when it changed hands, labor as well as land thus passing from owner to owner. This lack of mobility distinguished the *yanaconaje* from other nonslave labor institutions. At the same time, the *yanaconas'* continued residence on Spanish estates exempted them from the *mita,* although not from tribute. By 1600 the number of *yanacona* was almost equal to that of Indians living in Andean villages in Peru and Bolivia. They remained in northwestern Argentina into the seventeenth century and, under the name *origenios,* in Paraguay into the 1790s. In some places *yanaconaje* persisted after independence.

Indian Slavery

Chattel slavery was the most repressive form of Indian labor in the early colonial period. Where mineral wealth and surplus agricultural production were absent, enslaving the natives rather than assigning them to *encomienda* proved more attractive to Spaniards eager for immediate profit. But slaves were common in Central America even before the Spanish arrived in the early 1520s, as tribes fought to capture slaves for labor or sacrifice. In addition, thieves, rapists, and poachers, among others, could be enslaved by their own people. This tradition facilitated the continuation and expansion of slavery by the Spaniards, who had already enslaved Indians in the Caribbean. Under certain conditions, moreover, the Crown accepted the enslavement of Indians, notably those who refused to acknowledge its authority and submit to its rule peacefully. In addition to taking slaves in war, the Spaniards bought Indians who were already enslaved. Under pressure from the Spanish colonists, the *caciques* also sometimes enslaved free Indians.

The main reason for slavery in Central America was the demand for native labor elsewhere and the absence of other forms of quick profit. An *encomienda* in Honduras, for example, yielded little income. Nicaragua's principal economic activity in the 1530s was enslaving Indians who were then sent to Panama and Peru. Although there is no agreement on the number of slaves shipped out of Central America, estimates range from 50,000 (of 150,000 chattel slaves) to hundreds of thousands between 1524 and 1549.

Although slave raids continued on the Venezuelan coast until the early seventeenth century and native enslavement persisted on the Chilean and northern New Spain frontiers until the 1680s and in northern Argentina until even later, depopulation and the Crown's attack on the mistreatment of Indians in the New Laws brought it to an end in Central America by 1550. Alonso López de Cerrato, named to preside over the recently established *audiencia* for much of Central America (Los Confines), reached the region in 1548 and implemented the prohibitions on holding native slaves, much to the dismay of numerous colonists and traders.

The enlarged Portuguese presence after 1530 exacerbated the labor problem in colonial Brazil. As the sugar industry expanded, more laborers were necessary, and slaving expeditions became commonplace, despite the Jesuits' protests. The theory behind the expansion of slavery in Brazil was similar to that in Spanish America. "Just war," cannibalism, and the ransom of Indians captured by other natives in intertribal war in return for lifetime servitude were acceptable justifications for enslavement.

The coastal Indian population fell as a result of enslavement, increased warfare, and, beginning in 1562, the spread of disease. The slave traders then moved into Brazil's immense interior. By 1600, formal slaving expeditons *(bandeiras)* were becoming more frequent. Slavers from São Paulo, the famous *bandeirantes,* scoured much of south and central Brazil in the seventeenth century looking for Indians of any linguistic group to capture and enslave. Jesuit missions were particularly attractive targets, and the *bandeirantes* seized thousands of Indians from them in the early decades of the century. Although slaving expeditions continued in the interior until the mid-eighteenth century, the Indians captured were sent mainly to Rio de Janeiro, São Vicente, and São Paulo. On the sugar plantations of Pernambuco and Bahia in the northeast, African slaves had begun to replace Indian slaves in the 1570s, and by the 1620s the transition was nearly complete. Indian slavery persisted on Brazil's borders until the 1750s and illegally thereafter in a few areas. By that time, however, African slavery had long been the most important source of labor on Brazil's plantations.

Repartimiento de Bienes *and Indian Resistance*

Although the Spanish employed different forms of native labor, their purpose was always to convert labor into cash profit. Because many Indians participated reluctantly in the colonial economy, over time the Spaniards devised a system of compulsory purchase of goods and monopolization of Indian production. The *repartimiento* or *reparto de bienes* or *mercancías* reached maturity in the late seventeenth century and continued until outlawed in the 1780s. Under this system of forced exchange, *corregidores* and *alcaldes mayores* monopolized commerce between the Indians in their jurisdiction and the outside, forcing them to sell their goods—cochineal in Oaxaca, coca in the *yungas* of Bolivia, textiles in Quito—at fixed prices usually well below their free-market value. In addition, the officials compelled the natives to buy goods at artificially high prices. In the Andes the most common goods were textiles and mules, but some European merchandise was also included. The effect of this system was to create a permanent trade imbalance in the Indian communities that only native wage labor could make up.

Indians resisted labor demands in any way they could. Some fled their homes, surrendering their traditional right to land but retaining control over their lives. Sometimes native chieftains refused to cooperate and were imprisoned or lost their positions as a consequence. Local rebellions were common, notably in the Andes. Spanish authorities commonly responded to such challenges with force, beating, imprisoning, and occasionally even execution. Rarely able to improve conditions through force, the Indian communities quickly learned to use the colonial legal system, which included courts designated for their cases. For example, they could hire lawyers and initiate suits to win a smaller *mita* quota or the payment of their statutory wages. Although these victories were often costly and seldom lasted, the Indians' resourcefulness and persistence was remarkable.

Spanish demands for labor and the commercial requirements of the colonial economy often severed the close relationship between the natives and their land. The need to meet tribute payments, serve in labor drafts, and pay for unwanted goods forced on them by the *repartimiento de bienes* forced Indians from their villages and into the Hispanic culture. The transformation of Indian culture, however, was never complete. The Indians continued to resist the commercialization of their labor and production long after the Spanish Empire had collapsed.

Slavery and the Slave Trade

Before the Portuguese voyages of discovery in the early fifteenth century, slavery in western Europe had declined from its prominence in the latter stages of the Roman Empire to a marginal place in European social and economic life. But the Portuguese traders' explorations of Africa's Atlantic coast introduced them to the continent's indigenous slave trade, and by 1450 hundreds of African slaves were entering Europe each year. This flow seems to have peaked at about five hundred per year in the 1480s and then remained constant into the next century. Thus by the time that Columbus sailed, African slavery was well established in Iberia.

Slavery moved much closer to the legal and structural form it took in America when Portugal and Spain began to develop the Atlantic islands. The introduction of sugar cultivation from the eastern Mediterranean to Madeira and the Canary Islands hastened the adaptation of Iberian institutions and social forms to the special requirements of a colonial economic environment. Because these islands lacked an adequate labor force, sugar cultivation was linked to the African slave trade almost immediately. This stage in the development of slavery culminated in the Portuguese settlement of São Tomé. Located close to the African coast, it became the prototype of the plantation colony relying on heavy capital investment, monoculture, and a work force of African slaves.

Black Slaves in the Age of Conquest

Black slaves and freedmen arrived in America during the early stages of discovery and settlement. By the first decades of the sixteenth century, they were regularly participating in Spain's military expeditions. Conquistadors whose slaves accompanied them claimed an extra share of the spoils. The wealth gained in Mexico allowed them to purchase large numbers of black servants, and as a result, each succeeding expedition contained more blacks than its predecessor did. Black slaves were common in Panama by the 1520s and were present in all of the early voyages undertaken by Pizarro and Almagro. So important was black manpower and skill that Pizarro secured permission to import fifty slaves to Peru as part of his preconquest agreement with the Crown. One black man, in fact, served as second in command of Pizarro's artillery at Cajamarca. Another, Juan Valiente, was prominent in Almagro's ill-fated Chilean expedition, which included many blacks. He later returned to Chile with the conquistador Pedro de Valdivia and received land and an *encomienda*. A runaway slave from Mexico, Valiente—like many of his Spanish contemporaries—had overcome the liability of obscure origins and achieved a better life in the Indies.

Most African slaves and almost all freedmen in Spanish America during the conquest were born in or had lived many years in Europe. In contrast, the Portuguese settlers in Brazil, from the earliest years, relied heavily on the African slave trade. Whether slave or free, the thousands of black men and the handful of black women in the Spanish settlements of the Caribbean, Mexico, and Peru spoke Spanish, were baptized as Christians, and generally operated within the culture and technology of Europe. Although racially distinct and retaining some elements of African culture and practice, Hispanized blacks joined the Spanish conquistadors and settlers in imposing Europe's political domination and transmitting its culture.

Indians recognized the blacks' strong association with Hispanic culture and considered them "black white men." Although Spanish law defined the Indians as the legal equals of Spaniards in many regards and imposed a judicial and social inferiority on blacks, in the New World blacks held an intermediary social rank. Spanish masters considered Indians weak and unreliable workers and preferred Africans when their purchase was economically feasible. Sometimes Spaniards used their black slaves to supervise the labor and collection of tribute from free Indian populations. Blacks trained as artisans also directed Indian draft labor for large-scale public and religious construction projects. Others helped introduce European agriculture, especially the highly specialized production of sugar and wine. Had the Indian population remained stable and the black population continued to be drawn from Europe, the character of Latin American race relations and culture would have developed quite differently.

The Spanish preference for black workers overcame in large part the cost advantages of Indian labor and produced a ready market for imported slaves. Indeed, investing in slaves was a sound financial decision for many miners and sugar planters. The owners of Brazilian sugar plantations, for example, found African slaves more profitable than the cheaper but less healthy and less productive Indian slaves. Nonetheless, *encomiendas* and *repartimientos* of Indian labor provided the greatest economic benefits to the Spaniards because they required no capital investment and the laborers provided for their own maintenance. African slavery prospered only where a diminished Indian population could no longer sustain alternative forms of labor. In the wake of the high native mortality, the use of slaves in agriculture spread first to the islands and then to the tropical lowlands of the Caribbean basin.

As sugar cultivation began in Hispaniola in the early sixteenth century, the plantation model from the Atlantic islands started to take hold. Genoese merchants provided much of the capital and black slaves most of the labor. After the mainland conquests, however, large numbers of Spaniards, perhaps a majority, abandoned the older colonies of the Caribbean to seek their fortunes in Mexico and Peru. Shorn of investment capital and manpower, the islands could not compete successfully with the well-established sugar estates of the Atlantic islands.

Slavery was more successful in the early mining industry on the mainland. Placer mining with Indian labor had produced much of the wealth extracted from Hispaniola before 1520, and many early settlers in Central America had prior experience in this industry. Initially, the *encomienda* and enslaved Indians formed the labor gangs in the gold-mining industry in Honduras and Guatemala. But the high native mortality drove the miners to import expensive black slaves. Several major gold strikes provided the necessary capital, and by the 1540s slaves were arriving in substantial numbers, eventually reaching three thousand. When profits fell, however, the miners sold their slaves and returned to the cheaper Indian labor.

The African Slave Trade

Because Spain had surrendered its right to establish outposts in Africa as part of the Treaty of Alcaçovas in 1479, it developed a system of monopoly contracts, *asientos,* with foreign merchants, usually Portuguese, to supply its American colonies with slaves. To secure the maximum fiscal benefit for itself and to prevent contraband trade, beginning in 1518 the Crown sold exclusive licenses to private enterprises, individuals, or monopoly companies to import into the colonies a set number of *piezas de Indias,* young adult males or their labor equivalent, within a limited number of years. Because women, children, and older or disabled men counted as fractions, a ship delivering one hundred *piezas de Indias* could actually unload two hundred or more slaves. Because the *asientista* usually earned greater profits from the introduction of contraband goods, few fulfilled their obligation to import a full quota of African slaves. The *asiento* bid up the cost of slaves, and the fleet system limited efforts to market colonial production in Europe.

Between the early sixteenth century and 1810, Spanish America received nearly 1 million African slaves. The following table reveals that the late eighteenth century—a time of dramatic expansion in sugar and other tropical products—was also the time of greatest vitality in the slave trade. The booming sugar plantations of Cuba absorbed more than half of the slaves entering Spanish America after 1770, although Venezuela and the Río de la Plata region also imported many. Overall, however, the Spanish colonies received only about 13 percent of all the slaves imported into the Western Hemisphere before 1820. Brazil and the Caribbean sugar colonies of France and Great Britain were the preeminent destinations. British North America, in comparison, imported slightly fewer than 350,000 slaves, or one-third the number that entered Spanish America.

Estimated Slave Imports to Latin America, 1551–1810

	Total Imports		Average per Year	
Years	Spanish America	Brazil	Spanish America	Brazil
1551–1600	62,500	50,000	1,250	1,000
1601–1700	292,500	560,000	2,925	5,600
1701–1810	578,600	1,891,400	5,786	18,914

Source: Philip D. Curtin, *The Atlantic Slave Trade: A Census* (Madison: University of Wisconsin Press, 1969), pp. 116, 119.

An overwhelming majority of the slaves taken to America were from West Africa. On small islands off the coast and in fortified trading posts, the Portuguese, Dutch, French, and English maintained trading stations and exchanged manufactured goods, rum, and tobacco for the slaves offered by African middlemen. European merchants preferred young adult males because women, children, and older men cost the same to ship but sold at lower prices. The resulting permanent sex imbalance of two males to one female in the trade undermined the slaves' family life and prevented the possibility that the New World slave population would increase naturally. Colonial planters sometimes expressed preferences for slaves from a specific African region because certain cultures had reputations for hard work or docility—the two characteristics the owners valued most. Yet problems in organizing the African side of the trade prevented a systematic effort to meet these demands. Traders took slaves from wherever they were plentiful and cheap, and planters bought those that were available.

Brazil was the first American colony to introduce sugar agriculture on a large scale. The planters of the northeast coastal zone initially relied on forced Indian labor, but a succession of devastating epidemics beginning in 1562 pushed them toward black slavery as an alternative labor source, and by the 1620s they relied on it entirely. Portuguese traders already well established off the African coast, and carrying slaves to Europe gave the Brazilian plantations distinct market advantages. In addition, the proximity of Africa reduced transportation costs and the number of slave deaths in transit. The consequence of these advantages can best be seen in a comparative context.

During the seventeenth century, almost as many slaves entered Brazil alone as entered Spanish America and the French and British sugar colonies combined. Even in the eighteenth century, when the Caribbean's sugar production grew most rapidly, the Portuguese colony continued its dominance in the Atlantic slave trade. Although the total imports of the French and British Caribbean colonies were greater, no other nation's colonies imported as many slaves as did Brazil. By 1810 more than 2.5 million slaves had entered Brazilian ports.

Estimates of slave imports to the Americas tend to disguise the trade's effects on Africa and obscure its dreadful nature. Tens of thousands of Africans died even before arriving in the slave ports, and thousands more perished in the wars and civil unrest that the slave trade helped promote. Travel in crowded and pestilential ships claimed the lives of tens of thousands more Africans. The Caribbean sugar boom in the eighteenth century created a heavy new demand for slaves, and inhuman conditions and the resulting high mortality became even more common in the slave ships plying the Atlantic. In an extreme case, only 98 of the 594 slaves embarked on the *George* in West Africa in 1717 reached Buenos Aires alive. Overall, between 1 million and 2 million men, women, and children—10 to 20 percent of all slaves leaving Africa—died in transit. Probably almost half as many blacks died violently in Africa as a result of the trade or on board ship as reached the New World.

How profitable was the Atlantic slave trade? Some historians have argued that the profits from the trade and slave-based agriculture in the Americas played a central role in the development of modern capitalism. Others have claimed that the overall profit level of the trade was generally low and that many investors lost money. Common sense suggests that the trade would not have persisted for several centuries unless profits were fairly secure. The best estimates currently available indicate that profits averaged between 5 and 6 percent of invested capital during most of the time that the trade was legal. Nevertheless, many participants in the trade lost money, and some went bankrupt, including some of the most heavily capitalized monopoly companies. High profit levels were not uncommon, but the terrible mortality experienced on some slave ships and the unpredictability of slave prices in the New World limited profit levels over the long term.

The trade to Brazil was less limited by bureaucratic restrictions and, apparently, more dependably profitable. Brazilians themselves participated in the trade throughout the sugar boom. Though profitable in the long run, the slave trade's earnings were more modest than some early commentators alleged, and individual voyages often brought losses. In the broad context of the expanding Atlantic commercial network, however, the slave trade unquestionably promoted the growth of European economic activity and the development of specialized export economies.

Plantation Slavery

The African slave trade was tied primarily to the development of plantation agriculture. The sugar plantation more than any other part of the colonial economy rested on slave labor. Nonetheless, numerous slaves worked in occupations other than those in the cane fields. Blacks worked on estates that grew indigo, tobacco, and cacao; in urban crafts such as tailoring, shoemaking, carpentry, blacksmithing, and bricklaying; and as stevedores, cowboys, and street vendors. In seventeenth-century Lima, for example, Antón Mina was a journeyman bricklayer and Lázaro Criollo, a cobbler.

Most of the plantations of the Brazilian sugar zone had between sixty and one hundred slaves, a number similar to that on an average plantation in the Old South of the United States during the cotton boom. In contrast, the sugar plantations of the French and British Caribbean typically had hundreds of slaves, and holdings of five hundred to one thousand were not unknown. These differences in scale were, in the Brazilian case, rooted in the reduced capital resources available to planters and the slowdown of Portuguese commercial activity after 1650.

Slaves in Brazil lived in terrible conditions. Housed in poorly ventilated barracks, their limited diet included few fresh fruits and vegetables and only small amounts of meat. Because of the distorted male–female sex ratio that characterized the slave trade and the nature of the work on the sugar plantations, long-term, stable relationships between men and women were rare. Family life, defined by either African or European norms, could be sustained only with great difficulty. Low birthrates and very high infant mortality rates were common in the sugar zone.

The material conditions that masters imposed on slaves were also terrible. Many slaves dressed in rags, and few ever slept in real beds. Poor diet, crowded housing, a brutal work schedule, and constant exposure to tropical disease all contributed to a low average life expectancy. Yet owners made no consistent efforts to enhance life expectancy by improving conditions. Because the average slave on a sugar plantation would recover his initial cost in less than two years of labor, masters seldom viewed improved living conditions as a sound investment. Brazil's plantation owners quickly used up slaves, considering them a dispensable part of production.

Given their living conditions, it is not surprising that slaves struggled to gain some control over their lives. Usually they tried to limit their master's claims on their labor by feigning illness, breaking machinery and tools, killing livestock, or simply refusing to work efficiently. Thousands ran away. In many cases runaways stayed near the plantation and sought through intermediaries to gain some advantage, such as better food or a better job. Other slaves escaped completely, forming free communities, or *quilombos* (*palenques* in Spanish), in remote areas, often joining with local Indians. By the 1670s there were as many as twenty thousand runaways in Brazil, perhaps half of them living in organized groups. The largest *quilombo*, Palmares in Alagoas, held out against punitive expeditions for decades before finally falling in 1697. Runaway communities were also common in the Spanish colonies. Mexico, New Granada, Ecuador, and Venezuela all had large and long-lived *palenques*. In some cases, the Spanish authorities were forced to negotiate treaties that recognized the escaped slaves' freedom.

In contrast with Brazil, the mature plantation complex did not develop in the Spanish colonies until the late eighteenth century when Cuba emerged as a major sugar producer. Although the Spanish used slaves in agriculture on the mainland from an early date—principally along the Caribbean coast in the production of cacao, indigo, and sugar—slavery on the mainlands was less common, for several reasons. Mining drained risk capital away from tropical export agriculture, and Spanish commercial regulations also reduced the potential for profit.

Urban Slavery

Slavery had a much more urban character in colonial Spanish America than in Brazil. Slaves constituted between 10 and 25 percent of the populations of Caracas, Buenos Aires, Mexico City, Lima, Quito, and Bogotá by the mid-eighteenth century. Some wealthy households maintained fifteen or more slaves as domestics. But most slaves lived in smaller households, one or two per master. The small scale of slave holdings and the intimacy imposed by urban architecture produced a slave society necessarily more fluid and humane than that of the plantations in Brazil.

Few urban slaves experienced labor demands as brutal as those of the sugar harvest. Better fed and clothed than their rural counterparts, urban slaves lived longer and had higher birthrates. Sex ratios were generally normal, and slaves could form more stable and lasting relationships. Owners and slaves knew one another well, a familiarity that sometimes led to manumission, although only a small fraction of the slave population, often the American-born offspring of slave women and Spanish men, won freedom. Economic opportunities in the cities also promoted manumission. Male slaves often earned wages as artisans or laborers; female slaves washed clothing, sewed, and sold goods in city markets. Both groups were able to save some of their earnings, and the most fortunate of them purchased their freedom. Even those who remained slaves had some discretionary income and autonomy. As a result, it was in urban centers that various voluntary associations appeared first among blacks.

Whether in the city or on a plantation, slaves were at the mercy of their owners. Like those on plantations, some owners in the cities deprived their slaves of adequate food and clothing or indulged in cruel punishments. The most common complaints that slaves brought before Spanish courts involved whippings and other corporal punishments, inadequate medical care, and sexual abuse. Runaways were common in the urban environment, but the existence of a large number of black freedmen in the colonial cities helped shield them from the authorities.

The courts and the Catholic Church did help restrain the ill treatment of slaves in Latin American cities. Slaves sought and found help from the courts. Every *audiencia* assigned an attorney to protect the poor without charge. In many cases the courts, following Spanish law, forced owners to allow a slave to purchase his or her freedom and prevented owners from breaking up a marriage by selling one of the spouses. On occasion judges ordered particularly cruel owners to sell their slaves. In contrast with judicial practice in the United States before the Civil War, the Spanish courts regularly presumed that a black man or woman was free unless an owner had clear proof of slave status.

The lay brotherhoods of the Catholic Church gave slaves an opportunity to participate actively in the communities' civic and religious life. Some brotherhoods collected funds to help purchase their members' freedom. Although the Church and individual clerics owned slaves, the Church never embraced the racist justifications for slavery so common among Protestant denominations in the United States. Racial discrimination was an institutionalized part of both civic and religious life, but the Catholic Church recognized the essential humanity, the soul, of black slaves in Latin America.

The African slave trade provided the labor power that permitted the development of plantation economies in Brazil, Venezuela, and the Caribbean. In other areas, including coastal Peru and Ecuador, Argentina, and parts of Central America, slave labor was an important supplement to Indian labor drafts and wage labor. By the eighteenth century, black slavery was essential to the largest agricultural sectors in both Portuguese and Spanish America, and so these regions became the major centers of Afro Latin American culture. The importation of black slaves also added to the genetic pool of Latin America and to the multiracial and culturally complex society that characterized the colonial era.

Notes

1. John Hemming, *Red Gold. The Conquest of the Brazilian Indians* (Cambridge, Mass.: Harvard University Press, 1978), p. 144.

2. R. C. Padden, *The Hummingbird and the Hawk: Conquest and Sovereignty in the Valley of Mexico, 1503–1541* (Columbus: Ohio State University Press, 1967), p. 230.

Suggested for Further Reading

Borah, Woodrow, and Sherburne F. Cook. *The Aboriginal Population of Central Mexico on the Eve of Spanish Conquest.* Ibero-Americana No. 45. Berkeley and Los Angeles: University of California Press, 1963.

Bowser, Frederick P. *The African Slave in Colonial Peru, 1524–1650.* Stanford, Calif.: Stanford University Press, 1973.

Cole, Jeffrey A. *Potosi Mita.* Stanford, Calif.: Stanford University Press, 1985.

Conrad, Robert E. *World of Sorrow: The African Slave Trade to Brazil.* Baton Rouge: Louisiana State University Press, 1986.

Cook, Noble David. *Demographic Collapse: Indian Peru, 1520–1620.* Cambridge, England: Cambridge University Press, 1981.

Curtin, Philip D. *The Atlantic Slave Trade: A Census.* Madison: University of Wisconsin Press, 1969.

Denevan, William M., editor. *The Native Population of the Americas in 1492.* Madison: University of Wisconsin Press, 1976.

Engerman, Stanley, and Eugene D. Genovese. *Race and Slavery in the Western Hemisphere: Quantitative Studies.* Princeton, N.J.: Princeton University Press, 1975.

Gibson, Charles. *The Aztecs Under Spanish Rule: A History of the Indians of the Valley of Mexico.* Stanford, Calif.: Stanford University Press, 1964.

Klein, Herbert S. *The Middle Passage. Comparative Studies in the Atlantic Slave Trade.* Princeton, N.J.: Princeton University Press, 1978.

Mellafe, Rolando. *Negro Slavery in Latin America.* Translated by J.W.S. Judge. Berkeley and Los Angeles: University of California Press, 1975.

Newson, Linda. *The Cost of Conquest. Indian Decline in Honduras Under Spanish Rule.* Boulder, Colo.: Westview Press, 1986.

Palmer, Colin A. *Slaves of the White God: Blacks in Mexico, 1570–1650.* Cambridge, Mass.: Harvard University Press, 1976.

Queirós Mattoso, Katia M. de. *To Be a Slave in Brazil 1500–1888.* New Brunswick, N.J.: Rutgers University Press, 1986.

Rout, Leslie B., Jr. *The African Experience in Spanish America: 1502 to the Present Day.* Cambridge, England: Cambridge University Press, 1971.

Schwartz, Stuart B. *Sugar Plantations in the Formation of Brazilian Society. Bahia, 1550–1835.* Cambridge, England: Cambridge University Press, 1985.

Sherman, William L. *Forced Native Labor in Sixteenth-Century Central America.* Lincoln: University of Nebraska Press, 1979.

Simpson, Lesley Byrd. *The Encomienda in New Spain: The Beginning of Spanish Mexico.* Berkeley and Los Angeles: University of California Press, 1950.

Villamarin, Juan A., and Judith E. Villamarin. *Indian Labor in Mainland Spanish America.* Newark: University of Delaware Latin American Studies Program, 1975.

FIVE

PRODUCTION, EXCHANGE, AND DEFENSE

The Mining and Sugar Industries

Colonies existed to increase the economic well-being and political strength of their mother countries. Their production and markets were intended to benefit solely their metropolises which regulated trade and imposed taxes to transfer colonial wealth to themselves. The Portuguese Crown heavily depended on revenue derived from its factories and colonies, first from those in Africa and Asia and later from those in Brazil. The Castilian Crown, too, came to rely on New World income. American bullion enhanced royal coffers and added muscle to Spain's ambitions and expensive foreign policies. Controlling transatlantic trade to prevent gold and silver from reaching foreign hands and safely transporting bullion to the peninsula preoccupied the royal advisers from the early sixteenth century onward.

Most of the conquistadors in Mexico, Peru, and New Granada quickly squandered the enormous booty they had won. Few invested much in economically productive activities, and with the windfall gone, Spaniards in many settlements began to slip toward an impoverished life of subsistence farming and barter. Gold strikes in Mexico, Central America, and later New Granada slowed this decline briefly, but few deposits could be worked profitably for long. Gold mining, therefore, seldom could support the development of settled agriculture or the growth of Spanish towns. Silver mining, on the other hand, required large sustained expenditures of capital and labor and thus had a much greater impact on long-term settlement patterns. The discovery of rich silver deposits in Mexico and Peru stalled the process of economic contraction and initiated a period of unprecedented prosperity in Spain's American empire.

Starting with Columbus's avid pursuit of gold, Spain's experience in much of the New World largely revolved around precious metals. The gold and silver taken as booty in New Spain, Peru, and New Granada fed the search for their sources. By 1550 a number of major deposits had been found, and extensive mining was under way. Networks of urban centers and their rural dependencies were formed in response to the industry's special requirements. Even regions far away from the major mining centers of northern Mexico and upper Peru were organized to produce the food, fuel, livestock, and textiles that mines and miners needed. The production of silver and, to a lesser extent, gold also promoted the development of large-scale transatlantic trade and helped pay for Europe's growing trade with Asia.

Gold

The first American mining boom occurred in the Caribbean. Following the conquests on the mainland, goldfields were discovered in Mexico, Central America, New Granada, central Chile, and Peru. For the empire as a whole, the value of gold production exceeded that of silver in the years before 1540; after that, gold lost its lead. Although gold remained paramount in New Granada and, briefly, Chile, silver production in New Spain, Bolivia, and Peru far outstripped it in quantity and value.

Gold mining required little investment in machinery or plant. Miners used simple and inexpensive technologies to refine the gold flakes and nuggets. Most of the gold produced was panned or washed from the soil of riverbeds, although later there was some deep-shaft gold mining in Chile and New Granada.

Because miners could easily hide from royal officials the flakes and nuggets extracted from placer mines, no reliable estimate of colonial gold production is possible. Before 1550 more than 5 million pesos in gold was legally exported from Mexico, and another 10 million from Peru alone. By 1560 New Granada had produced over 6 million pesos worth of bullion, much of it in gold. Perhaps half of these totals was plunder taken from the Indians. Later gold exports reflect actual Spanish production. During the last half of the sixteenth century, somewhat less than 3.5 million pesos in refined gold was exported from Peru; Mexico produced another million pesos. Registered gold production reached its nadir in the 1660s when a significant contraband trade existed, but an expansion was under way by the early eighteenth century.

In the 1690s the first major gold deposits were discovered in Brazil. The strikes in Minas Gerais were among the richest found during the colonial period, and Brazilian gold production nearly quintupled between 1700 and 1720. It grew more modestly until 1735, peaking in the early 1750s. Estimated production reached nearly sixteen thousand kilograms between 1750 and 1754.

Silver

Large-scale silver strikes began about 1530 when Sultepec and Zumpango were discovered near Mexico City. Strikes in nearby Taxco and Tlalpuja-

hua follwed quickly. Major discoveries in the northern frontier zone—
Zacatecas in 1546, Guanajuato in 1550, and Sombrerete in 1558—greatly
expanded production in New Spain. In Bolivia, the richest silver strike in
America was at Potosí in 1545; a significant discovery at Castrovirreina in
Peru followed about a decade later.

Silver always required more processing and hence more capital investment and labor than did gold. At first the miners relied on smelting, a
refining technique that used simple and inexpensive technology. The ore
was broken up using heavy iron hammers and stamping mills, packed in a
furnace with charcoal or some other fuel, and fired.

Because smelting was labor intensive and required an abundant supply
of fuel, it was ill suited for mines in regions with small populations or without forests. Potosí's elevation, for example, was above fifteen thousand
feet, well beyond the timberline. Even well-forested areas were quickly
exhausted by the mining industry. Located north of the preconquest agricultural frontier, Zacatecas was far from the dense Indian populations
needed for a disciplined labor supply. Such disadvantages increased the
cost of fuel and labor and often restricted the use of the smelting process
to only the richest ores. This, in turn, placed a cap on total silver
production.

The amalgamation process, though more costly, greatly improved the
profitability of silver mining and spurred production. It first was used in
Mexico in the 1550s and in Peru in 1571. The *patio* process, as it was
known in New Spain, involved mixing finely ground ore—which had been
transported by wagon from the stamping mill—with catalysts (either salt
or copper pyrite) and mercury. Workers spread the resulting paste on the
stone floor of a large patio, and animals or bare-legged Indian laborers
mixed it. After the mixture had "cooked" for six to eight weeks, workers
washed it, removed the silver amalgam, and saved the leftover mercury for
the next batch. The process employed in Peru was similar except that the
mixture was cooked in large tanks rather than on a patio.

The need for mercury, or quicksilver, in the amalgamation process made
its supply and cost crucial determinants of production levels. When supplies were abundant, miners and their financial backers were willing to
invest in expensive new machinery and drainage shafts and to mine and
process relatively poor-quality ores taken from older mines. High prices
and short supplies tended to dry up credit and restrict exploitation to the
richest surface ores.

Crown policy was more important than the free play of supply and
demand in determining mercury's availability and price. The royal mine at
Almadén in southern Spain at first supplied all the mercury used in the
colonies. The discovery of a large mercury deposit in the early 1560s at
Huancavelica, 220 kilometers southeast of Lima, expanded its availability.
Quickly made a crown monopoly, Huancavelica's mercury mine supplied
all of Peru's needs and exported a surplus to New Spain until the early
seventeenth century. When its declining production proved unable to
meet Peru's demand, particularly after 1620, the Crown, which had been

sending Almadén's output to New Spain, assigned part of it to Peru and supplemented this supply between 1620 and 1645 with mercury from Idrija, Yugoslavia.

The Crown determined the price of mercury, although it auctioned to merchants the right to distribute it in the colonies. Responding to royal fiscal exigencies and not market conditions, the government demanded high prices and rarely considered the miners' economic plight. From 1617 to 1767 the price of mercury in New Spain remained constant, but at Potosí in 1645 it dropped from 104.25 pesos to 97 pesos a hundredweight (compared with 82.5 in New Spain) and remained at this level until 1779. In the seventeenth century, because miners were forced to invest heavily to drain the older mines and then often found lower-quality ores, the marketing and pricing of mercury worked to depress silver production. Then when the government experimented with lower mercury prices in the late eighteenth century, silver production rose.

Labor

Spaniards owned and supervised silver mines, and Indians—supplemented in many mines by black slaves and some *castas*—performed the arduous physical labor. The major Mexican mines were located a great distance from the sedentary native population of the central plateau, whereas the Bolivian and Peruvian mines were relatively close to the Andean population. This made important differences in the labor systems of the two viceroyalties.

After the initial use of *encomienda* and enslaved Indians, miners in central and southern New Spain benefited from *repartimiento* labor until the early seventeenth century. After this period it was no longer a crucial source of workers. In the northern mining districts, Indian and black slaves were numerous, but Indians hired as free wage laborers, sometimes bound by debt peonage, quickly became predominant. By 1600 free wage laborers constituted over two-thirds of a mining work force that at that time numbered just over nine thousand for all of New Spain.

Reliance on free labor meant that Mexican mine owners had to adjust wages and working conditions to market conditions, paying high wages and offering other inducements during periods when high profits increased the competition for labor. Among the most common and highly regarded benefits was the right of workers to work on their own account on Sundays or to keep some portion of their production, often a specified amount of ore. When mines were worked out or mercury was scare, however, workers had little protection. Wages fell, and even skilled miners were forced to seek other employment.

Because the colonial treasury derived substantial revenue from mining-related taxes and monopolies, officials consciously diverted scarce economic resources to support the vital mining industry. Thus faced with a declining Indian population in Peru, the state used its authority to ensure

Indian laborers forced to mine silver

adequate labor to meet the needs of the mine owners. Such aid increased labor costs and reduced profit levels in competing sectors of the economy, but added to capital, technology, and skilled overseers, this government policy guaranteed the mining sector's long-term primacy in the economy.

In Peru the *mitas* in the 1570s supplied 13,500 workers for Potosí and over 2,000 for Huancavelica. Although these forced labor drafts continued at lower levels into the nineteenth century, Indians hired for wages also became important participants, particularly in the jobs requiring skilled labor. Of the 9,900 workers in Potosí in the early seventeenth century, just over half were free wage laborers. Black slaves made up 14 percent of the mining labor force in New Spain but were almost totally absent from Peruvian mining.

Wage laborers, increasing numbers of whom were *castas,* handled most of the skilled tasks below ground at Potosí. These *barreteros* used pry bars and hammers to break loose ore that the Indian laborers, often *mitayos,* then hauled to the surface in straw baskets or cloth or leather bags. Typically they carried loads of over a hundred pounds up steep ladders and through narrow tunnels with only a single candle for light. The heavy burdens, the darkness, the long hours worked, the dangerous ladders, the blasting that became commonplace in the eighteenth century, and a host of respiratory ailments contributed to high levels of injury and death.

Production of Silver

The following graph shows silver production in Peru and Mexico from 1581 to 1810. Production rose until the early decades of the seventeenth

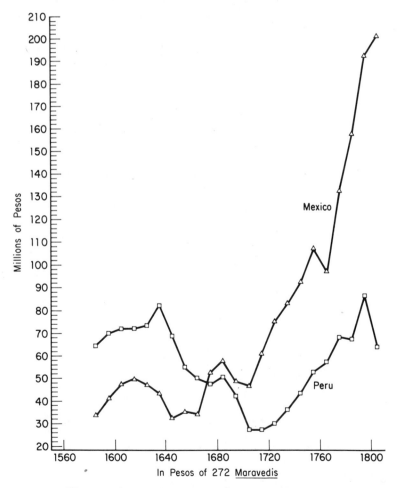

Silver production in Peru and Mexico, 1581–1810.

century. Then a long period of decline followed in Peru; a similar contraction began and ended earlier in Mexico, and by 1700 more silver was being mined than was a century earlier. Incredible growth followed in the eighteenth century: Peru's production again reached its early seventeenth-century peak. In Mexico, a tremendous boom in the first quarter of the century was followed by successive spurts of growth that propelled the output for 1805 through 1809 to 122 million pesos, over six times the amount mined in 1695–99. Having surpassed Peru's production in the 1670s, by the late eighteenth century Mexico was producing well over twice as much as its southern rival was.

Sugar

The importance of sugar as an export in late-sixteenth and seventeenth-century Brazil rivaled that of silver for Mexico and Peru. Although gold challenged its lead in the first half of the eighteenth century and tobacco, too, rose in prominence, sugar remained Brazil's most important export until supplanted by coffee in the 1830s.

The profitability of sugar production in Iberia and the Atlantic islands— Madeira, the Azores, the Cape Verdes, the Canaries, and São Tomé—led Portuguese settlers to introduce sugarcane into Brazil soon after Cabral's landfall. During the donatary period it became firmly established in São Vicente and Pernambuco. The extension of royal authority to Bahia in 1549 was accompanied by official efforts to foster a sugar industry. By the 1580s, the combined output of the northeastern captaincies of Pernambuco—the most important sugar region until the 1630s—and Bahia dominated the colony's production.

Sugar plantations *(engenhos)* required substantial capital to construct mills and purchase labor. Portuguese investors, including the original donataries, supplied much of the initial capital, but early profits enabled mill owners in Brazil to expand their operations. Typically an *engenho* had a mill that processed not only the owner's cane but also, for a charge of often 50 percent of the cane processed, that of a number of *lavradores,* cane farmers who were tenants, sharecroppers, renters, or independent landowners. This practice, unique in its extent in the Americas, enabled men with little capital to plant cane and, in good years, to profit handsomely. At the same time it gave the mill owner some protection against falling prices or a bad harvest, by spreading the risks and costs of planting. Because the planters relied on credit—primarily supplied by religious institutions and merchants—to build mills, purchase slaves, cover expenses, and enlarge their operations, limiting their potential losses through processing *lavradores* cane was a sound business practice. In addition, this relationship with the *lavradores* allowed the planters to benefit financially from economies of scale, by investing in more efficient, large-scale crushing and refining capacity.

Engenhos varied in value according to the amount and quality of land, the number of slaves, the condition of the mill and processing equipment,

Brazilian sugar mill

livestock, transportation equipment, and residential facilities. Land and slaves were the most expensive components of an *engenho*. Because most planters had over 20 percent of their capital tied up in slaves, fluctuations in slave prices could greatly affect their profit.

Unlike gold or silver, sugar had no intrinsic value. It was a bulky, perishable commodity that required rapid handling when harvested and timely transport to market and sale, to reduce storage costs that could drain profits quickly. These requirements limited the location of sugar plantations to coastal regions or near rivers on which sugar could be transported. The Bahian Recôncavo, the area surrounding the Bay of All Saints, enjoyed particularly good water transportation, a natural advantage that contributed substantially to its great success as a sugar-producing region.

Slave laborers performed a myriad of tasks associated with Brazil's sugar cultivation and processing. The slaves' supervisors might be whites, freedmen, or slaves themselves. Few *engenhos* had fewer than forty slaves; sixty to eighty was most common in Bahian mills. Field hands invariably outnumbered all other slaves combined, although individually they were less valuable than were house slaves, artisans, or skilled workers, to say nothing of labor foremen.

There was no technological breakthrough in sugar production to compare with the introduction of the amalgamation process in silver mining. Production rose principally from increased employment of land and labor. The most important technological improvement was the introduction by 1613 of a three-roller vertical mill to replace the older two-roller horizontal mill. Planters quickly adopted the new mill, for it was smaller, faster, easier, and less expensive to construct and more energy efficient than its predecessor. The new mill's advantages enabled some *lavradores* to open small mills and certainly contributed to a near doubling of mills from 192 in 1612 to about 350 in 1629.

Sugar production grew rapidly in the sixteenth century as rising prices stimulated investment. The heightened importation of African slaves after 1570 provided the labor supply necessary to sustain the expanding production that by 1580 was unrivaled in the world. Annual production increased from 6,000 metric tons in 1580 to 10,000 in 1610, and to between 15,000 and 22,000 in the 1620s.

With production remaining at 15,000 to 22,000 metric tons for over a century, the market price for sugar on the one hand and the cost of slave labor on the other largely determined the planters' profits. Sugar prices rose in the sixteenth century, declined in the 1610s, and increased again in the 1620s and early 1630s. Until mid-century, prices remained reasonably high, but general inflation reduced the planters' profit. Nonetheless, prices were strong enough for several more decades for planters to purchase slaves, whose prices had declined slightly since mid-century. A crisis for planters began in the 1680s when competition from foreign plantations in the Caribbean islands lowered sugar prices and drove up the cost of slaves. Although there were some good years subsequently, the overall position of the Brazilian planters was declining. The discovery of gold in Minas Gerais strengthened the competition for slaves. By 1710 a planter had to sell twice as much sugar to purchase a slave than had been necessary in 1635, a condition that persisted until 1750. Sugar's vulnerability to international competition meant that over the long term, planters had little control over their economic fortunes.

Bullion and sugar were the most important exports of colonial Latin America. Revenue from taxes, governmental monopolies, and other fiscal measures associated with these products were crucial supports for the Spanish and Portuguese Crowns. Consequently, colonial authorities directly encouraged and promoted mining and the sugar industry and sought to ensure the safe shipment of silver, gold, and sugar to Iberia. When necessary, these governments intervened to ensure a steady, cheap supply of labor. Thus officials in Peru maintained the *mita* for Potosí and Huancavelica. Portuguese laws encouraged slave imports into Brazil and limited the financial liability of plantation owners. Mining and the sugar industry tended to determine the cyclical behavior of the colonial economies' market-oriented sector. That is, when profits expanded, other areas of the economies grew. When profits fell, all of the economies tended to contract, as there was also less capital for investment and consumption. It was precisely the centrality of mining and sugar in the imperial economies that separated them from other colonial exports.

Although each region of the New World tried to produce goods that would command a market outside its boundaries, no other products affected such large geographic areas or contributed so much to imperial finance as did silver and sugar. The fortunes of cacao in Venezuela, cochineal in Oaxaca, indigo in Central America, and hides in the Río de la Plata, to cite four examples, were important to local and regional economies, but their value to the Spanish Crown in terms of revenue or their impact on other areas of the colonial economies was modest in comparison with silver. Not until the eighteenth century would such regional exports emerge from the long shadow of mining and assume a significant place in the imperial economy.

International Trade and Taxation

Trade and taxation transferred to Europe much of the wealth from American mines and plantations. By the end of the sixteenth century, Europe benefited from, but did not yet control, a network of exchange that included America, parts of Asia, and the African coast. High profits generated by American exports subsidized a more diversified, less valuable mix of European imports, which included wheat, rice, olive oil, cod, wine, and textiles. The wealth produced by Spanish America and Brazil promoted the growth of European industry and subsidized the consolidation of European commercial and military power in Asia and Africa.

Transatlantic trade in general operated under several constraints. Time and distance, two sides of the same coin, limited the range of tradable goods. Not absolute mileage but days at sea determined what could be transported profitably. Peninsular merchants could send perishable goods like wheat to Brazil but not to Peru and have it arrive in salable condition. Textiles and other manufactured goods, in contrast, could be sent anywhere. The limited availability and high cost of cargo space also affected what was transported across the Atlantic. On the American side, gold and precious stones, of course, were ideal, but silver was acceptable as well. Although both Iberian nations were only secondary actors by the eighteenth century, their New World colonies continued as important participants in European commercial expansion. Increasing the size of ships expanded the range of products that could be carried, but the cost of getting goods to colonial ports could be prohibitive. For example, transporting goods by sea from Lima to Panama and then by mule train across the isthmus for loading for export to Spain added substantially to their cost. In contrast, coastal Brazil and the Caribbean regions enjoyed lower freight costs and shorter transportation times to European markets. Thus products of less intrinsic value than gold and silver, even animal hides, could be exported profitably.

The Spanish Trading System

Trade between Spain and the colonies generally rose from 1504 to 1610 and then fell until well into the eighteenth century. Expansion coincided

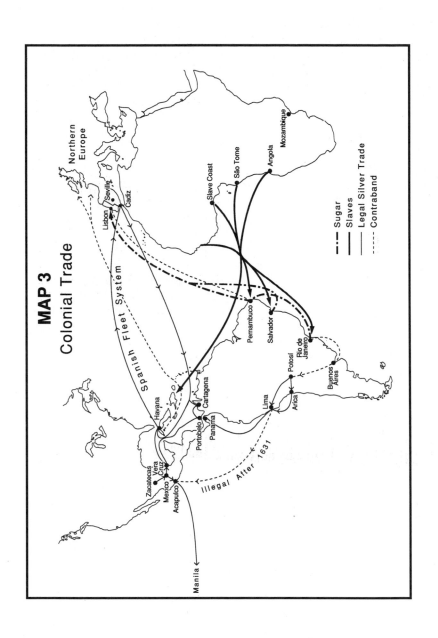

MAP 3
Colonial Trade

Northern Europe

Seville
Lisbon
Cadiz

Spanish Fleet System

Slave Coast
São Tome
Angola
Mozambique

Pernambuco
Salvador
Rio de Janeiro

Potosí
Lima
Arica
Buenos Aires

Havana
Cartagena
Portobelo
Panama

Zacatecas
Vera Cruz
Mexico
Acapulco

Illegal After 1631

Manila

- ·—·— Sugar
- ——— Slaves
- ——— Legal Silver Trade
- - - - - Contraband

with conquest, settlement, the development of the mining industry, and the early growth of markets for European goods that resulted from immigration and the natural increase of the white and Hispanized nonwhite population. The decline was related to Spain's growing inability to supply colonial markets, to contraband trade, to foreign threats, and to the growing capacity of the colonies to produce many items previously imported. Falling silver production accelerated this downard trend for much of the seventeenth century. By the time mining production began its spectacular rise about 1700, the trading system developed in the sixteenth century had long been in shambles.

At first transatlantic trade was only an adjunct to the transportation of men and supplies from Spain to the Indies. Settlers wanted wheat for bread, wine, olive oil, traditional sweets, horses and other livestock, weapons, and textiles but at first had little besides gold to exchange. As a result, many Spanish ships and sailors remained in the New World. Over half of the seventy-one ships arriving in 1520, for example, were purchased for use in interisland trade or voyages of discovery.

The conquest, plunder, and settlement of the mainland and subsequent development of silver mining in Mexico and Peru transformed the size and character of Atlantic trade. Thousands of Spaniards eager to duplicate the conquistadors' achievements arrived in the years after 1530. Added to a growing creole and Hispanized *casta* population, they dramatically increased the market for European products. From 1506 to 1550, the volume of trade increased nearly tenfold. Dyes, medicinal plants, sugar, tobacco, and chocolate produced in the circum-Caribbean colonies were added to the more valuable gold and silver of Mexico, Peru, and New Granada on a lengthening list of New World exports.

A serious downturn lasted from 1550 to 1562 because the Spaniards had taken over most of the Indians' treasure, but silver production had not yet expanded sufficiently to maintain a high level of imports. With goods shipped to the Indies selling slowly and profits declining, investors and merchants withdrew from the trade. The Crown went bankrupt in 1557 and then seized private stocks of bullion in Spain. This deepened the depression as investors looked for ways to keep their money in the Indies.

The rising silver production in the 1560s, credited to the amalgamation process, brought renewed expansion in trade until 1592 when thirty years of high levels of transatlantic trade began. The initial dependence on imported agricultural products dwindled rapidly as the colonies' production of wheat, wine, and olive oil increased. Textiles and other manufactured goods replaced comestibles as favored imports. Regular trade with Manila, which began in the late 1570s, expanded so much that beginning in 1582 the Crown took steps to restrict it. Nonetheless, by the 1590s Mexican merchants were intermediaries in a dynamic trade between Peru and Asia. Chinese silks, porcelains, and lacquered wares were exchanged for silver. By the early seventeenth century the value of the Manila trade actually exceeded that of the Atlantic trade. One measure of the extent of this trade was the use of the silver peso in much of Asia. The Crown finally responded by limiting the number and size of ships sailing from Acapulco to Manila and banning all trade between New Spain and Peru in 1631, a ban that remained until the late eighteenth century. Although designed to stem the hemorrhage of silver across the Pacific, this commercial prohibition had a chilling effect on intercolonial trade in dyes, cacao, and other products as well.

After 1622 the Atlantic trade declined in both volume and value. The total shipments of goods outbound and inbound between Spain and the Indies fell 60 percent between 1606 and 1610 and 1646 and 1650. The decline in New Spain's silver exports after 1635 was particularly notable. After 1650 the value of goods legally exported to Spain continued to drop. New Spain's total exports declined 75 percent from 1650 to 1699, and the value of Peru's exports plummeted even further. The total value of American wealth sent to Spain decreased from 17.4 million pesos in the 1650s to 3 million in the 1690s, although illegal shipments increased from the mid-1680s until 1700. The turnaround for increased legal trade with Spain awaited the 1720s.

Before the wealth of America was known, the Castilian Crown resolved to control the colonial trade for its own financial and political benefit. In 1503 it required trading ships to load and unload at the Andalusian port of Seville. Commerce with the colonies was placed under the supervision of the Casa de Contratación, or House of Trade, created in the same year. Some seventy miles up the Guadalquivir River, Seville was safe from foreign attack and was an established commercial, financial, and administrative center close to the supplies of grain, wine, and olive oil sought by colonial settlers. These advantages outweighed the city's inadequate facilities for docking, shipbuilding, and repair.

The first body created specifically to handle American affairs, the Casa authorized sailings, supervised the loading and unloading of ships, licensed emigrants, collected duties, kept track of American revenues, and handled judicial cases arising from the Indies trade until its abolition in 1790. The Casa was moved to Cádiz in 1717 because neither the Guadalquivir River nor Seville could handle the immense ships of the later years. Earlier, in 1668, the Crown had authorized the loading and unloading of transatlantic vessels in Sanlúcar de Barrameda. Cádiz became the major port in the trade after 1679, nearly four decades before the Casa was transferred.

The Casa worked closely with the wholesale merchants' guild, or *consulado,* of Seville after the Crown granted it in 1543 a monopoly over the Indies trade. Through the *consulado,* the wholesale merchants initially controlled colonial commercial activities by using agents they sent to the New World. In 1594 and 1613, however, the Crown authorized *consulados* for the wholesale merchants of Mexico City and Lima. Because these merchants had a monopoly over trade in their respective viceroyalties, they were largely able to determine the exchange value of silver and other colonial products. Consequently, commerce was generally more profitable than mining was, and over time, wealth in the colonies often accumulated in the hands of merchants rather than miners or other producers. This reduced investment in production and restricted the colonial economy's ability to grow.

The depredations of pirates and foreign rivals forced Spain to protect its Atlantic trade. The Crown's solution was to create a fleet system for conveying goods and to limit transatlantic commerce to three major American ports: Vera Cruz for New Spain, Cartagena for New Granada, and Nombre de Dios (later Portobelo) for Peru and the remainder of Spanish South America. By 1550 the system of regular convoys to and from the Indies was well established. In the mature system, one fleet (the *flota*) sailed in May for Vera Cruz where its merchants traded European goods for Mexican silver and sometimes dyes, hides and other products. A second fleet (the *galeones*) left Seville in August for Cartagena and then proceeded to the isthmus of Panama. At Nombre de Dios (or Portobelo), merchants traded goods for silver brought by sea from Lima and transported by mule train from Panama City. Once loaded with bullion and other exports of lesser value, the two fleets joined in Havana to sail in the spring for Spain.

Vera Cruz and the isthmian ports were steamy, pestilential, unhealthy sites nearly abandoned except when a fleet arrived. Word that the ships were offshore brought thousands of persons—including merchants, porters, muleteers, and prostitutes—to the ports to participate in the ensuing trade fairs. The inhospitable environment and pent-up demand promoted a feverish pace for these exchanges. *Consulado* merchants from Lima and Mexico City purchased European goods, principally textiles, in large lots and transported them to their warehouses in the capital cities. There they marketed the goods directly through their own outlets, through retailers and petty vendors, and through *corregidores* and *alcaldes mayores* who employed the *repartimiento de bienes* to sell to Indian communities.

Taxes on trade paid the cost of defending the fleets. The additional profit to be made through tax evasion, however, proved irresistible to many merchants. Bribing customs officials and sailors, mislabeling the contents of crates, and shipping more goods than were declared were three ways in which merchants cheated the Crown. Tax cheating reduced revenues, but the cost of effective protection for a fleet could not sink below a minimum level. Faced with inadequate revenues, the Crown responded by increasing taxes on trade, a step that in turn made tax avoidance even more attractive. The result was a trading system laden with fraud that mocked the Crown's efforts to maintain a commercial monopoly.

The Atlantic fleet system reinforced Seville's commercial monopoly and imposed a cycle of scarcity and glut on the colonial economy. By concentrating wholesale trade at one Spanish and three American ports, it favored heavily capitalized commercial houses able to buy and sell in large quantities and anxious to limit the volume of colonial imports in order to secure high prices and handsome profits.

In a free market, the arrival of the fleet would have dramatically lowered the price of European goods in the major colonial cities. The monopoly power of the *consulado* merchants, however, prevented this market adjustment and kept the price of imports artificially high. Unsatisfied colonial demand caused by the inefficient fleet system also created high prices for European goods. At the same time, limited competition among Seville's merchants and their American agents forced down the exchange value of American silver, dye stuffs, hides, pearls, and other exports.

In Castile, the Seville monopoly and the fleet system also transferred profits from producers to merchants and speculators, thus eliminating incentives to invest in new technology or to hire additional labor. Because the origin of goods shipped to the colonies hardly affected the merchants' profits, Seville's *consulado* comfortably accommodated itself to the decline of Spanish industry after the mid-sixteenth century and the substitution of foreign goods in the American trade. By the 1620s, foreign merchants used *consulado* members as front men, shipped foreign goods, and controlled most of Spain's Atlantic trade. French merchants in particular became increasingly prominent as the seventeenth century progressed. By 1700 perhaps no more than one-eighth of the goods shipped to the Indies originated in Spain.

The fleet system gradually failed to provide predictable and regular service. The system occasionally faltered after 1580, and by the 1620s a complete breakdown was clearly under way. Sailings became less regular; interruptions of several years were common. From 1650 to 1699, twenty-five fleets sailed to New Spain but only sixteen to the isthmus of Panama. By the end of the seventeenth century, the fleet system was nearly defunct; only four fleets sailed to the isthmus from 1680 to 1699. Both the Spanish economic decline and the growth of Dutch and English naval power had undermined the system. Nonetheless, in meeting its primary responsibility—getting American bullion safely to Spain—the fleet system was remarkably effective. Only in 1628 and 1656 did foreign rivals capture the bullion the fleet was carrying.

Contraband trade offered attractive possibilities for extra profits to colonial producers and serious fiscal problems for Spain because the traders paid no taxes. In addition, it sometimes undercut the prices of Spanish goods when the fleets did arrive. Portuguese merchants in Brazil gained limited illegal access to the silver of Potosí through an active contraband trade with Buenos Aires and Paraguay. British and Dutch competitors of Spanish merchant monopolies used their Caribbean colonies to penetrate overpriced, inefficient Spanish markets. Yet these exchanges were too irregular and unpredictable to create significant new colonial investment in export-oriented production. Perishable agricultural products, in particular, presented special problems for contraband trade. Nevertheless, in Venezuela, coastal Central America, and Argentina, contraband grew in importance during the seventeenth century and well into the eighteenth.

As long as the crippled fleet system and Seville's commercial monopoly remained in place and silver mining was depressed, colonial exports floundered, and investment capital tended to flow into urban and rural real estate. Only when a reforming Spanish government in the eighteenth century encouraged production through tax reductions and a liberalized commercial policy did colonial exports again thrive.

Brazil

Because Portugal during the sixteenth century focused its limited resources on developing the riches of the East Indies, it exercised little control over Brazil's early economic development. Until the mid-seventeenth century, the Portuguese Crown allowed almost unrestricted trade between metropolitan and colonial ports. In addition to Oporto and Lisbon, small ports like Caminha, Viana, and Aveiro regularly sent caravels to Brazil. Although each Brazilian captaincy had a port, the sugar ports of Recife, Bahia, and Rio de Janeiro were the most important. The ships transporting sugar were generally small, 80 to 150 tons, and lightly armed. Although convoys sailed in the 1590s in response to English privateering, their use was irregular. Portuguese participated in the trade, but English and especially Dutch shippers operating under Portuguese licenses were the most important carriers in the sixteenth and early seventeenth centuries.

Since Holland's rebellion against Philip II in 1568, Spain had sought to regain control over its former possession. As part of this broader objective, in 1605 Philip III excluded the Dutch from trading with the Portuguese world, joined to the Spanish realms since 1580. The Dutch retaliated by raiding ships carrying Brazilian sugar. During the Twelve-Year Truce (1609–21) between the Dutch and united Spanish and Portuguese crowns (1580–1640), Dutch commerce with Brazil boomed. Almost two-thirds of the ships in the trade were Dutch. They conveyed sugar to a number of European markets, including Amsterdam, where forty sugar refineries were operating in 1650. The end of the truce brought a renewal of hostilities and a Dutch invasion of Bahia in 1624–25 and the occupation of Pernambuco from 1630 to 1654. At last awakened to the threat posed by this unrelenting pressure, the Crown turned to protected convoys. It chartered the Brazil Company in 1649 to provide a fleet of warships to protect Atlantic routes in return for a monopoly of Brazil's most common imports— flour, olive oil, wine, and codfish—and the right to tax the colony's exports. New Christian investors resented by other important elite groups provided much of the leadership and capital. Undermined by religious bigotry and undercapitalized from the outset, the company never met its obligations, and the Crown took it over in 1664. Nonetheless, the fleet system survived this collapse and lived on for another century. Fleets of a hundred vessels were not uncommon, although one English observer remembered one early fleet as "the pitifullest vessels that ever I saw."[1]

A separate trade with Africa supplied slaves for the sugar industry. The Crown granted monopoly contracts, *asientos,* but, as with other imports and exports, put little effort into enforcing them. This relative laxness in the oversight of Brazil's trade with both Europe and Africa distinguishes the Portuguese commercial system from that of Spain and its colonies. Brazilian merchants, moreover, participated more in offshore commerce.

British trade with Portugal and Brazil remained insignificant for several decades after sugar from English plantations in the Caribbean replaced Brazilian sugar in the mid-seventeenth century. Beginning in the 1690s, however, the mining boom in Brazil brought back prosperity. By failing to protect the domestic production of manufactured goods and by outlawing colonial production, Portugal encouraged the capture of the Brazilian market by British factories working through Portuguese commercial inter-mediaries. By 1750 British exports to Portugal valued at little more than 1.1 million pounds were producing a favorable balance of trade of nearly 800,000 pounds. Although some historians attribute this commercial ascendency to the Methuen Treaty of 1703 and its antecedents, shifting European political rivalries and Britain's early development of cotton tex-tiles suitable for wear in the tropics were more important.

Taxation

The Spanish Crown taxed its American colonies enough that the empire as a whole not only paid the costs of its administration and defense but also produced a fiscal surplus for remission to the peninsula. New World revenues shipped to Spain became important about 1550 and expanded substantially during the reign of Philip II (1556–98). They totaled 20 to 25 percent of the Crown's revenue toward the end of Philip's rule, a sub-stantial sum that helped finance his expensive foreign policy in Europe. Remittances generally declined in the seventeenth century, especially after 1640 for New Spain and after 1660 for Peru. In the 1590s half of the revenue collected in New Spain was spent in the Indies; this amount increased to nearly 80 percent a century later. Indeed, the amount of pub-lic revenue sent from Mexico to the Philippines in some decades of the seventeenth century was over half the amount remitted to Spain. For Peru, only 36 percent of the revenue collected in the 1590s remained there, but the amount leapt to 55 percent the following decade and to 95 per-cent in the 1680s, a consequence more of declining income than rising expenditures.

The Crown levied a variety of taxes in the New World. It raised rates and introduced new impositions when possible. The treasury in seven-teenth-century Peru received income from over forty separate sources. Although the colonists paid less in taxes than did the Castilian peasantry, the American population bore a substantial burden relative to its resources. The importance of different taxes for royal revenue varied by district. Mining taxes and profits from the sale of mercury were paramount in the mining districts. Imposts on commercial transactions were central in the ports and administrative centers. And the importance of Indian tribute varied by region and with changes in population.

With the exception of Indian tribute, the Crown normally farmed out the tax collection, until the second half of the eighteenth century. Tax farmers paid an agreed-upon sum to collect a tax for a specified length of time, with their profit coming from collecting a sum larger than that owed. Both private entrepreneurs and corporations farmed taxes. During most of the seventeenth century, for example, the Lima *consulado* collected the *alcabala* and the port taxes.

As Brazil's major source of wealth, the sugar industry was taxed accordingly. These taxes, however, reduced the price competitiveness of Brazilian sugar in the international market and restricted the capital available for investment in land, labor, and technology. Until the gold boom, tithes levied after 1551 on agricultural products contributed most among the New World revenues. Although sugar was only one of many items subjected to the tithe, the value of its production made its yield extremely important. In the 1590s, an import tax of 20 percent and a sales tax of 10 percent were imposed on goods entering Portugal from Brazil. With rising imports and sales of Brazilian sugar, again the industry paid a heavy price for its success. Colonial municipalities also taxed sugar, their responsibility to provide "voluntary" extra support on occasion adding to the burden. Slaves, too, were taxed intermittently after 1699, thus hitting the planters once more. Tax farmers routinely collected these and numerous other impositions until the late eighteenth century.

In both Brazil and Spanish America, the efforts of metropolitan merchants and colonial bureaucrats to control and limit commercial relationships failed. Neither Iberian state had the human and material resources necessary to realize its colonial vision. Their efforts, however, greatly influenced the direction of subsequent economic growth in the colonies.

Defense

The papal donation as modified by the Treaty of Tordesillas in 1494 gave Spain and Portugal dominion over the Indies. As exploration and conquest proceeded, exaggerated accounts of New World wealth circulated in the Old, arousing the cupidity of European monarchs and common adventurers. The flow of wealth from the American colonies was seen by Spain's European rivals as the basis for its aggressive military and political policies. Individual ship captains, merchants, and adventurers simply resented being excluded from exploiting the wealth of the New World. Nearly incessant conflict in Europe provided an excuse for French and English attacks on Spanish and Portuguese shipping and colonial towns.

In the early seventeenth century, the newly independent Dutch became the most aggressive rival of the Iberian powers. Their unprecedented pressure opened the way for the first successful non-Iberian colonies in the Caribbean and North America as well as the temporary occupation of northeast Brazil. The subsequent age of buccaneers left a swath of destruction that lasted until the late seventeenth century. In the ensuing worldwide colonial conflicts of the eighteenth century, the Americas became a regular theater of combat.

For the Spanish Crown, protecting the transatlantic trade and the remission of bullion, defending New World towns and territory, and controlling the entry of foreigners into the empire all were parts of the same problem. Deep involvement in European conflicts precluded focusing on New World defense, but the need for American revenue to sustain these commitments forced Spain to invest resources in colonial defense. The result was the ad hoc evolution of a defensive policy remarkably successful in protecting the shipment of bullion to Spain and the territorial integrity of the colonies. It was far less effective in keeping unwanted foreigners out of the empire and, by the 1620s, progressively less able to control trade.

Defense of the Indies originally meant protecting treasure dispatched to Spain from Caribbean and Tierra Firme ports. Thus early military planning focused on both naval protection for ships carrying bullion and the defense of the circum-Caribbean ports. In the mid-1570s, however, the need to defend the Pacific coast and especially the movement of silver from Peru to Panama became apparent. The later development of the Manila trade extended the defensive perimeter as Acapulco emerged as New Spain's premier Pacific port.

As the area subject to attack expanded, the cost of defending it increased as well. Always penurious, the Crown's willingness to spend money on New World defense fluctuated with the severity of specific threats, the availability of revenue, and the financial demands created by its European conflicts. Throughout the sixteenth century, the Crown was generally able to defend the Indies and its trading system. Pressure from the Dutch in the Atlantic and Pacific during the early decades of the seventeenth century, however, nearly overwhelmed Spain's capacities. Coming all at once, the declining silver production and government revenue, the tremendous expenditures and losses incurred during the Thirty Years War (1618–48), the revolts of Catalonia and Portugal that began in 1640, and the growth of piracy prevented Spain from regaining control of the Caribbean.

The absence of significant bullion production until the close of the seventeenth century made Brazil less attractive than Spanish America was to foreign predators. Foreign threats were real, however, and French interest in the region persuaded the Portuguese to settle it. The greatest foreign threat to colonial Brazil came in the seventeenth century when the Dutch invaded and occupied northeastern Brazil in 1630. Their expulsion in 1654 did not end foreign incursions. Defending the vulnerable coastal ports remained a major preoccupation of colonial government, but Portugal's close ties with England and isolation from most European wars saved Brazil from becoming a major theater for conflict.

The Defense of the Americas in the Sixteenth Century

Spain's chronic immersion in European conflict began when Ferdinand intervened in Italian affairs in the 1490s. The accession of Charles I to the crowns of Castile and Aragon in 1516, his Habsburg inheritance of Burgundy and lands in central Europe, and his election as Holy Roman Emperor in 1519 intensified Spain's European involvement. Recurrent wars with France and, as the Reformation meshed with politics, Protestant territories continued until the Treaty of Câteau–Cambrésis in 1559. Charles's goal of a European empire, however, eluded him, and he abdicated in 1556. Philip II refocused Spain, turning it from central Europe toward the Atlantic, but he, too, spent his reign at war. Different enemies—Calvinist rebels in the Netherlands and, by the 1580s, England—brought the same financial consequence: bankruptcy.

Foreign threats to the Indies and its trade in the sixteenth century came from corsairs rather than national navies. Initially the corsairs inflicted their greatest damage on ships in the Atlantic triangle formed by the Strait of Gibraltar, the Canaries, and the Azores. Their focus shifted to the Antilles about mid-century, and their seizures increased. In addition, they raided coastal towns over one hundred times before 1585. The French capture, sack, and temporary occupation of Havana in 1555 was the most dramatic of these incursions. Stunned, Spain initiated a massive fortifications project that helped secure the key port until the British captured it in 1762.

In response to the corsairs' attacks, Spain first relied on armed convoys to transport merchandise and bullion across the Atlantic, on a patrol fleet in the Atlantic triangle, and on forts, artillery, and militia in the New World. As the corsairs increased their pressure in the Caribbean at mid-century, the coastal patrol squadrons became important. A French settlement on the coast of east Florida prompted Spanish retaliation. Pedro Menéndez de Avilés successfully expelled the intruders and placed a garrison at St. Augustine in an effort to prevent Florida from falling into enemy hands. When the corsairs turned to the Spanish Main and Central America, Spain was forced to shift its defensive strategy. Spain had general success against the thirty to forty small foreign ships, about half traders and half raiders, that operated in the Caribbean in the 1570s. By the eve of Francis Drake's celebrated invasion in 1585, it had a balanced defensive system in place that included forts with garrisons, coastal patrols, and armed convoys and intelligence collection. Although the system did have weaknesses—badly deteriorated coastal galleys, defectively designed fortifications that were inadequately armed and manned, and small and poorly equipped militias—the cost of improving it substantially without greater provocation would probably have exceeded any resulting benefits.

Because the wealth of Brazil was revealed more slowly, Portugal faced a much smaller military threat from European rivals. Much of the first brazilwood exported from Brazil was ultimately consumed in France. As a result, merchants and mariners from Normandy and Rouen began to frequent Brazil's coast. They both traded directly with the Indians for dyewood and raided Portuguese ships. By the 1530s both the Portuguese and French were allied with traditional Indian rivals. This French threat led King John III to encourage active settlement. A dramatic rise in immigrants followed. Nearly forty years of frontier warfare and Indian attacks resulted from this rivalry. Yet France was unwilling to invest significant military assets in this struggle, at least in part because it regarded Portugal as a potential ally against Spain. Finally, in 1565 France's major Brazilian settlement at Rio de Janeiro fell, marking the effective end of "La France Antartique."

The Portuguese and French were the first to breach Spain's trade monopoly. The English followed in 1562 when John Hawkins sought to introduce slaves and merchandise into the Indies. Denied permission to trade legally, he turned to contraband. Early success gave way to disaster, however, when the incoming Spanish fleet trapped his fleet off Vera Cruz. This experience demonstrated that Spain would deal harshly with any foreigner in American waters and tended to promote piracy rather than contraband.

As Francis Drake's career illustrated, piracy could be both profitable and respectable. The most celebrated sixteenth-century interloper, Drake's exploits eventually won him wealth and a knighthood from a grateful Queen Elizabeth I. Originally an illicit trader, "El Draque" turned to privateering after Hawkins's fleet was captured. In 1572 he reached the Caribbean with some 70 men and two ships. Supported by runaway slaves, he seized three mule trains laden with Peruvian silver as they neared Nombre de Dios. Emboldened and enriched by his success, Drake circumnavigated the globe in 1577–80, terrorizing the Pacific settlements on his way. He returned to the Caribbean in 1585 with an invasion force of more than twenty ships and over 2,500 men. His plan to attack Santo Domingo, Cartagena, Nombre de Dios, Panama, and Havana and to secure Cartagena and Havana with permanent garrisons, however, failed. Santo Domingo's capture produced only modest plunder and ransom. Cartagena fell too, but casualities and loss of manpower from disease aborted Drake's ambitious plan. He abandoned the city but later destroyed the fortifications under construction at St. Augustine. He returned to England where in 1588 he participated in the English victory over the Spanish Armada.

Drake's unprecedented invasion exposed the vulnerability of the Indies. Although failing to disrupt permanently the communication and trading system, it partially achieved its general objective of weakening Spain's ability to wage war by forcing Philip II to spend a greater proportion of American revenue on defense. He ordered military engineers to develop a comprehensive plan for fortifying the Caribbean ports, always the most likely targets for enemy attacks. Construction followed in fits and starts, depending on the intensity of the military threats, but eventually the most important ports of the Caribbean and Spanish Main were fortified.

The Treaty of London in 1604 ended the conflict between Spain and England and brought to a close the age of Drake, whose own death had occurred in 1596 off the coast of Veragua during a final expedition stymied by the revitalized Spanish defenses. Although French and English efforts to break Spain's hold on trade and territory in the Indies had been generally unsuccessful, the treaty emodied a principle that would underpin changes in the new century. A weakened and financially troubled Spain acquiesced to abridgment of its claims as set forth in the Treaty of Tordesillas. Henceforth, "effective occupation" would provide legal justification for non-Iberian countries that planted colonies in the New World.

Dutch Threats in the Caribbean and Brazil

The Dutch largely determined the course of events in the Americas between the Treaty of London and the glory days of the buccaneers. Their belligerence had deep historical roots. A part of Charles I's Burgundian inheritance, the United Provinces revolted against Philip II in 1566, initiating a costly conflict that continued, save for the Twelve Years' Truce (1609–21) until the Treaty of Munster in 1648 when Spain recognized the country's independence. In the New World, Dutch interlopers appeared before 1600 and occupied part of Guiana in 1616. Founded in 1621, the Dutch West Indies Company increased the threat to Spain, as it sought territory as well as booty. A major Dutch expedition on the Pacific coast caused near panic in Peru in 1624. In 1628 Piet Heyn seized an entire Spanish treasure fleet off Cuba in a spectacular and unprecedented exploit that brought agony to the Spaniards and an extraordinary dividend to company stockholders. The Portuguese Empire, however, suffered most from the company's attacks.

When King Sebastian of Portugal died on a disastrous and misguided invasion of Morocco in 1578, without leaving a direct heir, the throne was successfully claimed by Philip II of Spain in 1580 and retained by his successors until 1640. Even though Philip treated it as a separate kingdom and employed only Portuguese advisers and officials, Spain's enemies moved quickly to include these new territories within the orbit of their ambition. Portugal's far-flung possessions in Africa, the Far East, and the Americas soon felt Dutch military pressure.

The Dutch West Indies Company attacked Brazil for its sugar production and also because it was perceived to be a weak link among Spain's possessions. After briefly holding Bahia in 1624–25, the Dutch later returned to Brazil in force. They took Pernambuco in 1630 and expanded their control over much of the rich sugar-producing region. Occupation by Protestant heretics and a declining yield from sugar, however, were more than the Catholic natives could bear. In 1645 Brazilians of all races and classes rose against the intruders in a revolt that did not end until January 1654, with the surrender of Recife and the remaining Dutch possessions.

While establishing their colony at Essequibo and meddling in Brazil, the Dutch took the Caribbean islands of Curaçao, St. Martin, and St. Eustatius. Dutch pressure on Spanish shipping and defenses also facilitated the establishment of foreign settlements on other islands Spain had left unoccupied. Already in 1605 Spain had forced its settlers in northwestern Hispaniola to abandon the region. In the 1620s and 1630s, the English occupied parts of St. Kitts and Barbados, Antigua, and Montserrat. The French seized Martinique and Guadelupe and the remainder of St. Kitts. In the early seventeenth century as well, the Dutch, English, and French founded settlements in Virginia, New York, Massachusetts, and Canada in North America. Taken in 1655 as a consolation prize following an unsuccessful formal military invasion in the Caribbean sent by Oliver Cromwell, Jamaica became an important English possession in the West Indies. The island soon produced sugar for export, and its capital, Port Royal, became a major center for contraband and for several decades served as a base for English buccaneers.

The Age of Buccaneers

The Spanish abandonment of northwestern Hispaniola left a vacuum filled by growing numbers of cattle and swine. A few renegades, escaped slaves, and smugglers remained to collect the meat and hides. Their successors found attacking Spanish shipping and coastal towns more profitable. Originally called "cow killers" by the English and *flibustiers* (filibusters) by the French, these men are best known as "buccaneers" for their use of a *boucan* or grill, for roasting meat over a fire. A contemporary described them as

> dressed in a pair of drawers and a shirt at the most, shod with the skin of a hog's leg fastened on the top, and behind the foot with strips of the same skin, girded round the middle of their body with a sack which served them to sleep in. . . . When they returned from the chase to the *boucan,* you would say that these are the butcher's vilest servants who have been eight days in the slaughter-house without washing themselves. I have seen some who had lived this miserable life for twenty years without seeing a priest and without eating bread.[2]

By 1630, similar groups had formed on nearby Tortuga. Spain's repeated efforts to end attacks on shipping by the buccaneers were never more than temporarily successful.

Major Spanish naval losses encouraged the buccaneers' exploits. The defeat of the Spanish fleet carrying reinforcements for troops in Flanders at the Downs in 1639 and a later disastrous loss of a combined Spanish and Portuguese fleet to the Dutch at Itamacá off Pernambuco in early

1640 nearly destroyed Spain's one-great navy. Spain's inability to clear buccaneers and contraband traders from the Caribbean coincided with the reduction in the size and frequency of its fleets. Even coastal settlements were raided repeatedly by buccaneers seeking treasure and demanding ransom. By the early 1660s, there were some 1,500 to 2,000 buccaneers, with Port Royal, Jamaica, serving as their primary base. Among them was the Welshman Henry Morgan, one of the most successful, notorious, and cruel of these pirates.

Morgan's profitable attack on the unsuspecting interior town of Granada, Nicaragua, in 1665 served as a rehearsal for his bold attack on Portobelo in 1668. With some four hundred Englishmen, he struck the port city from the undefended interior side. After capturing the defensive fortifications, the force began two weeks of looting that yielded over 250,000 pesos, silks, linen, other European merchandise, and the finest guns the Spaniards had mounted in the forts. The following year Morgan raided the Gulf of Maracaibo, Venezuela, but because French filibusters had pillaged the region thoroughly in 1667, the pickings were slim. A surprise attack on three Spanish warships sent to trap him as he left the Gulf, however, augmented his coffers. The imaginative corsair's greatest victory occurred in January 1671. With a combined force of nearly 1,500 English and French buccaneers, he led a nine-day trek across the isthmus of Panama to attack its capital. Victorious once more, the assailants subjected the inhabitants to four weeks of pillage, rapine, and torture unprecedented in its length and viciousness. By the time they left, Panama City had been totally destroyed by fire, and when rebuilt, it was located on a new site. Morgan returned to Port Royal with loot and honor. He received commendation from the Council of Jamaica and ultimately knighthood and employment as lieutenant-governor of the island.

Morgan's sack of Panama was the last great English buccaneer raid. In the 1670 Treaty of Madrid, Spain officially recognized the English presence in the Caribbean, and both parties agreed to revoke letters of marque and reprisal so as to reduce the piracy. Enforcement was initially sporadic, but England's recognition that profits from trade ultimately were more valuable than the buccaneers' booty led to more peaceful relations. The French buccaneers continued raiding from their base in Tortuga and gradually moved into part of Hispaniola. This led to the effective Spanish cession of the western half of the island to France, by the Treaty of Ryswyck in 1697. With this treaty the era of the buccaneers at last drew to a close, and the economic devlopment of the Greater Antilles could proceed.

The Defense of the Pacific Coast

In addition to the Caribbean, Spanish Main, and Atlantic coast of South America, the Pacific coast had to be defended. From the first expedition by the English pirate John Oxenham in 1575 until the mid-eighteenth century, English, Dutch, and French interlopers bedeviled Pacific coastal

towns and shipping. By 1742 armed foreign contraband traders, priva-
teers, and pirates had appeared on the Pacific coast of Central America or
Mexico at least twenty-five times. Many of these expeditions also landed
on the Pacific coast of South America. Above all else, these interlopers
were drawn by the fabulous wealth carried by the Peruvian silver fleet to
Panama and the Manila galleon from Acapulco to the Philippines.

Drake captured several ships off South America in 1578–79, including
one with fourteen chests of silver pesos, 80 pounds of gold, 26 tons of
silver bars, pearls, and jewels. To prevent a repetition, Viceroy Toledo initiated a convoy system to escort the silver from Lima to Panama. The raids
of Thomas Cavendish in 1587, although yielding little booty from Peru,
reemphasized the threat from the sea and promped expanded protection
of the silver fleet.

The Dutch sent major expeditions to the Pacific coast in the 1610s and
1620s. One in 1615 defeated the Spanish Pacific fleet off Cañete, Peru,
and razed Paita. It failed, however, to capture either the Peruvian silver
fleet or the Manila galleon. A large expedition that reached the Peruvian
coast in 1624 intended not only to trade and raid but also to establish a
colony. Although it destroyed Guayaquil, it too failed in its primary objectives. In response to these threats, the Spanish began to fortify Acapulco
in 1616 and to strenghten the Pacific fleet.

Less frequent trade fairs at Portobelo meant fewer sailings to Panama
and fewer naval vessels for the Pacific fleet. But even these reduced needs
were hard to fulfill, despite greatly decreased remittances to Spain,
because of declining revenue in Peru. Coastal defense needs, however, had
increased, owing to attacks by buccaneers who, following Morgan's example, crossed the isthmus of Panama in pursuit of booty. From 1680 to
1690, English buccaneers caused enormous havoc from Panama to Chile.
By the end of 1686, they had captured almost two-thirds of the Pacific
merchant fleet. Faced with immense losses should the raiding continue, the
Lima merchant guild funded the arming of merchant ships to protect the
coast. This continued into the more peaceful decades of the early eighteenth century. Only after the terrible earthquake of 1746 destroyed
Callao and severely damaged the ships at port did the Crown send warships to Peru. They were removed in 1748 following the peace with England.

On the Pacific coast of New Spain, buccaneer depredations provoked
the use of a small permanent defense fleet beginning in 1690. The major
concern, however, remained the protection of the Manila galleon. In 1710
an expedition by Captain Woodes Rogers captured the smaller of two gal-
leons. The final noteworthy attack on the Pacific coast occurred in 1741
when Commodore George Anson led an English naval squadron into the
Pacific and seized eleven Spanish vessels off the South American coast. He
then crossed the Pacific to the Philippines, where he captured the west-
bound galleon carrying a million and half pesos. Only in 1762, during the
Seven Years' War, would Spain lose another galleon to the English.

Soldiers, Militias, and the Cost of Defense

Few full-time soldiers served in the Spanish colonies before the British capture of Havana in 1762. Small forces served as viceregal guards. Troops were stationed in garrisons at fortified coastal ports and towns and in *presidios,* or frontier military outposts, in northern New Spain, southern Chile, and the frontier zones of the Río de la Plata where they fought against unconquered and rebellious Indians. Taken together, the regulars totaled only several thousand men.

Rather than regular forces, from the mid-sixteenth century onward the Crown relied on militia for manpower in cases of military attack or invasion. In 1540 the Crown required all able-bodied men to serve if called. At first the size of the white male population determined the number of available men, but eventually colonial authorities called on *mestizos,* free blacks, mulattos, and even Indians for militia service. The colored militia in Lima performed so well during the Dutch threat in 1624 that its members won an exemption from tribute as a reward.

However many men were available for militia service, the Spanish government had a constant problem of supplying them with adequate weapons and ammunition. Royal strictures limited the importation of weapons by individuals and forced the Crown itself to supply most arms. Sixteenth-century corsairs in the Caribbean were regularly better armed than the militia, although the militiamen's preference for flight and preservation of life and property reduced the significance of their inferior weaponry and frequent shortage of powder. The viceroys of Peru in the seventeenth century repeatedly decried the shortage and poor quality and condition of their firearms.

The government expenditures for defense were modest until the mid-sixteenth century but then increased rapidly. By 1640 the Mexican treasuries were spending a third or more of their revenues on defense, as they provided heavy subsidies to the Caribbean and Phillipines as well as for the defense of Mexico itself. By the late seventeenth century, military expenditures regularly exceeded the treasuries' remission of bullion to Spain. Spending far more on defense than they were remitting to Castile in the mid-seventeenth century, viceroys of Peru watched their defensive needs increase relentlessly in the 1670s and 1680s while regular revenues were declining. In the first full year of the War of Jenkin's Ear, regular defensive expenditures consumed 57 percent of the Lima treasury's income, and extraordinary expenditures pushed the total to 85 percent, or 1.2 million pesos. Defending the empire was expensive, but not defending it was unthinkable.

The empire in general and its trade and bullion shipments to Spain in particular were vital to the Spanish Crown. Judged by the retention of New World territory on the one hand and the rare loss of a treasure fleet on the other, royal defensive policy was generally successful. Yet Spain won innumerable individual battles at a cost of losing political hegemony in the

Old World and commercial domination in the New. Its fronts were too many, its resources too thin to achieve victory. Every peso spent on defense in the Americas was one less available for expenditure in Europe; conversely, the court's constant demand for bullion forced New World officials to sacrifice military preparedness despite the constant expenditures. Ironically, even though Spain's power was waning on both sides of the Atlantic during much of the seventeenth and early eighteenth centuries, the greater retention and expenditure of royal revenue in the New World mitigated the government's financial demands and increased the colonies' self-reliance and self-sufficiency.

The Colonial Economy

The form and pace of economic development in colonial Latin America also helped determine both its social and political structures. Colonialism, of course, is a form of political subordination, but in the Latin American case the economy was often more important in forming a new social order from the remnants of indigenous culture and the migratory flows from Europe and Africa than were the institutions of empire. The geographical distribution of population, the class structure, and a legacy of state intervention in production and distribution all have roots in the colonial economy.

Conquest and the Indigenous Economy

European conquest and early settlement took a heavy toll on the indigenous economies of the Western Hemisphere. The destruction of Tenochtitlán, Cuzco, and other cities not only destroyed accumulated wealth in the form of public and private buildings but also disrupted traditional exchange relationships that encouraged specialized production and distribution. In addition, Iberians expropriated precious metals and other luxury goods. Because they invested very little in the colonial economy, Europe, not America, gained the economic benefits of this lost wealth. The conquest also wasted substantial human capital, the productive potential of skills and experience. The skilled sectors of Indian society—urban artisans, priests, and administrators—suffered the most in loss of life and forced migration in the aftermath of conquest, and the productivity of the Indian communities showed this. Epidemic disease, however, was what most affected the Indians' economic performance, and the collapse of the Indian population led to an equally large drop in their production and consumption.

Because the indigenous cultures of Brazil had not developed the levels of specialization and integration found in Mesoamerica and the Andean zone, the scale of postconquest contraction was reduced. Yet the near collapse of indigenous production that resulted from military action and dis-

ease contributed to the famines of the sixteenth century. Even without
mineral wealth, European settlement remained confiscatory through the
imposition of forced labor and slavery.

Despite the conquest's damage to the Indian population in Spanish
America, important changes in the years before the major mining strikes
of the 1540s set the stage for future growth. European technology and
skills, new crops, new animal species that provided locomotion and food,
and the flow of immigrants from Europe and Africa all contributed to
Spanish America's ability to produce wealth. The new colonial system created larger, more unified trading systems that connected local producers
to growing Atlantic and world markets, and the introduction of European
monetary and credit mechanisms enabled some to reach these regional and
international markets. It was mineral wealth, however, that defined the
fundamental character of the Mexican and Peruvian economies in the
same way that plantation agriculture did for Brazil and, later, the Spanish
colonies of the circum-Caribbean.

The concentration of resources at the silver mining centers of Mexico
and Peru and the sugar-producing regions of Brazil encouraged agricultural, grazing, and manufacturing production in adjacent areas. The
founding of colonial cities and the development of transportation networks also reflected the special needs of these mining and plantation districts. On the periphery of these central economic zones, regionally significant economic activities like the production of cochineal in northern
Oaxaca, cacao in Venezuela, and indigo in Central America helped guide
the development of urban networks. The early development of these local
export economies then influenced the distribution of colonial population
and wealth.

The Greater Peruvian Region

The silver mines at Potosí profoundly affected the economy of much of
South America. The introduction of the amalgamation process in 1572 led
to silver production's quintupling between 1571 and 1575 and continuing
to climb until the early 1590s. The population grew even faster. Potosí had
3,000 inhabitants in the 1540s, a reported 120,000 in 1580, and perhaps
160,000 in 1650. Its size and economic influence were unparalleled in the
Americas and perhaps equal to those of contemporary London. The mining center gave form and direction to the economic potential of a region
that included the Argentine *pampa,* the central valleys of Chile, coastal
Peru, and Ecuador.

The region around Potosí could meet only a small fraction of the city's
needs. As a result, a vast area entered Potosí's economic orbit in the boom
years of the late sixteenth century. Tucumán in northwestern Argentina
experienced two separate cycles of integration. In the 1580s it sent to the
mines cotton textiles produced on native looms. After early profits, local

encomenderos bought European looms and built *obrajes* staffed by Indians. The region also produced woolen cloth after the introduction of sheep. This precocious manufacturing industry was faltering by the 1620s, however, when other regions with competitive advantages entered the Potosí market.

The grazing industry, nonetheless, kept the jurisdiction of Tucumán tied to Potosí. Through the annual livestock fair at Salta, the region sent thousands of mules, oxen, cattle, and horses to provide food and traction for the mines. This trade grew from 7,050 head in 1596–1600 to a peak of 69,027 in 1681–85. This distant region's economy depended almost completely on the performance of the Potosí mines.

Other regions and economic sectors also followed this pattern. The economy of Lima was closely tied to the meteoric growth and later slow decline of Potosí. When Potosí's production began to decline after 1592, increases in silver production for the viceroyalty as a whole muted the effects until the 1640s when a drop began that continued almost without respite until about 1720. Silver went overland from Potosí to the port of Arica and then by ship to Lima/Callao. Because after 1613 the Lima *consulado* exercised monopoly power in the import–export market, miners were at a disadvantage when they exchanged silver for European goods. The profits from this unequal exchange as well as the tax revenues sent to the capital from provincial treasuries gave life to Lima, fueling the opulent display of its elite and sustaining its commerce.

The growth of Lima, founded in 1535, to a population of some 25,000 in 1610 and perhaps 75,000 by the early 1680s stimulated market agriculture and manufacturing along the Peruvian coast and in Chile. *Limeños* in 1630 consumed more than 150,000 bushels of wheat, 75,000 pounds of sugar, 25,000 head of sheep and goats, 3,500 cattle, and over 200,000 jugs of wine. Olive oil, cheese, almonds, honey, and hundreds of other local and regional products also found a place in its markets. High-quality European textiles, iron goods, books, and other luxury items faced little competition in this market. Cheaper imported textiles, furniture, pottery, and agricultural products such as wine and olive oil, however, met increasing colonial competition.

Potosí and, especially after 1687, Lima, depended on distant food producers. A major earthquake in 1687 lowered grain production near Lima and gave Chile an essential place in the city's market. Ships built in Guayaquil and owned by Lima merchants tied Chile's wheat fields to Peru's urban consumers. Potosí received most of its food from Cochabamba, but wine, olive oil, and later brandy were carried across the mountains from Arequipa and the coastal plain. Potosí's populace also consumed large quantities of *yerba,* tea from Paraguay, and coca leaves from the Bolivian *yungas.*

Other distant manufacturers also benefited from the Potosí market. The mines' large population of permanent and temporary laborers created a profitable market for cotton and wool textiles. The *obrajes* of Tucumán, Cuzco, Trujillo, Cajamarca, and especially Quito produced cloth for this market throughout much of the colonial period.

During most of the seventeenth century more than ten thousand workers were employed in *obrajes* in Ecuador. Some slaves and convicts worked in these primitive mills, but Indian *mita* laborers supplied most of the labor. Although Spanish law classified these workers as free and required that they receive wages, *obraje* owners commonly used debt peonage and coercion to maintain a permanent, inexpensive work force. Responding to the dynamic growth of the textile industry, the surrounding region increasingly specialized in sheep raising and related tasks—shearing, cleaning, carding, and spinning. By the late seventeenth century, a textile industry dependent largely on the Potosí market dominated Quito's economy.

The economic history of Potosí's vast region of influence can best be understood by the cycle of its silver production. During the period of expansion, the high prices for goods at Potosí awakened the economic potential of an enormous area. Producers in distant regions could profit from supplying this market despite high transportation costs. The resulting competition among producers drove down prices and pushed less profitable participants toward other types of production, as in the case of Córdoba which moved from textiles and agriculture to grazing.

After 1592 silver production at Potosí began a long downward trend that worsened substantially after 1640 and continued into the eighteenth century. Although its production, even during its most disastrous years of the seventeenth century, compared favorably with the best yields of Zacatecas at the time, Potosí's decline rippled through the regional economy and exacerbated competition among its suppliers by reducing demand and depressing prices. Mule prices, for example, tumbled over 80 percent from the 1620s to the end of the century. Falling prices and declining profits affected all parts of society, but the weight fell disproportionately on the colonial workers, especially the Indian masses. The elite, squeezed by the declining demand, used its economic and politcal power to maintain profits by transferring costs to the Indians. The most onerous device developed to sustain their profits was the *repartimiento de bienes*. Not surprisingly, the most common goods in this trade were mules and colonial textiles, two products hit hard by the shrinking demand at Potosí.

Mexico and the Circum-Caribbean

The silver mines of Mexico played a similar role in its economic zone, but with several important differences. First, Mexico's silver production increased more gradually than did Peru's and therefore distorted the regional economy less. Mexico's silver production did not exceed Peru's until the 1670s, and only in the 1740s did it reach the 85 million pesos that Peru had produced a century earlier. Second, the location of the richest mines far from the dense population of central Mexico brought about the mine owners' earlier reliance on wage laborers. This difference in the labor market occasioned a relatively more equitable distribution of wealth and promoted a greater investment in production for the domestic market. Finally, Mexico's economy did not share Peru's isolation. Its producers were more successful in seeking European markets for their exports, although they also faced greater competition.

After the conquest and following the dissipation of much of its booty, Cortés and others sought means of making the new colony pay. The labor and commodity tributes of the *encomienda* allowed Spanish settlers to force Indian producers into new market relationships. Within two decades a colonial commercial system had appeared: Nearly without exception, the products were traditional, and the producers were Indians. New towns— particularly Puebla and the mining camps of the northern frontier—and the newly rebuilt Mexico City provided ready markets for both traditional and European food crops, livestock, and local artisan production. Because the Spaniards controlled marketing and could hold down labor costs, they were the major beneficiaries of the expanding markets.

By the early 1560s, exports from Mexico and Central America were in a period of dynamic expansion, and by the end of the century their cyclical behavior largely determined the rhythm of the regional economy. Silver mining led this growth and also aided the domestic economy by contributing to a dramatic increase in the money supply. This, in turn, encouraged investment in production and helped direct labor toward the most profitable areas of the economy.

Dyes were the nonmineral exports with the largest market. Some precious and semiprecious stones, medicinal plants, and other products also were exported in small amounts. Cochineal, a red dye made from insects cultivated on the nopal cactus, remained an important export until the end of the colonial period. *Encomenderos* required their Indians to supply cochineal as tribute, diverting it from domestic consumers and into the export market, although most production remained under the control of the Indian communities. Despite strong demands for cochineal, requirements of climate and limited labor skills slowed its growth. Epidemic disease and the spread of European livestock in the Valley of Mexico gave northern Oaxaca undisputed domination of this market by the seventeenth century.

Indigo, a blue vegetable dye, was the principal Central American export by 1600, although the Yucatán was also an important producer. Indigo was a more "typical" colonial product than cochineal was; its producers faced stiff competition in the European market from similar products imported from other regions and rarely found prices stable. Forced Indian labor was common in indigo production, but *castas* and black slaves held many of the skilled jobs.

The presence of the largest white and Hispanized nonwhite population in Spanish America joined with a dynamic silver industry to create a diversified regional economy in Mexico. In the areas surrounding the silver mining centers of northern New Spain and the great urban center of Mex-

ico City, market agriculture and grazing developed quickly. Wheat for the
Spaniards and *castas,* maize for the lower classes, and a broad range of
other rural products from the intoxicant *pulque* to olive oil found ready
consumers. An enormous livestock industry also supplied the mules, oxen,
and horses that tied together the major population centers, provided
essential traction at the mines, and produced the hides used ubiquitously
in an age without plastic. Although the domestic markets were somewhat
less volatile than the export sector was, the fortunes of rural producers
generally rose and fell in response to changes in silver production and the
size of the mining centers.

Manufacturing in colonial Mexico took two forms, the *obraje* and traditional artisan production. Textile *obrajes* were major employers in Querétaro, Oaxaca, and Puebla. Puebla's textile industry, in fact, remained competitive with imports even after independence. Mexican *obrajes* also
produced pottery. Artisans provided consumer goods and industrial products ranging from luxury items to tools and implements for mines and
farms. But both forms of colonial production found their markets limited,
as wealthier private consumers generally preferred European goods, and
by the eighteenth century, many European producers actually enjoyed a
price advantage, owing to the development of the factory system. The
obrajes survived, therefore, by targeting lower-class consumers and using
the cheapest workers available—*repartimiento* laborers, convicts, and debt
peons. Artisans compensated for their high production costs by providing
individualized goods—jewelry, silverware, luxury clothing, coaches, and

Textile *obraje* (factory) with Indian laborers, Mexico

furniture—or specialized products for the mining and transportation industries.

Mexico was also the center of an important intercolonial commercial network. Wheat from the Puebla region found a market in Cuba. Central America relied on Mexican textiles, exporting livestock in return. However, cacao, or chocolate, a beverage once restricted to the Mesoamerican elite, was the preeminent product in this regional trading system. The conquest destroyed the indigenous elite's ability to enforce taboos against the lower class's consumption of cacao, and the Spanish *encomenderos* profited from this previously suppressed market. As consumption grew beyond the capacity of the traditional suppliers, new areas of production opened up.

Guatemala experienced an early cacao boom that peaked in the 1570s, owing to the decline in Central America's Indian population that helped create an opportunity for Guayaquil and Venezuela. But the Crown damaged Guayaquil's initial hold on the Mexican market when in 1631 it banned trade between Mexico and Peru in order to stop the flow of Peruvian silver to Asia. Although some Guayaquil cacao continued to enter Mexico by overland routes, from the 1630s into the eighteenth century, Venezuela controlled this profitable market. Exports rose from ninety bushels in 1622 to nearly fifteen thousand bushels forty years later and peaked in 1722 at forty thousand bushels. Although Mexico sent to Venezuela wheat and textiles in return, it maintained the balance of trade principally with silver.

Brazil and the Río de la Plata Region

After the desultory decades in which dyewood was Brazil's major export, sugar production took hold, and Brazil's economic history effectively began. Victory over the Indians of the northeastern coastal region gave planters a supply of cheap, if inefficient, slave labor. By the 1570s the planters had enough investment capital and labor to give Brazilian sugar an important share of the European market. Production grew rapidly until the Dutch seized Pernambuco, the major sugar-growing region, in 1630. During the quarter-century of occupation, Bahia emerged as the primary producer, a position it generally retained until the nineteenth century. After the expulsion of the Dutch in 1654, cyclical expansions and contractions resulted from disruptions in Atlantic trade and from new competition from Dutch, English, and French colonies in the Caribbean. Although there were interludes of prosperity after the mid-seventeenth century, sugar prices frequently were too low to match the generally rising price of African slaves. The discovery of gold in the 1690s and the subsequent mining boom exacerbated this serious problem for an industry already in economic trouble.

Even after the discovery of gold and diamonds, sugar remained the most important Brazilian export until the nineteenth century and continued to tie Brazil to Europe and less directly to Africa and Asia. It passed through Portugal to the Low Countries, England, and other European countries where it was exchanged for textiles and manufactured goods. Rum, tobacco, and other colonial products helped pay for slaves imported from Africa. Even an indirect Brazilian trade with Asia was sustained by Portuguese ships occasionally putting in at major ports to exchange spices and silks for sugar. As was true in the mining-dominated colonies of the Spanish Empire, merchants tied to Atlantic trade eventually gained ascendancy over producers. The planters' indebtedness to the merchants limited investment in production and, coupled with the heavy taxation of sugar, reduced Brazil's competitiveness as the production of Caribbean plantations both reduced markets in England and France and competed for sales elsewhere in Europe.

The sugar industry promoted the production and distribution of other goods and services. The costly refining equipment and slave labor of the sugar plantations required high production levels of cane in order to make a profit. As a result, few plantations were self-sufficient in food or livestock. Thus, the interior of the northeast and large areas of the southern coastal zone profitably produced manioc, maize, wheat, and livestock for plantation and urban consumption. As sugar exports rose, the regions economically tied to the northeastern plantation zone expanded. Eventually dried beef and other animal products from as far away as Buenos Aires entered this market. The concentrated nature and coastal location of the sugar industry further augmented this trade network. The plantation belt—indeed nearly all settlements in Brazil until the eighteenth century— was located along a narrow coastal strip that allowed distant producers to gain access to maritime shipping, thus avoiding the high overland transportation costs of the mining industries. It required the mining boom of the late seventeenth century to draw labor and capital into the Brazilian interior and create additional markets for regional producers.

Brazil was also linked to the Potosí mining complex through Buenos Aires. European goods and African slaves imported illegally via Brazil and Buenos Aires were cheaper at the mines than were those carried on the longer and more costly legal route via Panama. The rich profits of this trade were particularly important to Brazil, as it suffered a chronic shortage of specie until the discovery of gold. When Spain moved to cut off this hemorrhage of silver, by creating new interior customs barriers at Salta and Jujuy in the 1670s, Portugal founded, as a center for contraband, Colônia do Sacramento in 1680, across the Río de la Plata from Buenos Aires. Brazil also had commercial links to Venezuela and Paraguay, exchanging European goods for cacao and *yerba*. The collapse of the Spanish fleet system and a decline in silver exports from Spanish America in the seventeenth century helped contribute to a more integrated American commercial system, of which Brazil's ties to Potosí and the grazing frontiers of the Río de la Plata and Venezuela were a part.

Obstacles to Economic Development

The colonies of Latin America were dependent on economically weak European metropolises. During the sixteenth and seventeenth centuries, more dynamic economies in northern Europe eclipsed the economies of Spain and Portugal. As the colonies' needs for capital and technology grew after 1550, both Iberian nations began a long period of economic decline. Spanish authorities, in particular, attempted to compensate for the weakened home economy by increasing colonial taxes and legislating, often ineffectively, against American production of items that competed with Spanish exports; the colonial production of silk, olive oil, and wine, for example, were banned at various times. In addition, although some commentators in Iberia complained that emigration was damaging both Spain and Portugal, the colonies received too few skilled settlers to transfer the full range of European technology and skill.

A related problem was the development of a large public sector in both empires. Although the size and cost of the colonial bureaucracies were modest by modern standards, the costs of taxes and government intervention were substantial. Bureaucrats actively intervened in the colonial economies to drain capital from production and promote consumption; to the extent this consumption took place in Iberia, its effects damaged the New World economy. Import and export taxes, the tithe on rural production, and mining taxes all steered wealth away from mines, plantations, and farms to urban administrative centers, defensive installations, and naval forces protecting Atlantic shipping.

Other obstacles also hindered economic development. The colonies' chronic trade deficit with the metropolitan countries left them perpetually short of specie, despite the bullion production of Peru and Mexico. Inadequate monetary resources, particularly in Brazil before the discovery of gold and in colonies outside the silver-mining regions of Spanish America, inhibited growth in domestic and regional markets. A shortage of credit caused by the tardy development of banking and joint-stock companies worsened the problem. In the absence of banking services, wholesale merchants and religious institutions were the only sources of investment capital. The conservatism of these lenders pushed capital toward rural enterprises or real estate, for they provided land and buildings as collateral, and away from investment in new technology, especially in manufacturing. Finally, substantial amounts of capital were used to establish and maintain the colonial Church.

Geography also raised grave obstacles to economic development. Extremely rugged terrain separated the great mining centers of Mexico and Peru from populous commercial centers. Mountains, jungles, and deserts presented natural barriers to human enterprise. European goods unloaded in Buenos Aires had to travel more than a thousand miles on unimproved road before reaching Potosí, and this route was less difficult than the one from Arica. Freight carried from Quito to Guayaquil passed along a dangerous stretch of muddy road. In 1590 the engineer Juan Bautista Antoneli called the strategically important mule trail that connected Panama City with Nombre de Dios the "filthiest way in the world." Because few navigable rivers linked the major population centers, mules, humans, and, in flat terrain, ox carts moved the colonial produce. The resulting high transportation costs limited the profitability of both domestic and export production.

Despite the many obstacles, Latin America's colonial economies produced a wide variety of goods and distributed them, according to demand and competition, through local, regional, and international markets. The collective energy, initiative, and creativity of individuals were ultimately responsible for the region's achievements and individuals as well suffered the consequences of economic failures.

Notes

1. C. R. Boxer, *The Portuguese Seaborne Empire 1415–1825* (London: Hutchinson & Co., 1969), p. 224.
2. Arthur P. Newton, *The European Nations in the West Indies 1493–1688* (London: A & C Black, 1933), p. 170.

Suggested for Further Reading

Andrews, Kenneth R. *The Spanish Caribbean: Trade and Plunder 1530–1630.* New Haven, Conn.: Yale University Press, 1978.

Bakewell, Peter J. *Silver Mining and Society in Colonial Mexico: Zacatecas, 1546–1700.* Cambridge, England: Cambridge University Press, 1971.

Bannon, John Francis. *The Spanish Borderlands Frontier 1513–1821.* New York: Holt, Rinehart and Winston, 1970.

Boxer, C. R. *The Dutch in Brazil 1624–1654.* Oxford, England: Clarendon Press, 1957.

Boxer, C. R. *Salvador de Sá and the Struggle for Brazil and Angola 1602–1686.* London: University of London, 1952.

Chevalier, François. *Land and Society in Colonial Mexico: The Great Hacienda.* Translated by Lesley Byrd Simpson. Berkeley and Los Angeles: University of California Press, 1963.

Clayton, Lawrence A. *Caulkers and Carpenters in a New World: The Shipyards of Colonial Guayaquil.* Athens: Ohio University Center for International Studies, 1980.

Cushner, Nicolas P. *Lords of the Land: Sugar, Wine, and Jesuit Estates of Coastal Peru, 1600–1767.* Albany: State University of New York Press, 1980.

Davies, Keith A. *Landowners in Colonial Peru.* Austin: University of Texas Press, 1984.

Earle, Peter. *The Sack of Panama. Sir Henry Morgan's Adventures on the Spanish Main.* New York: Viking, 1982.

Exquemelin, A. O. *The Buccaneers of America.* Translated by Alexis Brown. Baltimore: Penguin, 1969.

Farriss, Nancy M. *Maya Society Under Colonial Rule: The Collective Enterprise of Survival.* Princeton, N.J.: Princeton University Press, 1984.

Haring, Clarence H. *Trade and Navigation Between Spain and the Indies in the Time of the Hapsburgs.* Cambridge, Mass.: Harvard University Press, 1918.

Keith, Robert G. *Conquest and Agrarian Change: Emergence of the Hacienda System on the Peruvian Coast.* Cambridge, Mass.: Harvard University Press, 1976.

Hoffman, Paul E. *The Spanish Crown and the Defense of the Caribbean, 1535–1585: Precedent, Patrimonialism, and Royal Parsimony.* Baton Rouge: Louisiana State University Press, 1980.

Larson, Brooke. *Colonialism and Agrarian Transformation in Bolivia. Cochabamba, 1550–1900.* Princeton, N.J.: Princeton University Press, 1988.

Lyon, Eugene. *The Enterprise of Florida: Pedro Menendez de Aviles and the Spanish Conquest of 1565–1568.* Gainesville: University Presses of Florida, 1976.

MacLeod, Murdo J. *Spanish Central America: A Socioeconomic History, 1520–1720.* Berkeley and Los Angeles: University of California Press, 1973.

Maltby, William S. *The Black Legend in England: The Development of Anti-Spanish Sentiment, 1558–1660.* Durham, N.C.: Duke University Press, 1971.

Martin, Cheryl English. *Rural Society in Colonial Morelos.* Albuquerque: University of New Mexico Press, 1985.

Newton, Arthur P. *The European Nations in the West Indies, 1493–1688.* London: A & C Black, 1933.

Powell, Philip Wayne, *Soldiers, Indians, and Silver.* Berkeley and Los Angeles: University of California Press, 1952.

Riley, G. Michael. *Fernando Cortés and the Marquesado in Morelos: A Case Study in the Socioeconomic Development of Sixteenth Century Mexico.* Albuquerque: University of New Mexico Press, 1973.

Salvucci, Richard J. *Textiles and Capitalism in Mexico. An Economic History of the Obrajes, 1539–1840.* Princeton, N.J.: Princeton University Press, 1987.

Schurz, William L. *The Manila Galleon.* New York: Dutton, 1939.

Smith, Robert S. *The Spanish Guild Merchant: A History of the Consulado, 1250–1700.* Durham, N.C.: Duke University Press, 1940.

Spalding, Karen. *Huarochirí. An Andean Society Under Inca and Spanish Rule.* Stanford, Calif.: Stanford University Press, 1984.

Stern, Steve J. *Peru's Indian Peoples and the Challenge of Spanish Conquest. Huamanga to 1640.* Madison: University of Wisconsin Press, 1982.

Taylor, William B. *Landlord and Peasant in Colonial Oaxaca.* Stanford, Calif.: Stanford University Press, 1972.

SIX

LIVING IN AN EMPIRE

Securing an Income

The colonial economy served as an arena where people struggled to satisfy their material needs, especially food and shelter. Social class, ethnicity, race, and gender defined discretionary material needs among privileged groups. Both culture and economic opportunities helped determine how individuals and groups defined and satisfied their material needs. That is, European immigrants sought goals different from those of Indians or creoles and *castas*. But securing an adequate income necessarily meant satisfying class and ethnic cultural norms and realizing individual ambitions for social status.

The colonial character of the Latin American economies, particularly the structural instability of the export sector, increased the vulnerability of all social classes. The profits of a merchant who imported European textiles, the income of a muleteer, the wages of a colonial weaver, and the ability of a sheep rancher to repay a loan all were tied to the volume of trade carried by Spanish fleets, the productivity of the colonial silver mines, and demographic changes. Alterations in any of these could redistribute income and opportunities among the colonial society's competing classes.

The Elites

The size of the New World and the distances separating the major centers of wealth meant that there was no single colonial elite. Rather, each city or region had a local elite of men and women who dominated the political, economic, social, and cultural life of both its urban core and the surrounding rural areas. Despite differences arising from location and the presence or absence of certain economic activities, for example, silver mining, it is possible to generalize about local elites.

The colonial elites were heterogeneous and often interlocking mixes of ranchers, planters, miners, merchants, high-ranking churchmen, and bureaucrats. Many members of the elite pursued activities that crossed economic boundaries. For example, wealthy miners and merchants often owned rural properties; some churchmen and royal officials used kinsmen and friends as front men for commercial undertakings; and merchants commonly invested in large-scale mining and agricultural activities. Except for high-ranking bureaucrats and churchmen, wealth, influence, family, and social connections were more important than was occupation in determining elite membership.

Long-term, large-scale changes in the performance of the economy—for example, the seventeenth-century decline of Potosí, the contemporary rise in Venezuelan cacao production, and the late seventeenth-century discovery of gold in Brazil—moved capital from sector to sector and altered the relations of wealth and power within and among the colonies. Alterations on this scale often profoundly affected the colonial elites: Many *encomenderos* failed to survive the sixteenth-century decline in the Indian population. A decrease in silver production due to mercury shortages or the exhaustion of rich ores transferred economic power from miners to merchant creditors. And in the case of the Brazilian gold boom, mining profits increased the competition for labor and forced up the cost of slaves needed for the colony's faltering sugar industry.

Colonial elites developed strategies to meet these crises. With few exceptions, elite families diversified their holdings to limit damage caused by failure in any one sector of the economy. João Peixoto Viegas, the illegitimate son of a Portuguese cleric who emigrated to Brazil around 1640 provides an example. He built a traditional commercial career exporting Brazilian sugar and importing wine and slaves. As pressures developed in the sugar trade, he developed large rural estates based on livestock and market agriculture. The Zacatecan silver miner Don Joseph de Quesada owned an extensive rural estate with thirty thousand head of sheep in addition to mining property at the time of his death in 1686. And Lima merchant Juan de Quesada y Sotomayor diversified his investments in the 1630s by purchasing an appointment to Lima's royal treasury.

The Bureaucracies of Church and State

The men recruited in Spain and Portugal to run the bureaucracies of state and church rarely were men of great independent wealth. Salaries and other material benefits placed high-level bureaucrats near the apex of colonial society. To equal the annual salary of nearly 5,000 pesos received by an *oidor* of the *audiencia* of Lima normally required investing capital of 100,000 pesos. Yet the wealth of the most prosperous miners, merchants, and planters far overshadowed the resources of this administrative class. As a result, bureaucrats and even high churchmen commonly considered themselves materially deprived and undercompensated, which led many to enrich themselves through the abuse of institutional power.

The use of government revenues for personal gain was common. Because the colonies lacked adequate credit mechanisms, access to institutional funds often gave officials a competitive advantage in the marketplace. In 1630 an official of the Tribunal de Cuentas of Lima alleged that the viceroyalty's *corregidores* owed the treasury 1,654,057 pesos. Similarly, a *visita* conducted by the president of the *audiencia* of Guatemala in 1717 found that the *contador* of the local treasury owed the Crown 30,000 pesos and that his predecessor owed 4,000. In all of these cases, officeholders had invested public funds in private-sector enterprises or lent them to kinsmen or business associates.

Spanish and Portuguese administrative practice clearly contributed to this problem. Officials at every level were relatively underpaid; few received more than one thousand pesos in annual salary. In addition to the expenses of travel to the colonies and setting up new households, European appointees often arrived with substantial debts incurred in securing office. Pariticularly in the seventeenth and early eighteenth centuries, many purchased their appointments outright, and others spent large sums to gain a favorable hearing for their applications. In the Spanish case, appointees after 1631 had to pay one-half of their first year's salary as a tax *(media anata)*. These and other burdens encouraged corruption.

Many bureaucratic appointments were sold to the highest bidder. Among them, the offices of *corregidor, alcalde mayor,* and *gobernador* offered the greatest potential for private gain through commerce. Because the salaries of all Spanish *corregidores* were nearly the same, the differences in the prices paid for the different jurisdictions suggest the range of extralegal income. For instance, in the late seventeenth century, a term as *corregidor* in the cotton- and cochineal-producing area of Oaxaca cost more than seven thousand pesos, whereas a similar post in the much poorer and less populated district of Chihuahua brought only seven hundred pesos. High officials also participated illegally in commerce. In 1629 the bishop of Popayán charged that the governor, Captain Juan Bermúdez de Castro, so monopolized the local textile trade that other merchants avoided the town.

Although less venal and corrupt as a group, churchmen also sought material advantage for themselves and their families. Archbishops and bishops commonly advanced the careers of nephews and other relatives. Archbishop Alonso de Montúfar of Mexico City, for example, appointed his nephew to the post of *maestrescuela* in 1555 over the opposition of the cathedral chapter. Others operated openly in the economy. In the 1620s Archbishop Juan Pérez de la Serna of New Spain was found to be operating a butchershop in his palace. More often bishops and archbishops used for private gain their control of the agricultural tithe and fees charged for the administration of the sacraments. Clearly the churchmen's greed often hurt the society's poorest members. In one notorious case, efforts by Bishop Alvarez de Toledo of Chiapas in 1712 to increase the tithe collection touched off a bitter Indian rebellion.

Merchants

No group more actively pursued ties with other elite groups than did the merchants. Spanish wholesale merchants, in particular the members of the *consulados* of Mexico City and Lima, were among the richest, most powerful residents of the New World. The monopoly trade system created by the Spanish government in the early sixteenth century was the basis for their position.

Because competition among these privileged merchants was limited, they were generally able to influence, if not control, the exchange values of American exports. In the mining regions of Peru and New Spain, merchants gained the upper hand through their control of credit and the supply of mercury and other essential imports. In the absence of other credit sources, they provided the capital needed for digging new shafts or buying new equipment. Some merchants bought semirefined silver at a discount or received commissions for exchanging minted coins for refined silver. Alonso de Peralta Sidonia summarized their behavior in 1603: "The merchant gives clothes or money for forty or sixty days, to be paid for in silver . . . on each mark, worth 65 *reales*. He takes six *reales,* and in many places, eight; and this is an established business."[1]

Although the great merchants benefited from the monopolistic commercial policy of the Spanish Crown, there was a natural tension between their pursuit of private gain and this inflexible system. Consequently, wealthy merchants frequently engaged in illegal trading. In 1646, authorities in Mexico discovered a number of merchants, including the former head of the *consulado,* shipping enormous quantities of illegal silver to the Philippines. Mexican merchants repeatedly violated laws prohibiting the shipment of European goods to Lima via the port of Acapulco.

Wholesale merchants also controlled the retail sale of imported goods. Many owned retail shops or had family ties to retailers in provincial centers, and through these connections they maintained profitable prices despite market fluctuations. On the export side, merchants advanced credit to *corregidores* and other officials and in return received special consideration in the purchase of Indian production. Cotton mantles, cochineal, coca, and, to a lesser extent, cacao flowed through this network of mercantile and administrative interests.

In Brazil and in peripheral regions of the Spanish Empire like Venezuela, the Río de la Plata, and the Caribbean islands, merchants faced more direct competition from legal rivals and from contraband. Nevertheless, in time these merchants also gained substantial advantages over colonial agricultural and grazing interests. In seventeenth-century Brazil and eighteenth-century Venezuela, the creation of state-sanctioned trading companies promoted this process. However, the merchants' ascendency in these regions was rooted in the largest merchants' ability to set exchange values by working in concert through short-term partnerships or price-fixing agreements and in the absence of adequate credit.

The Rural Elite

Elite families frequently invested in both urban and rural enterprises. In the mature colonies, an important segment of the elite derived much of its wealth and status from estates devoted to agriculture or grazing. More than any other class did, the colonial planters and *hacienda* owners lived a traditional seignorial life, enjoying great wealth and commanding large numbers of slaves and free dependents. Yet despite their considerable economic and social power, planters and *hacendados* often found their interests subordinated to those of the commercial elite.

The very nature of large-scale rural enterprise created a need for credit. Because income from agriculture was concentrated in the period following the harvest, landowners were forced to borrow to cover their expenses during the remainder of the year. In addition to these expected needs, the unpredictable effects of droughts, pests, and changes in market conditions generated extraordinary debts that endangered the very survival of a rural enterprise. Most rural elites, therefore, found it necessary to forge strong ties with the Church and the merchant community, the two major sources of credit during the colonial period.

Agriculture for Domestic Markets

There was a very large subsistence sector in colonial Latin America: Indian communities and *casta* peasants struggled to meet their own food requirements. In years of abundant harvests subsistence farmers were able to sell their surplus corn, potatoes, and other staples in the market. Good harvests, therefore, lowered prices and reduced profits for heavily capitalized, large-scale producers. In addition, the poor quality and high cost of transportation, slow rates of population growth, and the poverty of the masses further limited demand.

As a result, large-scale producers sought profits by subverting the marketplace. Individually and collectively the *hacendados* attempted to control the flow of goods to urban consumers in order to create artificial scarcity. Unlike smaller producers compelled to sell as soon as the harvest was complete, the *hacendados* sold most of their production later in the year when prices peaked. The largest producers actually held wheat and corn in their warehouses until famine years when their sale could earn enormous profits. Municipal councils attempted, often unsuccessfully, to limit the devastating consequences of these market strategies by buying grain and holding it in municipal warehouses and by setting retail prices. However, price gouging during famines was common.

Large-scale rural producers also sought increased profits by forcing down labor costs. Producers at various times used Indian slavery, *encomienda*, *repartimiento*, convict labor, debt peonage, and black slavery to depress labor costs, a practice that reduced the laboring masses' ability to consume other goods produced in the colonies. Low consumer demand was the natural result of widespread poverty.

Plantations

Only silver mining had larger capital requirements than did plantation agriculture. Plantations were generally located in tropical areas where Indian population losses were most dramatic: the Caribbean Basin, Brazil, and coastal Peru. As a result, colonial plantations depended on expensive African slaves. In addition to high labor costs, sugar planters competing in the international market needed to invest in costly refining machinery. Because there were substantial economies of scale in sugar production, plantation size and therefore cost increased with time. Cacao and tobacco production required less capital, but heavy indebtedness plagued many of these plantations, nevertheless.

Although the European demand for New World plantation products increased steadily throughout the colonial era, production tended to grow faster still. Tobacco production spread from the Caribbean to Río de la Plata. Cacao plantations were found in Brazil, Mexico, Central America, Ecuador, and Venezuela. In the late seventeenth and eighteenth centuries, heavily capitalized sugar plantations brought into production on the French, Dutch, and English islands of the Caribbean forced down the profits traditionally earned by Brazilian planters. Faced with intense international competition, the planters struggled to remain profitable.

Unlike the *hacienda* owners who tried to dominate local markets, planters who competed internationally were unable to influence prices by withholding their production from market. Indeed, debt service and the possibility of spoilage made it impossible to wait for favorable prices. These conditions led planters to seek government intervention to guarantee markets and stable prices. The prosperity of Venezuelan planters in the late seventeenth century, for example, depended largely on statutory obstacles to Guayaquil's cheaper cacao entering the Mexican market. Tobacco and sugar planters in both Portuguese and Spanish colonies sought similar monopolies.

The Role of Inheritance Law

The inheritance laws of Spain and Portugal undermined the elites' ability to accumulate wealth and invest in production. These laws severely limited discretionary authority over the disposition of an estate: All wealth acquired during a marriage was divided according to a rigid formula. One-half went to the surviving spouse, and the other half was divided among the children or their heirs. The wife's dowry, a common feature of marriages in the elite, was returned to her before the division. By the time the dowry was officially returned, of course, the wife was often a mother or grandmother and would pass on the money to her family. A groom's endowment to his bride, the *arras,* was treated similarly. Unless the family could agree to shared management, all agricultural or mining enterprise would be sold and divided to meet the law's requirements. This formula was particularly disruptive in commerce and manufacturing, in which the need for division undermined all forms of business partnership. To circumvent the forced division of properties, a few of the wealthiest colonial families used entailment, a legal device that reserved in perpetuity the largest portion of an estate for a single heir.

Middle Groups

At the top of the urban middle sector were manufacturers, master artisans, retail merchants, middle-ranking officials of the colonial government, and priests. Priests and bureaucrats were the most secure, as their status depended on institutional prestige and predictable, if modest, incomes. The other groups depended on unpredictable market conditions to maintain their status. Members of the urban middle sector routinely imitated elite practice and attempted to protect their status and income by creating institutional guarantees.

Master craftsmen in skilled trades were organized collectively to set quality control standards, work rules, and recruitment and training procedures and even to limit product lines. Their intent was self-consciously conservative. To prevent levels of competition that would endanger the group's status, they sought to limit individual freedom in the market. This ideal was beginning to weaken in Europe before the settlement of America and the nature of colonial society undermined it further. The slow trickle of European immigrants forced Spanish and Portuguese masters to train Indian, *casta,* and slave apprentices, and so the racially and culturally heterogeneous artisan community of the New World was freed in custom, if not statute, from many traditional restraints. Masters forced down labor costs by using slaves or by ignoring the apprenticeship system. The most successful were, in effect, manufacturers. Some owned *obrajes* dependent on Indian and *casta* labor. But more often, the masters depended on the help of one or more journeymen and apprentices to satisfy the needs of neighborhood customers. Nearly all of these artisan producers owned their tools and carried a small amount of inventory, but only a few owned their shops and homes.

Nearly every master artisan purchased his raw materials on credit and then found it necessary to offer credit to clients. Although essential to business, these relationships of debt and credit dramatically increased the vulnerability of artisans and small manufacturers during periods of economic recession. One result was the fairly common practice of fleeing creditors by moving to another city.

Retail merchants operated across a broad scale of enterprise. The most successful sometimes rivaled *consulado* members in wealth. The poorest operated small neighborhood shops or participated in the open-air markets that ringed the central plaza. Many were little more than agents for wealthy wholesalers, their income deriving from their ability to anticipate supply and demand. Profits were associated with risks: Would a fleet arrive next year? Would contraband undercut the prices of goods purchased on credit from a wholesale merchant? Could inventory be protected against theft? Were their customers good credit risks? Credit helped sustain retail sales. Even at the level of the neighborhood grocery, shopkeepers carried large numbers of small debts, and the retailer himself was commonly indebted to the wholesale merchant and to family and other kin.

Most retail merchants operated in a geographically restricted market. Many, in fact, served a single urban neighborhood. Because increasing the volume of trade by entering new markets or expanding credit to customers was very risky, retail merchants were more likely to seek additional profits through diversification. Most typically, they invested in real estate, particularly urban rental property, but investments in the retail sale of alcoholic beverages and the maintenance of gaming establishments were also common.

Petty bureaucrats, secular priests, and other religious had uniformly modest incomes but a relatively secure status. Many middle-level officials owed their positions to patronage. Once in office, these men sought to solidify and improve their association with their powerful patrons and local elite families. They sought marriages with the daughters of landowners or merchants, marriages that would bring dowries and potential inheritances. Most members of this group supplemented their salaries with tips and bribes. Others sought opportunities to enter commerce as investors.

By the end of the sixteenth century Spanish America was home to numerous secular priests, especially in urban areas. Those who acquired parishes through patronage or competitive searches received a small salary augmented by fees paid by parishioners; poor Indians and other commoners often complained that fees for baptisms, marriages, and funerals were exorbitant. Some parishes were so rich that the priest could, in effect, subcontract his sacramental duties to vicars in order to pursue other interests. Family-endowed chantries supported other priests. Many priests and nuns were also involved in business, and their personal ownership of urban and rural property was not uncommon. One nun, Catarina de Telles Barretto of the Desterro convent of Bahia, owned rental property, lent money, and owned twelve slaves who prepared and sold sweets. Her private estate at her death was worth half the annual income of her convent.

Some areas also had a rural middle group. On the northern frontier of the viceroyalty of New Spain, in the Bajío, and in Oaxaca, for example, were many ranches and small farms that produced food and livestock for local markets. The use of seasonal labor kept labor costs low, but the scale of enterprise and limitations in demand restricted profits. As a result, very few members of this group acquired the land and resources necessary to enter the elite.

This social type was, perhaps, best exemplified by the *lavradores de cana* of the Brazilian sugar zone. Although dependent on nearby plantations for refining and processing, in many cases, these cane producers were wealthy individuals who owned slaves and land. In other cases they were little more than sharecroppers. The high cost of land, slaves, equipment, and plant for refining limited their advancement. Although their place in the pro- duction process curtailed their profits during boom times, the *lavradores'* fixed costs and lower levels of indebtedness reduced their risk of catastro- phe during periods of falling prices.

The Poor

The poor in colonial Latin America conformed to no set pattern. In rural areas there were important differences between the subsistence and the market sectors. In regions with large Indian populations—for example, the Spanish colonies of Central America, Oaxaca, Yucatán, and the Andean region—traditional social institutions, religious sodalities, and kin networks mitigated the endemic material deprivation. These subsistence producers were often hurt by drought or epidemics, but the cyclical behav- ior of the market economy seldom ruined them. Some participation in the money economy was necessary, however, for tribute in most regions was collected in specie, and where the *repartimiento* of goods was employed, the *corregidores* required money payments for goods that the Indian commu- nities were forced to buy. Therefore, Indians had to sell their surplus pro- duction in local markets and to seek seasonal work on Spanish *haciendas* or in nearby towns to fulfill these obligations.

Poverty developed a different character in rural areas tied to the expanding marketplace. There the labor of the free poor was a commodity bought and sold in response to changing market conditions. Even the slaves' material conditions—diet, housing, clothing—followed these large cycles. During boom periods, life improved. But when bust followed, the poor had few recourses other than reentering the subsistence sector.

The cities of colonial Latin America had large and diverse underclasses. At the top were skilled journeymen, marketpeople, peddlers, servants, sol- diers, and sailors. At the bottom were beggars, thieves, prostitutes, and the impoverished victims of accidents or diseases like leprosy. All these groups were excluded from the traditional supports provided by the indigenous communities. In addition, unemployment or illness forced even relatively skilled members of this class to seek charity or perish.

Wage laborers worked from sunrise to sunset, just as slaves did. The workweek ran from Monday through Saturday, but numerous religious and secular holidays interrupted this routine. Such workers customarily received breaks for lunch and refreshment, and in many artisan shops and in some unskilled jobs, the employers provided meals. Apprentices and some journeymen slept in their employers' back rooms. For many workers, these forms of compensation in kind were essential to their struggle for survival.

Both the changing market demands for labor and wage custom determined the workers' pay. Wage custom was the association of a certain daily wage, *jornal,* with a specific job, and as a result, the wages of the unskilled changed very little over long periods. Only sustained high labor demands could break this pattern. A similar wage structure existed in the skilled crafts, in which all masters were likely to pay the same wage to their journeymen. Few men worked fifty-two, six-day weeks. Rather, many endured periods of unemployment each year. Because few skilled or unskilled wage laborers had any savings or investments, extended unemployment or illness often led to destitution. Some guilds offered medical assistance to their members, but most workers turned to the Church for assistance. Although women were barred by statute or custom from most skilled and unskilled manual labor, the evidence is overwhelming that they did work. Most often they were found away from the jealous scrutiny of guilds and magistrates, producing and selling goods made in the home or, particularly in regard to textiles, providing much of the *obraje* labor force.

Most colonial populations included some soldiers, government lackeys, and, in the ports, sailors. Uniformly underpaid, these men were often compelled by necessity to seek part-time employment. Their participation in the urban labor market accordingly depressed urban wages and often stirred resentment by the local population. Some Spanish soldiers actually had to beg when their wages were not paid.

Peddlers and market vendors shared the low incomes and vulnerability of the wage laborers. Often in debt, their meager inventories were subject to theft and spoilage. And unlike artisans and other skilled workers, these petty retailers could not rely on wage custom and institutionally established labor recruitment mechanisms. They thus lived on guile and pluck, and only a handful ever achieved material security. For many the eventual fall from peddler to thief or beggar was all too predictable.

Some urban slaves lived in material circumstances superior to those of the great mass of the free working class. All slaves suffered from racial prejudice and the other consequences of bondage. But slaves in elite households often lived much better than did the masses of free *castas.* Some slaves, particularly those owned by men and women of modest means, lived outside their owners' households and pursued employment on their own. In a minority of cases they were able to acquire small amounts of property and purchase their freedom. Many female slaves participated in market activities; in colonial Brazil, in particular, enterprising slave women dominated the urban markets.

Every colonial city also was home to prostitutes, thieves, and beggars. Propertied men and women demanded protection from their blandishments and attacks in the crowded streets, but little protection was offered. Most of the underclass lived lives of incredible deprivation, although fash-

Butcher selling meat in Mexico City

ionable prostitutes or skillful thieves might have fleeting moments of high income. For example, four *casta* women set up a house of prostitution in Lima in 1631 and enjoyed a brief period of good business: "These men come and go, in and out of the house day and night," complained the authorities.[2] But public outrage led to the dispatch of Pascuala de Cabeza and the others to a shelter for "lost women."

Latin Catholic culture was tolerant of beggars and poverty. The Church viewed the indigent poor as part of the God-given social landscape, not as a social aberration, and urged Catholics to remember them as fellow Christians and to give alms for their sustenance. Members of mendicant orders, in seeking to imitate Christ's poverty, begged for their daily bread. *Cofradías* and other religious sodalities who shared these sentiments regularly offered alms to beggars following the funerals of members and during special feast days. As a result, swarms of beggars congregated around the churches and public buildings in every colonial city. To sustain themselves, the very poor also relied on offal from municipal slaughterhouses, spoiled

Black laundress in Buenos Aires

and stale bread from bakeries, and the limited generosity of wealthy households.

The distribution of wealth and access to opportunity in colonial Latin America promoted gross inequalities. Nevertheless, despite their privileged position, the performance of the economy often placed members of the elite and middle sectors at risk, as well as causing suffering among the masses. As a result, all classes in society, even the poor, operated conservatively to protect themselves against declining fortunes and lost status. Structural limitations in the economy restricted the free play of ambition and the potential for upward mobility. Consequently, men and women of all classes sought security by exchanging independent access to the marketplace for statutory privileges such as commerical monopolies, *mayorazgos,* guilds, religious *fueros,* and licenses to beg. The resultant interplay of rational decision making and cultural norms worked to create an economically active population little inclined toward risk taking and novelty.

Urban and Rural Environments

European conquest and settlement altered the New World's architectural environment as well as its political and economic structures. In a remarkably short time, the conquerors' cathedrals, monasteries, administrative buildings, and private residences replaced the pyramids, elevated plazas, ball courts, and palaces of the indigenous elites. In important ways, both the surviving indigenous traditions and the imported European architectural forms helped create the context for the evolution of Latin America's colonial society.

The architectural progression from indigenous to mature colonial was clearest in central Mexico and Peru where large urban centers existed before contact. When the Spaniards settled in regions outside the great Andean and Mesoamerican civilizations, they established new towns unencumbered by the architectural legacies and city plans of the Indian past. Eventually, however, common features of a colonial style in construction and town planning appeared throughout Spanish America. Because the indigenous Brazilian people had not constructed urban centers, Brazil's colonial experience was similar to that of Spain's peripheral colonies.

The Conquest Period

The most important native cities suffered severe damage during the conquest: The battle for Tenochtitlán completely destroyed the city, and much of Cuzco was reduced to rubble as well during Manco Inca's rebellion of 1536. In both cases colonial authorities decided, for political reasons, to rebuild the cities as Spanish centers. Despite the capitals' distance from the sea, both Pizarro and Cortés understood that rebuilding them symbolically legitimized the authority of the new colonial order.

Many Indian cities, for example, Jauja in Peru and Tlaxcala in Mexico, survived the conquest period nearly unscathed. Their concentrated population and nearby agricultural resources attracted Spanish settlers, who asserted political authority and then moved quickly to impose a new urban landscape. As a result, they destroyed many of the Indian structures to make room for churches, governmental buildings, and Spanish residences.

In regions without previous settled agriculture and urbanization, the Spaniards founded towns to organize and control the indigenous population. Where native cultures had not produced authentic urban development, missionaries and civil authorities encouraged and, if necessary, forced the concentration of the Indian population to facilitate Christianization and compel participation in the colonial economy. In each case, Spanish and Portuguese settlers imposed their own concepts of urban social organization, architecture, and city planning. Yet even in this new environment, elements of indigenous experience survived in construction techniques, decorative motifs, and residential patterns.

The Early Colonial Period

The conquistadors and early settlers defined their colonization of the New World by founding cities, which they saw as their link with European civilization and culture. On his second voyage, Columbus founded the first Spanish colonial town, Isabela, on Hispaniola. Its precipitous failure foreshadowed the later collapse and abandonment of many early settlements, most frequently because their sites were unhealthy or the nearby Indian population declined. Yet Santo Domingo, the present capital of the Dominican Republic, and many smaller towns survived. By 1525 the historian Gonzalo Fernández de Oviedo compared Santo Domingo favorably with Barcelona, one of Spain's larger and more prosperous cities.

Spaniards had founded over 190 towns and cities by 1620, at least half of them before 1550. But Indian attacks, an unhealthy climate, and earthquakes, among other reasons, caused many of these early settlements to move to more favorable locations. For example, Vera Cruz, founded hastily by Cortés, was relocated to a more protected harbor. Nevertheless, by 1600 most of the major urban centers of modern Spanish America were in place. In Brazil, by comparison, fewer than 40 cities and towns, almost all within a few miles of the coast, had been founded before 1650.

The City Plan

From the outset of colonization, the Spanish Crown actively promoted urban planning. It urged the royal administrators and conquistadors to avoid swampy or insect-ridden terrain and admonished them to ensure the availability of adequate water and arable land before settlement. In 1573 Philip II promulgated ordinances that codified the Crown's conception of how Spanish cities in the New World should be built. The basic pattern was a grid: A large plaza at the center of the city served as a marketplace and hosted religious and secular ceremonies. The plaza was not to be smaller than two hundred by three hundred feet or larger than three hundred by eight hundred feet. In major administrative centers like Lima, Mexico City, Bogotá, and Guatemala, the cathedral, governor or viceroy's palace, and city council building bounded the plaza. Lesser cities had fewer and smaller public buildings, but the plaza still served as the political and religious focus of community life.

When geography restricted this form of orderly development, the grid pattern was found only at the city center. Uneven terrain imposed irregular street patterns on Potosí and other mining towns located in mountainous areas. In the very few fortified cities found in the Spanish colonies, the walls tended to deform the grid, as Lima and Cartagena demonstrate. On the frontier, where secular authority was often weak, the Church imposed similar requirements on the missions. Resettled Indian populations, *congregaciónes,* and mission settlements—for example, the famous Jesuit *reducciónes* of Paraguay—followed a grid pattern, with the church and other public buildings located on a central plaza. Their walled courtyards provided a defense against hostile attacks and offered a sheltered place for instructing crowds of Indian converts.

The Portuguese Crown was less directly involved in city planning than was the Spanish Crown, and so Brazilian colonial cities generally developed more spontaneously. Nevertheless, most of the important cities did have a grid pattern in the city center. Because Brazil's major commercial and administrative cities were located on the coast, they were vulnerable to attack. Defensive walls and other fortifications, consequently, often influenced the direction of urban growth.

A System of Cities

Within a century of the initial rush to establish towns in Spanish America, a durable rank order could be found among the region's larger cities and towns. The viceregal capitals of Mexico City and Lima quickly became dominant. By 1630, 58 percent of the Spanish population of the *audiencia* of Mexico lived in Mexico City, and 55 percent of the Spanish population of the *audiencia* of Lima lived in Lima. The two capitals were followed in importance by Bogotá, Guatemala, and Santo Domingo. The third rank included Panama, Quito, Cuzco, Guadalajara, La Plata, and Santiago de Chile.

Spanish immigrants initially settled near Indian population centers. The *encomienda* system reinforced this early attraction. Later the discovery and exploitation of rich mineral deposits brought rapid population growth in mining centers like Potosí and Zacatecas. The profitable commercial activity of port cities like Cartagena, Havana, and, to a lesser extent, Portobelo and Vera Cruz drew a civilian population as well as military garrisons. In each case, increased numbers of Spanish residents and the developing market economy brought imperial recognition in the form of fiscal and administrative structures. Once in place, the public sector's ability to collect and disburse funds reinforced the order established initially by demography, physical resources, and commercial activity.

This rapid proliferation of towns did not, however, result in strong economic ties among the major cities of Spanish America. The cities of British North America, by comparison, were significantly more integrated. Geography, cumbersome regulations, or, in some cases, statutory prohibitions inhibited regional and intercolonial trade in the Spanish colonies. Generally, colonial cities were tied more closely to Seville and Cádiz by their economic and political structures than they were to one another. Because the exportation of sugar so completely dominated the Brazilian economy from the mid-sixteenth to the early eighteenth centuries, this pattern of colonial isolation and dependence on the metropolis was even more sharply defined.

The Colonial City

The rectilinear core of the colonial city, the *traza,* was overwhelmingly European in culture and architecture. Around the central plaza crowded the most impressive secular and religious buildings. Nearby were the residences of the elite. Most Spaniards, both immigrants from Europe and their American-born descendants, lived with their servants and slaves in large homes in this central district. The most affluent *mestizos* and other *castas* emulated them in residences located as close to the plaza as possible.

Urban churches and convents were immense bastions towering over their surroundings and laden with ornate decoration. The finest ecclesiastical buildings demonstrated the centrality of religious sentiment in colonial culture as well as the Church's great wealth. Although architecturally derivative, the cathedral in Mexico City was the largest and most splendid in America. Other capital cities, too, boasted magnificent churches. In general, Brazil's churches also followed European models, although on a smaller scale. Yet the best of these churches is still able to impress a viewer. Visitors to Lima noted

> . . . the cathedral, the churches of St. Dominic, St. Francis, St. Augustin, the fathers of Mercy, and the Jesuits, are so spendidly decorated, as to surpass description. . . . The altars, from their very bases to the borders of the paintings, are covered with massive silver. . . . The walls . . . are hung with velvet or tapestry. . . . The whole church is covered with plate, or something equal to it in value; so that divine service is performed with a magnificence scarce to be imagined. . . .[3]

Even in the richest mining centers and administrative capitals of Brazil and Spanish America, no secular construction rivaled the cathedrals and the richest convents. In Brazil, government policy prohibited governors and other officials from constructing unnecessarily expensive residences and office buildings. The viceregal palaces of Lima and Mexico City were large, well-constructed buildings but lacked the architectural interest of the great palaces of Europe. Few secular buildings, other than perhaps the palace of Cortés, compared favorably with European ones.

Typically, the buildings of church and state as well as the residences of the wealthiest and most powerful royal officials, prelates, and elite families fronted on central plazas where the city's primary markets were held. Many buildings in colonial city centers had exterior arcades to shelter buyers and sellers from the elements. In some cities the municipal government provided separate market stalls.

The City as Arena

The central plaza served as an arena for a variety of public spectacles. During the year, numerous secular and religious processions concluded with a mass at the cathedral. The order in the processions reflected the colonial social hierarchy, with prelates, high-level secular officials, and *caballeros* enjoying places of honor. Deviation from this expected system of preferment provoked protests and even litigation. Commercial and artisan corporations maintained a similar hierarchy. Bullfights, *autos da fé,* and public executions also drew enormous crowds to the plaza.

The ostentatious display of the colonial elite impressed European visitors. Thomas Gage, an English-born Catholic priest resident in Mexico and Central America in the early seventeenth century, wrote admiringly about the richly decorated coaches that filled the streets of Mexico City. In the late afternoon fashionable men and women paraded around the tree-lined park in the center of the city. Young men dressed in their finest clothes rode horses, and older men and women rode in coaches driven by black slaves in bright liveries. Even the viceroy often appeared with members of his court. Venders sold cool drinks and sweets to those who stopped to watch this elaborate ritual.

Courting and flirtation were also part of the elite's life. Gage wrote of duels and other violent confrontations caused by overly direct attention to women by ardent admirers. Some contemporary accounts noted the scandal created by the visible presence of prostitutes or the mistresses of prominent citizens. By the eighteenth century, even lesser cities like Buenos Aires provided parks or shaded straight routes where their elites could amuse themselves.

The elite's houses were distinguished by their scale and construction. Most were two-story dwellings built of cut stone or brick, often with interior patios and attached carriage houses and stables. The exteriors were seldom decorated. Heavy shutters protected windows, but second-story balconies, their privacy protected by carved blinds, provided a view of the street below. An abundance of sitting rooms and bedrooms offered more privacy.

A contract signed in 1631 for the construction of a house in Popayán

Elite residence in Lima, Peru

illustrates: The master carpenter, Francisco González Leuro, built a two-story house facing the central plaza for the wealthy merchant Diego Daza. The first floor held four two-room shops and some storage space. The second floor contained four bedrooms and a sitting room with a balcony and large shuttered windows. Servants probably slept downstairs. Almost certainly the kitchen was a separate building behind the residence.

This type of floor plan was common. Even the wealthiest colonial merchants used the first-floor rooms of multistory homes and the corner rooms of single-story homes for retail activities. The floor plan of a merchant's home in Córdoba, Argentina, for example, shows the front left-hand corner room to be used for commercial activity. Many home owners not directly involved in trade or manufacture also rented space to small

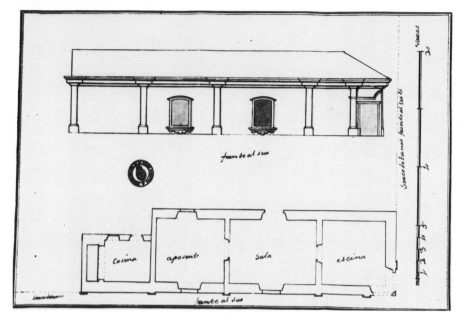

Architect's design for combination residence and artisan shop

shopkeepers and artisans. The result was a nearly universal intermixing of commerce, manufacture, and housing throughout the cities of colonial Brazil and Spanish America.

The homes of high-ranking officials, mine owners, wealthy merchants, and other members of the colonial elite were richly decorated. Their wills often specified in detail chairs and tables imported from Spain, china, carpets, and silk curtains carried by the Asian trade, and settings of silver produced by skilled colonial artisans. Some households contained musical instruments, and a few had libraries, mostly filled with religious and moral tracts. Paintings, statuary, and other decorative objects were also typically religious in nature, but by the eighteenth century, secular art, particularly portraits, was increasingly popular.

Away from the central plaza lived the majority of the poor, mostly Indians, *castas,* and free blacks, in sprawling impoverished *barrios* that generally lacked the orderliness of the central city's grid. Streets were narrower and unpaved. During rainy seasons the heavy carts and mule trains that connected colonial cities to agricultural and mining communities turned the streets into seas of mud where pedestrians passed at some peril. During dry seasons, winds coated passersby with the dust from the unpaved, often dung-covered, thoroughfares. The small, mud-colored adobe houses of the urban poor fronted directly on the street. Only parish churches and poorer convents afforded architectural relief from the monotonous and squalid landscape of these humble suburbs.

Yet significant differences in status and material conditions could be found in the *barrios* as well. Some poor Spaniards, usually recent immigrants, lived among the *castas*. Skilled Indian artisans and a small number of traditional Indian political authorities represented the upper end of the neighborhood social pyramid. Below them were market gardeners, laborers, porters, and petty merchants. At the very bottom were Indians temporarily drawn to the city as *repartimiento* workers or engaged in voluntary, unskilled day labor.

Housing conditions in the poor *barrios* differed dramatically from those in the central *traza*. Most desirable were the large apartment blocks owned by wealthy investors or the Church and privately owned single family dwellings. Very few urban wage earners, however, could afford to rent or own such housing. The majority of colonial urban working-class families lived in single rooms or rooms divided by a blanket and shared with other families. Single men and women often lived in the back rooms of the commerical and manufacturing establishments where they worked. The less fortunate found shelter in hallways, storerooms, or patios for a few *reales* a month. For the totally destitute, life on the street was a last resort.

The relatively high cost of housing, particularly housing adequate for family life, forced many young men and women to defer marriage and childbearing. It also meant that working-class women and children were much more vulnerable to intimidation, sexual assaults, and common insults. In this environment, husbands and fathers commonly found themselves defending their family's honor with knives or fists.

Members of the working class owned few material possessions. Probate

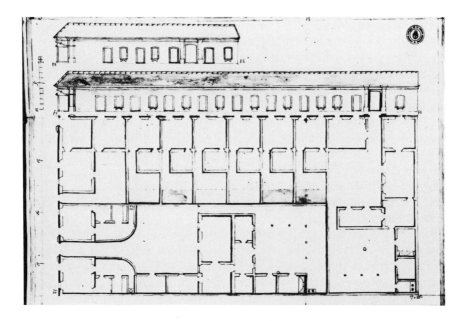

Architect's design for an apartment block

records suggest that the homes of unskilled workers, journeymen, and street peddlers contained little more than a few straight-backed chairs, rough tables, a chest, and straw-filled mattresses. Food was eaten with one's hands or with a knife or spoon from wooden or cheap ceramic plates. The entire wardrobes of most men and women were on their backs, although many did own an extra shirt or a poncho that could double as a blanket at night.

Most of the unsanitary, dangerous, and noisy urban businesses were located in suburban *barrios*. Bakeries and the kilns of brickmakers that posed fire threats, slaughterhouses and tanneries that exuded noxious odors, and the corrals that serviced local and long-distance freight businesses were scattered among the homes of the poor.

Numerous gaming and drinking establishments provided some pleasure and diversion for lower-class males. Mexico City, Lima, and other large cities had dozens of regulated dispensaries, but unlicensed bars were common throughout colonial Latin America. The beverages of choice changed from one region to another, but the urban poor consumed enormous amounts of *pulque, chicha,* rum, wine, and other alcoholic beverages. Drunkenness and related acts of violence, like the endemic poverty and political powerlessness that supported them, were familiar features of the urban landscape.

Rural Settlement

Two settlement patterns predominated in the countryside. Both Iberians and the indigenous high civilizations emphasized the village over dispersed rural settlement. Where these heritages overlapped, mainly in Mesoamerica and the Andean zone, rural life centered on the village. On the periphery of these areas, where grazing was more important than agriculture—for example, in Brazil, the Río de la Plata region, and the *llanos* of Venezuela—dispersed residential patterns were more common, if not always predominant.

Villages were not miniature cities. Few had a grid pattern or large-scale religious or secular buildings. The social focus was as likely to be the general store as the church. Smaller villages commonly had a church, but rarely a resident priest. In these agricultural communities, farmers lived near one another and walked to their fields. This pattern was particularly strong where Indian populations maintained their preconquest communal landholding system.

Residential construction depended on adobe and local timber. Houses typically had a single room and a separate kitchen constructed of less substantial material. More prosperous families added additional rooms to the original structure as their needs changed and resources grew. In some places, corrals were attached directly to residences, but in other regions they were located on the fringe of the village. Thomas Gage left a vivid portrait of rural housing in the Indian and *casta* villages of Guatemala:

> Their houses are but poor thatched cottages, without any upper rooms, but commonly only one or two rooms below. They dress their meat in the middle of one, and they make a compass for fire with two or three stones, without any chimney to convey the smoke away. This spreadth itself about the room and fillth the thatch and the rafters so with soot that all the room seemth to be a chimney. The next room, where sometimes are four or five beds according to the family, is also not free from smoke and blackness. The poorer sort have but one room where they eat, dress their meat, and sleep. . . . Neither have they in their houses much to lose, earthen pots, and pans, and dishes, and cups to drink their chocolate being the chief commodities in their house. There is scarce any house which hath not also in the yard a stew [sweat house], which is their chief physic when they feel themselves distempered.[4]

Large Estates

Large estates, many painstakingly amassed over years through numerous small grants, purchases, bequests, and usurpations of native lands, dominated much of the most valuable countryside in many parts of Latin America by the early seventeenth century. The lay and ecclesiastical owners of these estates earned profits by selling agricultural and pastoral products. Location, climate, and access to labor, however, affected both what they could produce and whether the market would be primarily local, regional, intercolonial, or international. The most heavily capitalized large estates were plantations focused on the international market. The sugar plantations *(engenhos)* developed in Brazil after the mid-sixteenth century served as a model for the later Spanish plantations *(ingenios)* in the Caribbean. Tobacco, indigo, and cacao also were often produced on plantations. Less capitalized estates often devoted to growing wheat or other grains or raising livestock were variously termed *haciendas* or *estancias* in Spanish America and *fazendas* in Brazil. Location frequently precluded their production's being sold beyond nearby markets. Northern New Spain was a classic example of colonial *haciendas* established to serve a regional market, in this case Zacatecas and other mining centers.

Plantations

The tropical plantation was the rural economic enterprise most completely integrated into the world economy. Its products were bought and sold in a highly competitive international market, yet its characteristic labor system, chattel slavery, was clearly a legacy of the precapitalist past. The social relationships and architectural forms of the plantation reflected these contradictions.

The Brazilian *engenho* shared two characteristics with the *hacienda:* its extensive landholding and, compared with urban environments, its physical isolation. Important differences were manifested in the architecture, however. First, sugar cultivation required a much larger and more expensive labor force than did the livestock raising and agriculture of the *hacienda*. The presence of more workers compelled planters to build larger residential compounds. In addition, the chronic problem of slave runaways added security considerations to the housing design. Second, sugar refining was a complex, multistage procedure, and plantations thus required large investments in physical plant. Separate buildings for crushing the cane, boiling and skimming the juice, and storing the final product were needed. Finally, because enormous profits were earned during boom periods, prosperous plantation owners had surplus capital with which to construct impressive residences.

The *casa grande* was commonly built in a Portuguese style. Its more prominent characteristics included a tower, roofs that inclined on all four sides, external stairs, and a long veranda. Most were two-story structures. Family life was largely confined to the second story, and the servants used the first floor for food preparation, laundry, and other household tasks. During the heady boom years of the early seventeenth century, successful planters were able to fill their homes with furniture imported from Europe and carpets and ceramics from Asia.

Most slaves lived in barracks, although some plantations had single-family housing. Barracks offered owners seeking to prevent runaways substantial security advantages but severely hampered the development of family life among slaves. The impoverished material conditions in which slaves lived reduced their cultural life to a minimum. Forced isolation limited their access to religious and secular instruction, and collective forms of expression, such as the lay brotherhoods found in the towns, could not be regularly sustained in the harsh work environment of the plantation.

Haciendas

In regions where the population density was very low, *haciendas, estancias,* and *fazendas* provided the physical focus for both social life and production. The owner's large house dominated the *hacienda*'s residential core. Like many plantation owners, however, the *hacendados* were frequently absent, preferring the social life and material culture of the city. Single male employees, particularly those without family in the region, lived in dormitories. Married employees resided in small adobe homes near the owner's house.

Haciendas produced subsistence goods as well as a market surplus and usually contained a blacksmith's shop and often a pottery and carpentry shop as well. Some of the wealthiest *haciendas* maintained a chapel, although resident priests were seldom present. The largest units covered many square miles and had outlying corrals, line shacks, and some dispersed housing for tenants.

Isolated Rural Dwellings

The small ranches and farms of freeholders and tenants shared the rural landscape with the *haciendas,* plantations, and, at times, Indian villages and missions. Isolated family housing was scattered along the northern frontier of New Spain, in the southern *pampa* of the Río de la Plata, and in the interior grazing area, the *llanos,* of Venezuela. The inhabitants were very poor. They used adobe or woven sticks covered with mud to construct their houses. Doors and window coverings, if there were any, were fashioned from animal skins. Furniture was almost unknown. Cattle skulls served as chairs, and packed-earth platforms covered with straw or skins, as beds. The physical isolation of these dwellings diminished the material and emotional supports of the traditional Iberian and indigenous social networks. Other forms of cultural support—literacy and access to religious consolation among them—also were directly dependent on population density.

The architectural environment of colonial Latin America helped shape and control a diverse mix of competing social groups. As in the advanced preconquest indigenous societies, colonial city planning and urban architecture contained a political message: The colonial cities asserted and sustained the authority of the small local white elites. The monumental architecture of the city center—the labor and wealth frozen in the walls and decorations of the cathedrals, convents, governmental offices, and palaces—served to awe and intimidate the masses. When used as an arena for *autos da fé,* bullfights, and executions, the central plazas helped direct the energies and anger of the masses toward safe symbolic targets.

At another level, the physical settings provided by houses, gaming establishments, taverns, shops, and small manufacturers operated more subtly to help fashion the values of family and class. This context was more directly the result of the inequalities imposed by the colonial economy and Iberian social attitudes. The physical environment sometimes shaped and sometimes reinforced colonial perceptions of race and gender, decisions about marriage and child rearing, and feelings of solidarity with or alienation from coworkers. More than a place to reside and work, the urban and rural living environments reflected both the highest aspirations and the deepest despair present in the colonial world.

Colonial Society: Race, Culture, and Class

The formation and evolution of colonial society occurred within a context of rapid and profound demographic and economic change. The initial simplicity of the society created by conquest could not be sustained, despite the efforts of the conquerors and churchmen. As time passed, social distinctions proliferated. The dramatic decline and forced relocation of the indigenous populations, the contemporary immigration of thousands of

Europeans whose claims of high status were not legitimized by association with the conquest, the development of the African slave trade, and the rapid growth of a racially mixed population combined to overwhelm the social categories and economic arrangements established in the first decades of colonial rule.

Spanish America

Social organization on the Iberian peninsula strongly influenced that of the colonial society. Both Castilian and Portuguese societies were divided into three estates—nobles, clerics, and commoners—and a number of corporate bodies, each with its own set of privileges or *fueros*. The first two estates enjoyed special privileges, such as tax exemptions and judicial rights, that separated them from the third estate which comprised over 90 percent of the population. Individuals from any estate who participated in certain activities or were members of certain institutions also enjoyed *fueros*. Artisan guilds, for example, exercised substantial control over their members and enjoyed significant independence from the influence of noblemen and royal bureaucrats. In specified circumstances, universities exercised judicial authority over students, faculty, and other members of their communities, an authority that could be defended against the competing claims of other powerful institutions.

The importance of military service in the formation of the Castilian nobility provided the backdrop for claims to nobility made by Spanish conquerors, early settlers, and their descendants. Few conquistadors or early settlers could legitimately boast the title *don*. Their daughters and especially grandchildren and later descendants, however, routinely used *don* or *doña* on the justification that their ancestors had been ennobled through participation in the conquest and settlement of the New World. This general assumption of *hidalgo* status was also based on the exemption of Spanish colonists from tribute, a fiscal privilege that corresponded to the nobility's exemption from the direct tax that commoners paid in Castile.

Once the conquest had ended and the conquistadors and first settlers had reaped their initial rewards, birth increasingly replaced personal action as the primary determinant of an individual's place in society. The concept of blood purity *(limpieza de sangre)*, the absence of any Jewish or Muslim antecedents, became extremely important in fifteenth-century Spain, and its transfer to the New World was inevitable. The child of two Spanish parents entered life with advantages denied other children. Spanish birth linked the child with the conquerors, brought exemption from direct taxation (tribute), and established special claims on patronage in civil and ecclesiastical careers. The *mestizo* children of the great conquistadors, of course, provided an exception to this general rule. However, this small group was absorbed by the Spanish elite within one or two generations.

Opportunities to enter the upper levels of Spanish society were greater in the age of conquest than at any other time in the colonial era. The most successful conquistadors, regardless of their social background, were able to turn their *encomiendas,* local offices, modest land grants, and assorted economic activities into a political and economic base that could sustain social prominence for themselves and their heirs. Their very success, however, attracted a new and larger flood of immigrants. In a remarkably short time, colonial urban centers contained elements of nearly every Castilian class and corporation, except for the absence or near absence of high-ranking nobles.

Spaniards

Conquest placed *españoles* atop the colonial social hierarchy. This group included Spaniards born in Spain (peninsulars) or in the New World (creoles) and, especially in the first generation, legitimate and legitimized children born of Spanish men and Indian women. The number of Spaniards who actually participated in the conquest, of course, was very small compared with the number of immigrants who arrived in the decades that followed. This enlarged flow of European immigrants added both social and occupation diversity to the society established by the conquest.

Some conquistadors, early settlers, and later arrivals were able to gain and sustain the wealth necessary to maintain a prominent position in the emerging urban centers of the new colonies. Tribute income from *encomiendas,* trade, mining, ranching, agriculture, or a combination of these activities provided substantial wealth for a fortunate few. These beneficiaries of the colonial order, along with high-ranking civil and ecclesiastical officeholders, formed small local elites constantly renewed through intermarriage and the incorporation of successive generations of newly successful entrepreneurs and royal appointees sent from the Old World.

In Lima and Mexico City, among other locations, a small minority comprising the landed elite sought to perpetuate their family's wealth and prestige through the feudal device of entail *(mayorazgo).* Following the owner's demonstration that an estate was valuable enough to justify entailment and paying required fees, the Crown approved the formation of a *mayorazgo.* This institution prevented the heirs from selling or dividing the entailed property, and thus it passed intact from generation to generation. It is, perhaps, an indication of the market orientation and materialism of colonial society that very few wealthy families, only about one hundred in colonial Mexico, sought to establish *mayorazgos.* More common procedures for achieving formal recognition of elite social status included securing membership in a military order or a title of nobility.

A knighthood in the military orders of Santiago, Calatrava, or Alcántara confirmed one's nobility and provided status and prestige without constraining economic flexibility. A handful of Americans had entered the Order of Santiago before the conquest of Peru, but few followed them until after 1620. By that year only forty-two American men had become knights in all of the orders combined. A rapid increase followed, however, and nearly four hundred more knighthoods were awarded before 1700 and over one hundred in the next half-century.

Although the Crown bestowed the title of marquis on both Cortés and Pizarro as a reward for their leadership in the conquests of Mexico and Peru, it subsequently granted few such titles until the 1680s. By 1680 only six titles had been granted to residents in Mexico, five to Spaniards, and one, the conde de Moctezuma, to a *mestizo* descendant of the Aztec royal family. The residents of Peru were more fortunate, probably a reflection of the immense mineral riches being funneled to Spain through the City of Kings until the late seventeenth century. By 1750 over eighty-five titles had been granted to residents in Peru, as opposed to only twenty-seven to residents in Mexico. These later titles rewarded a few prominent bureaucrats, organizers of militia units, and wealthy individuals who had donated large sums to the royal treasury in times of financial need and frequently in explicit exchange for a title. Although peninsulars often received the original titles, creoles routinely inherited them. Thus over time the titled nobility of Spanish America became heavily creole.

The majority of the Spanish population, in contrast with the elite, filled a host of less prestigious occupations. Some owned modest rural property or an urban store. Others filled ecclesiastical positions, practiced law or served as notaries, held minor offices, clerked in retail shops, owned or managed a tavern, supervised urban or rural laborers or mine workers, plied a trade, or even performed unskilled manual labor. Spaniards, in short, engaged in almost every economic activity. Most were neither wealthy nor socially prominent. Like the fabled poor *hidalgo* who sat beneath his coat of arms and ate a humble garlic soup, pride in birth and its accompanying privileges rather than substantial means separated most Spaniards from the remainder of the population. This ethnic identity tended to be more important among the least-advantaged immigrants. Peninsulars who entered the New World elite based their sense of social place on the more dependable supports of wealth and access to political power.

Although Spaniards shared pride in a racial heritage that at least theoretically they held in common, place of birth divided them in a way that transcended even their occupational heterogeneity. Spaniards who had emigrated from the peninsula retained strong local and regional loyalties. They were *sevillanos,* Andalusians, Extremadurans, or Basques rather than "Spaniards." Regardless of their birthplace, however, these peninsulars considered themselves superior to their New World cousins. Spaniards born in America also identified with their city or region of birth, considering themselves, for example, *limeños* or *caraqueños,* but for convenience historians usually refer to them as creoles.

Peninsulars engaged in the same range of activities as did creoles but were especially conspicuous in wholesale commerce and high posts in the colonial administration and the ecclesiastical hierarchy. In contrast, creoles dominated landowning and mining and by 1600 were also well represented in local offices. Their entry into most higher bureaucratic positions generally increased until the middle of the eighteenth century.

All Spaniards shared some cultural traits, joined in the avid pursuit of honors, office, and economic gain, and rejected employment as manual laborers whenever possible. The creoles, although they resented the peninsulars' arrogance, generally imitated their snobbishness as they looked down on the rest of society. Antagonism between creoles and peninsulars was far worse among the less affluent in each group than among the more successful. Socially ambitious creole fathers often provided rich dowries in order to arrange marriages between their daughters and Spanish immigrants who offered in exchange racial purity and undiluted metropolitan culture rather than great wealth. These marriage alliances between American families and immigrants created over time a socially coherent elite united by kinship and class interest. The apex of Spanish society in each major urban center of the New World was therefore made up of peninsulars and creoles frequently united by ties of family, godparentage, and economic interest. Although the rivalry between peninsulars and creoles was an inherent result of colonial status, most immigrants were eventually assimilated into preexisting networks of kinship and economic interest. During periods of increased immigration, when new arrivals actively sought to assert their metropolitan superiority, threatened creoles and long-established peninsulars usually acted in concert to protect their existing advantages.

Indians

Before the arrival of Europeans, the New World was home to a large indigenous population divided among numerous cultural and linguistic groups. Even in the vast territories subject to the Aztec and Inca states, significant cultural diversity existed. Each society was, in turn, internally diverse. Although all sedentary agricultural societies were socially stratified, this hierarchy was most complex among the highly urbanized cultures of Mesoamerica and the Andes. As Spanish colonial society matured, these distinctions of culture and class were compressed or eradicated.

This process began with the creation of a racial identity, Indian, that had not existed before the conquest. The development and implementation of Indian policy by agents of the Crown gave this artifact of colonial rule political and economic meaning. Policies intended to ameliorate injustice, as in the New Laws, or to enrich the exchequer, as in the imposition of tribute, had the effect of blurring distinctions of culture and class. In Mexico, for example, the application of tribute eliminated a traditional distinction between commoners with and without access to communal land. In Peru *yanaconas* improved their status relative to *ayllu* members by associating with the conquistadors.

Chastened by the demographic tragedy of the Caribbean colonies and committed to the conversion of the Indians, the Spanish Crown initially sought to promote the development of a racially segregated society on the mainland. Legislation barred Spaniards, other than missionaries, and *castas* from Indian settlements. Eventually, even *encomenderos* were restricted from visiting their tribute populations. But this attempt at social engineering soon collapsed. The effects of epidemic disease, resettlement efforts, and the growth of the market economy overwhelmed the statutory isolation of the indigenous peoples. The increasing pace and duration of contacts irrevocably altered the native culture.

The conquistadors and the Crown initially recognized the legitimacy of the native elites. Both Cortés and Pizarro tried to advance the process of pacification by using captive rulers drawn from the traditional ruling families, but the experiment quickly ended in Mexico. The last Inca pretender died in Spain in 1627, a completely Hispanized seeker of royal patronage. Some Spaniards married Indian women of the highest rank in order to lay claim to traditional tribute and other privileges. As a result, within two generations the upper ranks of the Indian nobility of central Mexico and Peru became racially mixed and culturally Spanish. The general pattern was for the indigenous royal families and great territorial nobles to lose ground or be pushed aside.

The progressive deterioration of the chiefdom of Tepaneca in the Valley of Mexico illustrates this phenomenon. Juan de Guzmán Itzollinqui became the native ruler in 1526. His inheritance included substantial property and the services of some four hundred retainers. He received an annual tribute of corn, wheat, chiles, tomatoes, salt, wood, and fodder in addition to labor services. His heir was less fortunate. The marqués del Valle, a son of Cortés, seized some traditional lands in the 1560s, and changes in the law forced the *cacique* to pay for labor that traditionally had been offered as tribute. By 1575 the patrimony of the grandson of the original colonial-era *cacique* was reduced to fifty-one retainers and a tribute of 23 pesos. In the late eighteenth century, the incumbent *cacique* financed a costly personal appeal at the Spanish court by working as a carpenter. The desperate act failed, and this pathetic remnant of the traditional Mesoamerican ruling class died in a Spanish prison.

Local authorities, however, survived because they were essential to the functioning of the colonial labor and fiscal systems. The *caciques* of Mexico, the *batabs* of Yucatan, and the *kurakas* of the Andes, for example, oversaw the collection of tribute payments and labor for the *repartimiento/mita*. The men who held these positions usually came from traditional families, but there were numerous cases in which ambitious commoners who proved useful to the Spanish or were tied to them by shared economic interests pushed aside rightful leaders. Although materially poor relative to much of the Spanish population, these Indian leaders often owned private land and livestock and were exempted from tribute and labor service.

As the colonial order matured, this class of cross-cultural intermediaries became increasingly Hispanized. Fernando Uz, a hereditary *batab* in the

Yucatán in the early seventeenth century, was granted the position of Indian governor and later served as translator and senior aide to the Spanish governor. Other members of this class used the Spanish legal system to further their own interests or the interests of their communities against *encomenderos* or landowners, or with *corregidores* and priests. In Peru, ethnic descendants of the Incas went to court to protect their exemption from the *mita*. Use of the courts to gain and retain the office of *kuraka* was also common. The proliferation of new secular and religious offices within the Indian communities provided additional opportunities for traditional families. Indian *alcaldes* and *regidores* were generally related to local rulers. Offices in church-affiliated institutions like *cofradías* and secular positions in the local church like choirmaster, teacher, and lay assistant were also filled from the traditional ruling families.

The great mass of Indians found the weight of the colonial order a nearly intolerable burden. In the decades immediately following the conquest, the goods they produced and the labor they provided sustained the combined weight of a growing Spanish population and the surviving vestiges of the traditional ruling class. Once the Indian population began to decline, demands for labor and tribute undermined communal bonds, and so large numbers of individuals, and sometimes entire families, migrated. They headed for the bush beyond Spanish control, or more often they sought work on Spanish farms and ranches or in other Indian communities. As peons or *forasteros* they were exempt from forced labor.

Indian communities survived the colonial experience, but only after being substantially altered. Communal landholding practices in particular proved remarkably resilient, despite the effects of population loss and the advent of market forces. The Indians' oversight of numerous local affairs also continued in many regions, especially those distant from Spanish urban centers. Yet the vitality and relative abundance of the precontact agricultural community were lost because of external demands for labor and land. In its place developed the impoverished peasant village still visible in Latin America.

Throughout the colonial period the population continuously flowed away from Indian communities and toward Spanish cities and towns. These migrants were pushed by the harsh realities of tribute and labor service and pulled by the appearance of greater independence and opportunity. Most lived the hand-to-mouth existence of day laborers or *obraje* workers, but a small minority learned trades and entered the class of propertied workers. Whether successful or not, these migrants were the primary contributors to a process of assimilation and cultural change that helped produce the colonial working class.

Blacks

Men and women of African descent first appeared in colonial Spanish America during the period of conquest and initial settlement. In Iberia the statutory and customary status of blacks was far inferior to that held by whites, regardless of their class or corporate identity. Black slaves were legally defined as chattel, despite a limited body of Spanish law and church teaching that recognized their humanity. Black freemen carried the stigma of their enslaved ancestors and were constrained by a broad array of discriminatory legislation.

In the New World the crushing military defeat suffered by the Indians and the rapid devaluation of Indian culture that resulted from the imposition of colonial rule and the Christian religion temporarily invested blacks with an intermediary social position. They were, in effect, representatives of European culture and power. As allies of the conquerors, blacks served militarily in the pacification of frontier zones, managed and supervised Indian laborers, and directed the urban household staffs of the wealthiest and most powerful Spaniards.

This unprecedented power led to accusations that blacks were abusing the Indian population. Although the actual abuses by blacks seldom were worse than those committed by Europeans, the Crown promulgated a series of unenforceable laws prohibiting contacts between blacks and Indians. Indian villages were placed off limits. Marriages were prohibited, and blacks who had sexual relations with Indian women were given one hundred lashes for the first offense and had their ears cut off for the second.

Throughout the colonial period, mutilations, whippings, and brutal executions were the all-too-predictable responses to transgressions by slaves and black freemen. Violent runaways and rebels, in particular, were frequently executed. Regardless of whatever material or political advantages that the blacks gained relative to the Indians, the white legal system always punished their crimes more severely.

With the development of the African slave trade, greater availability and lower prices led to the widespread use of slaves in mining and agriculture and enabled new groups to purchase slaves. By the end of the seventeenth century nearly every Spanish household, including those of artisans and others of modest means, had one or more slaves. Some members of the Indian elite also owned black slaves.

The development of the slave trade had important consequences for the evolving colonial social structure. Direct trade with Africa broke the close association between the black population and the dominant culture of the European conquerors. The cultural distinctiveness of an increasingly African slave population and the social effects of harsh labor and brutal discipline promoted negative racial stereotypes and reinforced the effects of discriminatory legislation and racial prejudice brought from Spain.

Because European immigrants never met the colonial demand for skilled labor, slaves and freemen in urban areas gained access to most manual trades, despite discriminatory laws issued to prevent slaves from competing with whites. Male slaves worked in nearly every artisan trade, in lesser-skilled jobs in transportation, and in domestic service. In many larger cities, black artisans even created their own guilds. Many skilled slaves hired

Peruvian woman beating her servant with an iron

their own time and provided their owners with a monthly income. Female slaves dominated most of the urban marketplaces. They also produced and sold sweets, did laundry, and, of course, provided the domestic labor in many Spanish households.

These positions in the urban economy gave slaves opportunities to earn and accumulate money, which led to manumission and the growth of a free black community. Spanish law provided a framework for determining a slave's fair market value and the supervision of his or her self-purchase. As a result, purchased manumissions became the most common road to freedom in both Spanish and Portuguese America. Masters also freed without payment other slaves, particularly children and the elderly. In was common for freed slaves to work for the freedom of family members who remained in bondage. Indeed, the commitment and enterprise of black families were as responsible for the rapid growth in the free black population as were Spanish law and Catholic beliefs. Although manumission was far more common in Latin America than in the British colonies, the majority of African slaves and their American-born descendants lived and died in bondage.

The most important organizations of the black community were based on European models. *Cofradías,* lay brotherhoods, played a crucial role in organizing the religious life of the black community. These also provided some medical assistance, burial services, and limited survivor benefits for members. Perhaps more importantly, they organized black participation in the secular and religious celebrations that gave expression to communal civic consciousness. In areas with large African-born populations, there were also social organizations based on African identities—Congos, Benguelas, or Yorubas, for example. Besides uniting individuals from distinct cultural and language groups, these associations helped keep alive elements of African tradition and also provided an organized means for adapting to the harsh realities of the colonial slave system.

Castas

Miscegenation among Spaniards, Indians, and Africans produced a large racially mixed stratum in colonial society. Colonists developed a confused and confusing nomenclature to describe the many physical types that resulted from contacts among the three original racial groups and their mixed descendants: *mestizos,* mulattos, *zambos, castizos, cholos,* and *chinos,* among others. These terms had the appearance of precision but were applied casually and unpredictably. There were also important regional differences in usage. The child of mixed Indian-African heritage was called a *zambo* in Mexico and a *chino* in Buenos Aires. The nomenclature suggests that colonial society recognized the difference between a *mestizo,* an Indian-white mixture, and a *castizo,* a *mestizo*-white mixture, and then favored the aspirations of the *castizo.* In actual practice, proximity to European cultural norms demonstrated in speech, dress, manner, occupation, and wealth proved more important to determining status of the racially mixed than did pigmentation or phenotype.

By the middle of the seventeenth century, *castas*—all free men and women of mixed ancestry—were the largest population sector in most urban centers and mining camps. Even in rural areas the *casta* presence was expanding rapidly relative to that of other groups. The increasing demographic significance of the racially mixed group resulted from the often precipitous decline in Indian population and the limited emigration of Europeans and from the workings of the racial nomenclature that assigned to the *casta* group all children born to parents from two different racial categories.

The disruptions of the early colonial period—in particular, the breakdown of traditional social controls in the Indian communities and the presence of large numbers of rootless, single men—encouraged casual sexual encounters and concubinage. Although some Spaniards married Indian women to gain access to traditional tribute and land rights, most cross-racial relations were temporary. In a few cases, Spanish fathers legitimized their offspring and provided an inheritance. More typically, *mestizos* were forced to accept the status and limited material circumstances of their

Español, y Mulato, Morisco.

Español, è Ynaio, Mestizo.

Two eighteenth-century representations of race mixing

mother's heritage or move to a Spanish city to seek their fortunes on the margin of the Spanish economy. Generally, as the *mestizo* population expanded, its social status fell. However, *mestizos* retained their advantages relative to those of the Indians. Some *mestizos* gained positions at the lowest levels of the Church and bureaucracy, and they also held a much higher proportion of supervisory and skilled positions.

By the mid-sixteenth century the Crown realized that the new racial groups were threatening the stability of colonial society. A 1553 order referred to "many orphaned *mestizo* youths badly inclined both by their nature and lack of instruction and employment." Another order spoke of *mestizos* in Peru committing murder, robbery, adultery, and other crimes. Still another order referred to the growing number of *mestizos* in Guatemala who needed employment. A half-century later this litany continued, with *mestizos* portrayed as "vicious and lost people" whose "evil inclinations and customs" threatened the social order. The mixed-race group of African descent was described in even more negative terms.

From the beginning, the Crown tried to prevent marriage, and more casual relations, between whites and blacks. Both racial prejudice and the stigma of slavery contributed to the genesis of this policy. Legal obstacles and common prejudice discriminated against all unions between whites and blacks, although occasionally there were marriages. When in the seventeenth century some Spanish officers in Santo Domingo married black women, the town coucil asked the king to bar them from future promotions. Concubinage, however, was sufficiently widespread to show up frequently in probate records and in court actions throughout the colonies. Many wealthy Spanish males maintained black mistresses. Some were kept in lavish surroundings that became scandals and led to the passage of largely unenforceable sumptuary laws prohibiting black women from wearing gold and silver jewelry and silk clothing.

Despite this context of legal discrimination and prejudice, the racially mixed black population became essential to the colonial structure. By the eighteenth century, mulattos (also called *pardos*) held many skilled manual jobs in mines, artisan shops, other manufacturing enterprises, and agriculture. The colonial military establishment depended on this sector of the population to fill its enlisted ranks, and the formation of segregated urban militia offered some *pardos* the opportunity to reach officer ranks. To the disgust of the white elite, the most affluent *pardos* purchased licenses, *cédulas de gracias al sacar,* that made them legally "white" in order to gain admission to universities and other institutions officially closed to them.

Most of the discriminatory colonial legislation focused on the racially mixed population, yet this same group clearly established itself at a midpoint in the socioeconomic hierarchy. Many historians have argued that this advantage arose from the racism of the white elite. No one can dispute that lighter color and European features benefited some *castas,* but the greater racial affinity between whites and *castas* was less important than were the cultural differences between whites and the subordinate Indian and African groups in determining social stratification.

The conquest did more than substitute one political order for another; it also created a new social system and a new economy. Colonial institutions and practices were derived with few alterations from the European experience. As a result, success, whether measured in terms of power or material wealth, was closely associated with the values, skills, and manners of the dominant culture. In this environment both Indian and African groups were disadvantaged. Slavery constrained the achievement and integration of the Africans. The persistence of the traditional culture and institutions worked to limit the Indians' adaptation to the new order, although it did offer some protections from the destructive effects of the marketplace.

Cut loose from these restraints, the *castas* adopted the Spanish language, Christianity, and European skills. Although this process was commonly greeted with derision and discrimination, the endemic shortage of European skilled laborers forced the colonial elite to reward assimilation materially. The *castas* were, then, both less inhibited in their pursuit of individual advantage and less protected from failure. By the eighteenth century, the results of *casta* assimilation were visible throughout Spanish America.

Brazil

The social structure of Brazil was essentially similar to that in Spanish America. In the mature colony, the distribution of wealth and power correlated closely with the racial status system. The elite was white; the impoverished rural masses were black or Indian; and the intermediary groups of the city and countryside were largely racial mixtures. However, there were important differences.

The political organization and economic structures of Brazil's indigenous population were less compatible with the new colonial order than were those of Mesoamerica and Peru. As a result, few Portuguese settlers married Indian women. There were no Brazilian social equivalents of the sisters and daughters of Moctezuma or Atahualpa. In addition, Brazil did not have a hereditary Indian leadership class that survived the conquest and evolved to assume an intermediary role in the colonial order. Nor did a semifeudal class of *encomenderos* develop in Brazil. Instead, the social order rooted itself in the materialism and fluid social relations associated with the Atlantic commercial system. Finally, the collapse of the Indian population and the compensatory development of the African slave trade occurred earlier and was more complete in Brazil than in the Spanish colonies.

At the top of the Brazilian social order were the Portuguese immigrants who dominated trade and the bureaucracies of church and state and the largely native born, *mazombo,* landowning class. Social contacts, business alliances, and intermarriage between these groups were common. Although rivalry and competition between the native born and Portuguese existed, it appears to have been less important than was creole-peninsular antagonism in Spanish America in defining political and economic life. The interpenetration of native-born and immigrant elite groups was enabled in large part by the volatile nature of the sugar industry, which led to high rates of turnover and required the constant injection of new capital, and by the geographic compression of the population along the coast.

Relative to Spanish America, a larger New Christian population, Portuguese-Jewish converts to Christianity, also distinguished the Brazilian social order. Particularly in the period before the Dutch occupation, New Christians in Brazil were able to gain positions of influence and power denied them in Portugal. They dominated commerce and were found in the Church and bureaucracy. They played a crucial role in sustaining contraband trade through Buenos Aires to the silver mines of Peru. Because some New Christians collaborated during the Dutch occupation of Pernambuco (1630–54), in some cases reasserting their Jewish faith, the entire New Christian community suffered a decline following the Portuguese triumph.

Another difference was the weakness of corporate institutions relative to those of the Spanish colonies. Some Portuguese *fidalgos* received land grants in Brazil, but very few members of the nobility ever resided in the colony. Nor did many wealthy planters, administrators, or merchants seek or gain noble status. The Church in Brazil was also much poorer and weaker than in Spanish America. The secular hierarchy was more completely in the pocket of the landowning class, and the regular orders, with the important exception of the Jesuits, lacked the independent economic base and political leverage commonly found in the Spanish colonies. Guilds of artisans and merchants were seldom established and, when present, were weak. Without these traditional corporate institutions, class and especially racial identities assumed more importance.

As the Indian resistance was crushed, thousands of Indians were enslaved. Although essential to the early economy, they had a poor reputation for disciplined labor. As epidemics and military defeat pushed the surviving Indians toward the frontier, African slaves and their Brazilian-born descendants inherited the lowest position in colonial society.

The presence of a large slave population in Portugal, nearly 10 percent of the population, created the legal context for the development of colonial race relations. In addition, the physical and cultural distinctiveness of the African population as well as the material deprivation and statutory inferiority imposed by slavery encouraged the development of negative racial stereotypes that further circumscribed the participation of blacks in society. Free blacks also suffered the discriminatory consequences of race prejudice, although an exceptional few rose to positions of influence. The best known of these exceptional individuals was Henrique Dias, who was one of the heroes of the resistance to Dutch occupation of the Brazilian northeast in the mid-seventeenth century. But even this hero was forced to complain, "I am treated with little respect, with unspeakable words to my person, and no one recognizes me as a soldier."[5]

Of particular note was the importance to the arts of Brazil's black population. Blacks were prominent in all the arts but were most influential in music, painting, and sculpture. The best-known artist was Antonio Lisboa, the son of a Portuguese immigrant and a slave woman. Afflicted with leprosy in middle age, he was known as Aleijadinho, the "little cripple." He designed both the interiors and the exteriors of many of Minas Gerais's finest churches, and he was also a good sculptor, best known for the *Twelve Prophets* at Nosso Senhor de Mattosinhos.

The racially mixed population filled interstices in both rural and urban society. Mixtures of the three original racial groups proliferated in the violent and unsettled early years of the colony. Indian-white and black-Indian mixtures were important in the early decades, particularly in frontier zones and in the grazing industry, but it was the black-white mixtures, the *pardos,* that came to hold the central place in the work force. Free *pardos* and blacks provided much of the skilled urban work force, although Portuguese immigrants made up approximately 30 percent of this group in the largest cities. Mixed-race persons often were supervisors in the sugar industry. Indeed, the *pardos* were essential to the peace and stability of the colony, filling the enlisted ranks of the military and the constabulary. Transportation, construction, and nearly all occupations associated with Atlantic shipping depended on the mixed groups, especially the *pardos.*

As the New World colonial societies matured, a complex mix of racial, cultural, and economic influences determined relations of wealth and power. Although all these societies were hierarchical, sharing an archaic European ideal of a static precapitalist social order, the colonial social realities were, in fact, more fluid and unpredictable than contemporary bureaucratic formulations suggest. The distinction between Indian and European, conquered and conqueror, proved to be remarkably durable. However, as time passed and racially and culturally intermediate groups appeared, the boundary between these two categories lost much of its early precision.

Differences in wealth and power, class differences, were also present from early times. As racial and cultural boundaries blurred, these distinctions increased in importance. A strong correlation between the system of racial stratification and the class structure can be found throughout the colonial period. This correlation was weakest in urban areas during periods of economic expansion and strongest in rural areas remote from market forces. There were obvious exceptions; some traditional Indian noblemen enjoyed relative material abundance, and some immigrants survived only as beggars. Color prejudice and discrimination were, however, mechanisms for distributing wealth and organizing labor: Race relations in colonial Latin America always had a class character.

The Family

The family was the basic social unit in the colonial world. Race, wealth, and occupation all helped define an individual's position in the social structure. These attributes, however, were usually evaluated in the context of the family, not only the biological family, but also the larger set of family relations created by marriage and *compadrazgo*. The advantages, or burdens, of familial associations had a longitudinal character as well. A family's lineage, services to the Crown, and privileges all helped place its individual members within the social order. Thus, to understand the most economically and politically powerful segment of colonial society over time, one must focus on the family—successive generations, marriages, in-laws, and other relatives—and the totality of the family members' economic and political activities, rather than on individuals. Family objectives framed and colored the opportunities and goals of its individual members. At least in part, this power to mold individual choices grew out of the family's ability to grant or withhold assets—for example, credit, land, and political influence—in a society that provided few opportunities for persons with only talent to recommend them. Education, marriage, occupation, and even travel were familial concerns that extended beyond the individual participant.

Although the nuclear family was the most common residential unit, the extended family was the effective social and economic unit for both Iberians and Indians throughout much of the colonial world. The Indian nobility prided itself on its lineage just as much as did the Iberians and was equally capable of exploiting the benefits of familial connections and resources. *Caciques* and nobles normally married within their own rank and thus maintained their social distance from Indian commoners. But even commoners perceived the family as a basic social unit and exercised control over marriage decisions. The continuing importance of kinship groups in Peru and central Mexico testifies to the strength of family ties. In Yucatán, patrilinear extended families of up to five related males, their wives, and unmarried daughters formed the basic economic unit. In many ways it was the strength of these familial associations that allowed Indian communities to survive despite the heavy demands of the colonial regime.

Marriage

In the eyes of the Spanish and Portuguese Crowns and the Catholic Church, the sacrament of marriage alone was the basis for a legitimate family. Although Iberian males in the colonies frequently had nonwhite mistresses before becoming established and supported a separate household for them after marriage, wedding a woman of their own culture and fathering a legitimate family was the usual goal. Although formal dissolution or divorce terminated some marriages, union for life, if not love, was the general rule that underlay Spanish and Portuguese matrimonial practices and the accompanying elaboration of the extended family.

Ancestry influenced the selection of marital partners, but typically marriages throughout colonial society joined persons from the same or adjoining social classes. Relatively few white men married nonwhite women, perhaps because such women were readily available for consenual unions free from marital responsibilities and because such marriages generally led to a decline in the man's status. Mixed-race males routinely married women of similar ancenstry, whereas the women married whites when possible. Indians normally married Indians, although unions with persons of mixed ancestry took place as well, particularly in cities and mining camps. Marriages among black slaves were infrequent, although there is evidence that many lived in long-term consensual unions. The sexual imbalance in the slave trade, obstacles inherent in the legal position of slaves, and often the active discouragement of masters worked to inhibit slave marriages. Nonetheless, over 60 percent of the adult slaves at the Engenho Santana in Ilhéus, Brazil, in 1731 were married or lived in consensual unions. In Peru before 1650, less than 8 percent of slaves aged twenty to twenty-five and less than 15 percent of slaves aged twenty-six to thirty-five married; in both groups women married more frequently than men did. Among free blacks, marriage rates were similar to those for whites.

Age at first marriage varied by sex. Among both whites and Indians, women almost always married earlier than men did. Youthful marriage helped ensure premarital virginity and thus the maintenance of family honor as well as high reproductive capability. White males in Spanish America were normally about four years older than their wives. In Vila Rica, Brazil, in the third quarter of the eighteenth century, white males married at about thirty years of age, whereas their wives were about twenty-two, the same as in the Spanish colonies. Within the white elite of Spanish America, males were often older and females younger at the time of marriage than was the case for nonelite whites. Women of the elite and middle groups were more closely controlled than were poorer women. Visitors to Brazil commonly noted the jealous restraints imposed on women. For example, women of both rural and urban elite families seldom left home without a chaperon, and when they did it was generally for mass or a religious festival. Custom banned their participation in dinner conversation. The males' concern with the chastity of their daughters and the honor of their wives could lead to violence. In fact, courts in both Spanish America and Brazil could send a woman suspected of infidelity to a convent merely on the testimony of her husband or father.

Nearly all women who married in the New World had been born there, although some peninsular women did emigrate to improve their prospects. If elite women married men who were in their mid-thirties or older, however, the husbands were often European immigrants who had reached the colonies in their youth and taken years to prove they were worthy additions to established aristocratic families.

The ongoing incorporation of successful immigrants into colonial elite families was a prominent feature of society in both Brazil and Spanish America. Few immigrant males who married in the Indies were minors; many were in their mid-thirties, and a substantial number were forty or older. Among immigrant merchants and bureaucrats, marriage was commonly deferred until the individual was well established and able to arrange an alliance with a woman who had a dowry. Colonial-born males of wealthy families, in contrast, tended to marry earlier, for they were already established in local society. For example, when Pedro Jiménez de los Cobos, a native and *regidor* of Mexico City, married Clara Leonor del Sen in 1684, he was twenty-seven and she was fourteen. Peninsular Juan Martínez de Lejarzar, in contrast, married a creole woman in Querétaro when he was forty-nine and she was twenty-three. And a number of high court judges of Brazil married much younger Brazilian women.

In Spanish America, where Indians survived in greater numbers than in Brazil, the limited evidence suggests that a higher proportion of Indians than Spaniards married and that Indian males married at an earlier age than did their Spanish counterparts. As did Spaniards, Indian males usually married younger women. *Casta* males commonly married even earlier than did Indians and, unlike whites or Indians, often married women older than themselves. *Casta* brides averaged about twenty-four years of age; the grooms, about twenty-three. The *casta* pattern differed, in part, because this group was largely denied access to both traditional Indian landholding rights and full participation in the Spanish economy.

A significant minority of free adults of all races and social standing remained single. Limited evidence suggests that this was especially true among the Spanish population, in which probably a quarter or more of the men and women over the age of twenty-five never married. This high rate probably reflected both the reluctance of whites to marry below their station and the relatively small pool of acceptable spouses. In addition, Spaniards were given opportunities to follow ecclesiastical careers or enter convents that were normally denied to *castas* or Indians. In Brazil the pool was further reduced, as many elite families sent unmarried daughters to convents in Portugal and the Azores. This practice was banned in 1732, but the foundation of the first convent in Bahia in 1677 had already given elite families a colonial alternative.

Practical concerns as well as romance determined the selection of marriage partners, especially among elite families. Cash and property were often more alluring than physical charms in selecting marriage partners, as marriage linked not just bride and groom but also their families. Marriage offered the opportunity for two prominent families to join and expand their economic and political activities or for a wealthy immigrant or his child or a rising but not yet socially prominent family to unite with a family richer in status than in worldly possessions. Although a woman did not need a dowry to marry, and a declining proportion of women were receiving them by the mid-eighteenth century, a substantial dowry clearly enhanced her ability to contract an advantageous marriage. A dowry provided a bride with some financial security as well as underwriting some of the new couple's expenses. The husband administered the dowry but was responsible for maintaining its value, for it remained the property of his wife and the potential inheritance of her children, or, if she died childless, her family.

The more prosperous a bride's family was, the more apt it was to dower her. The size of the dowry varied with the family's wealth and number of daughters. Few provincial families provided dowries of more than several thousand pesos. In Mexico City, Lima, and Bahia, in contrast, brides from rich noble families often received dowries of cash, jewels, slaves, clothing, art objects, and furniture worth over 10,000 pesos. Some dowries included a house, *hacienda,* or mine, but normally these properties went to male siblings. For instance, when Maria Antonia de la Redonda y Bolívar wed Francisco Delgadillo de Sotomayor in Lima in 1668, she brought with her a dowry worth 61,500 pesos. The future city councilman of Lima, in turn, provided her with *arras* of 20,000 pesos. Even among artisans and petty merchants, however, a small dowry of a few hundred pesos or a slave could provide the opportunity to expand a commercial undertaking or escape from debt.

Arras were the groom's gift to the bride. A sum equal to as much as 10 percent of the groom's assets at the time of the marriage, *arras* became part of the bride's personal estate. The amount reflected the new husband's financial resources while simultaneously improving the bride's own financial future. The wording of the gift often testified to the bride's honor, virginity, and social position.

Family Size

In the absence of any completely reliable means of birth control except sexual abstinence, family size in the colonial world was largely determined by the wife's age at marriage and infant, childhood, and adult mortality rates. A family's economic and social standing also influenced fertility and mortality rates and family size. In early modern Spain, a relatively late marriage age (twenty-five) limited a woman's reproductive period to approximately fifteen years, during which she would bear five or six children. Because the high infant, childhood and adult mortality levels almost always claimed the lives of half of all offspring before they reached adulthood or one of the spouses before the end of the wife's fertile years, the mature family usually included only four or five individuals. Remarriage was common, particularly among men and women with some property, and colonial families often contained children from two or more marriages. Evidence suggests that women in the Spanish colonies married about three years earlier than did women in Spain, and so their average reproductive span might have allowed many of them to bear more children.

Indian women had both higher fertility and a shorter life expectancy

than did *casta* women. Thus, after the devastating pandemics in the Indies
had subsided, Indian family size was about the same as for Castilian peasants. At the other end of the socioeconomic spectrum, elite families in the
Spanish colonies were often larger, as they were among the Castilian nobility, for the better a family's economic circumstances were, the better
chance there was that its children would reach adulthood. For women of
all classes, the complications associated with pregnancy and childbirth
were among the most common causes of early death.

The Family as an Economic Unit

Although all Spanish and Portuguese immigrants to the New World had
ancestors on the Iberian peninsula, the origin of a family that attained elite
status in the colonies could usually be traced to one man, although occasionally the activities of several close relatives, for example, the Pizarro
brothers, brought about a substantial improvement in family fortune. In
Spanish America, the windfalls of the age of conquest, early mining discoveries, the foundation of city councils, and the allocation of *encomiendas*
and plots of urban and rural land to early immigrants immediately created
the first colonial elite families. Able to marry Spanish women who came to
the Americas, the early elite males fathered children whose marriages were
used to further family ambitions. By investing in agricultural and pastoral
activities, trade, offices, mining, and urban properties as appropriate
within the region of residence, they sought to diversify the economic
sources of their wealth.

In the sixteenth century the immediate descendants of *encomenderos*
rarely passed on to their heirs resources equal to those they had inherited.
Few prominent families in the early and mid-seventeenth century traced
their origins to conquerors or *encomenderos*. Castilian inheritance laws
worked against elite families trying to retain their wealth intact, although
they did not lessen the privileges or immediately reduce the social eminence of a prominent family. In addition, the loss of *encomienda* income
due to the effects of epidemics and flight and the natural limits on mining
income both promoted a generational contraction in elite wealth. By 1650
the closing of the frontier in many areas of Spanish America and the beginning of a long period of economic stagnation restricted social mobility and
limited access to the upper levels of the social order. Opportunities in government also were fewer. Most municipal offices passed from generation
to generation; new royal offices were rare.

In seventeenth-century Brazil, expansion into the interior provided
opportunities to accumulate wealth and improve social status earlier than
in the Spanish colonies. Huge cattle ranches spread throughout the Brazilian northeast. The Dias d'Avila and Guedes de Brito families established
de facto sovereignty over the region, waging war against the Indians and
in 1696 even evicting the Jesuits from a nearby mission.

Many elite families died out after two or three generations because of infant or child mortality or their heirs' refusal to marry or inability to have children, and others were absorbed into the nonelite white population as a result of financial reverses or a surfeit of heirs. A notable exception to these general patterns was the Gómez de Cervantes family. Resident in central Mexico since the conquest, it remained prominent beyond independence. But even though its longevity was extraordinary, the means by which it preserved its elite status were not.

The Gómez de Cervantes family survived as an elite family not only because generation after generation of male heirs carried on the family name. Strategic marriages initially linked the Gómez de Cervantes to other families of conquistadors and *encomenderos* and later united heirs with families that could provide substantial cash dowries. Establishing an entailed estate that included both urban and rural properties maintained an economic base for successive generations. However, the entail also meant that many potential heirs received smaller material legacies and, as a result, entered the Church or created independent economic bases. As each generation filled public offices, often as provincial *alcaldes mayores,* it both secured income and demonstrated its service to the Crown that the next generation could emphasize when soliciting comparable positions. In addition, the practice of sending younger sons and daughters into ecclesiastical careers and convents enabled the family to maintain its estate. A willingness to reduce expenses by retiring to the family *hacienda* during difficult financial times also helped prevent the kind of economic disaster that overcame many elite families who, by the third generation, were dependent on *encomiendas,* mines, or commerce. None of these actions alone was adequate to maintain the family's economic position or social status, but together they were able to prolong its elite status for more than three centuries.

Within the parameters established by race and social standing, it was gender that determined occupation. Colonial society was patriarchal, and the activities of men and women, and thus hubands and wives, reflected a differentiation of roles that could be traced back to their Iberian heritage, on one hand, and the indigenous societies, on the other. Men held all civil offices, made political decisions, and dominated the most lucrative economic activities. Men performed most of the heavy manual labor in the fields and mines, constructed buildings and ships, worked on roads, and transported goods as carriers, muleteers, and seamen. They performed military service and held all ecclesiastical posts, except those in the convents. And only males could secure a higher education or enter a *consulado* or most artisans' guilds.

Women

This outline of a male-dominated society in which the participation of women was narrowly defined obscures the latter's important contributions. The capital investments, labor, and entrepreneurial skills of women were often significant, particularly for both the rural and urban working classes. Few families were able to survive on only the income earned by the male head of household, as the cost of basic necessities almost invariably exceeded the income of any one worker, whether peon, cowboy, artisan, or laborer.

Many women worked openly. Brazil's sugar estates and smaller cane farms depended on female labor throughout the productive cycle, but especially during the harvest. Small independent farmers and ranchers also relied on the labor of wives and daughters, as few produced enough income to hire temporary workers. Retail sales in many urban and rural markets were largely dependent on women, who produced and sold bread, pastries, and sweets. Women also held an important place in colonial manufacturing: Some skilled textile manufacture was completely in their hands, and in Mexico City as early as the sixteenth century there were female guilds with female officers. Women were also found in both textile

Indian woman weaving, Trujillo, Peru

and ceramic *obrajes.* Even in artisan trades, in which female participation was forbidden, women commonly contributed labor. Poorer masters who could not afford the set wages of journeymen or the expense of an apprentice relied heavily on the labor of their wives and children to prepare raw materials and maintain tools. Often the women of this class supplemented the family income by taking in washing, renting rooms, or working as domestics. All elite households required female domestics to cook, clean, and serve as wet nurses.

The primary responsibilities of Spanish wives were in the home. They were to bear and rear children, manage domestic affairs, and instill cultural values. Although the Spanish ideal called for married women to devote themselves to being mothers and wives, even elite women often took an active role in ensuring the family's economic well-being. Particularly in families in which the husband traveled to maintain distant investments in agriculture or mining or to undertake commercial ventures, wives often had the day-to-day responsibility for managing rental properties or shops.

Widows with property enjoyed the greatest freedom of action and participated most extensively in the colonial economy. A widow enjoyed full control over her dowry in addition to half of the wealth she and her husband had amassed while married, and a widow usually also administered her children's inheritances while they were minors. Thus women owned and operated, frequently with the aid of male relatives, rural and urban properties, mines, *obrajes,* and other economic investments. In addition, they actively borrowed and lent money. For example, Izabel Maria Guedes de Brito, a daughter of one of the largest landowners in northeastern Brazil, took full control of her family's business affairs following the death of her husband in the late seventeenth century. Widows in particular and women in general thus both worked and had substantial economic power in both Brazil and Spanish America.

A sketch of the Baquíjano y Carrillo de Córdobas illustrates the importance of marriage and kinship ties, diversified investments, varied occupations, and a widow's continuation of her late husband's business activities in an extended elite colonial family: Juan Bautista Baquíjano emigrated to Lima from Vizcaya in the early eighteenth century, joined a prominent compatriot merchant, worked hard, and prospered. At the age of forty-four he married the twenty-year-old *limeña* María Ignacia Carrillo de Córdoba, the daughter of a distinguished family that could trace its ancestry to conquistadors and early settlers in Chile and Peru. The marriage was a classic match between a wealthy, older peninsular and an established creole elite family with extensive familial ties in the region.

After marriage, Juan Bautista continued to prosper. One of Lima's wealthiest residents, he had investments in shipping, commerce, and agriculture. In 1755 he purchased the title conde de Vistaflorida. His death in 1759 left his wife with seven minor children. María Ignacia continued her late husband's business ventures with the assistance of her brother Luis, a chaplain at the viceregal palace. Her affairs prospered, and the estate she left her heirs exceeded Juan Bautista's.

The surviving Baquíjano y Carrillo children extended the family's influence and power. The elder son and second conde de Vistaflorida settled in Madrid where he invested in commerce, lent money, bought government bonds, and provided his relatives with a convenient voice at court. The younger son, José, became a minister on Lima's *audiencia*. Given the family's wealth, it is surprising that neither son married. Through marriage, however, the five Baquíjano daughters further strengthened the family's eminence in Lima. Their husbands brought expanded ties to the city council, the *consulado*, the militia, the *audiencia*, and even the viceroy. The diversification of political ties, incorporation of successful peninsulars, and continuing investment in shipping, agriculture, and trade typified an elite family's strategy to maintain and enhance its position.

The basic social unit in the colonial world, the extended family was most effective at its upper reaches. As each region in the Indies achieved economic and social maturity, its most prominent families intermarried as well as incorporated through marriage successful newcomers, normally peninsular males, into their midst. Although the timing varied, this establishment and consolidation of extended families took place in settings as diverse as Recife, Salvador, Santiago, Lima, Popayán, Guatemala, and Puebla. Indian societies also maintained families, although epidemics, forced relocation, and voluntary migration worked against their perpetuation. The centrality of family in the colonial world was hardest on the free mixed-race population. The prevalence of illegitimacy among the early generations in particular made impossible the kind of familial ties and support common to the majority of society. But as the number of persons of mixed ancestry increased, their families conformed to the colonial ideal of the extended family.

Daily Life in the Colonies

Daily life in the colonies reflected the extremes of social position and wealth, on the one hand, and the great disparity between urban and rural environments, on the other. For the rural majority, tedium broken only by religious activities and occasional secular celebrations was the rule. Generally, the richer and more complex life of ritual and social interaction of the precontact indigenous cultures subsided as the effects of epidemic disease, miscegenation, and the penetration of the market economy forged the colonial rural culture. Urban dwellers enjoyed more frequent and varied entertainment than did rural residents, but most of them, too, lived a precarious existence marked by a long working day, minimal diet, and poor health. Crime and violence threatened urban and rural residents alike. Although the elite alone had access to all of the pleasures present in the colonial world, the less advantaged groups could enjoy religious celebrations, drinking, music, games, and other diversions.

Labor

From the time they were children, most members of colonial society spent their daylight hours working. Whether engaged in agriculture, ranching, domestic service, mining, or other occupations requiring manual labor, the hours were long and the compensation modest. The struggle for survival consumed most of their energies.

Sundays and religious holidays offered the only respite for manual laborers, and the special requirements of planting and harvesting could cancel even these unpaid breaks. Indians and other free rural laborers routinely toiled from ten to twelve hours a day for up to three hundred or more days a year. Slaves, particularly on sugar plantations, often worked longer. On Jesuit sugar estates in Peru, for example, the day began at 4:30 A.M. in the winter and 5:15 A.M. in the summer. Slaves and other workers labored after morning mass and breakfast until sundown except in the grinding mills where, during harvest, the workday extended beyond midnight. Indian employees in the textile *obrajes* of Ecuador worked from 6:00 A.M. to 6:00 P.M. six days a week except for seven weeks per year when they were permitted to sow, weed, and harvest their fields. In the early seventeenth century, *mita* laborers had their work week reduced from six to five days, with Sundays and Mondays off. Their shifts, whether day or night, were theoretically twelve hours, but an oppressive quota system requiring them to deliver a specified amount of ore often extended the hours of toil.

As in Europe at the same time, wages paid to the majority of free workers in the colonial era hovered around the subsistence level. In the case of *mita* laborers and some *obraje* workers, wages were substantially less than the cost of subsistence, and as a result, those family members who remained in the villages had to provide a portion of the workers' food needs. Such minimal payment reinforced the social order. Spaniards and Portuguese considered nonwhites their social inferiors and believed that payment that would keep them mired in poverty was both just and appropriate. They thought, moreover, that low compensation encouraged productivity and discouraged idleness. Despite extreme fluctuations in the prices of basic foodstuffs, principally maize, wages generally remained stable in each category of employment after the mid-seventeenth century. Unskilled rural workers in Ecuador received fifteen to twenty pesos a year plus housing and food allotments, the total compensation being roughly equivalent to that received by an urban day laborer in Quito. Because Spanish employers deducted the tribute of eight pesos from the wages paid to Indian laborers, the workers' net pay was reduced substantially. Most *hacienda* peons in the Valley of Mexico were receiving two *reales* a day by 1650, a rate that remained standard 150 years later. The cash value of the total compensation—money, food, housing, and clothing—varied by region and date, but its worth was often too small to provide the necessities for survival. In Brazil, free rural laborers, in both grazing and agriculture, usually received some of their compensation in the form of permission to graze a few animals or plant a small garden. Only among the more skilled artisans of Brazilian cities did earning potential exceed subsistence costs. *Hacendados* and owners of mines and *obrajes* often advanced wages to workers to make up this shortfall, not out of kindness but to maintain a stable and dependent labor force. By combining such means with a frugal diet, minimal shelter, and a set of homespun or inexpensive clothing, laborers clung to life only precariously.

Urban manual laborers earned higher cash wages than did their rural counterparts, but they usually had correspondingly higher living expenses because they had to buy housing, food, and clothing. Cities, however, offered more opportunities for employment as artisans, retailers, or workers in a variety of services that offered higher compensation. Church and government positions, as well, were concentrated in urban areas. Combined and often intertwined with wholesale merchants and successful landowners, clerics and officials received and expended incomes that provided the cities with a rich and colorful social life.

Diet

Culture, taste, habit, availability, and price determined the composition of diet. European plants and animals quickly came to supplement indigenous staples such as maize, beans, squash, and chiles in Mesoamerica; potatoes and quinoa in the Andes; and manioc in the Carribean zone and Brazil. Europeans, Indians, and Africans altered their diets and tastes to incorporate previously unknown or expensive foods and obtained more variety and protein as a result. Regional products, moreover, gave Latin American meals a flavor distinct from the fare found on Iberian tables.

Maize remained the dietary staple of the indigenous population of Middle America after the conquest and was prominent in other regions as well. High in carbohydrates, maize kernels were often finely ground and cooked as tortillas, prepared in a gruel, or steamed. Whether served in these forms or others, maize provided as much as 90 percent of the calories in an Indian's diet in the seventeenth century and still accounted for some three-quarters in the mid-twentieth century. The rural *casta* population was similarly dependent on maize. Beans in their numerous forms also were a major source of protein throughout the colonial era, as they had been before. Squash, pumpkins, and gourds provided both calories and protein. Whether consumed raw or in sauces, chili peppers and tomatoes added both vitamins and flavor to the colonial diet.

Domesticated European animals were the most notable postconquest supplements to a diet that remained based on preconquest plants. Chickens, pigs, sheep, and cattle thrived in the New World and offered unprecedented amounts of protein. Indians prized eggs, and chickens soon became intrusive residents in most villages. Pork and mutton also won favor. Beef, in contrast, gained comparable popularity more slowly, initially perhaps because the Indians associated cattle with the destruction of their crops. By the eighteenth century, however, beef was a common dietary item in northern New Spain and in most of Brazil and the Río de la Plata.

Africa also contributed to the New World diet. Bananas, kidney beans, and okra followed in the wake of the slave trade. Although the slaves' diet was generally inadequate in calories and nutrition, Africans sought to imitate the cuisine of their homelands whenever possible. The legacy of these traditions survives in the recipes of modern Cuba and especially in Brazil.

Europeans and individuals emulating their taste in food ate very differently than did the majority of the population. Not only did they normally consume their meals at tables, absent in native houses and in the homes of many *castas*, but they tried to eat the kinds of food that were standard in Europe. This loyalty to the native cuisine explains the continued significance of wine, olive oil, and even wheat in colonial imports for decades after settlement. Urban markets and retailers generally offered a variety of foodstuffs that included local and regional products and imports. As income increased, family diets diversified and improved.

Wheat baked into bread was the principal ingredient of Europeans' and their creole cousins' diet. In fact, there was a distinct class identification associated with white and dark breads: The more affluent households consumed only white bread and considered dark bread to be a poor person's food. A prosperous male from the upper class consumed at least two pounds of bread, four ounces of meat, some vegetables, and oil or fat each day. Even country stores in the Mexican mining towns in the first half of the seventeenth century stocked a diverse mix of foods for those who could afford them. Shrimp, oysters, honey, lentils, spices, bananas, vinegar, salt, sugar, chocolate, beans, cheese, garlic, molasses, lard, and figs appeared on shelves far from Mexico City.

Unlike the indigenous population, Europeans and other advantaged groups acquired most of their protein from meat. Mutton was a favorite in the Spanish colonies. Despite a population of about fifty thousand, Lima in the mid-eighteenth century required just two or three head of cattle a week for the small number of peninsulars who alone ate it regularly. Pork was more popular, although the celebrated Spanish travelers Jorge Juan and Antonio de Ulloa considered it inferior to that served in Cartagena de Indias. Lard was used extensively in cooking, a custom begun before domestic olive oil was available. Proximity to the Pacific Ocean enabled residents in Lima to have fresh fish in their diet. Not only were the corbina and king's fish superior to those in Spain, but anchovies were plentiful as well. Crayfish from the River Rimac added another source of protein.

In Brazil, the Río de la Plata region, Chile, and Venezuela, the proliferation of European livestock, particularly cattle, made beef a fairly common part of the diet. By the early eighteenth century, slaves in Brazil were given small amounts of dried beef from the *pampas* region and *sertão,* or fresh beef, from the nearby ranches of the interior. Most Brazilian planters reduced the cost of feeding their slaves by allowing them to cultivate garden plots. Some slaves produced enough to sell the surplus to other slaves or in the local market. The very poor, beggars and prisoners, seldom consumed protein and relied almost entirely on the nutrients provided in bread. Prisoners in Bahia's jail received bread rations twice a week and a supplement of soup and a piece of meat on Sundays. This chronic undernourishment caused seventy prisoners to die of starvation between 1733 and 1736. Most prisoners throughout the colonies depended on charity for their survival.

Fruit and vegetables supplemented the bread and meat in the European diet. Both Spaniards and Portuguese planted gardens and fruit trees wherever they settled and the climate and terrain allowed. Travelers marveled at the variety and quantity of items available: Figs, grapes, pomegranates, oranges, lemons, bananas, other fruits, and green salads graced the tables in Mexico City. A seventeenth-century traveler to Lima was so struck by the abundance and excellence of its fruit and vegetables that he declared it to have "the richest Lent . . . in the world."[6] Even in inhospitable Potosí, high in the Andes, fruits of many kinds imported from lower valleys were available year-around in the markets.

As a dessert or a snack between meals, sweetmeats were extremely popular throughout the colonies. A traveler in Mexico City in 1625 noted their abundance with astonishment. In Cartagena they were not only plentiful, but residents considered eating some a necessary preliminary to drinking a glass of water. Juan and Ulloa noted much more restraint in Lima where, despite the quantity available, the inhabitants ate sweetmeats only as a dessert, and then but rarely. Slave and free black women produced and sold sugared sweets and pastries in all of Brazil's major cities.

The consumption of beverages accompanied and at times supplanted that of food. By the eighteenth century the most popular nonalcoholic beverage in much of Spanish America was cacao, or chocolate. Before the Spaniards arrived, nobles and warriors in Middle America had been its primary consumers. They drank it as a cold or tepid beverage made from ground cacao, water, maize flour, and chili. The consumption of cacao spread to the region's general Indian population after the conquest, and by the late sixteenth century the number of Spaniards in New Spain who drank the cacao beverage was growing. The Europeans changed the Indians' recipes, however, sweetening the beverage with vanilla, cinnamon, and sugar. With Guayaquil and Venezuela joining Central America as major centers of cacao production in the early seventeenth century, the market continued to expand. Cacao became the favorite beverage in colonial Mexico: Its consumption among the elite was high, and it was also a common drink in hospitals and convents. In South America, *yerba mate,* or Paraguayan tea, was also extremely popular, particularly among the creoles. In

Quito, Lima, the south of Brazil, and numerous other locations, many drank *yerba* in both the morning and the evening.

Alcoholic beverages were a frequent complement to meals and were drunk liberally at other times as well. Spaniards brought a taste for wine from Iberia and imported the drink in large quantities. Domestic production followed settlement quickly where the climate and soil were appropriate. By the late sixteenth century, substantial supplies of potable and sometimes fine-quality wine were available in major markets of South America. Arequipa emerged early as a major producer, but by 1600 landowners in Ica, Pisco, and Nazca had ended its original dominance. At mid-eighteenth century, Lima was importing an inferior white wine from Nazca and red and dark red wine from Pisco, Lucumba, and Chile. The latter's vintages included muscatel and held the highest reputation among connoisseurs in the city. Wine was produced in Mendoza by the late seventeenth century, and despite transportation difficulties the region helped supply the needs of Upper Peru and Buenos Aires. Imports from Spain and Peru supplied the markets in Mexico and Central America in the absence of a significant regional viticulture and because of prohibitions against interregional trade.

Brandy, the distilled, high-alcohol-content cousin of wine, emerged as the beverage of choice in the late seventeenth century, because of both its greater potency and better traveling characteristics. Originally used for medicinal purposes, the drink's popularity burgeoned, and imports from Seville, Cádiz, and, especially after 1679, the Canary Islands increased accordingly. New Spain, Cuba, and Venezuela were the major markets; production in Peru became important about 1700. By 1717 the Spanish miners there drank it in preference to wine, which they left to the lower classes. In Cartagena, Juan and Ulloa reported, even the "most regular and sober persons" invariably drank a glass of brandy daily at 11:00 A.M. to strengthen the stomach and whet the appetite. Among the less abstemious, however, *hacer las once,* as the custom was called, degenerated into a day-long activity. Brandy soon became the poor man's luxury among urban laborers, cowboys, and even slaves. In Quito, Peruvian brandy was a special favorite of peninsulars.

Whereas well-to-do Spaniards drank quality wine or brandy, most of society imbibed less pretentious beverages. These included *chicha,* a beer made from corn, drunk in the Andes; *pulque,* an intoxicant derived from the maguey or century plant, enjoyed in Mexico; and *aguardiente de caña,* a potent distilled drink derived from sugarcane and produced in Brazil, Paraguay, the Caribbean Islands, New Granada, and other locations where cane grew. On some Brazilian sugar estates slaves were given a rum ration before heading to the fields in the morning. In central Mexico during Aztec rule, commoners drank *pulque* on ritual occasions, but the nobility drank it more frequently. After the conquest, *pulque* consumption increased as commoners escaped traditional taboos and obtained access to imported Spanish wines as well. Indians considered drinking to stupefaction acceptable behavior in ritual situations. Among the Andean peoples, drinking was an expected part of ritual observance. The Mamaq of the Rimac River valley, for example, celebrated the maturation of their crops with the feast of Chaupinamca, at which men and women danced and drank for five consecutive nights. Such behavior drew the condemnation of Spanish authorities, although some Spaniards profited from the sale of alcohol to natives.

A heavy consumption of alcohol, in short, was a common feature of colonial society, as it was in the preindustrial societies of Europe. Owners of vineyards, canefields, and land devoted to maguey cultivation pushed to expand production and profit. Despite recognizing the social consequences of alcohol abuse, the Spanish government proved unable to limit its growth, at least in part because it benefited directly from taxes on its production. In Brazil, rum production and consumption was encouraged by a tithe exemption. Rum also became a significant export in the growing direct African slave trade. The masses, in particular, consumed alcohol in great quantity as they sought temporary relief from the misery always present in their daily lives.

Illness and Medicine

Epidemic diseases introduced from Europe and Africa repeatedly swept through Latin America, beginning before the fall of Tenochtitlán. Smallpox, measles, typhus, influenza, pneumonic plague, and pestilential fevers were the most prominent killers. Poor sanitation practices, inadequate water supplies, and a general absence of sound hygiene promoted disease and poor health. The streets of large cities were running sewers filled with human and animal excrement. Slaughterhouses discarded their waste where dogs and other scavengers could carry it near the houses. The city councils of Buenos Aires and other towns regularly repeated prohibitions against leaving the bodies of slaves and carcasses of livestock in the street. Few colonial residents had access to safe wells. Although aqueducts were constructed in some of the larger cities, most residents bought water from peddlers or used sometimes-contaminated rainwater that was collected in ceramic or wooden tubs. The dangers inherent in these conditions were compounded by poor personal hygiene. Few people bathed regularly; soap and clean clothes were luxuries limited to the more affluent groups in colonial society.

Against these grave health threats, contemporary medical practices offered little hope. Nor were medical practitioners very effective in curing the host of other ailments, notably rheumatic and other fevers, stomach ailments, catarrh, syphilis, abscesses, and tumors that weakened the population and frequently brought premature death. Treating injuries successfully was also usually impossible with the techniques and medicines at hand. As a result of these inadequacies, most of the people in the colonial world spent much of their lives ill or in pain.

Spanish physicians began arriving in the New World on Columbus's second voyage. The mainland conquests drew them in their train as wounded, diseased, or simply ill conquistadors sought and paid for medical assistance. Within a decade after their founding, the city councils of Mexico City and Lima were already trying to eliminate charlatans, by requiring licenses to practice, licenses for which only university-trained and -certified physicians were eligible. The Crown soon named royal medical examiners to continue this worthy objective. Despite such efforts, charlatans with fraudulent credentials were a common feature of colonial life throughout the Spanish colonies and Brazil.

Licensed physicians were the elite of the medical profession, but before the late eighteenth century, the profession itself had little to recommend it in either the New World or Europe. From the sixteenth to the nineteenth centuries, a baccalaureate in medicine entitled a man to begin practice. University instruction in medicine drew heavily on Hippocrates and Galen. Modernization of the curriculum began in the late eighteenth century, but very few students matriculated in this unattractive career.

Surgeons held a status far below that of physicians. Often associated with barbering and blood letting, surgeons seldom bothered to get official approval to practice. Most had no university training; rather, they apprenticed with an "approved" surgeon for four or five years. Tightened standards and more formalized instruction awaited the late eighteenth century.

Phlebotomists, or bleeders, ranked below even surgeons among medical practitioners. Apprenticeship of three or four years replaced any academic work. Oral examinations, moreover, meant that phlebotomists did not need to be literate. Examiners expected them to know only about veins and arteries and how to put on leeches and cupping glasses, to open ulcers and boils, and to extract teeth. Outside the major colonial cities, barbers usually provided these services. Barbering, a traditional artisan occupation, mixed medical and dental work with hair cutting and shaving. In small towns without guilds, there were few effective controls on the training and practice of these men, with malpractice and abuse the predictable results.

Unlike all other aspects of medical practice, delivering babies was almost exclusively a woman's profession, although wealthy women in larger cities often sought assistance from a licensed surgeon as well. Few midwives were formally trained or licensed, and most relied more on superstition than anatomical knowledge. The deadly combination of frequent pregnancies and poor medical practice made complications in childbirth one of the most common causes of death for colonial women. As in Europe at the same time, even physicians regularly recommended treatments that endangered both mother and child. The respected Mexican doctor Juan Manuel Venegas, for example, advised the following procedure for expelling a dead infant from the womb: application of an enema made from "'a chicken cut open down the back,' a mule's sweatpad cooked in urine, and infusions of feathergrass and leaves of senna," followed by a "drink of horse manure dissolved in wine."[7]

Inadequate opportunities for formal medicine instruction and the low status of medical practitioners in general combined to produce few physicians. The University of Mexico conferred only 438 baccalaureates in the faculty from 1607 to 1738, and the University of San Marcos in Lima probably conferred even fewer. In Guatemala the University of San Carlos graduated only 30 bachelors of medicine from 1700 to 1821. Graduates, moreover, established their practices in urban centers where the Spanish populations were eager for their services. Rural villages rarely if ever had a physician. Because Brazil lacked a university, all of the colony's Portuguese physicians were immigrants or colonials trained in Europe.

The small number of legally qualified physicians opened the way for quacks and healers who diagnosed illnesses, bled victims, and prescribed remedies for the majority of the colonial population. Sometimes foreigners, sometimes friars, often mixed-race males and females with a private stock of remedies or access to a local apothecary, these persons lacked any formal medical training, although some had observed physicians while working as hospital attendants. In regions with large populations of African slaves, native remedies that combined the bark, roots, and leaves of plants with spiritualist practices were frequently employed, even by the more affluent members of society.

Apothecaries stocked the items that physicians and other medical practitioners prescribed. The inventories contained oddities drawn from centuries of folk medicine and Galenism in Spain as well as items unique to the Indies. As in Europe, druggists sold products whose efficacy frequently rested more in the mind than the body: Tapir's hoof, human cranium, llama fetuses, lizard excrement, spider webs, dried and powdered earthworms, gander droppings, pearls, amber, and garnet sat on the druggists' shelves along with rose-colored oil and honey, several varieties of animal grease, mercury, and bezoar stones secured from the stomaches of llama, vicuña, and other ruminant animals. Purgatives included balsam, snake skin, corn meal, and tobacco.

Although the Spanish population lamented the persistent shortage of physicians, there was nonetheless a healthy skepticism about the efficacy of medical treatment. The Peruvian poet Juan del Valle Caviedes voiced disdain for physicians individually and as a group:

> And wherever the book says *doctor,*
> Be attentive, because you should read there
> *Executioner,* although the latter
> Is a little weaker.
> Wherever it says *prescription*
> You will say *sword*
> Because sword and executioner

End up being the same.
Wherever it says *bloodletting*
You should read *throatcutting*
and you will read *scalpel*
Wherever it says *medication.*
Wherever it says *laxative*
Read he finished off the patient.
And where it says *remedy*
You will read *certain death.*[8]

Poverty and disease go hand in hand, for the conditions creating the first produce an environment conducive to the second. Widespread poverty, an inadequate diet, hard labor, and unsanitary conditions at work and home combined to produce both high mortality and lower labor productivity. For most inhabitants in the colonial world, life offered few pleasures and fewer rewards.

Crime and Punishment

Crime and violence accompanied the settlement of the New World and remained permanent features of colonial daily life thereafter. Colonial authorities regularly dealt with cases of robbery, assault, and homicide, but many paid less attention to violations of legislation intended to protect Indians and slaves from physical and financial abuse. Colonists, moreover, proved adept at conniving with underpaid officials to defraud the government; evading taxes and customs duties was only one of many ways in which they did so. Ironically, although both hardened criminals and more genteel malefactors threatened society, their punishment at times provided grisly entertainment, particularly in the capital cities.

Because the law enforcement bureaucracy was very small, most crime was not detected by the royal authorities. Within rural Indian villages, local leaders dealt with cases of robbery, adultery, and rape. On the plantations and large ranches of Brazil and the Spanish colonies, landowners or their agents exercised de facto judicial authority, usually administering corporal punishment. The death penalty, however, remained a prerogative of the state. Homicide, sedition, and aggravated assault required the intervention of the colonial judiciary, but these cases accounted for comparatively few violations of the law. Local and royal officials in cities, in contrast, dealt with the full spectrum of crime.

Thieves found irresistible the urban centers with their unlit streets and few night patrols. The concentration of cash, jewels, and other movable property within their bounds and the desperate living conditions of the urban poor meant that neither the wealthy nor the impoverished were immune from theft. In August 1629, for example, robbers took more than ten thousand pesos from the downtown store of Lima merchant Christóbal Lario. An almost daily occurrence, such robbery prompted the *consulado* to hire three night watchmen to patrol the shopping district. Not even this action, however, was effective. The following year, burglars entered the residence of another merchant, Benito de Orozco, while he and his wife were sleeping. They threatened him with sword and dagger and stole his jewels and clothing. Robberies of a small grocery store and a mulatto silversmith's shop were reminders that thieves attacked persons of modest means as well.

Assault with a deadly weapon, often a butcher or household knife, was commonplace in both rural and urban areas. Armed assaults were so common in rural areas of Argentina and Uruguay that shopkeepers protected themselves and their merchandise with iron or sturdy wooden bars. The offenders were almost always male and usually young adults, and the victims also were usually young males. Only rarely were assailants and victims strangers, and many times they were family members, neighbors, or fellow workers. Primitive medical practices, furthermore, increased the likelihood that a wounded victim would die. Juan Antonio Suardo, a clerical diarist, recorded from 1630 to 1635 nearly sixty murders and deaths resulting from assault in Lima. On one of many occasions involving passion, an irate husband stabbed both his wife and a priest after discovering them in *flagrante delicto*. There was a particularly violent night in 1634 when within an hour and a half a Spaniard, a *mulatto*, and a black were killed in different parts of the city.

Civil authorities regularly administered punishments in public to remind the populace that robbery, violent acts, and other crimes could bring severe retribution. Judges routinely ordered terms of hard labor in *obrajes*, port facilities, the galleys, or military service. In the sixteenth and seventeenth centuries, numerous offenders held in the royal jail in Lima were sent to Chile to fight against the Indians. Whippings were another common sentence, even for minor offenses. In the Mixteca Alta region of New Spain, six to fifty lashes were the usual punishment for peasants in the seventeenth century. One day in 1634, eleven Indians were whipped in Lima as *ladrones famosos*, or "reknowned thieves." On occasion, judges combined whippings with a sentence of forced servitude. One slave was lashed and sent to the galleys for attacking a Spaniard with a sword and then resisting arrest. The use of lashings was discriminatory, for unlike the rest of society, Spaniards were spared corporal punishment.

Executions were less frequent in the Spanish colonies and Brazil than in the English colonies. This difference arose both from the Iberian legal systems' receptivity to pleas of extenuating circumstances and an appreciation that dead offenders could provide no labor. It is possible, moreover, that except for a concerted effort to clear central Mexico's main roads of highwaymen in the eighteenth century that led to numerous hangings, executions became less common after 1700 than earlier. Rarely ordered even for homicide in late eighteenth-century central Mexico, executions were frequent in early seventeenth-century Peru. Judges ordered execution primarily in cases of murder, attempted murder, robbery, and sodomy. From 1630 to 1635 alone, Suardo recorded over forty executions.

Executions, especially those for sodomy and bestiality, attracted sizable crowds of people. The burning in Callao of a *mestizo* and a mulatto convicted of sodomy drew numerous spectators from Lima. Even more spectacular was the execution of the Aragonese merchant Thomas Buesso, convicted of sodomy and bestiality. An "infinite number of persons on foot, on horseback, and in coaches" gathered at 4:00 P.M. on November 13, 1630, to watch the whipping of Buesso's black male lover and the burning of both the merchant and the unfortunate dog he had molested.

Entertainment

Daily life in colonial cities offered variety and excitement far removed from the routine of the countryside. Bells in churches and convents marked the hours. Processions honoring religious holidays mixed with civic celebrations to add color, sound, and festivity to urban life. The concentrations of wealth in the largest colonial cities enabled expenditures for public display rarely possible in other cities and beyond the imagination of villages. Even the funerals of wealthy residents became public celebrations.

Urban life focused on the plazas and streets. In Spanish America, bullfights were staged in a plaza whose entrances were closed for the event. The plaza was also the site for jousting on horseback with cane spears, military parades, public *autos da fé,* executions, religious and civil processions, and fiestas of all sorts. Vendors of fruit, sweetmeats, beverages, ices, and other tasty tidbits hawked their goods there. On crowded, dirty streets passed mules laden with goods, horse- and mule-drawn coaches and chaises, ambulatory vendors selling their wares, wives and servants on their daily shopping trips, persons going to and from work, and children playing or going to school.

The presence of viceroys, archbishops and other prominent civil and ecclesiastical authorities, wealthy merchants and *hacendados,* and a variety of corporate bodies stimulated an especially active social life in Mexico City, Lima, and Bahia. Several examples of social life in Lima illustrate the types of entertainment available: On New Year's Eve, 1629, Viceroy Conde de Chinchón staged a dramatic presentation in the palace at 3:00 P.M. for the *audiencia* ministers and their wives. Five days later he invited them to celebrate his son's birthday amid general rejoicing and fiestas. On January 12, 1630, a private citizen, Don Francisco Flores, sponsored a bullfight and party for a large number of male and female friends at a town near Lima. When an Augustinian secured a chair at the University of San Marcos later in the month, his friends informed the populace by awakening them with trumpets and drums; great bell ringing and fireworks continued the celebration the following night. The arrival of a new archbishop in early February prompted another round of celebrations, bell ringing,

Three youths playing with tops

and fireworks highlighted by a "splendid dinner" at which sixty-four different dishes were served. On occasion, the viceroy, his wife, and a large
retinue joined in the daily stroll around the *plaza mayor* and nearby streets
that enabled people to show off their finery, see friends, and be seen by
the populace present.

The humble as well as the wealthy participated in fiestas. The day after
an elaborate official celebration in honor of the birth of Prince Baltasar
Carlos in 1629, petty retailers in Lima decorated their stalls with hangings
and flowers and the central plaza with trees and fourteen large figurines.
Persons of all walks of life filled the plaza in the afternoon to celebrate,
and fireworks entertained the entire city in the evening. In the next several
weeks, guilds of confectioners, grocers, hatmakers, tailors, shoemakers, sil-

versmiths, and merchants each provided fiestas, many complete with bull-fights and fireworks. Smaller cities and towns offered similar celebrations on a reduced scale. Even Indian villages invested their scarce resources in the celebration of feast days and secular holidays.

Although the plazas and streets were the centers of city life, elite families also entertained at home. Residences of the wealthy contained silver utensils and serving pieces; numerous paintings, often religious; books; mirrors; gilded chairs; a large table; and an ornate desk. The principal residential amusement for the elite was card playing, accompanied by gambling, an activity popular among Iberians before settlement of the New World. Participants included nearly anyone with enough pesos to lose. Despite prohibitions to the contrary, Dr. Antonio de Morga, president of the *audiencia* of Quito from 1615 to 1636, entertained prominent citizens nightly in an atmosphere reminiscent of a gambling parlor. During his tenure, his wife oversaw their illicit gains reach some 200,000 pesos. In Guatemala City at about the same time, audiencia President Gonzalo de Paz y Lorezana prohibited gambling at cards in private houses in order to monopolize it in his own. In Mexico City, Thomas Gage reported that gambling was so popular that women invited gentlemen to visit them for no purpose other than to bet at cards. Gambling was also a passion among the lower classes, and there were few *cantinas* or *pulperías* that did not offer the opportunity to play cards or dice or wager on games of skill. Here suspected cheating or unexpected losses often led to knife fights and brawls.

Work, inadequate compensation, tiresome meals, and illness were the lot of most persons in colonial society. For them, life offered almost no possibility of improvement. Only occasional fiestas broke the routine. For the elite, on the other hand, daily life was markedly different. Their income allowed them to purchase luxury goods both imported from abroad and produced locally. Their diets were varied, their entertainments, numerous. The divergence in daily life for nobles and commoners apparent in Aztec and Inca society as well as Spain and Portugal before the conquest continued in the colonial world, as the local elites enjoyed a material and social existence that bore little resemblance to that of most of society.

The Cultural Milieu

Colonialism subordinated the indigenous and later creole cultures to European cultural hegemony. Undergirded by Catholicism, cultural colonialism proved to be more durable and resistant to American efforts to establish an independent cultural identity than did the more visible political and economic structures it helped sustain.

The cultural milieu in colonial Latin America varied according to the intensity of a region's contact with Europe, its wealth, and the composition of the local society. The elites in major administrative centers tried to replicate Iberian cultural institutions and practices. The movement of officials, churchmen, merchants, and others to and from the colony and metropolis resulted in an ongoing transfer of Iberian high culture—European books and ideas, music, and art—to the major colonial cities, whether located on the coast or inland. In poorer and geographically isolated colonial towns and rural areas, the limited high culture available revolved around religious instruction and celebrations. Wherever there were large indigenous populations or numerous African slaves, the inhabitants drew on non-European traditions and modified Iberian cultural expression into a unique popular culture.

Origins of a Colonial Culture

In any clash between literate and preliterate societies, historical understanding, the past itself, becomes the possession of the literate culture. In the case of Latin America, the creation of colonial societies through conquest and settlement was seen through the lens of European chronicles and histories. Written from the victors' perspective, these accounts enshrined a concept of European cultural superiority that persisted long after the colonies became politically independent.

The origins of this colonial culture began with the chronicles and histories written soon after the discovery of the Americas. In letters, reports, and logs filled with inaccurate European and biblical references, Columbus made the first attempt to recast American realities according to European intellectual categories. The creation of this mythical New World coincided with the conquest and settlement of the real America. Bernal Díaz del Castillo, for example, identified the great cities of Mesoamerica with places mentioned in the popular romance *Amadis of Gaul.* Not only the reports of Cabeza de Vaca but also the mythological flight of seven Portuguese bishops from the invading Muslims defined the search for the "Seven Cities of Cíbola."

The conquistadors were rough and generally unlettered men who wrote few works of lasting historical or literary value. A major exception was the foot soldier Bernal Díaz. His *True History of the Conquest of Mexico,* a highly personal and readable narrative of the epic event, has been translated into English, German, French, and Hungarian and still finds many readers. Cortés's *Letters From Mexico* demonstrates his high intelligence and curiosity and provides an unequaled glimpse into the great leader's mind. Nicolaus Federmann, one of the Welser's captains in Venezuela, and Pedro de Valdivia, the conqueror of Chile, also left similar, although lesser-known, chronicles of their exploits. A number of the participants in the conquest of Peru later also wrote about their experiences. The most important early chroniclers of Brazil were Pêro de Magalhães de Gândavo, the Jesuit Fernâo Cardim, and Gabriel Soares de Sousa.

The missionaries were anxious to discover and understand the languages, customs, and histories of the indigenous peoples. Although the results of their findings were uneven in quality and even the most important of their works found an extremely limited contemporary audience, many scholars still consult them. The writings of the Jesuits Manoel de Nobrega and José de Anchieta remain particularly valuable sources for Brazilian history. By 1572, at least 109 books to aid evangelization had been written in New Spain alone, most of them by Franciscans. Far from being pedantic scholarship, these and many similar works were intended to facilitate the process of conversion and cultural change.

The early churchmen also wrote a number of historical and ethnographic works, which were often marked by a genuine sympathy for the indigenous peoples as well as thoroughness and intellectual rigor. The Dominican Bartolomé de las Casas, bishop of Chiapas, exemplified this close identification with the plight of the conquered peoples. In his numerous writings he portrayed the Indians as innocent victims of Spanish cruelty. The Franciscan Fray Toribio de Benavente, known as Motolinía, wrote an extremely informative *Historia de los Indios de la Nueva España*. Fellow Franciscan Fray Bernardino de Sahagún put the learning of a lifetime of missionary work and study in Mexico in his monumental *Historia General de las Cosas de Nueva España*. Unfortunately, Philip II ordered the manuscript confiscated in 1577 as part of a general prohibition against published descriptions of native customs and superstitions. This effort to prevent the subversive effect such knowledge might have on Christian doctrine meant that Sahagún's *Historia General,* Motolinía's earlier completed *Historia* or numerous other valuable ethnographic works were not published until centuries later. Felipe Guaman Poma de Ayala's depiction of Incan and colonial life in Peru was not printed until the twentieth century.

Education

Iberian settlers naturally wanted to raise their children in the religious and intellectual traditions of Europe. To avoid the high cost and danger of transatlantic travel, colonists established schools, seminaries, and universities in the New World. After the conversion of the native peoples, the Church achieved its greatest success in founding institutions that protected and transmitted the intellectual authority of Europe through education. By the end of the sixteenth century, most of the orders had shifted their scarce educational resources from the native nobility to meeting the needs of boys and young men from the Spanish and creole elites. The Jesuits, in particular, were successful in attracting to their *colegios* the sons of well-placed colonial families. They founded the first of ten *colegios* and four seminaries in Brazil in 1556, their first *colegio,* San Pablo, in Lima in 1568, and *colegios* in Mexico beginning in 1574.

Colegios offered courses in humanities, philosophy, theology, and languages. The school day was long, as students started at 7:45 A.M. and took courses and participated in mandatory religious services until after 5:00

P.M. By the early seventeenth century, the *colegio* of San Pablo had five hundred students, and from the 1660s to the 1760s, it had over a thousand students.

In the Spanish colonies, settlers, ecclesiastics, and civil authorities pushed from an early date for the creation of universities. In 1551 the Crown authorized the founding of universities in Mexico City and Lima. Both were modeled in curriculum, governance, and administration on Spain's great University of Salamanca. During the sixteenth and seventeenth centuries, universities proliferated in the Spanish colonies, and by the end of the colonial period, well over twenty institutions had conferred nearly 150,000 university degrees. Ten "major" universities offered doctorates in all the conventional faculties: arts, theology, law, canon law, and medicine. The remaining "minor" universities conferred degrees in only some faculties, usually arts and theology, and were frequently run by the Jesuit or Dominican orders. Until the late eighteenth century, Aristotelian logic, metaphysics, and physics dominated the three-year arts curriculum.

In contrast with Spanish America, no university was established in colonial Brazil. Portugal had a well-established educational system, and so Brazil's most important thinkers and writers graduated from its prestigious University of Coimbra. The seventeenth-century Brazilian poet Gregorio de Matos, for example, was educated by the Jesuits in Bahia before studying at Coimbra, where he received a doctorate in law. One reason for the absence of a university in Brazil was the relative weakness of the Church.

Courtyard of the University of San Carlos, Antigua, Guatemala

With only three bishoprics established by 1700, the potential patronage for learning and the opportunities for university graduates were limited.

At first, professorial appointments were based on the results of open competitions judged by the university's governing body, students, and alumni on the faculty. Cronyism and aspirants catering to students' taste, however, soon corrupted the system. As a result, by the late seventeenth century, the students had lost their vote in the selection process. Most salaries were quite low and remained unchanged throughout the colonial era. Consequently, most professors relied on income from outside positions in the Church or government.

Student bodies were composed solely of males, most of whom came from ambitious middle- and well-to-do creole families in the capitals and provincial cities. By law the Indians, particularly Indian nobles, were permitted entry into universities, but few attended. The racially mixed children of wealthy or well-connected Spaniards had little trouble overcoming the racial proscriptions designed to exclude all persons with "tainted blood." Blacks and mulattoes had the greatest difficulty entering universities. They repeatedly met prejudice and protest and found it difficult to receive degrees even after completing the required course work and examinations.

By the end of the seventeenth century, the general intellectual level in the colonial universities, as in Castile, was very low. Professors often did not attend class or, when they did lecture, did so perfunctorily. In some cases they actually knew nothing about the subjects they were supposed to be teaching. The worst abuses in Mexico were associated with the chairs in Indian languages. In part the corruption of colonial universities was the natural result of the selfish vocationalism that drove ambitious youths to seek degrees, particularly in civil and canon law, that were required for some of the most desirable and powerful positions in the church and state.

Books and Printing

Books were carried by the Iberian discoverers, conquistadors, and settlers from the earliest days of colonization. Light reading, for example, romances of chivalry, found room in at least a few conquerors' luggage as they trekked across the New World. Clerics imported religious works that included breviaries, Bibles, and missals. Despite routine examination by the inquisitors of Seville and the colonial Inquisitions, prohibited literature could be found in many libraries.

Although the literate colonial population of Spanish America continued to import a wide variety of books from Spain, the introduction of printing presses in the colonies enabled the publication of New World editions of Old World classics and also offered local authors an opportunity to see their prose and verse set for posterity. The first press in Mexico began publishing in the mid-1530s; its oldest extant book, a catechism in Spanish

and Nahuatl, dates from 1539. By the end of the century, close to two
hundred books had been published in the viceregal capital. Printing
presses began functioning in Lima in 1583, Puebla in 1640, and Guatemala during the following year, although the Guatemalan experiment had
to be renewed in 1660. In the eighteenth century, another fourteen cities
boasted presses. Never allowed to compete seriously with Spanish publish-
ers, the New World presses initially focused on works for evangelization
and subsequently published a broader range of works, which included
books on history, geography, law, medicine, and other fields. Numerous,
and at times short-lived, newspapers appeared in the late eighteenth
century.

Colonial publications in Spanish America were overwhelmingly religious. Churchmen, the most avid devotees of literature, published numerous sermons, theological studies, and works to assist evangelization, as well
as biographies of outstanding clerics. Sermons were usually printed
through the largesse of a benefactor interested in advancing the career or
satisfying the ego of a particular cleric. By the mid-seventeenth century
some sermons contained a strong element of creole nationalism. In New
Spain this was particularly evident in works devoted to the Virgin of
Guadalupe.

The audience for both colonial publications and imported books was
extremely small. Probably no more than 10 percent of the colonial population was ever functionally literate, that is, actually used their reading and
writing skills. The active intellectual community was much smaller, probably never more than a few thousand at any one time. In the late seventeenth century, only a few hundred individuals in Mexico City participated
in its intellectual life and were aware of the major controversies and new
ideas that were stimulating the European intellectual community.

In contrast with Spanish America, no printing press was available in Brazil until 1808. As a result, Brazilian authors sent their works to Lisbon for
publication. Without a printing press, the dissemination of ideas and the
essential connection of writer and audience was nearly impossible. Without
universities and the libraries, the concentrated intellectual energies of faculty and students, and the fiscal resources that they brought together, Brazil lacked the critical mass necessary to promote creative activity at the level
found in the great cities of Spanish America. Although literary production
was limited, the major themes and styles noted in Spanish America were
nonetheless present.

Colonial Intellectuals

Despite the problem of isolation, censorship, and limited audience, Spanish America produced a number of significant intellectuals, although few
of the first rank. This failure—if failure it was—resulted from the heavy
weight of the colonial situation itself. The work of colonial intellectuals was
necessarily derivative, imitating European style and theme. Originality was

instead found in the evocation of the American landscape or the celebration of American heroes.

A number of works celebrated the heroic era of colonial history, such as *La Araucana* (1569), the epic poem by Alonso de Ercilla, and *Comentarios Reales de los Incas* (1609), by the Peruvian *mestizo* Garcilaso de la Vega. The American themes of *La Araucana* and *Comentarios* were representative of what became a general pattern of increased creole self-confidence and self-consciousness in the Spanish colonies.

The outstanding seventeenth-century literary figure in Brazil was the Jesuit Antonio Vieira. Born in Lisbon in 1608, Father Vieira migrated to Brazil at the age of six and was educated at the Jesuit college in Bahia. There he fought hard in the order's effort to improve the condition of Brazil's native peoples, and when he returned to Portugal to pursue this battle, his prose became well known in Europe.

The Baroque period, roughly the seventeenth and early eighteenth centuries in Latin America, was marked by great technical skill, exuberance in decoration, and a concern for the fabulous and supernatural. Entries in poetry tournaments, popular from the late sixteenth century, frequently demonstrated a Baroque spirit. This period also was characterized by a growing interest in nature, an interest pursued increasingly through rational inquiry and measurement. In the next century, this marginal intellectual direction gained in prestige, through the reflected glories of the European Enlightenment. Yet the triumph of rationalism and scientific method was never complete in Latin America.

The inherent tension between the competing claims of reason and religion that was typical of the Baroque era can be detected in the lives of two of colonial Spanish America's great intellectuals. Pedro de Peralta y Barnuevo, eventually the rector of the University of San Marcos in Lima, was an early eighteenth-century mathematician and cosmographer known to contemporaries as a "monster of erudition." He also devoted himself to practical projects, such as supervising the city's fortifications. Yet toward the end of his life Peralta expressed disillusion with learning and worldly concerns. His last great work, *Passion and Triumph of Christ,* was an archetypical Baroque expression of religious enthusiasm that alleged that knowledge of God is not subject to rational inquiry.

The Mexican creole Carlos de Sigüenza y Góngora was an even more remarkable individual. His father had been tutor to a son of Philip IV, and his mother, also a Spanish immigrant, was related to the poet Luis de Góngora. Sigüenza entered the Society of Jesus as a youth in 1662 but was expelled for a breach of discipline. Although he later became a priest, his efforts to gain readmission to the Society failed. Turning to an academic career, he secured the chair of mathematics and astrology at the University of Mexico in 1672 at the age of twenty-five.

Sigüenza's achievements can be grouped into two broad categories, archaeology and history and mathematics and applied sciences. He learned Indian languages and collected artifacts and manuscripts. Most of his research on the indigenous civilizations of Mesoamerica was either not published or failed to survive, but we know that he examined topics as diverse as the ancient calendar and the genealogy of the Aztec royal house. He also wrote histories of the University of Mexico and the city cathedral. Although not a theoretical mathematician, Sigüenza made a well-recognized contribution to engineering projects and to astronomy. He owned a telescope with four lenses and labored tirelessly to measure the movement of heavenly bodies.

Sigüenza's interest in comets led him into a heated debate with the noted Jesuit Eusebio Kino. In this dispute the creole scholar upheld the role of reason and science against the authority of the classical sources and the church fathers. Like other Baroque intellectuals, he did not find it necessary to resolve apparent contradictions between faith and science. In his history of the Corpus Christi convent, he uncritically narrated a series of miracles associated with the institution's development.

Sigüenza's final testament, like his life, left unresolved the contest between reason and superstition. He requested that surgeons examine his mortal remains to discover the cause of his painful death, leaving explicit suggestions as to which organs might hold the key. At the same time, he noted that he owned a hat worn by Francisco de Aguiar y Seijas, a deceased friend and the former archbishop of Mexico. Because some sick people had experienced relief when they touched the hat, Sigüenza provided for it to be placed in a church where the sick could continue to seek its miraculous powers.

The most remarkable colonial intellectual of the Baroque era was the Mexican nun Sister Juana Inés de la Cruz (1651–95). An illegitimate child from a modest provincial family, the precocious and beautiful young woman attracted the attention and patronage of the viceroy's wife. Despite these advantages, she entered a Carmelite convent at age fifteen. Unhappy with this order's strict discipline, she left it for a Jeronymite convent, where she remained until her death.

Unlike most of the colonial period's literature, Sister Juana's poetry still finds an audience. Its durability is largely the result of her mastery of the lyric form and the emotion and intelligence that it communicates. Unlike most of her contemporaries, Sister Juana escaped the deadening habit of mere verbal cleverness and decoration. Her best verse illuminates the inherent tension and conflict between the claims of reason and emotion, and science and revelation:

> My soul is confusedly divided into two parts,
> One a slave to passion, the other
> measured by reason.
> Inflamed civil war importunately
> afflicts my bosom. Each part
> strives to prevail, and amidst
> such varied storms, both contenders
> will perish, and neither
> one will triumph.[9]

Sister Juana Inés de la Cruz

Sister Juana was also aware of the unequal and unfair burdens she carried because of her sex. Indeed, some of her critics viewed her passion for knowledge and willingness to question as rebellious and unfeminine. Given her personal history, her questioning of society's double standard was particularly powerful:

> Which has the greater sin when burned
> by the same lawless fever:
> She who is amorously deceived,
> or he, the sly deceiver?[10]

As her fame increased and her work, much of it secular, won an audience in the Old World as well as the New, Sister Juana was criticized by some religious authorities: Members of her order, her confessor, and the hierarchy, including the bishop of Puebla, revealed their displeasure. In 1693, after going through a period of self-doubt and unhappiness, she finally gave up her unequal struggle with the representatives of conservative opinion in the Church. She renounced her worldly possessions, including her beloved library and mathematical and musical instruments, signing what was in effect a surrender in her own blood: "I, Sister Juana Inés de la Cruz, the worst in the world." Turning to a harsh discipline of fasting and mortification of the flesh, her health declined rapidly, and she died in 1695.

Popular Culture

Most of colonial society experienced cultural life in forms different from those enjoyed by the literate population. The statutory and material subordination of the colonial masses resulted naturally in the devaluation of the artistic and intellectual values that survived from the indigenous or African cultures or were created along with an evolving creole folk culture. Yet, despite the elite's prejudice and the limited resources, elements of these minority cultural traditions did contribute to the artistic and literary development of Latin America.

Because the masses were denied access to a formal education, the popular culture escaped some of the inhibitions found in the works of the great creole intellectuals. Illiteracy and, in many cases, cultural distinctiveness permitted a cultural independence and exuberance denied to the completely Hispanized and educated minority. As a result, dance, music, theater, and, to a lesser extent, literature in Latin America carry the thematic, rhythmic, and mythological imprint of the popular culture.

Because the culture of Christian Spain was officially that of the colonies, the popular culture developed by expropriating some of the forms of symbols sanctioned by church and state. The people created a tradition that celebrated their values and needs by insinuation rather than conflict. The forms most susceptible to this process were dance, religious theater, music, and the *máscara* or *mascarada*. The *máscara* was a parade of costumed men and women, sometimes associated with a theme and sometimes not. Over time, these various forms of expression developed rules of style and theme, one being a tendency to lampoon the pretensions and conceits of the metropolitan culture.

One *máscara* in Puebla, New Spain's second city, included a float on which effigies of the viceroy and his wife were beaten. Lesser public officials and even religious leaders often shared this humiliation. It was also common for social conventions to be stood on their head. For example, dressing as a member of the opposite sex was a popular feature of *máscaras*. Even within the more constrained confines of religious processions and plays, the people found opportunities to express their cultural distinctiveness. One scholar has found strong evidence of rites associated with

Dance of the Condors, Trujillo, Peru

Huitzilopochtli in the celebrations devoted to the Virgin de la Soledad. Folk music and dance also helped perpetuate native American or African traditions and represented the struggle of the colonial masses for dignity and autonomy.

Cultural life in colonial Latin America was overwhelmingly derivative, as the New World intellectuals of this era looked to Europe for literary and artistic themes and styles which they then applied to the colonial culture. Despite this limitation, however, there were significant intellectual achievements in many of the region's major urban centers. The inherent tension between a pride in things American and deference to European canons of taste led in some cases to the tentative development of an intellectual nationalism, in particular, in studies of the great indigenous civilizations. Eventually, in intellectual life, as in the marketplace, men and women grew restive within the constraints of the colonial order.

Notes

1. P. J. Bakewell, *Silver Mining and Society in Colonial Zacatecas 1546–1700* (Cambridge, England: Cambridge University Press, 1971), p. 211, n. 3.
2. Luis Martín, *Daughters of the Conquistadores. Women of the Viceroyalty of Peru* (Albuquerque: University of New Mexico Press, 1983), p. 165.
3. Jorge Juan and Antonio de Ulloa, *A Voyage to South America,* The John Adams Translation (New York: Alfred A. Knopf, 1964), p. 181.
4. Thomas Gage, *Thomas Gage's Travels in the New World,* ed. J. Eric Thompson (Norman: University of Oklahoma Press, 1958), p. 221.
5. Carl N. Degler, *Neither Black nor White; Slavery and Race Relations in Brazil and the United States* (New York: Macmillan, 1971), p. 80.
6. Antonio Vázquez de Espinosa, *Compendium and Description of the West Indies,* trans. Charles Upson Clark (Washington, D.C.: Smithsonian Institution, 1942), p. 428.
7. John Tate Lanning, *The Royal Protomedicato: The Regulation of the Medical Professions in the Spanish Empire,* ed. John Jay TePaske (Durham N.C.: Duke University Press, 1985), p. 309.
8. Ibid., pp. 226–27.
9. Irving A. Leonard, *Baroque Times in New Mexico* (Ann Arbor: University of Michigan Press, 1959), p. 178.
10. Ibid., p. 189.

Suggested for Further Reading

Chance, John K. *Race and Class in Colonial Oaxaca.* Stanford, Calif., Stanford University Press, 1978.
Cohen, David W., and Jack P. Greene, editors. *Neither Slave nor Free: The Freedmen of African Descent in the Slave Societies of the New World.* Baltimore, Johns Hopkins University Press, 1972.
Cushner, Nicolas P. *Farm and Factory: The Jesuits and the Development of Agrarian Capitalism in Colonial Quito, 1600–1767.* Albany: State University of New York Press, 1982.
Cushner, Nicholas P. *Jesuit Ranches and the Agrarian Development of Colonial Argentina, 1650–1767.* Albany: State University of New York Press, 1983.
Diffie, Bailey W. *A History of Colonial Brazil, 1500–1792.* Edited by Edwin J. Perkins. Melbourne, Fla.: Krieger, 1987.
Hanke, Lewis. *The Imperial City of Potosí: An Unwritten Chapter in the History of Spanish America.* The Hague: Martinus Nijhoff, 1956.
Harris, Charles A. III. *A Mexican Family Empire: The Latifundio of the Sanchez Navarro Family, 1765–1867.* Austin: University of Texas Press, 1975.
Hoberman, Louisa Schell, and Susan Migden Socolow. *Cities and Society in Colonial Latin America.* Albuquerque: University of New Mexico Press, 1986.

Juan, Jorge, and Antonio de Ulloa. *A Voyage to South America.* Tempe: Arizona State University Press, 1975.

Karasch, Mary C. *Slave Life in Rio de Janeiro, 1808–1850.* Princeton, N.J.: Princeton University Press, 1986.

Kinsbruner, Jay. *Petty Capitalism in Spanish America: The Pulperos of Puebla, Mexico City, Caracas, and Buenos Aires.* Boulder, Colo: Westview Press, 1987.

Konrad, Herman. *A Jesuit Hacienda in Colonial Mexico: Santa Lucia, 1576–1767.* Stanford, Calif.: Stanford University Press, 1980.

Kuznesof, Elizabeth A. *Household Economy and Urban Development: São Paulo, 1765–1836.* Boulder, Colo.: Westview Press, 1986.

Lanning, John Tate. *The Royal Protomedicato: The Regulation of the Medical Profession in the Spanish Empire.* Edited by John Jay TePaske. Durham, N.C.: Duke University Press, 1985.

Lanning, John Tate. *The University in the Kingdom of Guatemala.* Ithaca, N.Y.: Cornell University Press, 1955.

Lavrin, Asunción, editor. *Latin American Women: Historical Perspectives.* Westport, Conn.: Greenwood Press, 1978.

Leonard, Irving A. *Baroque Times in Old Mexico.* Ann Arbor: University of Michigan Press, 1959.

Leonard, Irving A. *Books of the Brave.* Cambridge, Mass.: Harvard University Press, 1949.

Liss, Peggy K. *Mexico Under Spain, 1521–1556: Society and the Origins of Nationality.* Chicago: University of Chicago Press, 1975.

Lockhart, James. *Spanish Peru, 1532–1560: A Colonial Society.* Madison: University of Wisconsin Press, 1968.

Martín, Luis. *Daughters of the Conquistadores. Women of the Viceroyalty of Peru.* Albuquerque: University of New Mexico Press, 1983.

Martín, Luis. *The Intellectual Conquest of Peru: The Jesuit College of San Pablo, 1568–1767.* New York: Fordham University Press, 1968.

Miller, Robert Ryal, editor. *Chronicle of Colonial Lima. The Diary of Josephe and Francisco Mugaburu, 1640–1697.* Norman: University of Oklahoma Press, 1975.

Mörner, Magnus. *Race Mixture in the History of Latin America.* Boston: Little Brown, 1967.

Morse, Richard M., editor. *The Bandeirantes: The Role of the Brazilian Pathfinders.* New York: Knopf, 1965.

Ramirez, Susan E. *Provincial Patriarchs: The Economics of Power in Colonial Peru.* Albuquerque: University of New Mexico Press, 1985.

Russell-Wood, A. J. R. *Fidalgos and Philanthropists: The Santa Casa da Misericordia of Bahia, 1550–1755.* Berkeley and Los Angeles: University of California Press, 1969.

Sweet, David, and Gary Nash. *Struggle and Survival in Colonial America.* Berkeley and Los Angeles: University of California Press, 1981.

Taylor, William B. *Drinking, Homicide and Rebellion in Colonial Mexican Villages.* Stanford, Calif.: Stanford University Press, 1979.

Twinam, Ann. *Miners, Merchants and Farmers in Colonial Colombia.* Austin: University of Texas Press, 1983.

SEVEN

IMPERIAL EXPANSION

The Spanish Colonies, 1680s to 1762

Problems apparent in the waning Habsburg era persisted as the eighteenth century opened. In the critical areas of trade, revenue, and administrative control, the military and financial pressures of the War of the Spanish Succession, 1700 to 1713, brought further deterioration. Although the empire's population increased slowly, the consumption of legal imports remained at low levels. One important reason for this commercial stagnation was the aggressive intervention of foreign traders, especially the French, along the Pacific coast. In addition, empirewide mining production reached it nadir during this period. Mexican silver output grew, but the increase failed to overcome a drop in Peruvian silver production.

Philip V faced familiar problems: how to increase American tax revenues, how to protect the empire, and how to expand Spain's commercial relationship with the colonies. More efficient administration, better revenue collection, an effective defense, and the elimination of contraband were related objectives. An improved defense required greater revenue which in turn required the reinvigoration of legal transatlantic trade. A more effective administrative system was a clear precondition in order for the Crown to gain the greatest benefit from efforts to increase revenue. Between 1713 and 1762, the Crown took a number of steps to realize these objectives. It generally pursued the conservative strategy of seeking to eliminate abuses, rather than attempting structural change. However, some new policies were dictated by the financial and defensive requirements arising from war or the threat of it.

War, Foreign Threats, and the Empire

French pressure during the War of the Spanish Succession forced the new Bourbon monarch Philip V to grant his ally commercial access to New World trade. This marked an important legal break in Spain's long-defended claim to monopolistic control over colonial trade. The Treaty of Utrecht confirmed Philip on the throne but also gave the English important economic concessions—the *asiento,* a monopoly contract to import slaves, and the annual ship. A quarter-century of recrimination between Spain and England over contraband trade associated with these privileges finally culminated in the War of Jenkins's Ear (1739–48).

A dispute between Spain and Portugal over colonial boundaries resulted in a conflict over the Portuguese Colônia do Sacramento on the Río de la Plata in the first half of the eighteenth century. The Treaty of Madrid in 1750 called for an exchange of territory, but the failure to implement the provisions fully led to nullification of the agreement and a renewed but inconclusive war. The issue was far from resolved when Charles III became king in 1759.

New Spain's northern boundary of occupied territory, although sparsely settled, expanded substantially in the late seventeenth and early eighteenth centuries. Threats from the Indians, the French, and the English underscored the need to provide additional defense in the borderlands. The Jesuits established missions in northwestern New Spain as far north as Arizona. After the loss to Indian forces in the disastrous Pueblo revolt of 1680, New Mexico was not resettled until the 1690s. In Texas a series of missions and garrisons were built in the early 1720s as a buffer against French threats to northern Mexico. The establishment of Fort San Carlos on Pensacola Bay in 1699 and its recapture in 1723 after four years of French occupation solidified the Spanish presence on the northern Gulf coast, although French traders remained in Louisiana. In Florida the successful defense of St. Augustine against the English during the wars of the Spanish Succession and Jenkins's Ear emphasized the importance of this northern redoubt in New Spain's defensive perimeter.

Challenges to Spanish authority in the viceroyalty of Peru led to a major administrative reorganization. The vulnerability to enemy attack of lands adjoining the Caribbean and the problem of contraband trade led the Crown to create a third viceroyalty, out of the northern portions of the viceroyalty of Peru. This new viceroyalty, of New Granada, combined the *audiencia* districts of Santa Fe de Bogotá and Quito and the coastal districts of Venezuela. Initially established in 1717 and suspended six years later, New Granada was permanently reestablished in 1739. In this final organization, New Granada lost control of Quito but gained Panama.

Administrative Reforms: An Uneven Course

International recognition of Philip's rule in the Treaty of Utrecht in 1713 was followed by his victory over Catalonia, which in 1714 had joined the rest of the Crown of Aragon in supporting the Habsburg claimant Archduke Charles. Peace enabled the monarch to consolidate his authority in Spain. He immediately indicated that the Habsburg's patrimonial approach to ruling would yield to a more unitary and centralized vision, by terminating the autonomy of the Crown of Aragon in 1716. Tighter control, more efficient administration, a reduction in special privileges that ran counter to royal financial and political interests, and the greater centralization of authority in Madrid were the order of the day for Spain. The same approach would be extended to the colonies in the succeeding decades.

Philip V appointed secretaries of state with specific responsibilities that cut deeply into those previously exercised by councils. In this administrative reform, the Council of the Indies lost a great deal of its authority after 1717. Although it remained unchallenged in its judicial powers and continued to enjoy patronage over judicial and ecclesiastical positions, the council lost power to the secretary of state for the Indies in financial, military, commercial, and general administrative matters. Henceforth one person—the secretary—rather than a committee was responsible for general oversight of the Indies.

Besides restructuring colonial administration at court, the Crown made several efforts to improve administration in the Indies. New Spain, the major source of American bullion since the 1660s and the most populous colony in the New World, received increased attention. Beginning in 1710 Philip sent a series of special investigators to examine the viceroyalty's administrative institutions and to secure additional revenues to support his wartime expenses. For more than two decades these agents found accounts in arrears, evidence of fraud, and numerous other abuses. These royal agents proved better at identifying than rectifying abuses, however.

From the late seventeenth century to the mid-eighteenth century, the fiscal demands of war repeatedly frustrated efforts at administrative reform in the colonies. The systematic sale of appointments to *audiencia* positions that began in 1687 continued until 1750. During this period, efforts to gain control over the courts by appointing meritorious outsiders floundered with each outbreak of war. Renewed sales brought a rush of purchasers who, particularly in Peru, erased the modest gains. Beginning in the 1750s, however, improved finances enabled the Crown to stop selling *audiencia* appointments and slowly to start regaining authority. Probably over 80 percent of the creoles but scarcely 10 percent of the penisulars named from 1687 to 1750 purchased their initial *audiencia* appointments. Almost 40 percent of the Americans named, moreover, were native sons, men appointed to the tribunal located in their region of birth.

The termination of sales at mid-century began a decline in the number of native sons, and before 1763 the new direction of appointments was unmistakable. Of twenty new men named, only four were creoles. The simultaneous royal reluctance to permit additional ministers to establish local ties set the stage for a dramatic assault in the 1770s on the remaining native sons and *radicados,* or locally rooted ministers.

The continued sale of appointments to provincial administrative positions until the mid-eighteenth century undercut intermittent efforts to control exploitation of the natives by provincial administrators. Indeed, the cost of an appointment intensified the financial pressure on purchasers and undoubtedly resulted in even greater abuse of office, especially the forced sale of goods to Indian communities. In response to a situation that its own actions had exacerbated, the Crown attempted in 1751 to regulate the prices that officials could charge for forced sales to Indian communities. Its efforts to curb abuse failed, however, and the much resented exploitation continued unabated.

The Crown sought also to improve revenue collection. The Habsburgs had relied on tax farming for the collection of taxes. In contrast, the Bourbons gradually began to place tax collection directly in the hands of royal bureaucrats. Early moves in this direction affected the powerful *consulados* of Lima and Mexico City. In 1724 the Crown assumed direct control over the *alcabala* and other commercial taxes long administered by Lima's *consulado*. Thirty years later it extended this approach to Mexico.

Demographic Expansion

The population of the Spanish colonies as a whole increased during the first half of the eighteenth century. Precise data for the period are not available, but a number of regional examples point toward demographic expansion. The population of New Spain, for example, grew by nearly 50 percent between the mid-seventeenth and mid-eighteenth centuries. The growing Spanish and *casta* populations accounted for a disproportionately large share of this increase, although the Indian population was also growing. The native population of Peru fell briefly as a result of severe epidemics in the 1720s, but growth resumed by mid-century. Caracas grew slowly but steadily throughout the early eighteenth century and by mid-century had perhaps 30,000 people. Buenos Aires increased from a population of about 11,600 in 1744 to 26,125 in 1778. Chile increased from 95,000 people in 1700 to 184,000 in 1755. In Cuba, the population perhaps tripled between 1700 and 1760, numbering some 160,000 in the latter year. Aided by the increased availability of labor and a larger pool of consumers, both economic production and trade grew substantially.

Mining

The combined silver production of New Spain and Peru reached a very low level in the 1680s and remained depressed into the early eighteenth century. Conditions were different, however, in the two viceroyalties. After 1660, New Spain had emerged as the premier silver producer. Buoyed by increased mercury supplies from Spain and rising silver production at Zacatecas, Mexican output climbed until 1690 before falling briefly. Silver production rose from nearly 20 million pesos in 1695–99 to 50 million in 1720–24. It then dropped nearly 25 percent for the next twenty years. Production rose again after 1746 to an average of 12 million pesos a year until a shortage of mercury in the early 1760s brought a temporary decline.

Silver production in Peru hit bottom in the 1720s but then began to improve slowly, accelerated by the 1736 reduction in the tax rate from a fifth to a tenth. Comparative production levels fell further behind those of New Spain, despite the recovery. By 1750 the northern viceroyalty was producing roughly almost twice as much silver as Peru was, a margin that grew larger by 1800.

Gold production in Colombia in the seventeenth century was worth about 20 percent of the silver mined in the viceroyalty of Peru (170 million to 752 million pesos). The yield in the Chocó appears to have been higher in the first half of the eighteenth century than later. In Antioquia, on the other hand, production grew rapidly after 1750. Total Colombian output in the eighteenth century exceeded that for the seventeenth century by about 15 percent. In Chile, gold mining regained ground in the 1690s and grew throughout most of the eighteenth century.

Remission of Bullion and Imperial Profit

Mexico's replacement of Peru as the foremost silver-producing viceroyalty after 1660 was reflected in the amount of public revenues sent to Castile. Between 1651 and 1660, Peru sent 8.6 million pesos to the metropolis, and New Spain sent 4.3 million. In the 1660s, New Spain's remissions exceeded Peru's. By the decade from 1741 to 1750, Peruvian remissions had fallen to 500,000 pesos, whereas those from New Spain had increased to 6.4 million. In the following decade, New Spain's contribution rose to over 16 million pesos, but Peru sent nothing.

Bullion remitted to Spain was only one source of revenue that the Crown derived from the Indies. Comparing the remission of bullion from New Spain and Peru with figures from Cádiz's treasury office records for the Indies reveals that the bullion regularly provided less than 40 percent of the funds collected. Peninsular taxes on the Indies' trade and various fees, fines, and loans collected on the peninsula contributed, from 1731 to 1770, up to three-quarters of the revenues. The highest average revenues were collected during the reign of Ferdinand VI and thus coincided closely with the higher level of silver production in New Spain.

Although the significance of American bullion for both the Spanish Crown and the expansion of European trade around the world was immense, its glitter has unfairly overshadowed an even more important source of royal revenue for much of the eighteenth century: The Crown created a royal monopoly over Cuban tobacco in 1717. Although the contraband sale of Cuban tobacco was often triple the amount of tobacco sent legally to Spain in the 1720s and 1730s, the monopoly made enormous profits from processing and selling the Cuban leaf. From 1740 to 1760 about 85 percent of the tobacco processed by the royal factory in Seville came from Cuba. This monopoly produced annual profits that grew from nearly 4 million pesos in the early 1740s to over 5 million by the late 1750s. Profits from the tobacco monopoly in the 1740s, in other words, exceeded the revenues remitted from New Spain and Peru by more than 400 percent. In the 1750s, the royal income from the tobacco monopoly was still more than twice as large as the extraordinarily high remissions of bullion.

Commerce

The transfer of the House of Trade from Seville to Cádiz in 1717 once again housed administrators, merchants, and ships together in a single port. José Patiño, for example, was an administrative official in the navy and president of the House of Trade in the same year, thereby demonstrating the Crown's recognition that seapower and commerce went together. Later secretary of state for the Indies, navy, and treasury, Patiño tried to strengthen Spain through greater commercial exploitation of the empire.

Under Patiño's leadership, Spain pursued a mercantilist economic policy. Spain had traditionally sought to exclude European rivals from colonial trade in order to ensure its monopoly of bullion. After the 1730s this policy was tied to an effort to promote American production outside the mining sector. Because importing goods from sources outside the empire upset the balance of trade, mercantilist policies encouraged, for example, sugar production in Cuba and cacao production in Venezuela.

Although beginning in 1618, it had allowed 2 small ships to sail each year from Seville to Buenos Aires and had always permitted a modest number of single ships to transport goods to the Indies, the Crown refrained until the eighteenth century from authorizing major changes in the fleet system. Beginning in 1701, French ships were allowed to stop at Indies ports for repairs and provisions, which opened the door to illicit trade with Peruvian and Chilean ports. The value of French ships for defense against England and the impossibility of providing regular fleet service during the War of the Spanish Succession prevented the suppression of this contraband. By 1724, 150 French ships had sailed for Spain's Pacific coast colonies. On occasion colonial officials blatantly skimmed off a percentage of the profit. The quantity of merchandise lowered prices and spelled ruin for the long-decadent fleet system going through Portobelo and the isthmus of Panama. It also weakened the Lima merchant class. The Treaty of Utrecht granted the *asiento* to the South Sea Company which established a commercial post in Buenos Aires. From 1715 to 1738, over 60 English ships entered this port carrying slaves and an unknown quantity of merchandise. In addition, illicit goods funneled to Buenos Aires through Portuguese Colônia further diminished the markets for legal goods shipped through Lima.

The annual ship authorized by the *asiento* for the Portobelo fair also caused difficulty for Spanish merchants. The English sent a larger ship than authorized and sold their less expensive textiles tax free. Because English goods sold for 30 percent less than did goods imported by Spanish merchants, the appearance of an English ship at the fairs of 1722, 1726, 1729, and 1731 disrupted the market. Competition from French and English goods dramatically altered traditional commercial ties between Peru and Spain.

In 1720 the Crown stated its desire to reestablish an effective fleet system. This effort to reinstate regular fleet sailings also expanded the use of single, licensed ships sailing directly from Cádiz to designated Atlantic ports. Ironically, this provision undercut the larger objective of maintaining a fleet system, for it challenged the high transportation costs and monopoly prices of the trade fairs at Portobelo and Vera Cruz. Buenos Aires, in particular, benefited from the greater use of register ships. Through it flowed goods to Upper Peru and Chile, although such transfers required special permission. As a consequence, Peru was less well stocked than Chile was. Faced with a shrunken market, the *consulado* merchants in Lima, some of whom engaged in contraband trade, opposed holding new fairs.

Although seven fleets sailed to Vera Cruz and four to Portobelo between 1717 and 1738, single ships sailing with purchased licenses transported over 20 percent of the total transatlantic tonnage. The outbreak of the War of Jenkins's Ear, however, marked the true transition from the fleet system to reliance on register ships. With Portobelo destroyed and the fleet system for South America moribund, the Crown in 1740 extended the use of register ships to the Pacific. The change arose from the sensible belief that fast single ships could more easily escape English naval squadrons than could convoys.

The length of the war also demonstrated that register ships provided faster and more dependable transportation. Purchased permits authorized register ships to sail from any Spanish port to any South American port between Concepción and Callao. Nearly twenty ships reached Callao by 1748, and over thirty-five more by 1761. The quantity of merchandise reaching Chile and Peru was so great that only by lowering prices and raising the pressure on the Indians through forced purchases could the merchants sell their wares. One contemporary in Lima reported that "the convents are filled with merchants who have closed their doors and declared themselves bankrupt."[1] Merchants who were no longer protected from competition by means of monopoly sought a return to the fleet system. The new ties created through register ship trading, however, could not be overturned. Despite the merchants' complaints, both consumers and the Crown benefited from an increased volume of trade. As the postwar years demonstrated, between 1717 and 1738, register ships carried a greater average volume of goods than had the fleet system. Between 1739 and 1756, register ships handled nearly all the trade between Spain and the

Indies. Although six more fleets sailed to New Spain in the following two decades, register ships accounted for 80 percent of the ships sailing from Spain to the viceroyalty.

Comparing the average annual shipments to Spain of selected colonial exports from South America (excluding Venezuela) reveals substantial growth in the legal trade. In the 1720s and 1730s, an average of five ships a year carried approximately 2 million pesos of silver and 850,000 pesos of gold, 210,000 pounds of cacao, 50,000 pounds of cascarilla, and 7,500 hides. After the War of Jenkins's Ear, between 1749 and 1755 an average of ten ships a year transported 3.2 million pesos of silver, 2.75 million pesos of gold, 995,000 pounds of cacao, 160,000 pounds of cascarilla, and 42,000 hides. Figures for ship sailings demonstrate the dramatic expansion of trade from 1700 to 1761. There was an average of 195 sailings in each of the first two decades, a number that increased to an average of 370 in the following two decades before jumping to 447 in the 1740s and 582 in the 1750s. In 1760 and 1761 alone, the number of sailings, 189, was equal to the total between 1700 and 1709.

The estimated tonnage *(toneladas)* transported between Spain and the Indies rose substantially as well. Between 1681 and 1709, the annual average was 6,041 *toneladas,* which between 1710 and 1740 increased almost 50 percent, to an average of 8,696 a year. In the first twenty years in which register ships were used extensively, the amount of goods carried averaged 17,636 *toneladas,* nearly triple the average for the first period.

The introduction of monopoly trading companies charged with handling trade and eradicating contraband from a specified region was another innovation of the first half of the eighteenth century. The most successful company was the Caracas Company, established in 1728. This group of primarily Basque merchants received a monopoly over trade with Venezuela. There was constant friction between Venezuelan cacao planters and company officials, especially over the prices imposed in Venezuela and the curtailment of the planters' participation in the more profitable contraband trade. Nonetheless, cacao production and legal exportation increased substantially under the company's administration. Before the company's establishment, cacao exports totaled approximately 2.5 million pounds annually, which rose to 5.25 million pounds annually between 1730 and 1748 and to 6.4 million between 1749 and 1765. Under company rule, moreover, Venezuela for the first time became fiscally self-supporting. Instead of draining Mexican resources for subsidies, the region actually returned a profit to the Crown starting in the early 1730s.

In Cuba, trade and population expanded in the first half of the eighteenth century. Largely as a result of natural increase, the population grew from perhaps 50,000 in 1700 to about 160,000—about a quarter of which were slaves—in the late 1750s. The shortage of regular shipping between Cádiz and Havana, however, had long hindered the development of a legal tobacco trade, although contraband flourished. After earlier experiments proved unsuccessful, the Crown awarded a contract in 1740 to a group of Havana merchants, who formed the Havana Company. The company tried to cut tobacco production so as to eliminate a surplus sold illegally and to increase the production of sugar. It gained a monopoly over the purchase and export of 3 million pounds of high-quality Cuban tobacco to Spain for manufacture at the royal factory in Seville. It also received special tax treatment for exported sugar and hides. Under the company, Cuban trade expanded to a higher level. In the mid-1730s, for example, there were only twenty sailings in five years, a number that grew to fifty-nine between 1758 and 1762. Havana's trade with other American ports, particularly Vera Cruz and Portobelo, also rose, although the total volume was far less than that of the Spanish trade.

The expanding trade reflected increased colonial production. At the same time, the greater regularity of shipping induced producers of agricultural and pastoral products to raise their output even further. An important consequence of this was the economic growth of regions distant from the commercial centers of the old fleet system, and previously able to import only a limited quantity of expensive goods. The Río de la Plata, Chile, Venezuela, and Central America, areas previously on the periphery of imperial trade, had already grown economically before the elimination of further barriers to trade in the second half of the eighteenth century. Each region also had a growing population and rising exports of agricultural or pastoral products. The Río de la Plata benefited, too, from exporting bullion obtained by sending imported goods—textiles, slaves, iron, and other items—into the mining areas of Upper Peru and from trade with Chile. Chile's renewal of gold production in the 1690s further strengthened an economy already expanding as a result of substantial wheat shipments to Peru.

Despite the widening colonial trade, Spanish exports remained limited primarily to agricultural products—wine, brandy, olive oil, and spices— and iron and iron tools not manufactured in the Indies. Indeed, until the late colonial period, most textiles sent to the Indies continued to be reexports of foreign goods. In addition, Spanish exporters in Cádiz remained mainly front men for foreign merchants.

Economic expansion was the most important development in the Indies between the late seventeenth century and the British capture of Havana in 1762. The more efficient exploitation of colonial exports and the expansion of colonial markets were mandatory for Spain in order to participate again as a great power in European affairs. Its conservative approach to trade, however, meant that government initiatives focused on reestablishing and making more efficient the old fleet system. European affairs outside colonial concerns, moreover, occupied most of the Crown's attention during the early decades of the century. Consequently, the greater use of register ships after 1740—the most important alteration in Spain's transatlantic trading system since the development of the convoy system in the sixteenth century—largely took place as a result of individual initiatives to supply American markets through direct trade and as a necessary defensive response to English naval superiority. The results demonstrated the superiority of register ships over the fleet system and prepared the way for its final elimination in 1789. By that date, however, the Crown had long ceased relying on halfway measures and ad hoc defensive responses to make the empire stronger economically and militarily. Building on the stronger economic base developed during the first half of the century, the Crown was following a conscious and persistent policy of increasing royal authority and colonial revenues instead of the earlier piecemeal and inconsistent efforts.

Map 4
Colonial Latin America:
Political Organization

Disputed by England, Russia and Spain

Effective Frontier of Spanish Settlement

NEW FRANCE

ENGLISH COLONIES

Mississippi

Viceroyalty of New Spain

Atlantic

Ocean

Tropic of Cancer

Mexico City

Haiti (ceded to France, 1697)

Santo Domingo

Jamaica (conquered by English, 1655)

Caracas

1494 Line of Tordesillas

Original boundary between viceroyalties of New Spain and Peru

Viceroyalty of New Granada (established 1717,1739)

Guiana

Pernambuco (held by Dutch, 1630-54)

Bogotá

Equator

Quito

Grão Pará

Maranhão

Viceroyalty of Peru

Mato Grosso

Pacific

Ocean

Lima

Cuzco

Goiás

Bahia

Salvador

Minas Gerais

Topic of Capricorn

Viceroyalty of La Plata (established 1776)

São Paulo

Rio de Janeiro

Rio Grande do Sul

Santiago

Buenos Aires

Spanish America: Viceroyalties

Portuguese America (Viceroyalty of Brazil): Captaincies-general ca. 1780

Brazil in the Age of Expansion

The discovery of substantial gold deposits beginning in the mid-1690s inaugurated a boom in previously unsettled areas in the Brazilian interior. The rapid growth of population and the attraction of mineral wealth in Minas Gerais and other mining regions led the Portuguese Crown to enlarge the colonial bureaucracy. New transportation networks and commercial relations were developed to supply the mining camps. The prosperity of the mining region placed pressure on the established sugar-producing regions of the northeast by introducing price inflation and greater competition for labor and capital. By the mid-eighteenth century, Brazil's economic center had moved south, although the value of sugar exports continued to exceed that of gold. The transfer of the viceregal capital from Bahia to Rio de Janeiro in 1763 culminated a series of administrative changes that reflected the south's greater economic and political importance as well as heightened tension with Spain on the southern frontier.

But boom became depression as gold production descended steadily after peaking in the early 1750s. The interior's days of glory passed quickly, but by the early 1780s the coastal provinces enjoyed a renewed prosperity. Bolstered by the importation of unprecedented numbers of slaves and improved market conditions, sugar production expanded rapidly in the 1790s. The greater demand for tobacco, cotton, rice, coffee, indigo, and cacao also contributed to coastal Brazil's renewed economic vitality. New government policies helped stimulate this recovery and channel benefits to Portugal.

Charcoal delivered to city of Rio de Janeiro

Administration

The growth of mining centers far from established settlements forced the Portuguese Crown to create new administrative, judicial, and treasury districts. Subdividing the immense territory previously under the jurisdiction of the governor and captain-general of Rio de Janeiro into smaller territorial units was the first step. In 1709 a new captaincy-general, São Paulo e Minas do Ouro, was separated from Rio's jurisdiction. This was later divided, in 1720, into the separate captaincies-general of São Paulo and Minas Gerais. In 1748 two additional captaincies, Goiás and Mato Grosso, were created. After further reorganization in the early 1770s, Brazil had nine captaincies-general and nine subordinate captaincies.

In 1752, a second colonial high court, the new *relaçao* of Rio de Janeiro, was established. The great distance separating the frontier mining camps from the old administrative centers led to the subdivision of captaincies into judicial districts *(comarcas)*. Both Minas Gerais and Bahia, for example, were divided into four *comarcas*. Judicial committees made up of the governor and the senior treasury official of the captaincy and the senior judge of the *comarca* provided justice in the new districts.

The administration in Brazil was centered on the towns. By formally elevating mining camps to townships, the Crown committed itself to providing at least skeletal royal administration. The simultaneous extension of land grants and other privileges to these new towns and their officials encouraged further settlement of the interior. Beginning in 1693 a number of new towns were created to improve law and order and to streamline the collection of royal revenue. Although the establishment of towns and the introduction of administrative institutions definitely strengthened royal control in Minas Gerais, there still was little effective control in the sparsely inhabited captaincies of Mato Grosso and Goiás.

A central feature of these administrative reforms was the creation of new treasury offices. Foundry houses were built in each major mining area, to which miners brought their gold for weighting, extraction of the royal fifth, and casting into bars. In addition, the Crown tried to limit access to the mining areas so that taxes could be collected on imports. Colonists in mining areas were also subject to the usual crown monopolies of salt, wine, and olive oil. Taken together, these taxes, the tithe, and local taxes contributed both to the rising royal revenues and the exorbitant cost of living in the mining regions.

During the second half of the eighteenth century in particular, the Crown sought to tighten its grip on Brazil. Sebastião José de Carvalho e Melo, after 1770 the marquis of Pombal and the powerful royal minister who dominated affairs of state from 1750 to 1777, correctly perceived that Portugal's fortunes rested on the prosperity of its huge American colony. Expanding the Brazilian economy and trade with the metropolis, collecting and expending its tax revenues, and securing its defenses, particularly in the lands adjoining Spanish America, were central to his goal of strengthening Portugal.

Under Pombal the Ministry of the Navy and Overseas Territories, established in 1736, gained control over colonial affairs. It oversaw general policy implementation and proposed high-ranking civil, military, and ecclesiastical appointments to the king. Pombal expanded the authority of the Board of Trade created in 1755 to develop Portuguese industry and reduce the kingdom's reliance on British imports. Its enlarged scope was recognized in 1788 when it became the Royal Committee for Trade, Agriculture, Factories, and Navigation for Portugal and the Colonies.

The establishment of a new royal treasury in 1761 centralized accounting for Portugal and the empire. Headed by Pombal himself as inspector-general, this agency centralized the supervision of revenue collection and expenditure. The next step in the Crown's fiscal reorganization was the creation during the 1760s and 1770s of treasury boards in each captaincy-general. Within their jurisdictions, the boards oversaw the activities of all departments of the royal exchequer. Double-entry bookkeeping was introduced in Brazil in 1764, but the shortage of trained personnel limited its effectiveness.

The Church

The stronger and more centralized Portuguese monarchy of the eighteenth century took numerous actions that reduced the power of the Church, its foremost institutional rival. Under Pombal the government broke the long-standing tradition of equal and complementary authority exercised by church and state.

The rapid economic and demographic expansion of the interior gold-mining regions was not accompanied by a parallel expansion of clerical influence and authority. The first friars on the scene were deeply involved in gold smuggling, and consequently the Crown banned all religious orders from Minas Gerais in 1711. This ban was not, however, accompanied by an effort to attract secular clergy to the region. Efforts to eliminate the extortionate practices of greedy priests, by paying clerics from the royal treasury and limiting the fees charged for the sacraments, proved ineffective. In fact, these policies kept the Church from establishing itself as securely in the mining zone as it had in northeastern Brazil during the first stages of settlement.

The expulsion of the Society of Jesus from Brazil in 1759–60 demonstrated the Crown's ability to destroy its opponents. The Society was solidly entrenched in Brazil when the Crown signed the Treaty of Madrid in 1750. Jesuit opposition to this treaty, exaggerated rumors of the Society's wealth, and Pombal's outrage at the Jesuits' opposition to his creation of a joint-stock company to exploit the resources of the interior led to the expulsion of the Society from Portugal and the empire and the seizure of its properties. The Crown sold some rural estates but maintained others as royal domain. Jesuit churches passed to the secular clergy, and the Society's colleges were often converted into government or military facilities. Because of the Jesuits' central role in education, the expulsion had a chilling effect on Brazil's cultural life. The diversity and scale of Jesuit holdings meant that the government's action affected urban real estate, ranching, sugar production, and farming. And because the Society was also the colony's largest institutional slave owner and a source of investment credit, Pombal's decision had unforeseen consequences for the labor and capital markets as well.

The Crown then turned its attention toward the assets of the other orders. It seized the rich cattle ranches and other property of the Mercedarians and forced other orders to lend it money in exchange for government bonds. Coupled with the state's lukewarm support for the secular clergy, these actions toward the Jesuits and other regular clergy represented a significant weakening of the Church in Brazil.

Demographic Expansion

The population of Brazil increased from perhaps a million in 1700 to about 1.5 million at mid-century and over 2 million in 1800. Although the mining boom shifted the population south and west, the traditional agricultural economies of the coastal regions maintained their larger, more densely settled populations. Nonetheless, the great gold rushes to the interior were clearly responsible for attracting new immigrants, expanding the slave trade, and stimulating internal migration. This process, in turn, led to the creation of a more diversified, more integrated colonial economy.

Immigrants from Portugal averaged perhaps three thousand to four thousand annually during the first twenty years of the century. The flow was sufficiently heavy that in 1720 the Crown strictly limited it through new licensing procedures. After that the annual total probably never reached two thousand. During the first half of the century most of these immigrants went to the mining zones.

In the mining camps Portuguese immigrants soon outnumbered the Paulista frontiersmen who discovered the mines. The mining camps also received an enormous influx of black slaves. In the eighteenth century, Brazil imported approximately 1.7 million slaves from Africa. Despite this large number, the labor demands and capital resources of the mining districts drove up prices and created an internal trade that took slaves away from the plantations of northeastern Brazil. African slaves thus soon formed the backbone of the work force. In Minas Gerais the number of slaves had reached about thirty thousand by 1715, and in Minas Novas slaves were the majority of a population that reached about forty thousand within three years of the initial gold strike.

The drop in gold production that began in the 1750s reoriented the African slave trade toward the newly developed agricultural areas of the coast and, after 1791, to the sugar zone near Bahia. The imports of slaves during the second half of the eighteenth century almost certainly equaled those between 1700 and 1750. Between 1800 and 1810 another 200,000 slaves were imported. Because the slave trade continued to carry a high proportion of males to females, there was a low rate of natural reproduction in the slave population. However, a high mortality rate—the result of tropical diseases, poor nutrition, inadequate medical care, rudimentary housing, and harsh working conditions—was the major obstacle to the growth of the native-born slave population.

The racial composition of Brazil in the early nineteenth century naturally reflected the massive importation of slaves, nearly two-thirds of the population was African or of African descent. Slaves were the most numerous class, 38 percent of the population. Free blacks and mulattoes together made up 28 percent, an amount equal to that of the white population. Within the settled regions of Brazil, Indians represented only 6 percent of the population.

Brazil's population at the turn of the nineteenth century was densest on the northeastern coast. The captaincies-general of Pernambuco, Bahia, and Rio de Janeiro accounted for nearly 60 percent of the population. The mining region of Minas Gerais was the most populous single captaincy-general, with over 400,000 inhabitants, 20 percent of Brazil's population Brazil's two largest cities were on the coast: Bahia and Rio de Janeiro, both major exporting cities, hovered around 50,000, and both increased by 50 percent or more after 1750. In contrast, the third largest city, São Paulo, grew little in this period. Although only thirty miles from the Atlantic, the city's transportation and communication with the coast were impeded by difficult terrain. Still, São Paulo had 24,000 inhabitants in 1803. The ports of Recife and Sâo Luis were the only other cities with populations in excess of 20,000 persons. Vila Rica de Ouro Prêto, the most populous city of Minas Gerais, demonstrated the volatility of boom-town populations, falling from some 20,000 inhabitants in the 1740s to just 7,000 in 1804.

Society

Brazilian society in the eighteenth century remained hierarchical. Place of birth, wealth, occupation, race, and legal status were used to classify individuals and assign privileges and rights. The mining boom and later agricultural recovery altered the demographic components of this colonial society and extended the social apparatus of class and race across new territory. Although the society in 1808 shared important characteristics with that of 1700, it was more dynamic and fluid and also more violent and unpredictable.

The mining boom attracted a wave of immigration from Portugal. Only a tiny minority of these new arrivals made fortunes in gold and diamond mining, but their presence altered society significantly. As a result of this relatively large population of recent immigrants, the settlements of the mining district and southern coastal region confronted much more directly the cultural and political meaning of colonial status. The inherent tension between metropolitan assertiveness and the natural proprietary sense of the colonial natives eventually led to armed conflict in 1708–9. The War of the Emboabas (tenderfeet) pitted the Paulistas against the Portuguese and northern Brazilian migrants. Significantly, the interlopers prevailed.

Another important result of the century's economic dynamism was the creation of a large number of newly wealthy men. The mining elite of boom towns like Ouro Prêto and Sabará were generally rough, uncultured men with little prior experience in the exercise of power or the enjoyment of social leadership. Their wealth gave them the ability to build and consume on a grand scale, but their combination of exuberance and limited cultural breadth produced as many excesses as works of art. As one contemporary put it,

> Those who had amassed great wealth from their diggings were led thereby to behave with pride and arrogance. They went about accompanied by troops . . . ready to execute any violence and to take the greatest and most frightful revenge, without any fear of the law. The gold incited them to gamble lavishly, and heedlessly to squander vast sums on vain luxuries. For instance, they would give one thousand *cruzados* for a Negro trumpeteer; and double that price for a mulata prostitute, in order to indulge with her in continual and scandalous sins.[2]

One example of this type was the millionaire diamond contractor Dr. João Fernandes de Oliveira, who built an artificial lake in order to sail a scaled-down ship manned by a crew of ten. This extravagance was prompted by the complaint of his mistress that she had never seen the ocean.

The cotton, rice, and cacao booms produced their nouveau riche as well. The recovery of sugar prices and an expanded Atlantic trade reinvigorated these sectors of the landed elite, but in the late eighteenth century, social power in Brazil was more dispersed than before. The social and political consequences of this geographical disperison were magnified by the new elite's predisposition to stay in the countryside. Governor Luís Antônio de Sousa complained in 1766 that São Paulo was a desolate place because plantation owners visited town only on the most important occasions.

These centrifugal forces were partly compensated by greater economic integration. Merchants, government officials, and large-scale agriculturalists diversified their investments to protect themselves from changing market conditions. There was a reciprocal social integration as well. Increased physical mobility, the diversification of economic activity, and a set of social presumptions that emphasized family-based associations all encouraged elite families to establish cross-sectoral linkages through marriage and godparents.

These patterns could also be found in the middle sectors, but an added racial dimension made them more complex. Skilled artisans, lower-level functionaries, junior officers, retail merchants, and other groups that made up the middle groups of the colony's cities were drawn from immigrant and native-born whites and from racially mixed populations, and none was likely to be deeply rooted in a region. Instead, they often sought marginal economic benefits by moving to new locations. The most successful acquired property, owned and employed slaves in their households and businesses, and were officers in the colonial militia. This diverse class also provided the social arena in which miscegenation played an important role. Unsure of their status and ambitious for upward social mobility, the members of this class were careful to measure the racial antecedents and economic prospects of their prospective mates.

In rural areas the middle sector included the *lavradores de cana,* the independent cane growers who helped supply larger refiners; tenants who traded labor or a portion of their crops for the right to farm or ranch on another's land; and skilled rural workers, including overseers, artisans, skilled refining workers, and ranch foremen. With the exception of the *lavradores,* they were usually racially mixed persons. Both *lavradores de cana* and tenants were particularly vulnerable to fluctuations in the economy. Because they were often in debt and unprotected by diversification, falling prices, drought, and other natural disasters could ruin them.

The urban and rural underclass formed the base of Brazil's free black and mulatto population. Illegitimacy, family instability, and criminal behavior were common. Because the colonial economy invested little in education or training, the underclasses of both city and countryside had few opportunities for upward social mobility. During boom periods most could secure steady employment and, as a result, adequate food and minimum housing. But when bust followed boom, the demand for labor fell, and many poor people were forced into begging, crime, or migration. Slaves, however, still remained the largest class of deprived colonial residents.

Gold Production

Efforts to estimate Brazil's gold production are limited by the unreliability of the surviving tax records. Whether based primarily on tax or foundry records, production estimates must be increased to include contraband. Sixteen times more valuable than silver per unit, gold tempted miners to employ all manner of ruses to avoid the heavy taxes levied by the Portuguese Crown. Indeed, one contemporary estimated that over two-thirds of the gold mined in Brazil was never declared.

Recent estimates of gold production indicate a rapid expansion from 1700 to 1720, slower growth for the next fifteen years, and a second boom until mid-century. The overall peak was reached in 1750–54 when production in Goiás reached its apogee and that of Minas Gerais, consistently Brazil's largest producer, was still very high. Overall production then decreased steadily. The total between 1795 and 1799 was almost identical with that between 1706 and 1710. A conservative estimate of real production would double the production figures found in tax records. The result is an average annual gold output from 1735 to 1764 of over 27,000 kilo-

Closely supervised slaves mining diamonds in Brazil

grams. This amount was equal in value to the production of more than 14 million silver pesos in the Spanish Empire, thus exceeding in value Peru's best comparable thirty-year period (1581 to 1610). The value of Mexico's bullion production did not surpass that of Brazil's peak years until the 1770s.

Sometime after 1720, diamonds were discovered near the gold boom town of Vila do Principe. Miners and colonial officials initially tried to keep the discovery secret to avoid taxes and regulation. By 1730, however, the Crown moved aggressively to organize and control exploration and development. The flow of Brazilian diamonds caused a crash in European prices and led the Crown to send military units to enforce an outright ban on production. Controlled production was then permitted by a system of monopoly arrangements, although smuggling remained common.

Brazil's gold production and the simultaneous boom in diamond mining in northern Minas Gerais increased the flow of funds to the royal treasury. At the same time, the development of these mining regions produced countervailing demands. Although never adequate to deal with the needs of the turbulent interior, the establishment and continued operation of administrative, judicial, military, and ecclesiastical organizations were nonetheless expensive. This cycle of taxation and expenditure worked to redistribute wealth away from the mining sector to other social groups and geographical regions, most importantly to the metropolitan economy. It may well be that the public sector's role in Brazil tended to limit investment in exploration, technology, and labor—thereby hindering the growth of production—but it also helped expand the colony's middle sectors, thus encouraging a more broad-based consumer class and stimulating domestic as well as transatlantic commerce.

Economy and Trade

As had occurred in the mining districts of Spanish America, rich mineral strikes in Brazil quickly brought together entrepreneurs, laborers, adventurers, freeloaders, clerics, and royal officials. All required food and drink, housing, and clothing. The more successful also sought luxury items whose consumption would reveal their good fortune.

There were numerous beneficiaries of the growth of the mining regions. The salted beef industry of the northeast, for example, profited by the demand for nonperishable food in Minas Gerais. An abundance of gold and a scarcity of nearly every article of basic consumption led to massive price inflation in the mining zone. This, in turn, promoted the rapid development of livestock raising, agriculture, and artisan manufacture. Cattle raising near the mines prospered as miners sought to reduce their dependence on beef imported from other regions. Royal land grants of several square leagues enabled cattlemen to settle near the mines or along transportation arteries. Land grants also enabled small farmers and stockmen to produce staples like pigs and chickens and manioc and other crops. Slaves cultivated a variety of crops for their own subsistence and in limited amounts for market. Thus prosperous agricultural and pastoral activities flourished with the rise in number of miners, slaves, and other residents.

The decline in the gold and diamond production that began in the late 1750s inaugurated a period of economic depression for Brazil. Economic recovery was not evident until the early 1780s and was largely confined to the agricultural belt along the coast. International conflicts, increased industrial demand in Europe, and the devastation of Haiti's sugar production after 1791 as a result of revolutionary violence combined to promote Brazilian agricultural exports. Total sugar exports roughly doubled between 1790 and 1807, reaching nearly 25,000 metric tons in the last year.

Grown commercially beginning only in 1760, cotton emerged as Brazil's second leading export by the close of the century. Production began in Maranhão, and for some forty years the captaincy held the lead among Brazilian regions. By the early nineteenth century, however, Pernambuco was exporting a greater amount of higher-quality cotton. The growth of French and especially English cotton textile industries during the early stages of the industrial revolution inflared prices and spurred production. Although dependent on expensive slave labor, cotton could be processed for less money than could sugar. In addition, because there was no cost equivalent to that of the necessary grinding and refining of sugar, cotton could be produced more quickly in response to escalating demand. In 1782 England imported about 9,000 pounds worth of Brazilian cotton.

Within five years Brazil's cotton exports to England surpassed 150,000 pounds in value and occasionally surpassed 200,000 pounds in succeeding decades. Although Brazil supported an unfavorable balance of trade with Portugal and England at mid-century, by 1791 England was exporting silver to pay for Brazilian imports.

In the late eighteenth century, tobacco, produced primarily in Bahia, continued to be exported legally to Portugal and as contraband to Buenos Aires and Upper Peru. It was particularly important to sustaining the trade in slaves on the African coast. Far surpassed in value by both sugar and cotton as the century closed, tobacco nonetheless remained a vital export for Bahia. Other exports included hides, rice, wheat, coffee, cacao, and a number of lesser products. Rio de Janeiro was the colony's export leader, followed by Pernambuco, Bahia, and Maranhão.

The continuation of a profitable trade in Brazilian agricultural exports, especially sugar, and the windfall profits of the gold and diamond booms led Portugal to abandon its efforts at industrialization begun in the late seventeenth century in the face of serious deficits and fiscal crisis. The Brazilian bonanza, coupled with the Methuen treaties of 1703, tightened Portugal's commercial ties with England. In exchange for preferential treatment for its wine, Portugal increased imports of English cloth, ready-made garments, tools, hardware, and metals. Brazil's gold and diamonds were used to balance Portugal's chronic trade deficit. The unexpected and rapid decline in gold and diamond production after 1750 reduced the royal revenues substantially, at a time when Lisbon was still being rebuilt after the destructive earthquake of 1755 and Portugal was having to pay the costs of war with Spain.

Faced with declining trade and a revenue shortfall in the 1760s and 1770s, the Crown tried to improve the quality of Brazilian sugar and tobacco exports and develop more profitable marketing arrangements. In addition, it attempted to stimulate northern Brazil's economy and revive the long-suffering northeastern coastal zone. The marquis of Pombal created local boards of inspection in Brazil's leading ports and established monopoly trading companies to stimulate agricultural production and promote exports. Inspection boards were set up in Bahia, Rio de Janeiro, São Luis do Maranhão, and Recife. They mediated disputes between producers and merchants and supervised weights and measures and quality control. More importantly, they set wholesale prices, theoretically at levels to maximize the market share of Brazilian exports. In practice, however, this strategy increased profits for the Portuguese shippers and merchants at the expense of the colonial growers and refiners. Colonial manufacturing, on the other hand, was actively discouraged. This approach culminated in 1785 with the prohibition of colonial textile manufacturing other than rough cloth used for slave clothing.

In 1755 the Crown established the Company of Grão Pará and Maranhão, granting it a twenty-year monopoly over shipping and the slave trade with the northern captaincies. This action was accompanied by a prohibition against itinerant Portuguese traders participating in colonial trade. A second Company of Pernambuco and Paraíba was founded in 1759 to handle trade with these two captaincies. Together these companies represented a conscious effort to rationalize the Luso-Brazilian trading system. Until their demise following the death of José I and Pombal's fall from power in 1777, the monopolistic companies increased slave imports and provided more reliable shipping for the regions they served. They also promoted the consumption of products produced in new Portuguese state-supported factories whose creation Pombal had encouraged. When local economic interests and the Jesuits protested against the creation of the first of these monopolies and a simultaneous change in Indian labor policy, Pombal reacted forcefully to silence the dissent.

British opposition to changes in the Luso-Brazilian trading system and the threat of renewed warfare on the border with Spanish settlements in the Río de La Plata prevented Pombal from extending the monopolistic trading companies to Rio de Janeiro and Bahia. Instead, he sought to expand trade by ending the fleet system in 1765. Henceforth, licensed individual ships carried most of the goods between Portugal and Brazil. In the following year, the prohibitions against coastal trade among Brazilian ports were removed.

Expanding Brazilian trade helped Portugal enjoy a favorable balance of trade with other European nations. Even its historic imbalance with England was reversed by 1791, largely as a result of the reexport of Brazilian products. However, these favorable trade statistics merely disguised Portugal's long-term structural disadvantage in commercial competition. Not only did Portuguese ships carry large amounts of British goods to Brazil, but from 1801 to 1807, metropolitan manufactures and legal reexports of English goods declined substantially as a result of increased British smuggling. In 1800 alone, thirty British ships reached Rio de Janeiro. As a consequence Portugal frequently had an unfavorable balance of payments with important Brazilian captaincies. Unable to compete with England's increasingly efficient manufactures, Portugal was also losing its profitable position as a transportation and commercial link between Brazil's plantations and England's factories.

Luso-Spanish Rivalry

Beginning in 1680 with the first foundation of Colônia do Sacramento across the estuary of the Río de la Plata from Buenos Aires, Portugal challenged Spain's control of a region that extended from the estuary north to the captaincy of São Paulo and from the Atlantic west to the Uruguay and Paraná rivers. Portugal was interested mainly in commercial access to the silver of Potosí. Spain, in turn, wanted to close down the contraband trading post of Colônia and gain a buffer zone between Buenos Aires and Brazil. These conflicting objectives led to repeated Spanish attacks on Colônia in the 1760s and 1770s.

By the Treaty of Madrid (1750), Portugal gave up its claims to Colônia and the lands adjoining the Río de la Plata. Spain relinquished the lands between the Uruguay and Ibicui rivers, where the Society of Jesus had seven missions and some 30,000 neophytes and agreed that the Society and its charges would withdraw from the region. This compromise agreement failed, however, because of opposition by powerful interests in Portugal and Spain. Resistance by the Jesuits and mission Indians led to open warfare between 1754 and 1756 and convinced royal advisers in both Iberian countries to push for the expulsion of the Society. The treaty's abrogation in 1761 left war as the final recourse.

In October 1762, Spanish troops led by Pedro de Cevallos, governor of Buenos Aires, took Colônia and then conquered coastal Rio Grande in Brazil. Under the terms of the Treaty of Paris, Spain returned Colônia but continued to occupy coastal Rio Grande. Intermittent armed conflict and ineffective efforts to blockade Colônia led to decisive action in 1776. An expeditionary force of nearly twenty thousand men led by the first viceroy of the Río de la Plata, Pedro de Cevallos, took Santa Catarina Island and Colônia in 1777 but failed to recover Rio Grande. The Treaty of San Ildefonso signed in October 1777 finally settled the boundary conflict. Portugal regained Santa Catarina and coastal Rio Grande but lost Colônia. Spain retained the Seven Missions lands and the Banda Oriental. This boundary remained unchanged until the Portuguese seized the Seven Missions lands in 1801.

Luso-Spanish rivalry carried a heavy price. Both countries committed vast sums of colonial revenue to support soldiers, sailors, and ships. Falling mining revenues and depressed trade in the 1760s and 1770s left the Portuguese Crown particularly hard-pressed. Administrators in Brazil curtailed unnecessary expenses, borrowed money, and delayed paying bills whenever possible. The costs of maintaining a large army created a budget deficit and diverted funds from investment in infrastructure. From the mid-1770s onward, the viceregal treasury's debt increased substantially, despite reduced remittances to Portugal.

The Enlightenment

As the eighteenth century progressed, the writings of the French *philosophes* and other "enlightened" writers entered the intellectual cultures of Portugal and Spain. The Enlightenment's challenge to traditional authority, its emphasis on the use of reason, and reliance on observation, experience, and experimentation reached the colonies, but only a few colonial residents in urban centers actually read and discussed the new ideas. However, a larger number were initiated indirectly through sermons, informal discussions in academies and salons, and illegal pamphlets and graffiti.

With no university in the colony, young Brazilian men had to travel abroad for higher education and professional training. Portugal's University of Coimbra attracted the most Brazilian students, but others attended

Montepellier in France and a few studied at other universities. Following the expulsion of the Jesuits, who had dominated education in Portugal as well as Brazil, Pombal reformed Coimbra's curriculum. After 1772 a reinvigorated faculty employed modern methods emphasizing experimentation, observation, and the critical use of reason. Students of this era returned to Brazil carrying exciting new ideas and recent publications that circulated in a wider circle.

One manifestation of the Enlightenment in Brazil before 1808 was the serious examination of the natural environment. Geography and biology gained a wider audience. The collection and classification of indigenous plants became popular among some intellectuals. And naturalists helped instill a growing pride in Brazil and an awareness of its uniqueness.

The Enlightenment's arsenal of ideas also contained revolutionary political and economic implications, many of which were manifested in the American and French revolutions. The ideals of independence, liberty, equality, and fraternity quickly found Brazilian partisans, although few people actively argued for a revolution against Portuguese authority. In Brazil, educated men and women generally worked to reform commercial and political structures rather than to instigate violent change. This moderation was rooted in the colony's dependence on slave labor and a racial caste system that inhibited the development of Brazilian nationalism. In the decades before 1808 there were only two major conspiracies against Portuguese rule, and both failed.

Conspiracies

Among those who participated in the Mineiro conspiracy in Vila Rica de Ouro Prêto in 1789 were intellectuals who admired the emerging United States and whose libraries contained works by Voltaire and other popular *philosophes*. More important than ideology as a spur to revolt, however, were the massive debts that some of the captaincy's richest men owed to the treasury. Fear that the Crown was about to collect these debts led these more powerful conspirators to view the end of Portuguese rule as the only answer to impending financial doom. Discovered before they could take action, the plot's leaders were arrested. Social eminence, economic resources, and the questionable actions of the captain-general saved almost all of the plotters and their silent partners from death. Only one participant, of modest means, was executed.

In Bahia nine years later, a group of conspirators, which included some slaves, several free mulattoes, and a few whites. issued a call to overthrow the colonial government and establish a republic that would provide "freedom, equality, and fraternity." The social and economic implications of mass emancipation and a definition of citizenship without racial requirements in a captaincy in which whites made up only one-fifth of the population stirred the authorities to action. Four leaders were executed, and the other participants were punished. Regardless of their birthplace and individual grievances, the white merchants, planters, and officials of Bahia believed that their self-interest required the maintenance of the slave system and racial discrimination.

In the opening years of the nineteenth century, Brazil was at a new peak of prosperity. Far more of the colony was settled and economically productive than in the 1690s before the mining boom. The colony's population had more than doubled, and vast areas of the interior had been brought within its economic and political spheres. Both the value and the diversity of exports had grown as well. More and more enlightened residents praised Brazil's progress and welcomed the promising future. Already the economic center of the Luso-Brazilian empire by the end of the eighteenth century, Brazil became its political center as well with the arrival of the Portuguese court in 1808.

New Spain, Peru, and the Reforms of Charles III

The British capture of Havana in 1762 compelled Charles III and his advisers to institute reforms that were more ambitious and costly than those of their predecessors. The preservation of the empire and the guarantee of its economic and fiscal benefits for the metropolis required a better military defense. Military preparedness, however, was costly. To obtain the necessary additional revenue, the Crown turned to the colonies, with reforms intended to integrate the colonies more effectively with Spain. The Crown improved tax collection and instituted new royal monopolies, took steps to raise the colonies' production of exportable primary goods and the importation of Spanish goods, and moved to tighten control over their administration. As was true in Portugal under Pombal, a greater centralization of authority and regalism characterized Spanish rule from the fall of Havana to the Napoleonic invasion of Spain in 1808.

The Peace of Paris in 1763 ended the military hostilities between Spain and Britain known as the Seven Years' War. Although Havana and Manila returned to Spanish rule after a brief British occupation, and France ceded Louisiana to Spain, the loss of Florida underlined the empire's continued vulnerability. In 1765 the Crown moved to increase revenues in New Spain which subsidized the defense of Cuba, the Philippines, and Louisiana, by dispatching a visitor general, José de Gálvez, to the empire's richest and most populous colony. When later named secretary of state for the Indies in 1776, Gálvez also sought improved fiscal benefits from South America. The reform effort in both viceroyalties succeeded in expanding revenue and improving defense. However, the pace of demographic growth during the half-century before the wars of independence was probably more important in determining the contours of daily life in these long-time cores of the empire.

Military Threats and Military Reforms

Faced with the threat of renewed British attacks, the Spanish Crown took the unprecedented step of creating colonial armies. Despite differences in the timing and nature of the reform in each viceroyalty, in both New Spain and Peru the number of authorized regular forces more than tripled between 1760 and 1800, reaching 6,150 in New Spain, excluding the frontier outposts in the north, and about 2,000 in Peru. Colonial militias were also expanded substantially after 1760, but these troops were seldom adequately armed or trained. In 1800 militiamen numbered almost 24,000 in New Spain and probably no more than 18,000 in Peru.

The creation of standing armies in the colonies brought unprecedented numbers of peninsular officers and soldiers to the New World. The consequent predominance of peninsular officers in the highest ranks aggravated the discrimination that creoles already felt in the civil and ecclesiastical hierarchies. In contrast with the regular officers' positions, creole representation was heavy in the militia, in which positions could be purchased. Suspicions about the reliability of creoles, however, led the Crown routinely to assign each unit a regular army officer from the peninsula to supervise training.

As inducements to enlistment, the Crown extended to the colonial armies a number of benefits, including the military *fuero,* the judicial right for officers, soldiers, and their dependents to be heard by a military rather than a civil court in a variety of civil and criminal cases. The benefits offered, however, were inadequate to lure many volunteers into colonial armies that featured low pay, harsh discipline, and poor prospects for advancement. Consequently, recruiting teams scoured taverns, gambling dens, and jails. The alcoholics, gamblers, and vagabonds they enlisted joined convicted criminals sentenced to serve their terms in the army. New recruits in New Spain and other colonies often received defective weapons and were sometimes charged for repairs. Provincial militia units received weapons that were scarcely usable. Because they often were not paid, some soldiers pawned or sold their weapons, uniforms, and shoes in order to survive or for drinking and gambling or, sometimes, to aid their desertion. Not surprisingly, contemporaries frequently considered soldiers more as scourges than defenders of the land, and as a result, the army failed to become an honored and prestigious institution in the colonies.

Despite the poor condition of both the regulars and militiamen, the defense of New Spain and Peru was expensive. In late eighteenth-century New Spain, often over 60 percent of the central treasury's expenditures went for defense. Although the total outlay was large throughout the period, it more than doubled between the early 1760s and the early 1780s. In Peru, Indian rebellions raised military costs even more.

Armed resistance rose in the eighteenth century among the exploited Indians of the Andean colonies. There were five uprisings in the 1740s, eleven in the 1750s, twenty in the 1760s, and twenty in the 1770s. The violent climax of Indian protest occurred in 1780 under the leadership of

José Gabriel Condorcanqui, also known as Tupac Amaru II. This *kuraka* from the Cuzco region led a general insurrection that pulled together a mixed force of Indians and *castas*. This protest against a harsh existence sought the redress of long-standing abuses and the implementation of specific reforms. Tupac Amaru wanted the *repartimiento* of goods ended, the *corregidores* removed, better working conditions instituted in the mines and *obrajes,* the *mita* terminated, and an *audiencia* created in Cuzco. The rebels executed a hated *corregidor* in November 1780 and gathered supporters, particularly near Cuzco. An army sent from Lima soon was victorious, and in May 1781 the captured leader was executed. The death of Tupac Amaru, however, did not end the rebellion; leaders in neighboring regions kept up the struggle. Before peace was restored in 1783, the rebellions had cost 100,000 lives, making them the most violent and costly uprisings since the period of Manco Inca in the sixteenth century. Even though these protests failed militarily, they forced the termination of the *repartimiento* system and led to the establishment of the *audiencia* of Cuzco. By raising the specter of race and class warfare, moreover, they strengthened the creoles' allegiance to Spanish rule and delayed Peru's independence.

The Expansion of Bureaucracy

The need for greater revenues to support defensive expenditures in the New World and to provide resources for its policies at home prompted the Crown to tighten its control over administrators, to assume direct responsibility over previously contracted activities, and to increase the number of crown monopolies. Although the origins of bureaucratic expansion predated the fall of Havana, the most dramatic efforts to reassert and increase royal control came afterwards. In both New Spain and Peru, the number of bureaucrats increased, and the cost of administration grew.

The Crown's loss of administrative power relative to that of the local elites was apparent in 1750. By selling appointments and positions, the Crown had created the kind of corrupt, inefficient bureaucracy it deplored. Lacking the funds to buy out the purchasers, often young native sons, the Crown embarked on a policy of attrition accompanied by a conscious policy of favoring peninsulars to fill vacancies as they appeared. By favoring the peninsulars for the most important new offices in the colonies, the Crown further diluted, although never eliminated, local influence in government.

The consequence of these changes in appointment policy and the termination of sales was visible in both viceroyalties. In 1750 only one of fifteen ministers on the *audiencia* of Mexico had been there less than five years. Thirty years later, thirteen of eighteen ministers were newcomers. In Lima, thirteen of eighteen ministers in 1750 had been born in the colony, but by 1780 only five native sons remained. Later appointments clearly revealed the heightened and continued discrimination against native sons.

Complementing its conscious efforts to reduce local representation in established administrative institutions, the Crown also attempted to expand its authority through directly administering previously farmed or alienated activities. Doing so increased the number of bureaucrats. Overall, the number of government employees in Lima nearly doubled between the mid-1770s and 1790. In New Spain the number of well-paid posts probably quadrupled as a result of these reforms.

The best-known administrative innovation was the establishment of the intendant system, a direct response to the abuses of the *corregidores* and *alcaldes mayores*. As José de Gálvez, the most vigorous supporter of the system's introduction, noted on concluding his *visita* in New Spain, it will be

more satisfactory and practicable for the chief executive of this kingdom to have under his immediate orders twelve *intendentes*, carefully chosen, whose character is above reproach, than to have to suffer and contend with two hundred wretches who, with their empty title of judges, have come to constitute an independent judicial sphere, wherein, driven by their own greed, they work out their own fortunes at the expense of the royal treasury and the ruin of the people.[3]

Adopted from French and Spanish precedents, the intendants represented a new layer of colonial administration linking district administrators to central authorities. The 7 intendants named for Peru in 1784 were directly in charge of 58 subdelegates who replaced the previous *corregidores*. In New Spain, the 12 intendants named in 1786 oversaw roughly 150 district administrators. By creating larger administrative units under officials with substantially greater authority than the previous *corregidores* and *alcaldes mayores* had, the Crown sought to make its power as effective in the countryside as in the cities and towns.

Intendants were responsible for public administration, finance, administration of justice, and military preparedness within their provinces. The improvement of the local governments, promotion of economic growth, encouragement of public works, and especially oversight of the collection of revenue were among their specific obligations. In contrast with the previous district administrators, intendants also exercised royal patronage over the ecclesiastical institutions within their provinces.

These powerful, prestigious, and well-paid new positions went almost exclusively to peninsulars. Many were professional soldiers, but some were lawyers and treasury officials. They secured their appointments by merit, not purchase, and—far more frequently than the *corregidores* whose authority they subsumed—intendants placed the royal interest above personal gain.

Despite Gálvez's great hopes, the intendant system did not yield the anticipated benefits. Although income rose substantially in Peru immediately after the system was introduced, it then fell. In New Spain, Crown revenues actually rose during the 1770s, before the introduction of the intendants. The intendant system also failed to provide good administration and justice in the countryside because it was flawed at the district level. The subdelegates who replaced the *corregidores* and *alcaldes mayores* were at first prohibited from using the *repartimiento* of merchandise; their legal compensation was limited to a small percentage of the tribute they collected. Protests against the prohibition of the merchandise *repartimiento* followed immediately in New Spain. When it became clear within a decade that strigent enforcement was impossible, many subdelegates, particularly those in parts of southern and southeastern Mexico and in the highlands of Peru, returned to the old system of forcing Indian communities to purchase often unwanted and expensive goods.

The intendant system fared better in the provincial capitals than in the countryside. Typically, the intendant sought to revitalize a city council by enlarging its membership, often by recruiting prominent, long-resident peninsulars of the city, raising its revenues, and making a variety of improvements in public services. Improved roads and bridges, street lights, and better sanitation and water supplies increased civic pride. With the limitations placed on the employment of native sons in a number of other government institutions, the *cabildos* increasingly became the primary political arena for local grievances in many parts of the Spanish Empire.

The Expulsion of the Jesuits

In the eighteenth century, the Spanish Crown, like its Portuguese counterpart, followed a broad policy of expanding royal authority at the expense of other institutions and interest groups. Unlike his predecessors, Charles III moved to change the balance between Crown and Church, previously equal and interdependent partners. Believing the Church's jurisdiction should extend over lay persons only in matters of conscience, the Crown reduced ecclesiastical immunity, principally the privilege of asylum, and also the personal legal immunity that clerics enjoyed in many areas.

The Crown's willingness to challenge ecclesiastical institutions became evident in 1767 when Charles expelled the Society of Jesus from his realms. Although the immediate cause was a series of municipal riots in Spain in 1766—believed by some to have been instigated by the Jesuits— the roots of the expulsion lay elsewhere. The Jesuits' refusal to acknowledge monarchical authority as being above papal authority defied regalist doctrine. In addition, the Jesuits had obstructed in the past the implementation of royal policy. Their preeminence in education and close ties to wealthy and prominent lay persons also gave them extensive influence. Finally, the Society's wealth tempted a monarch whose resources were stretched.

The expulsion of 680 Jesuits from New Spain and over 500 from Peru, a majority of whom were native born, shocked colonial opinion. Rioting broke out in the mining region of New Spain and also in Valladolid and Pátzcuaro, where workers were already dismayed by the more stringent tax collection and the imposition of excise taxes on *pulque*. José de Gálvez himself led a ruthless expedition to restore peace. In Peru the expulsion provoked astonishment, but the Jesuits were deported without significant protest.

Following their expulsion, the Crown confiscated the Society's estates and other assets. In Peru the value of the 203 *haciendas* and over 5,200 slaves seized was approximately 6.5 million pesos. In less than a decade, over half of these had been sold. The Society's rural holdings in New Spain brought the Crown over 5 million pesos. This rapid transfer of property created a local vested interest opposed to the Society's return and thus acted to counter pressure from those families angered by the expulsion of sons, kinsmen, and teachers.

The Enlightenment

The expulsion of the Jesuits deprived New Spain and Peru of their most prominent educators and created a shortage of qualified teachers. At the same time, the expulsion removed the foremost advocates of scholastic thought and thus facilitated the widespread introduction of a more modern approach to knowledge. By the close of the eighteenth century, skepticism of authority, observation of nature, experimentation, and analysis based on inductive reasoning had transformed the intellectual milieu of the colonies.

Even before 1767, in both viceroyalties, there were glimmers of an unmistakable swing toward modern approaches to knowledge and an emphasis on science and useful knowledge. The most noted supporters of these changes were active in the 1780s and 1790s. Their intellectual heirs sustained their reform agenda and, after 1810, added the political enthusiasms of the American and French revolutions.

The most widespread expression of enlightened ideas in Peru appeared in the *Mercurio Peruano,* a biweekly paper published in Lima in the early 1790s by a local variant of the many economic societies founded in the Spanish world since 1763. Through the *Mercurio,* the supporters of progress tried to provide Peruvians with useful knowledge of their region and information relevant to their daily lives. Thus the *Mercurio* published articles that advocated burial outside churches for reasons of health, supported more efficient mining techniques, and analyzed the viceroyalty's commerce. Although its publication demonstrated the presence of a number of self-proclaimed adherents of modern ideas, the *Mercurio's* demise in 1795 reflected how small that number was. At no time did the number of subscribers reach four hundred.

As in Peru, periodicals reached a broader audience in New Spain than did *colegio* and university courses. The foremost Mexican publicist was the cleric José Antonio Alzate y Ramírez (1729–99), an advocate of scientific knowledge and its application to contemporary problems. His *Gaceta de Literatura* (1788–95) provided a stream of informative articles on medicine, applied science, agronomy, and a host of other scientific topics. As did the writers of the *Mercurio Peruano,* Alzate focused on the viceroyalty of his birth and wrote articles intended to improve it.

Accompanying and further accelerating the spread of modern ideas in the colonies were Crown-sponsored scientific expeditions and the creation of new, specialized institutions designed to encourage specific activities. The decade-long botanical expedition of Hipólito Ruiz and José Antonio Pavón reached Peru in 1778 to collect samples and make drawings of plants that would enhance the Royal Botanical Garden in Madrid or be of medicinal value. A similar expedition was undertaken in New Spain in 1787. In related initiatives, a chair of botany was created at the University of Mexico, and a botanical garden was established. The Royal Academy of San Carlos was established in the capital in 1784 to teach painting, sculpture, and architecture, and the Royal College of Mines followed in 1792.

Although efforts to establish a school of mines in Peru failed, in the late 1780s the viceroyalty hosted an expedition of European mining experts led by the Swedish baron Thaddeus von Nordenflicht. Part of a royal effort to introduce the latest European mining techniques into the viceroyalty, the experts labored without notable success until 1810. A similar expedition led by the Basque Fausto de Elhuyar, who was trained at Europe's finest mining centers, reached New Spain in the late 1780s. Both missions confirmed the Crown's willingness to encourage experimentation and the initiation of new methods for utilitarian ends.

Demographic Expansion

Populations grew throughout the Western World during the second half of the eighteenth century. New Spain and Peru shared in this general growth, although at substantially different rates and with significant regional variations. There was internal migration in both viceroyalties, but neither received large numbers of immigrants from Europe.

Between 1742 and 1810, the population of New Spain rose from about 3.3 million to 6.1 million inhabitants. This impressive upward trend occasionally suffered reverses, most notably in 1785–86 when an estimated 300,000 persons died as a result of a catastrophic harvest failure and attendant epidemics. Growth was particularly rapid in the regions north and west of Mexico City as a result of both migration and natural increase. Northern New Spain had 26 percent of the viceroyalty's population in 1742 and 38 percent by 1810. The city of Guadalajara more than tripled in population from 1750 to 1810, largely as a result of migration from the surrounding rural areas. Mexico City was also a magnet for migrants, growing from 113,000 in 1793 to 137,000 in 1803.

The population of Peru reached its low point in the early 1720s as a result of a series of devastating epidemics. Recovery was well under way by 1750, however, and except for a temporary loss after the Indian rebellion led by Tupac Amaru in 1780, the population grew for the remainder of the colonial era. The census of 1792 listed 1,076,122 inhabitants. By 1812, natural increase, particularly among the Indian population, and territorial reorganization brought the total to about 1.5 million.

Breaking down the population totals reveals the substantial increase in the mixed-race and white populations. In the mid-seventeenth century, *castas* comprised a little over 5 percent and Indians some 86 percent of the population of New Spain. Despite an actual increase in numbers, Indians had dropped to about 74 percent of the total population by the 1740s and to only about 60 percent by the close of the eighteenth century. The population considered white grew to 18 percent, and the *castas,* with 22 percent, emerged as the second largest socioracial group in the viceroyalty. The 1792 census indicated that Peru had a smaller proportion of Spaniards (13 percent) and Indians (56 percent) than New Spain did. *Castas* accounted for the remaining 27 percent. Although the slave population in New Spain was negligible, Peru had over forty thousand black and mulatto slaves, most of whom resided in the intendancy of Lima.

The population change in both New Spain and Peru in the second half of the eighteenth century was almost entirely dependent on natural increase. Unlike Brazil and Cuba, to cite extreme cases, neither viceroyalty was a major participant in the African slave trade. The immigration of whites was also numerically inconsequential. In the early 1790s, Mexico City had only 2,359 peninsulars, almost all males. The booming mining center of Guanajuato had only 314 adult male peninsulars, Querétaro just 190, and Antequera 274. The viceroyalty as a whole probably contained fewer than 15,000 peninsulars at the close of the century. Peninsular immigration to Peru was even smaller than to New Spain. With fewer opportunites in trade and in civil, military, and ecclesiastical positions, the attractions were limited. Although individual peninsulars sometimes secured wealth, power, and prestige, especially through commerce, they were not demographically important in these two viceroyalties.

The white population was concentrated in or near the cities and towns in both New Spain and Peru. According to contemporary accounts, 67,500 whites, almost half of the city's total population, lived in Mexico City in 1803. Guanajuato and Antequera both had over a third of their population classified as Spaniards, the census term for whites. In Peru, the provinces of Lima, Arequipa, and Cuzco together contained 42 percent of the viceroyalty's Spanish population in 1792, and the majority of these whites lived in cities.

Society

The hierarchical socioeconomic structure based on race, occupation and wealth, culture, corporate affiliation, and legal privileges that had developed in the sixteenth century persisted in the late eighteenth century. At both the top and bottom of this hierarchy, race and class correlated closely. Peninsulars and creoles dominated the upper class, which included

Peruvian creole woman

owners of large estates and mines, wholesale merchants, high-ranking royal officials and clerics, professionals, and large-scale retailers. Indians made up the majority of the very large lower class of unskilled manual laborers and servants in the countryside. In a number of cities and larger towns, *castas* and slaves numerically dominated the lowest-paid, least-skilled positions. Between these extremes was a growing middle stratum. Characterized by racial heterogeneity, this stratum was expanding in response to the increased complexity of the economy and new opportunities promoted by a growing population and the reforms of Charles III. In urban areas the majority of employed white males could be found in artisan, retail, and other middle-level occupations. Even more numerous were the *castas*, particularly *mestizos* and mulattoes. A small number of Hispanized Indians were present as well. In rural areas, independent farmers with small or middle-sized holdings included creoles and, in some regions, *castas* and Indians.

An expanded population and the growth of mining production, trade, and commercial agriculture in New Spain after 1750 led to a growing gulf between rich and poor. Those families that owned estates that sold wheat, corn, meat, *pulque,* and other products to expanding urban markets, and those that owned productive silver mines or invested in wholesale trade achieved unprecedented prosperity. In the late eighteenth century, about one hundred, primarily creole, families in Mexico City, and perhaps ten elsewhere in the viceroyalty had assets of approximately one million pesos or more. Their immense fortunes, rather than titles or other honors, separated them from the other members of a larger elite of lesser landowners, mine owners, merchants, and high-ranking bureaucrats and ecclesiastics. Unable to enter their ranks through marriage or to compete with them economically, this lower elite was tied to their superiors by shared business interests and a common aversion to the lower orders. The great families owned numerous estates in different regions of New Spain, both as protection against natural disasters and as collateral in a society based heavily on credit. They integrated their agricultural investments by controlling the processing and marketing of goods produced on their estates, and they attempted to dominate the marketing of imported goods in regions in which they held properties. Lima had more titled nobles than Mexico City did, but only a handful of millionaires.

At the opposite end of the socioeconomic spectrum in New Spain was a growing underclass. Access to adequate land to sustain a family became more difficult as the villages' expanding populations exceeded their resources and as inheritance divided farmers' rural properties into parcels insufficient for subsistence. Consequently, a steady flow of migrants from the countryside sought a better life in the cities. As the largest city in the empire, Mexico City, not surprisingly, had the largest underclass. During periods of economic crisis or famine, the city's destitute may have constituted a third or more of its population. Unskilled workers found permanent employment difficult to obtain and usually were forced to look for work each day. With urban wages remaining nearly static during the eighteenth century and prices increasing after 1775, the plight of the poor worsened. Unfortunate Indians, *castas,* and some whites found themselves trapped in this broadening pool of poverty. But in 1796 a third of the persons arrested by Mexico City criminal authorities were whites; Spanish birth was no guarantee of prosperity.

With a much smaller base population and a slower rate of growth after 1720, Peru was spared the demographic pressure on land that caused such suffering in portions of Mexico. Lima's population experienced only modest change from the 1740s to the 1840s, hovering between fifty thousand and sixty thousand inhabitants. There was no equivalent of the stream of migrants responsible for Mexico City's rapidly rising population in the decades immediately before 1810. Although a gulf between a small, wealthy white elite and a large, poor working class had long been present, Peru did not experience the expansion of poverty or of a large underclass as had occurred in New Spain.

Few persons born in New Spain and Peru after 1750 enjoyed substantial upward social mobility. Downward social mobility, as defined by the society's racial prejudices, on the other hand, was commonplace. Examinations of marriages in Antequera, Querétaro, Guanajuato, and León, New Spain, in the 1790s reveal incomplete but suggestive information. Intermarriage between Spaniards and nonwhites was not uncommon. Even in cases in which mulatto or Indian women married Spaniards, the offspring suffered the general prejudice of the white population against *castas*. Because Spaniards in interethnic marriages were usually poor artisans or laborers, their children enjoyed none of the advantages that a well-to-do family could provide: education, capital, and influential friends and relatives. In the modest provincial town of Antequera in 1792, an elite of 327 contained only 4 nonwhites. Although there were another 17 nonwhites in the intermediate professional and shopkeeper group, this number paled next to 290 whites. The increasing size of the underclass in New Spain's cities, moreover, underscored the frequency of downward social mobility; the presence of members of every racial background emphasized its pervasiveness.

A major exception to this general pattern of downward social mobility was achieved by a small but highly visible number of peninsulars. The most successful arrived in the New World to work as business apprentices for peninsular uncles or other kinsmen who had sent for them. After years of training and forgoing marriage, the most promising married cousins or the daughters of business associates, joined their fathers-in-law's businesses, and prospered. The wealthiest peninsulars used international trade as the basis for their fortunes but usually diversified as quickly as possible by investing in rural properties and other real estate. In New Spain, Antonio de Bassoco, a Basque merchant and investor in mines, agriculture, and loans, parlayed his father-in-law's legacy of 250,000 pesos in 1763 into a fortune of 2.6 million pesos by the time of his own death in 1814. In Peru, the Navarese millionaire Pedro de Abadia invested in international trade, agriculture, and mining. Peninsulars were also active merchants in the provinces. Creoles participated in trade as well, both in the provinces and in the viceregal capitals, but were seldom among the most successful.

The expansion of the bureaucracy also brought more peninsulars into the elite. The introduction of standing armies and efforts to revitalize the militias augmented the numbers of peninsular officers serving in the viceroyalties. Archbishops and bishops, too, were usually peninsulars during the late eighteenth century.

The economic, social, and political power and visibility of a few peninsulars should not obscure the failure of many to improve their position. From the perspective of creole males, however, all peninsular males held jobs that might have gone to them. Moreover, the successful peninsulars who married almost invariably married creole women of good family, thus reducing the most attractive pool of potential wives for ambitious American-born males. Among the most prominent creole families, nevertheless, a wealthy or well-placed peninsular son-in-law was an asset. The peninsulars, in turn, benefited from incorporation into established families whose political connections and economic resources could further their ambitions.

Silver Production

Silver continued to be the major export for both New Spain and Peru from the mid-eighteenth century until 1810. Although the creation of the vice-royalty of the Río de la Plata in 1776 severed Potosí and the rest of Upper Peru from the viceroyalty of Peru, silver production in Lower Peru ultimately exceeded that of the older mining region. Starting from a low base of about 2.3 million pesos produced during the decade between 1700 and 1709, Lower Peru's production rose to 16.2 million pesos in the 1760s. Silver continued to be produced at a faster rate in Peru than in New Spain, rising to a peak of 44 million pesos in the 1790s, although Peru's total production remained far lower than New Spain's.

Silver production in New Spain reached 106 million pesos during the decade from 1716 to 1725. It then dropped nearly 25 percent, hovering at about 8 million pesos a year for the next twenty years. Production rose after 1746 but fell once more in the early 1760s owing to a shortage of mercury. Starting in 1769, however, the annual output reached 10 million to 15 million pesos a year. The most spectacular single year was 1804, when over 25 million pesos were produced. Descent from this height was rapid. The output between 1806 and 1810 was nearly 23 million pesos less than the remarkable 103 million produced between 1801 and 1805.

The great growth in New Spain's silver production that began in 1776 was aided by large infusions of capital drawn from international commerce and expensive drainage projects, improved supplies of mercury, the use of gunpowder for blasting, and a variety of tax incentives. Approximately ten operations, each with over a thousand workers and a capital investment of more than a million pesos dominated Mexican mining. The largest mine, the Valenciana, had more than three thousand workers. In some years its owners, the newly titled condes de Valenciana, received profits of over a million pesos.

In Peru, mercury supplies from Spain, necessary when the Huancavelica mine was exhausted, raised production at the older mines, and new strikes in the province of Trujillo led to a rising overall production that peaked in 1799. In contrast with New Spain, Peru's mining was characterized by numerous small-scale, undercapitalized enterprises averaging scarcely a dozen employees per mine.

The Rural Economy

The glitter of precious metals should not obscure the importance of agricultural and pastoral production in the two viceroyalties. The cultivation of maize, wheat, potatoes, and other staples occupied most of the viceroyalties' working populations. In the closing years of Charles IV's reign, livestock in New Spain provided about 30 percent of the viceroyalty's gross domestic product. This sector was dominated by large-scale producers, some with herds of cattle and sheep in excess of 100,000 head.

In contrast with the natives of New Spain, Indian commoners, chieftains, and communities in Peru more commonly raised livestock. In southern Peru, flocks of sheep and herds of cattle were small according to Mexican standards, but their ownership was more dispersed. Few estates had as many as thirty thousand sheep. As in New Spain, livestock production fell, beginning in the 1780s. The Tupac Amaru revolt and a depressed market for wool also led to a decline in Peru. Although Mexican producers sent cattle and sheep five hundred to six hundred miles from the northern pastures to Mexico City, Puebla, and other central Mexican markets, Peruvian producers rarely sent their animals more than sixty miles away, because of higher transportation costs and smaller markets.

The demands of a growing population and static or declining livestock herds increased beef prices in New Spain after mid-century, and inflated food prices emerged as a general problem in the viceroyalty about 1775. Workers were caught between higher prices for maize, wheat, beef, and other basic comestibles and stagnant wages. In Peru, prices for agricultural and manufactured goods apparently declined from 1755 to 1790. Sheep were far more important than cattle in Peru, and a collapse in the demand for wool in the 1780s, in large part because of the increased importation of European textiles, lowered prices. Although inflation appeared in Peru about 1790, it was less destructive than that in New Spain.

Trade

Beginning in 1765, the Spanish Crown slowly reduced its restrictions on colonial trade. After experimentally opening the Spanish Caribbean to trade with selected metropolitan ports, it expanded this "free trade within the empire" to Louisiana, Yucatán, and Campeche. In 1778 the new system was extended to the remainder of the mainland empire except New Spain and Venezuela. By 1789 these two colonies were also allowed to trade with sixteen Spanish ports. Reductions in duties and restrictions on intercolonial trade opened up trade further. The result was a remarkable tenfold expansion in the value of exports from the colonies to Spain from 1778 to 1796, when war with England initiated a permanent alteration in colonial trade.

Under the new trading system, a flood of European products, a growing proportion of which were of Spanish origin, reached Peru. Indeed, its higher silver production enabled Peru to remain Spain's most valuable trading partner in South America, and Peru's cities and mining centers were growing markets for imported goods: Between 1785 and 1796, Peru received 22 percent of all exports sent to America from Cádiz.

The influx of imported textiles and other goods reduced prices for consumers and led to more commercial activity. Numerous new retail stores opened, frequently under the ownership of peninsular immigrants. At the same time, lower-priced imported textiles manufactured in Spain and England weakened the market for the *obraje*-produced textiles already competing with inferior but cheaper cloth woven in small local establishments in the highlands.

The volume of Mexican trade depended heavily on the quantity of silver available for exportation. A jump in silver production beginning in 1776 was followed by a substantial expansion of trade. Between 1785 and 1795, imports from Spain averaged about 5.8 million pesos. Despite enormous variations in volume as a result of Spain's frequent involvement in wars, the average grew to about 8 million pesos between 1796 and 1810. Goods from other colonies and neutrals raised the total trade to over 11 million pesos. At the same time, private bullion exports averaged 8.3 million pesos. Overall, bullion accounted for nearly three-quarters of the value of Mexico's exports. Cochineal, sugar, and other products comprised the remainder.

Revenues

Royal revenues in New Spain rose dramatically from 1740 to 1775. Mining, increased trade, the first shifts from tax farming to direct collection by royal officials, and a growing population helped fuel this growth. In the 1770s, there was another spurt in revenue when the Crown imposed new taxes, increased some old ones, and took over the collection of the sales tax *(alcabala)*.

The higher tax revenue based on trade reflected a general growth in commerce. Commercial taxes exceeded revenues from mining beginning in the 1780s, yielding an annual average of more than 4.8 million pesos for the years 1780 to 1809. The revenues from monopolies were even greater. Excluding tobacco, they nearly tripled in the 1780s and averaged 6 million pesos from 1780 to 1809. The establishment of a tobacco monopoly in 1765 initiated a new and highly lucrative source of revenue that produced net profits approaching 3 million pesos a year by the late 1770s and averaged over 3.5 million pesos two decades later. Mining revenues exceeded 4 million pesos annually in the 1780s and 1790s but dropped to under 3.4 million from 1800 to 1809. Tribute grew with the native population, rising above 1 million pesos annually in the 1770s and contributing over 1.6 million pesos each year from 1800 to 1809. After 1780, new taxes and loans related to the expenses of war became the most important sources of royal revenue, growing from 28 percent in the 1790s to 63 percent of the total from 1800 to 1809 as the viceregal government fell deeper and deeper into debt.

After 1775, inflation accounted for much of the nominal growth. Although the real value of revenues increased over 2.5 times from 1712 to 1793, there was no increase from 1793 to 1810. The revenues of Mexico's central treasury grew in nominal value from 69 million pesos in 1791–95 to 112 million in 1806–10, but at the same time real per-capita income dropped.

In Peru, revenues collected in the Lima treasury in the 1750s were slightly less than from 1701 to 1710. The first sign of real growth was in the 1760s when sales tax revenue more than doubled. Total revenues remained almost the same until the 1780s, when the growth of sales tax revenues and income from mining and from other treasuries in Peru pushed the totals to their highest level of the century. Despite the onset of inflation, revenues fell by over 10 percent in the 1790s and continued to decline in the following decade. As in Mexico, the government borrowed to bridge the gap between normal revenues and expenditures. Although Mexico's treasury remitted over 90 million pesos in public revenue to Spain from 1761 to 1800, Peru's treasury sent none.

In 1808 Mexico was by far the richest and most populous colony in the Hispanic world. Lower Peru, in contrast, was struggling to retain its second rank against the emerging regions of the empire's periphery. In both viceroyalties, however, the population was larger, and mining production and trade were greater than a half-century earlier. Reforms had strengthened the royal authority and increased tax revenues. Yet all was not well. Mining production had peaked in the 1790s. Although government revenues continued to rise in the following decade in New Spain, extraordinary measures underlay the increase, and deficit spending had become the rule. In Peru, revenues dropped after reaching their apogee in the late 1780s. Both viceroyalties were experiencing inflation, which reduced the real value of taxes and, especially in New Spain, brought increasing misery to an expanding underclass. There had been economic growth in both viceroyalties after 1760, but its peak had passed by 1800. Moreover, this growth had not been accompanied by development. New Spain and Peru remained thoroughly colonial in their economies, societies, and institutions on the eve of independence.

The Emergence of the Periphery in Spanish America

During the late colonial period the population and economies of the once-stagnant peripheral colonies in Spanish America grew radpidly. At times famines and epidemics or short-term disruptions of both the Atlantic commercial system and regional trade interrupted this growth. Nevertheless, the economic expansion of the periphery during the last hundred years of the empire equaled the rapid growth experienced during the early stages of the mining boom in Peru and New Spain.

The emergence of Cuba, Venezuela, Chile, the Río de la Plata region, and New Granada added substantially to the empire's economic vitality. While Peru's and Bolivia's silver mines partially recovered from a lengthy

Argentine gaucho hunting American ostrich

depression and Mexico's economy grew substantially, the simultaneous expansion of European manufacturing and American agriculture transformed the character of the Atlantic economy. Within the peripheral colonies, merchants and landowners involved in the production and sale of agricultural exports—tobacco, cacao, *yerba,* wheat, coffee, sugar—and hides and processed animal products were the primary beneficiaries of this altered economy. Many small farmers supplying the food needs of growing colonial cites, retail merchants, and, in at least some cases, urban workers also earned more income, consumed more goods, and lived more comfortable lives.

It is difficult to determine precisely what promoted growth in the peripheral regions. The performance of their economies during this period reflected improved conditions in Europe generally and in Spain particularly. After over a century of metropolitan economic stagnation, there were clear signs of a renewed dynamism. By the end of the eighteenth century the greater consumer demand and the development of new markets in America and elsewhere stimulated Spanish manufacturers to introduce new and more efficient technologies in textiles and metallurgy. This led, in turn, to greater productivity and lower prices. To maximize these benefits, manufacturers needed new markets and new sources of raw materials. These opportunities and challenges stimulated investment and entrepreneurship in the long-dormant economies of the Caribbean and Southern Cone colonies.

Population growth and empirewide tax and commercial reforms enhanced the beneficial effects of the growing European demand for regional products. Changes in administrative structure also encouraged economic growth. The creation of two new viceroyalties, New Granada and Río de la Plata, pumped money and people into Bogotá and Buenos Aires and facilitated regional commercial integration. Finally, military expenditures tended to redistribute wealth from the older mining economies to the agricultural and grazing economies of the periphery.

Administration

Spain's efforts to improve its colonial defenses, increase its revenue collection, and tighten its administration touched the peripheral colonies even more than it did the old viceregal centers. Defensive considerations had already led to the permanent establishment of the viceroyalty of New Granada in 1739. Cuba became a captaincy-general in 1764 following the return of Havana to Spanish rule. Venezuela gained greater political and fiscal autonomy in 1777 when Caracas was made the capital of a captaincy-general. The creation of the *audiencia* of Caracas in 1786 severed Venezuela's dependence in judicial matters on distant tribunals and confirmed the capital's dominance within the captaincy-general. Although long identified as a captaincy-general, in the late colonial era Guatemala also won additional regional authority.

The most significant change in colonial political organization occurred on the viceroyalty of Peru's southeastern flank. This vast, sparsely populated region was vulnerable to both military attack and commercial penetration by Spain's rivals. Until finally evicted in 1776 by a large military force led by Pedro de Cevallos, the Portuguese maintained Colônia do Sacramento as a center for contraband trade on the east bank of the Río de la Plata. Cevallos's victory was followed by the creation of a new viceroyalty in 1777 that included Argentina, Uruguay, Paraguay, Bolivia, and part of Chile. The establishment of an *audiencia* in 1783 in the capital of Buenos Aires completed the reorganization.

In addition to major territorial reorganizations and the creation of new *audiencias,* the colonial administration was structurally altered through the introduction of the intendant system. First installed in Cuba in 1764, the system was extended to Venezuela in 1776 and to the viceroyalty of Río de la Plata in 1782. By 1790 intendants were present throughout the American empire except in New Granada. Among their most important contributions was an enhanced ability to collect taxes. These officials and other tax initiatives led to increased revenue, much of which was expended locally for defense and internal improvements.

The Church

The Church was much weaker in the peripheral colonies than in the wealthier and more populous viceroyalties of Peru and New Spain. Nevertheless, it was a significant part of their cultural life and often important

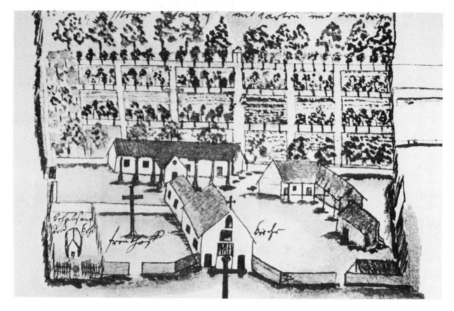

Jesuit church and mission in San Javier, viceroyalty of Río de la Plata

to their politics. Because the peripheral colonies were generally poor until late in the colonial period, the Church as a whole lacked the manpower and economic resources to match the rapidly expanding power of the secular bureaucracy after 1750. The Jesuits, however, were nowhere more powerful than in their famous reductions in Paraguay. To a regalist Crown, these reductions symbolized the Society's arrogance and, more importantly, the political danger of its geographically concentrated power.

When Charles III followed the Portuguese precedent by expelling the Jesuits from his realms in 1767, the action had enormous consequences in the Río de la Plata. The removal of the Society dramatically changed land and labor relations in Paraguay. Subsistence agriculture declined while *yerba* and tobacco production grew. After 1767 the Jesuits' ranches and plantations, powerful economic actors in the peripheral colonies, were sold to private individuals, given to rival orders, or run by local secular authorities. In the end this process of religious divestment seconded the general progress of market expansion in frontier zones and further reduced institutional constraints on the penetration of capitalist cultural values.

Population

Between 1750 and 1850, Latin America's population grew rapidly. Overall, the colonial population expanded at the rate of 0.8 percent per year, roughly twice the rate of contemporary Europe. As a group, the peripheral colonies grew faster than did the rest of the empire. In some cases, this expansion far exceeded even that of New Spain. Venezuela, for example, increased from an estimated 330,000 inhabitants in 1780 to 780,000 in 1800. Chile grew from 184,000 in 1775 to 583,000 in 1810.

Unlike in New Spain and Peru, immigration played a crucial role in population growth in the peripheral colonies. The most important sources for new migrants were Spain and Africa. The faster flow of free migrants from Spain and slaves from Africa not only stimulated the peripheral economies but also profoundly altered their social structure and, in some cases, culture. Migrants from other European countries and from the older, more established colonies supplemented the two main migratory streams.

The drop in the mortality rate from that of the sixteenth and early seventeenth centuries also added to the population. Although in New Granada the number of natives kept falling until the end of the colonial period, in general the Indian population was recovering by the late seventeenth century. Nonetheless, Indians generally remained more vulnerable to epidemic disease than other groups were and also were more likely to be victims of violence. In the frontier zones of Chile, the Río de la Plata region, and along the Brazilian border, slave raids and conflicts with settlers disrupted Indian family life and depressed fertility. Where peace and a stable agricultural regime could be established—for example, in the Jesuit holdings in Paraguay before the expulsion—Indian populations grew steadily after 1750.

The rapid growth of the *casta* population was particularly important because of the social and economic changes that accompanied it. The *castas* operated in the money economy as producers and consumers, thus contributing to the general economic expansion. By 1800 they were the largest racial group in most of the peripheral colonies. In Cuba, on the other hand, the rapid expansion of the African slave trade after 1762 reduced the demographic and cultural significance of the racially mixed population.

There are no reliable estimates for Spanish migration to the colonies in the eighteenth century. A total net migration to the peripheral colonies of forty thousand to fifty thousand, however, seems plausible. More important than the actual number was the fact that most of these immigrants arrived after 1762, which magnified the migration's political and social effects.

The increased vitality of the colonial economies attracted emigrants from Spain. The larger civil administration and military forces also drew Spaniards to the colonies, although most immigrants found employment outside the public sector. Trade was a steady magnet. In Buenos Aires after 1780, for example, 85 percent of the wholesale merchants were peninsulars.

The scale of European immigration to Spanish America was dwarfed by that of enslaved Africans. Between 1761 and 1810, colonists imported over 300,000 African slaves, most of whom entered the labor force of the

peripheral colonies. The Cuban economy rested increasingly on sugar production, and as a result slavery expanded rapidly into the nineteenth century. In 1760 the island was home to approximately 35,000 slaves. The
sugar estates in the region of Havana averaged 45 slaves each. Beginning
with Britain's promotion of slave imports during its occupation of Havana
in 1762, sugar production soared. After Spain reasserted control, colonial
authorities found it necessary to remove most of the obstacles that had
previously limited slave imports. As a result, 140,000 slaves entered the
Cuban work force between 1764 and 1810.

In response to a bigger but more competitive international market for
cacao and the profitable introduction of tobacco, coffee, and sugar cultivation, Venezuela also received significantly more slaves. Because the colony depended heavily on the contraband trade in slaves reexported by the
British in Jamaica and the Dutch in Curaçao, the currently accepted
import estimate of 30,000 slaves between 1774 and 1810 is suspect. In
1810 the bishopric of Caracas alone had 64,462 slaves and 197,738 free
blacks, out of a total population of 427,203.

The remainder of the viceroyalty of New Granada—the modern nations
of Colombia, Ecuador, and Panama—received a similar level of imports.
Because the labor-intensive gold-mining industry of Colombia depended
on slaves, the fourfold increase in production from the mid- to late eighteenth century suggests a significant overall growth in the region's supply
of slaves. In the Chocó region, however, the number of slaves actually
dropped after 1780.

The Río de la Plata region did not prove hospitable to the development
of plantation agriculture. Nonetheless, customs records indicate a dramatic rise in slave imports after the creation of the new viceroyalty. At least
45,000 slaves entered the port of Buenos Aires between 1750 and 1810.
The majority labored on the farms and ranches of the *pampas* or entered
the urban labor force. Many slaves were in domestic service, whereas others provided much of the artisan and transportation work force. Those
slaves not absorbed into the growing economy of Buenos Aires and its hinterland were sold in the interior, especially to the miners of Potosí.

Society

The demographic changes after 1750 led naturally to alterations in the
social structure. The loosening of commercial restrictions after 1765 and
the more important administrative and territorial reforms attracted Spanish merchants to the peripheral ports and capital cities. Peninsulars dominated the merchant elites of Buenos Aires, Caracas, Santiago, and
Havana. In Buenos Aires, Tomás Antonio Romero grew wealthy from the
mercury trade to Potosí and the importation of slaves. His contemporary,
Gaspar de Santa Caloma, imported European goods and exported silver
as a commission agent for Spanish commercial houses and also independently on his own account. As was common among wholesale merchants,

both men provided credit to local producers and retailers. In Caracas, men like Domingo Zulueta and Juan Bautista Echezuría extended large amounts of credit to planters. Although Spanish merchants provided market intelligence, transportation and warehouse services, and essential credit, their social position and economic power ultimately rested on the dependable functioning of Spain's Atlantic lifeline.

In Venezuela and Cuba in particular, immigrant merchants married into rural elites. Many also invested directly in plantations and ranches so that by the end of their careers they were indistinguishable from wealthy creoles. In Chile and New Granada, merchants and civil administrators forged lasting business and social ties. By the 1790s, merchants' fortunes were among the largest in these colonies, and the relative liquidity of their wealth gave them disproportionate economic influence.

New opportunities created by the expanding markets provided a fertile environment for the development of new rural elites—cacao planters in Venezuela, cattlemen in the Río de la Plata, *yerba* growers in Paraguay, wheat farmers in Chile, and sugar planters in Cuba. Most of the members of these new elites were "new men" from modest provincial backgrounds. Their ranches, plantations, and farms were located away from the traditional urban centers of social power, and this geographic dispersal and fragmentation of wealth and social power had important consequences in the period after independence.

The dominant cities of the peripheral colonies attracted artisans and lesser-skilled immigrants as well as merchants and bureaucrats. But in this expansive era, immigrants sought to escape manual labor by purchasing and training slaves or recruiting free *casta* apprentices. Nevertheless, the arrival of assertive new immigrants often led to bitter conflicts with the native born. In Buenos Aires, for example, such conflicts led guilds of silversmiths and shoemakers to fail in the 1790s. In some cities underpaid soldiers from local garrisons sought jobs in the civilian economy, undercutting wages and competing for employment. Although their absolute number was limited, the immigrants' visibility and assertiveness helped promote creole nationalism among the urban masses.

The slave trade had an impact on evolving social relations in all of the peripheral colonies except Chile. This tragic commerce alleviated the chronic labor problems and helped unleash the economic potential previously held in check by the fleet system. Yet the influx of African slaves also led to racial and cultural conflicts and further reduced the prestige of manual labor. In every occupation in which slave labor became important, both income and status tended to decline significantly. As a result, interpersonal violence, attacks on property, and other antisocial behavior developed an implicitly racial as well as class character.

By the end of the eighteenth century the peripheral societies generally were more racially and culturally heterogeneous than they had been fifty years earlier. There also was more social and geographic mobility: Where the slave trade had expanded, there was greater racial consciousness, but there was also more miscegenation and a proliferation of ambiguously defined social types.

The Peripheral Economies, Public Expenditures, and Trade

Demographic growth was crucial to the economic expansion of the late eighteenth century. Given the labor-intensive nature of the colonial economy, an expanding population reduced labor costs and promoted the exploitation of formerly marginal mineral and agricultural resources. More farm workers and ranch hands meant more rural production. Mining, transportation, and construction also were stimulated by the greater availability of workers.

All of the major cities of the peripheral colonies mushroomed during this period. Buenos Aires, Caracas, Bogotá, and Santiago more than doubled in size between 1770 and 1810. By 1780 Havana became the second largest city in the empire, with more than eighty thousand inhabitants. This growth of the urban population stimulated the development of market agriculture, construction, and services. The demand for European goods also increased substantially.

Another characteristic of the late colonial economic surge was the expansion of the market economy relative to that of the subsistence sector. This resulted in part from expanded silver production and mintage in both Peru and Mexico. The colonial money supply at last overcame some of the chronic cash shortage that had previously held back economic growth. The advantages of this increased monetarization were particularly important to the economies of the peripheral colonies, where both production for market and wage labor lagged far behind the levels in New Spain and Peru.

The administrative and territorial reorganizations of the Bourbon period, particularly those implemented during the reign of Charles III, increased tax revenues, whose expenditure stimulated the peripheral economies. By the end of the colonial period, the public sector was the single largest employer in most colonial cities. For example, the creation of new viceregal courts in Bogotá and Buenos Aires and the enhanced administrative authority of Caracas resulted in the appointment of numerous new officials who spent their salaries locally. Consumption expanded accordingly, most often at the profitable upper end of the market for goods, services, and housing. The administrative reforms also led to major new investments in government buildings and other internal improvements.

Expenditures by the municipal authorities often matched in scale those by the royal administrators. New office buildings, customs warehouses, harbor improvements, and a range of investments in street paving, water supply, public hygiene, and other forms of civic improvement injected public money into the economy. Skilled and unskilled workers and the local suppliers of building supplies benefited from these expenditures.

The creation of state-run tobacco monopolies had dramatic and unforeseen consequences in the peripheral colonies. Once imposed, the monopolies limited tobacco production, set prices, processed and manufactured tobacco products, and controlled retail sales. Even though consumer demand in the colonies and in Europe pushed upward, tobacco growers gained only limited benefits. Consumers also found these poor man's luxuries increasingly expensive. The Crown, however, earned heady profits. Because the monopoly paid cash, the tobacco-producing regions of Venezuela, New Granada, and especially Paraguay were able to develop new commercial relations with regional and even international markets. As cash replaced barter, the largest urban centers established more effective domination over the countryside.

The period after 1760 was also a time of renewed and expanded military commitments. Spanish garrisons were increased in size and readiness, and colonial militias were enlarged and provided with better weapons and training. This greater military commitment placed a heavy burden on the colonial treasuries. Regular army units in Cuba alone absorbed 647,775 pesos per year in salaries, but the local treasury had only 178,000 in income. Governmental solvency depended on subsidies from the Mexican treasury. In the jurisdiction of Buenos Aires, military salaries cost the treasury more than 3 million pseos between 1796 and 1800. Two smaller interior cities of the viceroyalty, Córdoba and Santa Fe, devoted nearly 90 percent of their public expenditures to military salaries and subsistence.

The secondary economic consequences of military expenditures were often significant. Major fortifications projects at Havana and Cartagena

Rural militia patroling Indian frontier in Argentina

affected local labor markets and pushed up wages for both skilled and unskilled workers. Even in regions where military construction was limited, enlistments in regular army units and part-time militia service tended to alter the labor supply. In the region around Buenos Aires, for example, the military buildup exacerbated the preexisting labor shortage, thus encouraging the expansion of the grazing industry which used less labor than did farming or manufacturing. The greater manpower of the Spanish garrisons and colonial militias also affected the economies of these regions in other ways. The increased demand for food, shelter, and clothing stimulated production and led to higher employment levels. The fact that the government paid cash was in itself helpful to the entire economy, as this promoted more complex commercial relations. The military in Cuba spent more than 30 million pesos during Spain's participation in the British colonies' struggle for independence. This infusion of capital, in turn, directly underwrote the local elite's ambitious plans to enlarge the sugar industry.

The already-evident growth of the transatlantic trade received further stimulation as the Crown slowly initiated "free trade within the empire" after 1765. By 1789 all major Spanish American ports were participating in the new system. When war with Britain began in 1796, Spanish exports were disrupted, and the Crown further compromised the limitations on colonial commerce by permitting trade with neutral nations. The major beneficiaries of this policy were United States merchants, who quickly moved into the Cuban market, in particular.

The most spectacular example of economic expansion after 1760 occurred in Cuba. During the brief British occupation, Havana and its surrounding agricultural region responded hastily to the influx of cheap slave labor, commerical credits, and a ready sugar market. Although Spanish sovereignty was soon reestablished, the liberalized trade laws and tax breaks stimulated sugar production. The now-dynamic sugar sector continued to grow, pushing aside tobacco and other agricultural rivals. Between 1759 and 1789, the number of sugar mills tripled, and overall production grew nearly eightfold. Then in 1791 the slave rebellion in Haiti drove up world sugar prices and further accelerated the growth of Cuban production.

Each year Cuba's plantation economy moved inexorably toward its mature form; the average plantation size grew, and the average number of slaves per plantation increased. This in turn caused a social revolution in the captaincy-general. The new sugar aristocracy became Cuba's first authentic creole elite, eclipsing in wealth and prestige the local representatives of the Spanish Crown. In the countryside, many rural small holders, tobacco producers and market gardners, were pushed off their land. In Havana and other cities, *castas* and free blacks in artisan and lesser-skilled jobs lost status and income in competition with slaves. Although the sugar boom made Cuba wealthier in absolute terms, the masses of this society suffered a relative decline in status and material well-being.

Both New Granada and Venezuela saw a substantial increase in exports,

Plaza de Armas, Havana, Cuba, in the early nineteenth century

as well as some general economic expansion, in the late colonial period, but neither matched the incredible performance of Cuba. In the district of Antioquia in New Granada, gold production increased from 27,150 gold pesos in 1750 to approximately 250,000 in 1800. Imports followed the same upward curve, increasing fivefold between 1760 and 1800. Trade with Spain and taxation, however, removed much of this bullion from the colony's economy. Gold contributed nearly 90 percent of New Granada's average of 2 million pesos in annual exports in the last decades of colonial rule. Instead of stimulating significant real growth, the increased gold production brought inflation and helped finance imports, especially textiles, that competed with local manufacture. New taxes and monopolies wrung additional consumer demand out of the economy.

Venezuela followed the Cuban model more closely. The creation of the Caracas Company in 1728 had provided the colony with both a commercial link to Spain and a source of capital. As cacao cultivation spread, slave imports increased. Competition from other cacao producers in the late eighteenth century led Venezuelan growers to diversify into other exportable products. Livestock raising became a major industry that sent thousands of mules to the sugar islands of the Caribbean in exchange for slaves. Tobacco production increased after the creation of the state monopoly, but government policy limited the potential for growth. Exports of coffee, indigo, and sugar all went up after 1780. Geographical advantages gave Venezuelan producers and consumers access to the British and Dutch markets.

Chile was less affected by imperial reform and the development of the Atlantic market than were the three colonies geographically located along the dynamic Caribbean Basin or the Río de la Plata region. Still, between mid-century and 1800 the value of Chile's mining production more than doubled, to approximately 1 million pesos a year, and silver, gold, and copper became important exports. Wheat exports to Peru, a mainstay of the economy, continued to grow after 1750, although more slowly than in the first decades of the century.

The viceroyalty of Río de la Plata was a great success story. By opening Buenos Aires to direct trade with Spain and other Spanish colonies and by linking the mines of Potosí to this port, the Spanish government provided the fiscal and monetary resources necessary to energize the region's long-dormant agricultural and grazing potential. Although the area continued to suffer from a chronic labor shortage, the slave trade and internal migration provided some relief.

By 1810 the combined economic weight of Buenos Aires's expanding consumer base and the capital resources of its wholesale merchants made the city both the undisputed center of an integrated regional commercial system and an entrepôt for the Atlantic economy. The capital's emergence tended to diminish the vitality of provincial towns such as Santa Fe, Asunción, and Córdoba that had previously controlled the regional markets for *yerba,* local wines and textiles. By the end of the colonial period, only two Spanish American ports, Vera Cruz and Callao-Lima, ranked ahead of Buenos Aires in volume and value of commerce.

After the commercial sector, the grazing industry was the major beneficiary of the creation of the viceroyalty. Hide exports rose from 150,000 at mid-century to a high of 1.5 million in 1786 and averaged 1 million until 1806. Typical of this form of dependent colonial development, however, Buenos Aires imported most of its tanned leather from Spain. Salted-beef exports to the plantations of Cuba and Brazil grew, but production was inhibited by high salt prices and limited labor supply. Dried beef and lard also found export markets. As livestock requirements at Potosí increased after 1730, traditional producers in the interior provinces largely met the demand. Pastoralists around Buenos Aires, too, sent thousands of mules to the mining district each year.

The region's agricultural sector also expanded during the final four decades of the colonial period. As the city of Buenos Aires grew, orchards and farms spread across the neighboring *pampas,* but labor was so short that Indians, convicts, and vagrants were forced to help with the harvests. In the interior, transportation difficulties often hindered development. The wines and brandies of San Juan and Mendoza found eager consumers in both the capital and in Potosí, but rugged cart roads and long trips hurt quality and raised prices. Nevertheless, the growth of Buenos Aires stimulated the interior's production of wine, *yerba,* wheat, and textiles.

The economy of Paraguay underwent complex changes during the eighteenth century. Throughout the late Habsburg period, *yerba* production dominated this isolated colony. A chronic currency shortage and the dominant role of the Society of Jesus in production and distribution, however, held back market expansion. In the early eighteenth century the Jesuits produced roughly 25 percent of the total volume and 40 percent of the value of *yerba*. The Jesuits' success was furthered by their interregional network of correspondents and warehouses that provided better market intelligence than that received by independent producers and also by their ability to wait out price swings. The Society's expulsion in 1767 enabled rival producers to reallocate Indian laborers, purchase improved lands, and attract new capital. As a result, production increased, and more markets were found in Chile, Peru, and Brazil. This commercial vigor did not, however, improve, the lot of the Paraguayan masses, who were increasingly pushed into debt peonage and tenancy.

Despite the remarkable growth of the peripheral economies, fundamental structural weaknesses remained. Much of the new growth was in exports, particularly of agricultural and grazing products. Yet bullion continued to dominate the relationship between several colonies and the metropolis. Chile exported nearly 900,000 pesos in gold and silver annually. Despite the growth in hide exports from Buenos Aires after 1776, silver from Potosí still contributed 80 percent of the value of all exports from the region. In New Granada, bullion provided 90 percent of export value. This hemorrhage of bullion drew down the colonial capital stock, limited the spread of commercial exchange, and hindered investment. The tardy development of banking, credit, and insurance in these colonies exacerbated the negative effect of the bullion loss.

Responding to new commercial opportunities, the producers of Cuban sugar; Venezuelan cacao, hides, and *yerba* from the Río de la Plata; and Chilean wheat increased their investments, improving the land and buying slaves or hiring free labor. The prosperity of these largely creole producers depended heavily on the fragile and unpredictable geopolitical relationships of the European powers. After 1792 Spain's shifting military alliances with England and then France led to the breakdown of the reformed commercial system that had helped stimulate growth. Unlike the bullion-based commercial system of the Habsburg era, the agricultural export economies promoted by the Bourbon reforms in the peripheral colonies could not wait out the disruption of the Atlantic trade. As a result, colonial producers successfully sought and developed new markets outside the legal commercial system. The United States, Britain's Caribbean colonies, and Britain itself replaced the old partners and further promoted exports of tropical products as well as bullion. This process loosened ties with Spain, encouraged economic nationalism, and strengthened the social power of creole elites.

The Enlightenment

The ideas of the Enlightenment circulated among a small minority of the urban elites and educated members of the middle sectors of the peripheral colonies. Nearly all of the great works of philosophical speculation, political and economic inquiry, and natural science were known in these colonies. Usually Spain played an intermediary role in the transmission of these ideas, either through the education of well-to-do creoles in the metropolis or through the discussion of the French and English works in Spanish books exported to the colonies.

Despite the official hostility of church and state to many of the most important Enlightenment authors, priests and royal administrators were among those persons most likely to own and lend forbidden works. European and American travelers, participants in scientific expeditions, and technological advisers also acted as intermediaries in this intellectual revolution. Even sailors and merchants from the newly independent United States contributed to this process by distributing in port cities potentially subversive tracts on republicanism.

The penetration of new ideas was advanced by the creation of secular organizations devoted to the twin totems of the new age: reason and progress. By the 1790s, economic societies had been established in many of the largest cities of the empire's periphery: Buenos Aires, Havana, Quito, Caracas, Guatemala, and Bogotá. Committed to promoting economic progress, these bodies typically published weekly journals that supported education, technological innovation, and broadened commercial relations. As educated colonials examined economic questions, some came to consider the Spanish commercial system as an obstacle to progress. Monopolies, special privileges, and restrictions on foreign trade—the very economic structure of empire—were attacked publicly. In Buenos Aires in 1809 the creole lawyer Mariano Moreno marshaled the economic liberalism of Adam Smith on behalf of free trade. Freemasons were also active in many peripheral cities. More explicitly political than the economic societies and organized in secret groups that led naturally to a conspiratorial style, the Freemasons later provided many leaders of the independence movements. Often their members were drawn from local elites tied to the export sector.

Protest and Popular Insurrections

There were a number of violent popular uprisings during the late colonial period, but they were not consciously connected with the intellectual ferment of the Enlightenment, and most of their leaders used the language of traditional Spanish law and Catholic theology to justify their actions. Most historians also separate these events from the later struggles for independence.

Popular violence and mob actions provoked generally by administrative corruption, new taxes, and high prices were common in colonial political life from the early seventeenth century onward. Royal officials were often targets for public frustration. In fact, competition and disagreement among civil bureaucrats, clergy, and their supporters repeatedly ignited violence and defined the political objectives of these conflicts. In the eighteenth century, however, the scale and duration of violent uprisings increased, and the most important of them directly threatened the metropolitan authority.

This change in the political character of popular protest originated in the administrative and fiscal reforms of the Bourbon monarchs. New taxes or the more efficient collection of old taxes provoked bitter protest. This was especially true when higher tax rates or new taxes pushed up the price of common consumer goods. The creation of private- and public-sector monopolies—the tobacco monopoly and the Caracas Company, for example—also led to litigation, protest, and, in some cases, rebellion. This occurred because the Spanish fiscal reform transferred the colonial tax burden away from the mining sector and Atlantic trade to articles of common consumption that directly affected the popular classes.

In Paraguay, conflict between colonists and the Society of Jesus over Indian labor and access to *yerba*-producing zones led to the overthrow of four governors and open warfare between 1721 and 1735. Led by local farmers and merchants, the *comunero* movement provided some evidence of a growing creole consciousness. The creole-dominated *cabildo* of Asunción's defiance of imperial authority foreshadowed the vanguard role of city councils in the independence period.

In 1749 cacao producers in Venezuela rebelled against the Caracas Company's heavy-handed monopoly. Led by the Canary Islander Juan Francisco de León, cacao growers resented the company's imposition of below-market prices and its inefficient provisioning of essential imports. More specifically, efforts by the company to prevent English and Dutch contraband threatened a further decline in earnings. Although the rebels gained the initial advantage, they disbanded their military force when a new governor promised remediation. After nearly two years of tense stalemate, the arrival of military reinforcements permitted Spanish authorities to arrest and exile the most prominent rebel leaders and reestablish the company's monopoly in a limited form.

In 1780 a large rebellion in Peru led by Tupac Amaru II helped ignite an uprising by the Indian masses of Upper Peru that lasted nearly three years. Although this rebellion of Aymara speakers maintained a loose alliance with Tupac Amaru's forces in the Quechua-speaking region of Cuzco, real cooperation against the Spanish was hindered by ethnic rivalries that antedated the Spanish conquest. Victorious Spanish authorities treated some white sympathizers mercifully but brutally executed Tupac Catari and other Indian leaders.

Although clearly directed against the conquest's social and economic consequences, these rebellions by the Indian masses in the Andes colonies did not directly challenge the king's authority or the legitimacy of the colonial regime. Like the earlier, less violent uprisings by white and *mestizo* colonists in Paraguay and Venezuela, Indian leaders proclaimed their loyalty to the king and focused their demands on eliminating or reforming the most corrupt and abusive elements of the colonial system, especially the *mita,* the forced sales of goods, and the sales taxes.

Right after the onset of the Indian uprisings in Peru and Bolivia, the colonial authorities in New Granada confronted a popular political protest. In order to pay for the defense of the colony against possible English attack, Spanish authorities increased the *alcabala,* raised tobacco and brandy prices, and limited the area where tobacco cultivation was permitted. The imposition of these tax and price increases combined in 1781 with the effects of bad harvests and an epidemic to produce rebellion.

The participants in this *comunero* revolt were drawn from the middle and lower sectors of provincial society and included *castas* and even Indians. Eventually a rebel force that numbered in the thousands marched on the nearly defenseless capital of Bogotá. Representing the Bogotá elite, Archbishop Antonio Caballero y Góngora appeared to surrender to most of the rebel demands, but once the armed *comuneros* dispersed, loyal troops reestablished control. Only a small rebel force led by José Antonio Galán refused to accept the settlement. But he was soon defeated and later executed.

Spain's peripheral colonies experienced dramatic changes in the late colonial period. Population grew at unprecedented rates, and the mix of races, classes, and cultures was altered as well. At the base of the social pyramid, the flood of imported slaves undermined the dignity and independence of free labor, introduced greater cultural diversity, and heightened racial tensions.

At the middle and upper levels of the social order, the arrival of Spanish immigrants helped heighten the creoles' sense of cultural distinctiveness and a nascent nationalism. The increased European demand for colonial products led to a territorial expansion of grazing and agriculture. This in turn meant the physical dispersal of those groups that wielded social and economic power. After independence the political consequences of this process were manifested in numerous rebellions against the political elites of the capital cities. The fact that the "new men" of the late colonial period often produced goods that carried little traditional prestige—hides, sugar, coffee, *yerba*—itself contradicted established assumptions about social rank.

The more fluid character of the recently formed elites of these colonies—New Granada is a significant exception—was little constrained by the recently reformed and expanded colonial state. Viceroys and governors appointed to the peripheral colonies were commonly military men or career civil servants with little independent wealth or prestige. Intendants and subdelegates did not intimidate or awe the newly rich of the frontier regions. Even the hastily constructed or poorly converted commercial buildings that housed the new representatives of the Bourbon monarchs in these regions lacked the intimidating scale of the architectural props for royal authority in New Spain and Peru. In many ways the Bourbon state was more irritating than awe inspiring.

The relations of production and exchange in place by the 1790s were profoundly different from those inherited from the Habsburg period. At the beginning of the eighteenth century, the peripheral colonies sustained only small-scale interregional and international exchange relations. But by the 1790s their economies were closely linked with Europe and the United States. As a result of this transformation, they were richer as well as more dependent. Fluctuations in distant markets, foreign wars, and shifting European alliances all came to play crucial roles in determining local economic conditions. Although these changes were set in motion by Spain's administrative and commercial reforms and funded in part by the investments of Spanish merchants and joint-stock companies, the Spanish market could not absorb the productive potential of the increasingly dynamic peripheral colonies.

Notes

1. Sergio Villalobos R., *El comercio y la crisis colonial* (Santiago, Chile: Universidad de Chile, 1968), p. 77.
2. C. R. Boxer, *The Golden Age of Brazil, 1695–1750* (Berkeley and Los Angeles: University of California Press, 1962), p. 53.
3. C. E. Castañeda, "The Corregidor in Spanish Colonial Administration," *Hispanic American Historical Review* 9:4 (November 1929), 448.

Suggested for Further Reading

Alden, Dauril. *Royal Government in Colonial Brazil with Special Reference to the Administration of the Marquis of Lavradio, Viceroy, 1769–1779.* Berkeley and Los Angeles: University of California Press, 1968.

Archer, Christon I. *The Army in Bourbon Mexico, 1760–1810.* Albuquerque: University of New Mexico Press, 1977.

Arrom, Silvia Marina. *The Women of Mexico City, 1790–1857.* Stanford, Calif.: Stanford University Press, 1985.

Barbier, Jacques A. *Reform and Politics in Bourbon Chile, 1755–1796.* Ottawa: University of Ottawa Press, 1980.

Barbier, Jacques A., and Allan J. Kuethe, editors. *The North American Role in the Spanish Imperial Economy, 1760–1819.* Manchester, England: Manchester University Press, 1984.

Boxer, Charles R. *The Golden Age of Brazil, 1695–1750.* Berkeley and Los Angeles: University of California Press, 1962.

Brading, D. A. *Haciendas and Ranchos in the Mexican Bajío Leon 1700–1860.* Cambridge, England: Cambridge University Press, 1978.

Brading, D. A. *Miners and Merchants in Bourbon Mexico.* Cambridge, England: Cambridge University Press, 1970.

Brown, Jonathan C. *A Socioeconomic History of Argentina, 1776–1860.* Cambridge, England: Cambridge University Press, 1979.

Brown, Kendall W. *Bourbons & Brandy: Imperial Reform in Eighteenth-Century Arequipa.* Albuquerque: University of New Mexico Press, 1986.

Burkholder, Mark A. *Politics of a Colonial Career: José Baquíjano and the Audiencia of Lima.* Albuquerque: University of New Mexico Press, 1980.

Burkholder, Mark A., and D. S. Chandler. *From Impotence to Authority: The Spanish Crown and the American Audiencias, 1687–1808.* Columbia: University of Missouri Press, 1977.

Campbell, Leon G. *The Military and Society in Colonial Peru, 1750–1810.* Philadelphia: American Philosophical Society, 1978.

Descola, Jean. *Daily Life in Colonial Peru, 1710–1820.* London: Allen & Unwin, 1968.

Fisher, John R. *Commercial Relations Between Spain and Spanish America in the Era of Free Trade, 1778–1796.* Liverpool: Centre for Latin American Studies, University of Liverpool, 1985.

Fisher, John R. *Government and Society in Colonial Peru: The Intendant System, 1783–1814.* London: Athlone, 1970.

Fisher, John R. *Silver Mines and Silver Miners in Colonial Peru, 1776–1824.* Liverpool: Centre for Latin American Studies, University of Liverpool, 1977.

Hamnett, Brian R. *Politics and Trade in Southern Mexico, 1750–1821.* Cambridge, England: Cambridge University Press, 1971.

Hussey, Roland D. *The Caracas Company, 1728–1784: A Study in the History of Spanish Monopolistic Trade.* Cambridge, Mass.: Harvard University Press, 1934.

Jacobsen, Nils, and Hans-Jürgen Puhle, editors. *The Economies of Mexico and Peru During the Late Colonial Period, 1760–1810.* Berlin: Colloquium Verlag, 1986.

Kicza, John E. *Colonial Entrepreneurs: Families and Business in Bourbon Mexico.* Albuquerque: University of New Mexico Press, 1983.

Kuethe, Allan J. *Cuba, 1753–1815: Crown, Military, and Society.* Knoxville: University of Tennessee Press, 1986.

Kuethe, Allan J. *Military Reform and Society in New Granada, 1773–1808.* Gainesville: University Presses of Florida, 1978.

Ladd, Doris M. *The Mexican Nobility at Independence, 1780–1826.* Austin: University of Texas Press, 1976.

Lanning, John Tate. *The Eighteenth Century Enlightenment in the University of San Carlos de Guatemala.* Ithaca, N.Y.: Cornell University Press, 1956.

Liss, Peggy K. *Atlantic Empires: The Network of Trade and Revolution, 1713–1826.* Baltimore: Johns Hopkins University Press, 1982.

Lombardi, John V. *People and Places in Colonial Venezuela.* Bloomington: Indiana University Press, 1976.

Lynch, John. *Spanish Colonial Administration, 1782–1810: The Intendant System in the Viceroyalty of the Rio de la Plata.* London: Athlone, 1958.

MacLachlan, Colin M. *Criminal Justice in Eighteenth-Century Mexico: A Study of the Tribunal of the Acordada.* Berkeley and Los Angeles: University of California Press, 1974.

Maxwell, Kenneth R. *Conflicts and Conspiracies: Brazil and Portugal 1750–1808.* Cambridge, England: Cambridge University Press, 1973.

McKinley, P. Michael. *Pre-Revolutionary Caracas. Politics, Economy, and Society 1777–1811.* Cambridge, England: Cambridge University Press, 1985.

McNeill, John Robert. *Atlantic Empires of France and Spain: Louisbourg and Havana, 1700–1763.* Chapel Hill: University of North Carolina Press, 1985.

Moreno-Fraginals, Manuel. *The Sugar Mill: The Socioeconomic Complex of Sugar in*

Cuba, 1760–1860. Translated by Cedric Belfrage. New York: Monthly Review Press, 1976.

Nunn, Charles F. *Foreign Immigrants in Early Bourbon Mexico, 1700–1760.* Cambridge, England: Cambridge University Press, 1979.

Phelan, John Leddy. *The People and the King—The Comunero Revolution in Colombia, 1781.* Madison: University of Wisconsin Press, 1978.

Ronan, Charles E. S.J. *Francisco Javier Clavijero, S.J. (1731–1787), Figure of the Mexican Enlightenment; His Life and Works.* Chicago: Loyola University Press, 1978.

Sharp, William F. *Slavery on the Spanish Frontier: The Colombian Choco, 1680–1810.* Norman: University of Oklahoma Press, 1976.

Socolow, Susan Migden. *The Bureaucrats of Buenos Aires, 1769–1810: Amor al Real Servicio.* Durham, N.C.: Duke University Press, 1988.

Socolow, Susan Migden. *Merchants of Buenos Aires, 1778–1810: Family and Commerce.* Cambridge, England: Cambridge University Press, 1978.

Steele, Arthur R. *Flowers for the King: The Expedition of Ruiz and Pavon and the Flora of Peru.* Durham, N.C.: Duke University Press, 1964.

TePaske, John J., translator and editor. *Discourse and Political Reflections on the Kingdom of Peru by Jorge Juan and Antonio de Ulloa.* Norman: University of Oaklahoma Press, 1978.

TePaske, John Jay. *The Governorship of Spanish Florida 1700–1763.* Durham, N.C.: Duke University Press, 1964.

Van Young, Eric. *Hacienda and Market in Eighteenth-Century Mexico: The Rural Economy of the Guadalajara Region, 1675–1820.* Berkeley and Los Angeles: University of California Press, 1981.

von Humboldt, Alexander. *Political Essay on the Kingdom of New Spain.* Edited by Mary Maple Dunn. New York: Knopf, 1973.

Walker, Geoffrey G. *Spanish Politics and Imperial Trade, 1700–1789.* Bloomington: Indiana University Press, 1979.

Whitaker, Arthur P., editor. *Latin America and the Enlightenment.* 2nd edition. Ithaca, N.Y.: Cornell University Press, 1961.

Woodward, Ralph Lee. *Class Privilege and Economic Development: The Consulado de Comercio de Guatemala, 1793–1871.* Chapel Hill: University of North Carolina Press, 1966.

Wortman, Miles L. *Government and Society in Central America, 1680–1840.* New York: Columbia University Press, 1982.

EIGHT

CRISIS AND COLLAPSE

An Era of War and Crisis for Spain and Portugal

Charles III died in late 1788, leaving Spain and the empire peaceful and reasonably prosperous. The Crown's normal income was almost adequate for routine expenditures, and the royal debt was modest. By January 1, 1808, however, the imperial panorama looked very different. Except for occasional interludes of peace, Spain had been at war since 1793. Its costly naval fleet had been destroyed in the battles of Cape St. Vincent and Trafalgar. Napoleon was exacting financial tribute and largely determining Spain's foreign policy. Colonial trade increasingly benefited neutral shippers rather than Spanish merchants and producers, and a rapidly growing debt burdened the royal treasuries in Spain and the colonies. In addition, the prominence of the powerful royal favorite Manuel Godoy, grandiloquently entitled duke of Alcudia, prince of the Peace, and admiral-general of Spain and the Indies, had discredited the royal family. Yet despite the numerous difficulties of these years, almost no one in Spain or the colonies expected that in less than two decades the entire mainland empire in America would be independent of Spanish rule.

The Cost of War

The execution of the French King Louis XVI on January 21, 1793, led Spain into the coalition of countries fighting against the spread of revolution. The nation was united against regicide, and initially the war enjoyed popular support. Military defeats, however, cost Spain its remaining portion of the island of Hispaniola in 1795.

Angered over Spain's ending hostilities with France unilaterally, England attacked Spanish shipping. These provocations, a belief that a land war with France was more dangerous than a conflict with England, and varied dynastic ambitions led Spain to sign an alliance with the French republic. War with Britain began in October 1796. The defeat of the Spanish fleet off Cape St. Vincent in 1797 opened the way for a British blockade of Cádiz until 1800. The Peace of Amiens in 1802 restored peace to Europe once more, and Spain, which already had ceded Louisiana to France, lost Trinidad. Spain, by now little more than a French satellite, found itself in renewed conflict with England beginning in late 1804. Victory over the combined Spanish and French fleets at Trafalgar in 1805 gave Britain uncontested dominance over the seas.

Spain's repeated involvement in war between 1793 and 1808 proved extremely costly in terms of both direct financial expenditures and the loss of trade and regular remittance of bullion from the colonies. An important consequence was that earlier policies to integrate Spain and the colonies economically gave way to short-term fiscal considerations. Reciprocity within the "colonial compact" succumbed to the Crown's desperate attempts to extract as much revenue as possible from the Indies, regardless of the consequences for the colonial economies.

An Overwhelming Debt

Spain's tax system proved unable to provide the funds necessary to meet the extraordinary expenses of war. Initially the Crown borrowed from foreign lenders, government trust funds, and special treasury funds. Faced with rising interest rates as the price for further loans, however, the Crown turned to Spain's own money market. In 1794–95 it issued treasury bills *(vales reales)* worth over 64 million *pesos de vellón,* a sum equal to nearly 75 percent of the total regular peninsular revenues in these years. Buoyed by the sale of treasury bills and bonds, the treasury's income in 1795 was the largest of the era. The deficit, however, was almost equal to total income in 1792, the last year of peace. The initiation of conflict with Britain in 1796 forced the Crown to issue bonds and treasury bills whose total value exceeded *all* normal treasury income from the American colonies between 1792 and 1807. Napoleon's demand for financial subsidies beginning in 1803 and the renewal of hostilities with England late in 1804 quickly pushed the Crown to the brink of bankruptcy.

Neutral Trade

The rapid deterioration of Spain's finances after 1793 and the subsequent disruption of normal trading patterns profoundly affected Spain's commercial and political relations with its colonies. The strength of the Spanish fleet and the alliance with Britain during the French war enabled American treasure to continue to reach Spain. Protected convoys carrying bullion managed to maintain a reasonable level of trade with the colonies, although the number of sailings dropped. Conditions changed rapidly, however, following the initiation of hostilities with Britain in late 1796.

The British blockade of Cádiz paralyzed Spain's transatlantic trade. Whereas 171 ships sailed from America to Cádiz in 1796, only 9 ships arrived in 1797. Spain's inability to maintain its trade with the colonies spurred colonial officials in Cuba and Venezuela to open their ports to neutral traders. In Madrid, policymakers recognized that the colonies needed some trade outlets and that state services such as mail delivery and the provision of mercury and administrative supplies had to be continued. In addition, they wanted to maintain some portion of the traditional market share to prevent the colonies from establishing new industries and trade links that would ultimately undermine the entire colonial system. These goals underlay the Crown's decree of November 18, 1797, sanctioning neutral trade. Although intended as a temporary wartime expedient to keep the imperial system afloat, the new policy facilitated the elaboration of non-Spanish commercial ties for colonial merchants and producers that were never eradicated.

The merchants of Cádiz fought tenaciously against neutral trade and secured a brief suspension in April 1799. Widespread noncompliance in the colonies and the continued need for revenue, however, led the Crown again to allow neutral trade in January 1801. After a brief peace and an attempt to reestablish the prewar system, renewed conflict with England in 1804 forced the reauthorization of neutral trade.

The commercial pressures experienced by the colonies were varied. Those regions that relied on the exportation of agricultural and pastoral products for their economic well-being—notably Cuba, Venezuela, and the Río de la Plata—had to sell them in a timely manner or watch them deteriorate. In contrast, New Spain and, to a lesser degree, Peru could store bullion until the return of peace and withstand two or three years of disrupted commerce by reducing consumption and promoting local manufactures and agriculture. The most immediate and persistent pressure for neutral trade thus came from the empire's emerging peripheral regions.

The United States' trade with Spanish America expanded immediately with the advent of neutral trade. Exports of American flour and some reexported British textiles flowed to a number of Spanish American ports; Havana and other West Indian ports were especially profitable markets. The United States' exports to the Spanish West Indies grew sixfold from 1795–96 to 1800–1, reaching nearly $11 million in the later period, and expanded fourfold for Spanish America as a whole. The average number of U.S. ships entering Chilean ports grew from three or four a year in the early 1790s to an average of eighteen a year from 1798 to 1807.

Consolidation of Vales Reales

The cumulative deficits resulting from war and the French alliance led Spain to desperate measures to solve its financial problems. The massive issues of *vales reales*—essentially unbacked paper money—posed a particular difficulty because they had depreciated so much in value. In 1798 the Crown ordered the sale of property held by a variety of public and religious institutions in Spain. The proceeds from these sales were to be delivered to the Crown in exchange for a royal promise to pay annually 3 percent of the value of these expropriated funds to the Church. Although the Crown planned to retire the *vales reales* with these funds, they were diverted to meet current expenses. The second war with Britain forced the Crown to search for additional resources, and on December 26, 1804, it extended to the colonies the royal decree of 1798 for the consolidation of *vales reales.*

In Spain, religious institutions affected by the consolidation held real property whose sale might lead to some land redistribution as properties held in mortmain returned to the open market. In the New World, however, most of the funds of the religious institutions and pious works were invested in loans extended to *hacendados,* merchants, miners, and others. Consolidation, therefore threatened a powerful debtor class, principally in New Spain, with the loss of property or bankruptcy. Anger over the implementation of consolidation was widespread. Although the Crown collected more than 15 million pesos, over two-thirds of it from New Spain, it paid a heavy political price. Both creoles and peninsulars grew dissatisfied with a government that so cavalierly disrupted local economies and undermined personal finances.

Among the many individuals affected by the law of consolidation was Gabriel de Yermo, a Vizcayan-born landowner and merchant whose wife had inherited rich sugarcane *haciendas* in Mexico. Yermo owed a total of several hundred thousand pesos, the largest single debt being 131,200 pesos. As did other debtors, he sought to avoid payment whenever possible and protested the seizure of his *hacienda* by the state in 1806. His case concluded in October 1808, just fifteen days after he led the coup that overthrew Mexico's viceroy. Yermo eventually regained his estate without payment.

Royal Family and Favorite

The prestige of the Spanish Crown diminished substantially during the reign of Charles IV (1788–1808). A well-meaning but lazy monarch, Charles took his wife's advice and devoted many hours daily to hunting rather than affairs of state. By 1808 the Spanish people viewed him with both pity and scorn. Hatred they reserved for Queen Luisa and Manuel Godoy, reputedly one of the queen's lovers. Rising from a modest position in the palace guard, Godoy came to dominate the royal family. Some even claimed that Godoy had fathered two children born to the queen in the 1790s. Whatever the truth, in 1792 the young favorite replaced the count of Aranda as the prime minister. Save for a brief hiatus at the end of the decade, Godoy was the most powerful man in Spain until 1808. Thus as the country endured the effects of war, fiscal crisis, and commercial decline, disgruntled opponents blamed Godoy for Spain's misfortunes. Despised by the aristocracy, distrusted by intellectuals and professionals, and hated by most people, his sole supporters were the king and queen. There was little sympathy when he fell from power in March 1808.

The hatred toward Godoy—or the prince of the peace as he was titled in 1795—vented itself in a corresponding enthusiasm for Prince Ferdinand. As the heir apparent, he embodied the hopes of all persons dismayed by Charles IV's virtual abdication of authority to a royal favorite. In March 1808, Ferdinand's supporters rioted in Aranjuez, where the royal family was then resident, and forced Charles IV to dismiss Godoy. On the following day, Charles abdicated in favor of Ferdinand. The Spanish populace greeted joyously the news of Godoy's fall and Charles's abdication, but the arrival of a French army of forty thousand men in Madrid dampened the festivities.

Napoleon and Iberia, 1807–1808

The French emperor Napoleon I made two decisions in 1807 and 1808 that had profound consequences for the Spanish and Portuguese empires. Having inaugurated in November 1806 the "continental system" prohibiting the European importation of British merchandise, in mid-1807 he tried to force Portugal to declare war on England and close its ports to British traders, a demand that Prince Regent John rejected. Angered, Napoleon secured passage across Spanish territory for a French army. French troops then captured Lisbon on November 30, 1807. Less than a week earlier, Prince John and the royal family; administrative, ecclesiastic, and military hierarchies; and numerous nobles—some ten thousand to fifteen thousand people in all, sailed to Brazil under British escort with the royal treasury, official records, and a printing press. As a result of this unprecedented move, from 1808 to 1821 John ruled his empire from Rio de Janeiro rather than Lisbon.

Napoleon's second decision was to withhold recognition of Ferdinand as monarch, to rid Spain of the Bourbons, and to place a ruler of his own choosing on the Spanish throne. At Bayonne, Napoleon demanded and obtained on May 6 an abdication from Ferdinand in favor of Charles. He had already persuaded Charles to abdicate in favor of himself. For six years Ferdinand remained in exile in France. Napoleon then placed his brother Joseph on the Spanish throne. The French emperor's decision to remove the Bourbons from Spain provoked an unprecedented constitutional crisis that soon spread to the colonies.

Spanish Governments of Resistance, 1808–1814

The majority of Spaniards refused to acknowledge the legitimacy of orders issued by Napoleon's representatives in Spain or the Spanish officials who worked with them. In the absence of a monarch, sovereignty had returned to the people to be exercised by their representatives. Provincial juntas were formed by the end of May to oversee resistance to the French and rule in the name of Ferdinand until his return to Spain. Hesitant members of the traditional elite found themselves forced to take control and provide leadership or face violent removal and possibly death.

The defeat of the French at Bailén in Andalusia in July 1808 led Joseph Bonaparte to withdraw temporarily from Madrid. By late August the provincial juntas had agreed to create a single body—the central junta—for the purposes of winning the war, securing English military assistance, and retaining the colonies. The central junta convened in Aranjuez in September 1808, but military defeats drove it to Seville in December. With about 350,000 French troops in Spain, the junta evacuated Seville and turned over its authority to a five-member regency in January 1810.

Lurking behind the junta's transfer of power to the regency were the issues of sovereignty and legitimacy. In general, Spaniards had accepted the reversion of sovereignty from Ferdinand to the people as represented in the popular provincial juntas and the central junta. The creation of a nonelected regency, however, raised the question of legitimacy. Aware of the problem, the central junta had called for a *cortes* (parliament) to convene for the purpose of writing a constitution. This was a clear break with Spanish constitutional experience and was tied to the same ideological assumptions that had underpinned the American and French constitutions. On September 24, 1810, the General and Extraordinary Cortes opened in a besieged Cádiz.

On the day it opened, the *cortes* passed a decree asserting that it had been legitimately established and rested on national sovereignty, that Ferdinand VII was Spain's legitimate monarch, and that the government should be divided into legislative, executive, and judicial branches. A decree of November 10, 1810, gave unprecedented freedom to the press. Authors could publish political, although not religious, ideas without prior censorship.

In March 1812, the *cortes* promulgated a constitution. Commonly known as the Constitution of 1812, this liberal document declared that sovereignty resided in the nation which alone had the right to establish fundamental laws. Although the constitution retained a hereditary monarch, it vested many powers formerly held by the monarch in the hands of an elected *cortes* that the king must allow to meet annually. The *cortes*, for example, created laws, determined public expenses, established taxes, and approved treaties. The old mingling of legislative, administrative, and judicial powers that characterized old-regime institutions gave way to a separation of these powers into distinct institutions. Viceroys in the colonies, for example, were replaced by *jefes políticos* who exercised limited authority and had to work with an intendant and elected members of a provincial deputation. In short, the constitution provided for a new unitarian state that eliminated many features of the old regime.

Politicization of the Colonial Elites

Starting with the creation of the first juntas in 1808, the successive governments of resistance sought to retain the empire and to receive financial assistance from it. In their efforts to do so, the central junta, the regency, and the *cortes* of Cádiz contributed to the politicization of the colonial population. The initial message was clear: An unprecedented equality between Americans and Spaniards was forthcoming. As early as October 1808, the central junta decided that it should have American representatives. Accordingly, on January 22, 1809, it issued a decree that the four viceroyalties and six captaincies-general should each elect one representative to serve on the central junta. Received warmly by creoles, this decree signaled the beginning of what promised to be a new era in the relationship between the colonies and Spain. Never before had Americans been summoned to Spain to participate in governance.

The regency also encouraged the belief that a new equality was at hand, in a decree of February 14, 1810, that called for the election of deputies to the *cortes*. The decree's explicit admission that Americans had been oppressed in the past but now were "free men" and thus equal to Spaniards both raised colonial expectations and reinforced the sense of grievance that was so common among creoles. The assertion that the past oppression had ended could be interpreted by Americans only as a promise that political and economic changes were near. Elections were held, and there was public discussion of the grievances as colonial city councils prepared instructions for the deputies. By the time the *cortes* opened in Cádiz on September 24, 1810, a newly formed junta in Caracas had already refused to acquiesce to the regency's authority. This first open challenge to continued Spanish rule in the New World demonstrated that retaining the empire would not be easy.

The most important issue that the *cortes* had to resolve was the extent of American representation. Most of the thirty American deputies sought equal representation with the peninsulars, initially seventy-five in number. With American expectations of justice in this matter raised by earlier declarations of equality, a successful resolution was imperative. Spanish Americans also pressured their peninsular counterparts on free trade and an end to restrictions on agriculture and manufacturing in the colonies. Other reforms they sought included an end to monopolies, a guaranteed percentage of bureaucratic appointments going to native sons, and the restoration of the Society of Jesus.

By 1814 perceptive Americans recognized that the touted equality between the New and Old World provinces of "the Spains" was just rhetoric. The Peruvian bureaucrat and intellectual José Baquíjano y Carrillo, for example, noted that the *cortes* had failed to fulfill the promises made in 1810. By refusing to establish equal representation and free trade, its "antipolitical conduct has been the true origin of the desperation of the American peoples; [the Cortes] never wanted to hear their complaints, nor to listen to their propositions."[1] Broken declarations of equality had revealed that regardless of the terminology employed, the American colonies remained colonies.

Parts of the constitution and some specific laws passed by the *cortes* galled numerous Americans. Colonial officials, especially the viceroys of

New Spain and Peru, exacerbated these political problems by refusing to accept the results of elections mandated by the constitution and to allow freedom of the press as decreed in 1810. Their selective enforcement of legislation undercut the legitimacy of the Spanish government. Nonetheless, there remained in 1814 a willingness on the part of the elites in Mexico and Peru to remain loyal to Spain, despite their dashed hopes.

Ferdinand and the Failure of Absolutism

Ferdinand's return to power in 1814 quickly dispelled illusions of equality and a political solution to the conflicts besieging much of the empire. With his popularity demonstrated by the public enthusiasm that welcomed him on his journey from France to Madrid, Ferdinand decided to abrogate the Constitution of 1812. By a decree signed on May 4, the king declared all acts of the *cortes* null and void. Absolutism had returned, amid wild popular acclaim and the imprisonment of a number of liberal leaders, including several Americans. Instead of reform, Ferdinand would rely on military force.

The return of Ferdinand underscored the expanded range of political possibilities that had appeared since 1808. Before the French intervention, the elites of Spain and the colonies, like the rest of society, were loyal to the absolute monarchy. During the intervening years, representatives of a liberal minority had turned Spain and the empire into a constitutional monarchy, albeit without a resident monarch, thus dividing supporters of monarchy into constitutionalists and absolutists. This division extended to the Indies where many creoles responded enthusiastically to the elections and open political discussion allowed by the constitution, while rejecting the more radical republican ideas.

In the Indies, the question of the kind of relationship that should exist between Spain and the colonies separated supporters of increased colonial autonomy from those who approved of the pre-1808 colonial relationship. A third group, most evident in Venezuela, actively sought political independence. Ferdinand's return reduced the options to two: a pre-1808 absolutism with minimal modification or independence. The middle position of increased colonial autonomy and reform that many American loyalists advocated was unacceptable to the king and his ministers.

Having rejected compromise, Ferdinand embarked on the dangerous course of using military force to reimpose order in the colonies. Unhindered by war on the peninsula, he was able to dispatch military forces to the Indies on a scale far greater than that possible for the regency or *cortes*. With the sailing of the Pablo Morillo expedition of 10,500 troops to Venezuela in 1815, the king committed himself to the military pacification of his colonial empire.

Ferdinand's resort to force pushed the elites in the affected regions a step closer to independence. The physical destruction of assets and loss of property affected numerous elite families in Venezuela and New Granada.

As was the case in Chile when a military force sent from Peru exacted harsh reprisals on the civilian population, punitive measures undermined the allegiance of members of the elite who had earlier supported continued Spanish rule.

The failure of Ferdinand's policy was clear by the end of 1819. The cost of sending and maintaining troops in the New World had been greater than normal Crown revenues could support. Already in debt in 1808, royal treasuries throughout the Indies were awash in accumulated deficits by 1819. The destruction of war and the breakdown of regular shipping had taken their toll on the empire. Chile, Argentina, and Paraguay were effectively independent, and northern South America was on the eve of independence.

The Riego Revolt and Liberal Rule

A military revolt that began in Spain on January 1, 1820, initiated the final stage in the disintegration of Spain's mainland empire. On that date Major Rafael Riego called on troops gathered in Cádiz in anticipation of another large military expedition to the New World to rise against absolutist government and restore the Constitution of 1812. Anxious to avoid service in the New World and dissatisfied with Ferdinand's treatment of the army, a sizable number of troops joined the uprising. In early March, Ferdinand reluctantly and insincerely proclaimed his allegiance to constitutional government. At a stroke the possibility of sending an army to the Americas had vanished. Again, events in Spain had directly affected the fate of the colonies.

The reinstitutionalization of a constitutional monarchy brought the liberals—many of whom Ferdinand had imprisoned or exiled in 1814—back to power. Progressively moving beyond the positions taken in 1812, the new regime not only abolished once more the administrative institutions of the old regime but also launched an attack on the privileges of the church and the military. In Mexico in particular, these reforms led many representatives of the elite to reassess their opposition to independence. Everywhere in the colonies where Spanish armies and loyalist governments persevered, these actions divided and weakened the forces opposing independence.

The events of 1808–14 had first raised and then dashed the expectations of equality and substantive changes in the colonial relationship. Although in 1814 most members of the colonial elites in regions still under Spanish control were prepared to give Ferdinand VII a chance to end the conflicts in rebellious regions and to accept absolutist rule rather than the unknown risks of independence, nothing occurred between 1814 and 1820 to strengthen the bond between monarch and subjects. On the contrary, the government's resort to force alienated its former supporters, as taxes and the direct expropriation of property were clearly not in the loyalists' interests. The same desire for self-preservation that initially led the elites to continue their loyalty to the crown as the best protection against social upheaval now led them to abandon a crown unable to maintain its authority in Spain itself.

Portugal

There was little immediate resistance to the French invasion of Portugal. With the court safely in Brazil, most of the elite that had remained began to accommodate itself to the new order. When news of popular uprisings in Spain reached Portugal in 1808, however, a popular revolt began. British naval forces that had already established a blockade moved to support this anti-French rising. Soon a military force composed of British regulars and Portuguese volunteers cleared the French from most of the kingdom. French invasions in 1808, 1809, and 1811, however, caused extensive property damage and perhaps nearly 250,000 Portuguese deaths. The nation's already-weak transportation system was particularly hard hit, and as a result, commerce suffered. By the time the French were finally expelled, the Portuguese treasury was encumbered with debt, and the economy was in crisis.

During the resistance, juntas similar to those in Spain sprang up in Portugal, but there was little republican radicalism. Many of the most important liberals were exiled in 1810 as a result of a conservative initiative supported by General William Carr Beresford, the British officer who had become a proconsul in the absence of the royal family.

The decision of John VI, king after 1816, to remain in Brazil and elevate the former colony to the status of a cokingdom created dissatisfaction in Portugal. Britain's impolitic policies further promoted a rising tide of opposition. With a British general as regent, Portuguese commercial interests were consistently sacrificed to those of Britain. The decision to open Brazil to direct trade with friendly nations—meaning primarily Great Britain—and the revocation of prohibitions on colonial manufacturing further confirmed the arrival of a new era, formalized in a commercial treaty signed in 1810. Despite legislation designed to benefit Portuguese merchants and shippers, the old monopolistic system was gone, and trade between Brazil and Portugal plummeted between 1809 and 1813 to less than a third of its level between 1800 and 1804.

Political and economic subordination to Britain and anger over the monarch's decision to remain in Brazil led to the development of a potent liberal opposition. This political tendency was most popular in the commercial class of the port cities and the small urban intellectual class. With the spread of Masonic lodges, military officers—many influenced by British colleagues—joined the opposition. In some rural areas, elements within the aristocracy were also unhappy with administration during the regency, although this group had little sympathy for liberalism.

In 1817 Beresford was informed of a conspiracy that included General Gomes da Freire, a leader of the Masonic movement. The regent quickly moved to crush this threat, even executing the popular military officer. When news of the 1820 military mutiny in Cádiz reached Portugal, a rebellion began in Oporto. As the movement spread, liberal political leaders in Lisbon and Oporto established juntas. Their first objective was to eliminate Beresford, the symbol of Portugal's humiliating subservience to Britain. They also sought the return of John VI from Brazil.

John resisted the pressure to return to Portugal, as he correctly recognized that once in Lisbon he would be reduced to a constitutional monarch subject to the whims of a popular government. Simultaneously, competing factions within the military struggled for control of the junta in Lisbon. Eventually the Spanish system of indirect suffrage was used to elect members of a constituent *cortes* in 1821. This first representative assembly held in Portugal since 1689 wrote a constitution that acknowledged popular sovereignty and established a unicameral legislature. The king's power was greatly limited, but the church and aristocracy retained many of their privileges.

John VI finally returned to Portugal in 1821. Despite his earlier fears, he had to live with the liberal constitutional order only briefly. Important elements within the church hierarchy and the aristocracy fought to return to the old regime, and an "absolutist" rebellion began in remote areas of the country. When a French army invaded Spain in April 1823 to restore Ferdinand VII to absolute power, a conservative military revolt began in Portugal. The constitutionalist government quickly fell, and John again ruled as an absolute monarch.

The traumatic events that began in 1807 led to irreparable changes in the colonial relationships between the Iberian metropolises and their New World colonies. War and its attendant economic disruption crippled the colonial commercial systems. Financial havoc plagued the peninsular governments. John's move to Rio de Janeiro elevated Brazilian aspirations to the point that restoration of the traditional colonial rule was impossible. The liberal revolts of 1820 and the subsequent absolutist resurgence in 1823 revealed the serious domestic conflict present in both Spain and Portugal. By 1826 each country had lost its American mainland possessions, and the following decades were marked by political instability and economic travail.

Independence in South America

The collapse of traditional monarchical power in Spain in 1808 followed a lengthy crisis and foreshadowed the disintegration of empire. Historians have identified a number of causes for the fall of Spain's empire. Among them are creole-peninsular hostility, a growing creole self-consciousness, trade restrictions, the Enlightenment, the precedent of the American Revolution, and the revolutionary ideology of the French Revolution. Neither individually nor collectively, however, are these "causes" responsible for the initiation of the insurgent movements. Rather, the constitutional crisis of 1808 and subsequent warfare and political developments in Spain triggered the colonial responses that ultimately, and with substantial provocation from peninsular authorities, led to the emergence of independent countries. Once these conflicts were under way, however, many of the mislabeled causes did affect the course of the war, justify actions that the insurgents took, and influence new forms of political organization. Because the Portuguese royal family escaped from Napoleon in 1807 and established their court in Brazil, that colony necessarily experienced a fundamentally different trajectory toward independence than did the Spanish possessions.

The independence movements in both Spanish South America and Brazil lacked the coherence of ideology and leadership present in the American Revolution. Because Spain's governments of resistance were fighting French armies until late 1813 and Ferdinand VII's resources were limited, the effort to retain the Spanish colonies depended primarily on the political will, economic resources, and military capacity of loyalists in the New World. Yet despite these grave limitations on royalist power, Spanish American insurgents won independence with great difficulty. In some regions the military campaigns and the resultant destruction of resources lasted more than a decade. Both the duration of these bitter contests and the equivocal political legacies inherited by the newly independent governments wre linked historically to the colonial experience that had promoted class and race conflicts. Where these divisions were deepest, independence was achieved with difficulty, and democracy quickly failed.

The Río de la Plata Region

The movement toward independence in the Rió de la Plata, a sparsely settled viceroyalty, began with Great Britain's failed effort to wrest control of the region from Spain. In June 1806 a small military expedition led by Sir Home Popham took Buenos Aires. When Viceroy Marqués de Sobremonte left the city, the citizens of Buenos Aires organized a political resistance and created a new military force that forced the English garrison to surrender in August. The euphoria that followed the retaking of the city was short-lived, for a second, much larger British force entered the estuary and took the well-fortified city of Montevideo in February 1807. Viceroy Sobremonte's inept defense of this crucial port led the *audiencia* of Buenos Aires to decree his suspension from office and to declare Santiago Liniers, the hero of the reconquest in 1806, acting viceroy. When the British forces moved to retake Buenos Aires, however, Liniers and his army failed to stop the landing. Rather, irregular forces and militia units led by Martín de Alzaga, a Spanish merchant and senior *alcalde* of the *cabildo,* successfully defended the city.

Ethnic conflicts among the victors followed the British defeat. Alzaga and other Spanish loyalists tried to force Liniers to reduce the size of the creole militia and move actively to suppress contraband trade. When the viceroy refused to act, Alzaga and other wealthy Spaniards plotted his overthrow. Although Liniers recognized the central junta, Alzaga's faction still doubted his loyalty. Some creoles, on the other hand, saw the abdications of Charles IV and Ferdinand as an opportunity to push for autonomy or even independence. Among other strategies, they pursued a covert diplomacy with Ferdinand's sister Carlota, who had fled to Brazil with her husband, the Portuguese prince regent.

Peninsular loyalists in Montevideo and Buenos Aires were the first to challenge Viceroy Liniers. The ultraroyalist governor of Montevideo, Francisco Javier Elío, convoked a meeting of leading citizens, a *cabildo abierto,* that repudiated the viceroy's authority and created a junta made up entirely of peninsulars. Martín de Alzaga and the peninsular ultrists in Buenos Aires organized an abortive effort on January 1, 1809, to replace the viceroy with a junta. Liniers was saved when creole militia commanders intervened. In a brief two-year period, the peninsular-dominated *audiencia* had deposed one viceroy, and the peninsular-dominated *cabildo* had narrowly failed in its effort to depose a second. Real power increasingly resided in the hands of politicized creole militia commanders.

In July 1809 the veteran naval officer Baltasar Hidalgo de Cisneros arrived to replace Liniers as viceroy. Cisneros recognized quickly that he must favor creole interests in order to hold the colony's loyalty. When two English merchants requested permission to sell goods in the city, for example, Cisneros accepted the recommendation of powerful local interests and opened the port.

Similar conflicts shook traditional authority in Upper Peru, the source of the mining revenues that sustained Spanish administration and military power in the Río de la Plata. In Chuquisaca (modern Sucre) the audiencia of Charcas imprisoned the governor-intendant in 1809 in a struggle between two factions of peninsulars. A much more violent rising followed in La Paz, where a mix of creoles and mestizos overthrew both the intendant and the bishop. The radical junta created in the wake of these events directly challenged Spanish rule and looked to enlist Indian allies. Such republican and egalitarian objectives terrified the majority of the white propertied class. A small, well-disciplined army organized by José Manuel de Goyeneche, the Arequipa-born president of the *audiencia* of Cuzco, easily reestablished Spanish authority in both La Paz and Chuquisaca. Most of the radicals from La Paz were executed.

Spanish rule soon faced a greater challenge in Buenos Aires. Cornelio Saavedra and other powerful members of the creole military pushed for a *cabildo abierto* to discuss the crisis in Spain. Viceroy Cisneros resisted this overture and was placed under what amounted to house arrest. A meeting was finally called for May 22, 1810. Ultimately only 251 of the 450 invited participants attended, as some peninsulars were kept away by youthful militants who took over the central plaza.

In the end the *cabildo* was empowered to appoint a junta. When the *cabildo* announced on May 24 that the junta included the viceroy as president, outraged creole leaders demanded his removal. The most powerful military figures not only signed the petition but also placed armed militia men near the homes of the *cabildo*'s members. The *cabildo* yielded on May 25 and formed a new, more radical junta with the militia commander Saavedra at its head. This new government claimed to represent Ferdinand VII and made no effort to formulate a constitution. After this May revolution, Spanish authority was never again reasserted in Buenos Aires or its hinterland.

The eclipse of Spanish power brought little agreement on the form or content that an independent political life should take. Buenos Aires was the epicenter of this eruption of political energy, but its leaders sought to sustain the city's traditional political authority and economic domination in the remainder of the viceroyalty. Few members of the provincial elites welcomed this continued ascendancy. Even within Buenos Aires there was bitter personal and ideological disagreement over the pace of political and social reforms.

Revolutionary militants led by the creole lawyer Mariano Moreno pushed to radicalize the government in Buenos Aires. Among their victories were exiling the viceroy and other peninsular officials and subjecting other peninsulars to confiscatory taxes and a discriminatory civic status. When these policies promoted organized resistence, the militants responded by executing opposition leaders in the capital, and in Córdoba former viceroy Santiago Liniers. Finally, in 1811 the Committee of Public Safety, modeled after its namesake of the French Revolution, was created to discipline the unenthusiastic. This radical stage peaked with the execution of Martín de Alzaga, the other hero in the defense of Buenos Aires against the British.

Conservatives gained the advantage when like-minded provincial deputies were seated in the junta. Moreno resigned, accepted a diplomatic mission to Europe, and, to the relief of many, died en route. Political passions now began to escape the confining structure of the junta of Buenos Aires. The formation of provincial juntas and the forced resignation of some radical members as a result of mob pressure reduced the junta's power. By September 1811 a triumvirate led by Saavedra briefly assumed executive power. Following a failed mutiny by the city's most prestigious militia regiment, conflict between the junta led by provincial conservatives and the more radical urban leaders in the triumvirate was resolved by the expulsion of the provincial deputies.

In 1812 Bernardino Rivadavia, one of the leading liberals, drew up a skeletal constitutional system that began the process of educational reform, ended the slave trade, and established basic civil liberties. His document also provided for a National Assembly made up of the *cabildo* of Buenos Aires and representatives from the municipal councils of the interior. However, even this limited form of representation proved unacceptable to the triumvirate which dissolved the assembly in April.

Within this context of disintegrating central authority, the interior provinces gained greater independence from Buenos Aires. A series of military expeditions to annex the rich mining province of Upper Peru failed. The arrogant, shortsighted behavior of military leaders from Buenos Aires left a legacy of poisoned political relations that eventually led to the independence of Upper Peru.

In Paraguay, a region that had long resented its subservience to Buenos Aires, creoles supported the peninsular governor in defeating a military expedition from the capital. Having disposed of this threat, the local elite then deposed the governor and created a rival junta. By the end of 1811 Buenos Aires was forced to recognize Paraguay's de facto independence. One of the most remarkable men of the era, José Gaspar Rodríquez Francia gained effective political control by 1813. Later named dictator for life, Francia kept Paraguay away from the wars of independence.

Uruguay

Montevideo and Buenos Aires were natural rivals. Although Buenos Aires was the capital of the viceroyalty, Montevideo had compensatory advantages. It had the finest deep-water harbor in the estuary and was well connected to the region's richest grazing lands. Despite familial and commercial links to the export merchants of Buenos Aires, the wealthiest peninsular merchants of Montevideo resented their rivals' commercial and political domination. Consequently, in the wake of the British invasions and the later collapse of the Spanish monarchy, they supported the creation of a separate junta headed by Governor Francisco Javier Elío.

Because the political life of the Banda Oriental diverged from that of Buenos Aires, Uruguayan rebels found themselves sidelined by a conflict between the declining colonial power of Spain and the territorial ambitions of Buenos Aires. Elío's loyalist junta had limited their options. To reject the pretensions of Buenos Aires meant accepting Spanish rule; to throw off colonial status meant accepting continued domination by Buenos Aires.

In early 1811 José Gervasio Artigas offered a political alternative to domination by either Spain or Buenos Aires. Artigas was the son of a prominent ranching family. He now emerged as one of the first *caudillos* of the independence era, a man whose authority and legitimacy were based on personal characteristics rather than on ideology or institutions. Artigas's political movement was genuinely popular, especially in the Uruguayan countryside, but this very popularity tended to thwart the development of democratic institutions or stable political parties.

Artigas supported the Buenos Aires junta when the loyalist Elío, now viceroy, declared war on it. But when the viceroy ordered the Uruguayan ranchers to prove title to their lands or to pay a fee to legitimize their holdings, he played into Artigas's hands. Because few ranchers had bothered with the formality of securing legal title to their properties, they deeply resented this measure and turned to Artigas and his army to protect their interests. As a result, Spanish authority was quickly limited to the city of Montevideo. Viceroy Elío sought to break this deadlock in 1811 by inviting in a Portuguese army from Brazil. When it became clear that the Portuguese had their own objectives, however, Elío sought peace with Buenos Aires. Excluded from these negotiations, Artigas undertook an independent course. Diplomatic pressure from Britain, Portugal's major trading partner, eventually secured the removal of the Portuguese army.

The Constituent Assembly of the United Provinces of the Río de la Plata met in Buenos Aires in 1813. Artigas instructed his delegates to demand a loose federation that would grant each province commercial and political autonomy. This position attracted the support of other regional *caudillos* and led the assembly to refuse to seat Artigas's deputies and to brand their leader an outlaw. Military forces from Buenos Aires finally occupied Montevideo in June 1814 but were forced to turn over the city to Artigas after seven months.

In 1815, Artigas controlled Uruguay and dominated the Federal League, a loose confederation of the provinces of Corrientes, Entre Ríos, Santa Fe, and Córdoba. Years of war, however, had devastated the region. The depredations of competing armies had depleted its herds of livestock and disrupted trade through Montevideo. Artigas responded to the need for economic recovery by allowing the British limited commercial access through the two major ports but restricted their penetration of the interior. In the countryside he undertook a radical agrarian reform that gave *castas* and poor whites preferential access to abandoned and unused land. He also pushed legislation that benefited the traditional landowning class, such as laws forcing vagabonds to work, but the principal effect of his populist rural policy was to weaken his support among wealthy ranchers.

Collusion between the government in Buenos Aires and the Portuguese monarchy led to a new Brazilian invasion of Uruguay in 1816. Driven from Montevideo by a Brazilian army, Artigas's forces suffered a decisive defeat in early 1820 at Tacuarembó. Even his allies turned against him, forcing him into exile in Paraguay, where he died thirty years later.

Uruguayan resistance to the Brazilian occupation continued, and after 1826 much of the countryside was in patriot hands. Independence was finally achieved through the lengthy mediation of the British. Peace came in 1828 and a constitution was adopted in 1830. This constitution was more conservative than the political objectives sought by Artigas; most of the rural and urban poor who had supported the cause of independence were denied the vote. Instead, the major liberal achievements of this new order were the abolition of slavery and the slave trade.

The Victory of Federalism in Argentina

By 1814 it was clear that experiments with collective administration, the junta and the triumvirate, had failed in Buenos Aires. There was neither effective leadership nor meaningful accountability. The capital's increas-

ingly hostile relations with the interior provinces prevented the establishment of a national legislature, for the city's radicals feared that representatives from the more conservative provinces would ally themselves with
their local enemies. As this conflict evolved, the centralists were identified
as Unitarians, and those seeking provincial autonomy, as Federalists. These
increasingly bitter enemies agreed only on the rejection of Spanish rule.
The remainder of political life was reduced to mere controversy and struggle over power and spoils as one weak executive followed another. Yet two
important events relieved this otherwise bleak picture: the calling of a new
constituent assembly in Tucumán and the commitment of resources to
José de San Martín's campaign to carry the war against Spain to Chile and
Peru.

When the"national" congress met in Tucumán, the corrosive effect of
ideological and regional conflicts was clear. Artigas and his allies in Entre
Ríos, Corrientes, Santa Fe, and Córdoba sent no delegates, whereas Paraguay under Francia pursued a completely independent course. Upper
Peru remained under Spanish control. Despite these weaknesses, the
assembly decided to throw off the increasingly shallow subterfuge of loyalty to Ferdinand and declared complete independence from Spain on July
9, 1816. There was less agreement over the form of government.

Among the representatives gathered in Tucumán were a significant
number of monarchists, including José de San Martín. Although able to
defeat the monarchists, republican deputies could not agree on a new institutional formula. In the end Juan Martín de Pueyrredón was given the
Napoleonic-sounding title of supreme director, and the congress decided
to move to Buenos Aires. The constitution completed in 1819 was unre-
alistically centralist, giving the national executive the right to appoint provincial governors. In reality Pueyrredón had little power, and the constitution could not be enforced. Outraged *caudillos* of the interior eventually
brought this rump national government to its knees by inflicting a crushing
defeat on Buenos Aires in 1820. Argentina was independent, but the stability of colonial rule had given way to anarchy.

Chile

In 1810 a junta had been established in Santiago without significant loyalist opposition. The competing ambitions of a handful of strong person-
alities, however, quickly divided the junta. With the election of a national
congress, a regional political struggle began, reminiscent of the contest
between Buenos Aires and the interior provinces of Argentina. In the Chilean case the capital's deputies were generally more conservative. Dissident
supporters of independence withdrew to the southern port city of Concepción where they organized a competing junta that worked to undermine the authority of Santiago.

José Miguel Carrera dominated the next stage of the independence struggle. Like San Martín in Argentina, Carrera had served with distinction in the Spanish army. He also benefited from the social prestige of his wealthy and powerful family. Committed to neither democratic institutions nor the rule of law, Carrera was a populist who proved adept at framing political issues to fit the aspirations and prejudices of the masses. Frustrated by opposition within the congress that convened in July 1811, Carrera organized and successfully carried out Chile's first military coup.

Carrera's ascendency was short-lived. The capable and strongly royalist Viceroy José de Abascal of Peru sent an army against which Carrera's forces campaigned ineffectually. As Carrera dithered, the Santiago junta replaced him as commander with Bernardo O'Higgins, the son of a former captain-general of Chile and viceroy of Peru. O'Higgins proved no more successful than his rival in defeating the royalist army. Through the mediation of a British officer, he did manage what appeared to be an acceptable political compromise that would have given autonomy to Chile. Abascal's opposition, however, rendered the agreement stillborn. When patriot forces were defeated at Rancagua in 1814, Carrera, O'Higgins, and many other Chilean leaders fled across the Andes.

José de San Martín secured an appointment as intendant of the Andean province of Cuyo from the government in Buenos Aires. With financial support provided by the hard-pressed government of Director Pueyrredón, he built a small, well-disciplined army with the intention of flanking the Spanish strongholds of Peru and Upper Peru by launching an attack on Chile. By late 1816, he had prepared a well-equipped army of nearly five thousand men, a majority of whom were blacks and mulattoes. San Martín divided his forces and in January 1817 began to cross the Andes in a feat reminiscent of the extraordinary achievements of the conquest period. With the majority of his army reunited, he defeated the royalist army at Chacabuco and entered Santiago.

Royalist forces regrouped in southern Chile and gained some successes against O'Higgins and San Martín but were unable to take Santiago. The final important battle of this campaign, fought at Maipú in April 1818, secured Chile's independence. With the first part of his plan accomplished, San Martín was now ready to pursue an attack on Peru. O'Higgins, returning the loyalty San Martín had earlier shown him, committed Chilean military forces and financial resources to this campaign. Although the support was crucial to San Martín, it weakened O'Higgins's strength in Chile.

O'Higgins ruled Chile for five years. He was a brave, honest politician committed to the independence and well-being of his country, but he distrusted democracy and failed to build a political base of support adequate to sustain his reform agenda. O'Higgins promoted education for the Chilean masses and sought to reform and secularize the educational institutions inherited from the colonial period. He attacked privilege, abolishing titles and attempting to end the system of entail, thus angering members of the landed elite. These policies led to a successful armed rebellion in

1823. As was true in Argentina, Chile had gained independence but lacked stable institutions and a broad-based political agreement on economic and social policy.

Bolívar and the Liberation of Venezuela and New Granada

Venezuela was one of the major beneficiaries of Bourbon economic policy. Most of the economic growth, however, was in export agriculture, a sector that depended on slavery and tenancy. Even before the French invasion of Spain, Venezuela experienced a series of unsettling social conflicts tied indirectly to the French and Haitian revolutions. In 1795 slaves and free laborers seized a number of plantations in the sugar-producing region of Coro, putting some owners to the knife before being ruthlessly suppressed. Two years later a conspiracy that included both blacks and poor whites was uncovered and repressed in La Guaira, the port city of Caracas. These and other signs of potential race and class war served temporarily to tie the region's creole elite to Spain.

Yet there were countervailing pressures on the elite as well. As Spain stumbled into the European wars that disrupted the Atlantic trade and cut off the colony from legal markets, planters began to calculate the cost of empire. Open ports and free trade seemed to promise prosperity for the elite. However, they feared that open conflict with Spain would unlease the violent passions of the exploited underclasses. As a result, Francisco de Miranda found no local support when he arrived in 1806 with a small expedition of North American volunteers to initiate a war for independence.

As in Buenos Aires, it was news of the royal abdications and the French invasion of Spain that began the process that would lead ultimately to independence. When a group of prominent creoles presented a petition for a junta in July 1808, Spanish authorities moved quickly to imprison or exile the leaders. Efforts to create a junta in December 1809 and April 1810 met similar fates. News of the dissolution of the central junta in Spain and the creation of the regency in Cádiz gave new life to the effort to push aside the colonial administration. On April 19, 1810, the creole-dominated *cabildo,* supported by street demonstrations, deposed the captain-general and the *audiencia* of Caracas. A junta was created that included both moderate autonomists and revolutionary nationalists drawn from the elite. Though their political aspirations diverged, these groups agreed on economic issues. The junta reduced taxes and established free trade, policies that benefited the elite. It also abolished the slave trade, although retaining slavery. Property qualifications barred most of the population, especially the black masses, from participation in politics. A congress convened in March 1811, replaced the junta with a three-person rotational executive, declared independence in July, and wrote a federalist constitution.

The two most important radical leaders of the era were Francisco de Miranda, a man who had spent most of his adult life conspiring and agitating among Spain's European rivals for intervention on behalf of independence, and Simón Bolívar, the well-traveled and well-educated son of one of the colony's wealthiest families. Neither man was prepared to bridge the gap between the egalitarian ideology of the early revolution and the harsh social realities that inflamed the black and *casta* majority. In the wake of royalist-inspired black uprisings, Bolívar referred to "this inhuman and atrocious people, feeding on the blood and property of the patriots. . . ."[2]

The republican government was threatened by royalist military challenges and popular uprisings. Then on March 26, 1812, a massive earthquake struck Venezuela and especially the Caracas area. Encouraged by royalist priests, the masses believed this natural disaster to be God's judgment on the republic. Although granted dictatorial powers, Miranda was defeated and forced to negotiate an end of republican government for a royalist promise to respect the republicans' lives and property. Bolívar viewed these negotiations as treason and conspired to permit the royalists to capture Miranda. With Miranda on his way to a Spanish prison where he would die, Bolívar inherited the leadership of the radical faction.

With the royalists victorious in Venezuela, Bolívar fled in 1812 to Cartagena in the temporarily independent New Granada. After brief military service there, he gained support for another campaign in Venezuela. Frustrated by the initial failures of democracy and federalism, Bolívar now advocated a strong centralized government and a more independent military power as necessary tools in the struggle with Spain. The campaign begun in May 1813 was particularly brutal, with both sides destroying the property of their adversaries and then executing prisoners. Despite some successes, Bolívar was defeated by the royalist *caudillo* José Tomás Boves who had organized the cowboys of southern Venezuela on behalf of the king. Even after Boves's death, republican fortunes continued to decline.

The recently restored Ferdinand VII sent to Venezuela a large military expedition under General Pablo Morillo. The Spanish forces entered Caracas in May 1815 and by October had pacified most of New Granada as well. In order to pay for this costly military venture, General Morillo confiscated and sold the property of well-known republican leaders and that of their noncombatant supporters as well. This harsh policy proved counterproductive because it forced the creole elite to see independence as the best guarantee for their property.

Although Bolívar was unable to gain British aid, he did find valuable new allies. Alexandre Pétion, the president of Haiti, provided significant assistance in return for a pledge to abolish slavery. Bolívar also won the support of two groups that had previously provided the Venezuelan royalists with their most effective troops, the *casta* cowboys of the interior and the free blacks. José Antonio Páez was a natural military leader who organized the cowboys of the Venezuelan plains into an efficient cavalry. Circumstances had forced this cross-class alliance on Bolívar and the socially conservative creole elite. Once in place, however, this new military force provided the means for unprecedented upward social mobility. Páez, the poor illiterate plainsman, eventually became president of Venezuela.

A national congress meeting in Angostura in 1819 named Bolívar president. Even as the congress met, however, an audacious military campaign was determining the future of Venezuela and New Granada. Bolívar crossed the Andes and defeated the Spanish armies in New Granada. He then returned to Venezuela where Spanish resistance was overcome at the battle of Carabobo in 1821.

The Congress of Angostura had declared the union of Venezuela, New Granada, and the still-unliberated Ecuador in the republic of Colombia, often called Gran Colombia by historians. A constituent assembly that met in 1821 produced a new constitution. Reflecting Bolívar's more authoritarian outlook, this centralist document gave the chief executive much greater power than the legislature or judiciary had and narrowly restricted the franchise.

Royalist forces in Ecuador were overcome in a pincer's movement. José de Sucre, one of Bolívar's most skilled lieutenants, was sent south to secure the coastal city of Guayaquil and then to move inland to take Quito. Bolívar himself undertook a difficult campaign through the royalist province of Pasto. There were, however, significant political obstacles to Bolívar's plan to integrate Ecuador into the new Republic of Colombia. Many Ecuadorians argued for complete independence, and some supported the idea of union with a free Peru. Ultimately the former group was successful.

Peru and Upper Peru

Once the independence of Chile was secure, San Martín moved to attack Peru. The governments of the United Provinces of the Río de la Plata and Chile pledged troops and financial support for the expedition. Pledging resources was easier, however, than finding them. Both governments faced internal opposition, and both economies were weakened by a decade of violence and disrupted commerce. San Martín's expedition included 4,500 soldiers and a strong supporting naval force under the British mercenary Thomas Cochrane. Because this force was not clearly superior to the army available to Viceroy Joaquín de la Pezuela, San Martín's natural conservatism drew him into a cautious strategy that avoided risky military confrontations. Instead, he sought to win the support of Peruvian creoles for independence and to disarm the Spanish army through negotiations.

This strategy ultimately proved unsuccessful. Peru's creoles were divided and unreliable as allies, and they distrusted the Argentines and Chileans of San Martín's army as much as they distrusted the Spaniards. Furthermore, the military capacity of the liberating army was limited, for it was underfunded and poorly led. Severe differences between San Martín and Cochrane, who chafed under San Martín's policy of restraint, also weakened the cause of independence.

San Martín's monarchism and social conservatism further impeded a rapid resolution of the struggle. He tried to avoid drawing the masses of Peruvian society into the conflict, fearing that this might lead to the reappearance of the hatreds manifested in the 1780s during the Tupac Amaru rising. He negotiated with royalist commanders and the British, looking for a formula that would produce independence within the context of a monarchy acceptable to Ferdinand and the other European rulers.

Reluctantly, the creole elite of Lima at last declared Peru independent in July 1821 and named San Martín the protector with supreme civil and military power. San Martín abolished tribute and the *mita,* ordered that the word "Peruvian" be used instead of "Indian" in official documents, and freed the children born to slave mothers. The creole elite, however, made no effort to enforce these reforms, and San Martín soon lost much of their support. The departure of Cochrane and his fleet in September further weakened the protector's position.

Recognizing his political, military, and financial weakness, San Martín turned to Bolívar, and the two met at Guayaquil in July 1822. Bolívar had the better cards. He had a larger, better-trained army and also a stronger economic base. San Martín returned to Peru, resigned his position in the Peruvian government, and left for self-imposed exile in Europe, where he died in 1850. Bolívar and his allies undertook the final campaign against Spanish power.

Before Bolívar could move against royalist forces in the Andean provinces, he had to overcome the infighting among rival creole leaders and a mutiny by the remnants of San Martín's army. He pushed aside his rivals in Lima and formed a new military force from the surviving fragments of San Martín's force, his own Colombian troops, and Peruvian creole units. Divisions among the Spanish commanders improved his prospects. Following news in 1823 that Ferdinand VII had again overturned the liberal constitution of 1812, the leading Spanish officer in Upper Peru, Pedro Antonio de Olañeta, broke with Viceroy José de La Serna, who was associated with the ousted liberal regime in Spain. This action forced the viceroy to send an ineffective punitive expedition against his former ally at the very moment that Bolívar's forces sought a conclusive battle.

On the Andean plateau of Junín in August 1824, Bolívar and Sucre defeated the royalist forces. While Bolívar then moved to reestablish control over the coastal zone and the capital city, Sucre commanded the liberating army in the final decisive battle for Peru. On December 8, 1824, Sucre's forces defeated the royalists and captured Viceroy La Serna at Ayacucho. Bolívar now was the virtual dictator of Peru. He reformed the educational system and established the first political institutions of an independent Peru.

Only Upper Peru remained in Spanish hands. The region was governed by General Olañeta who had rebelled against the Spanish viceroy. His political support was provided by conservative creoles rather than peninsular Spaniards. Olañeta represented, in fact, the widespread desire among the regional elite to protect and preserve the social and economic order of the colonial era rather than a genuine loyalty to the Spanish monarchy. Once Sucre and his victorious army entered Upper Peru, Olañeta's supporters calculated his chances and then deserted him. Thus when the final battle of independence was fought at Tumusla on April 1, 1825, Olañeta's fate was already sealed. It was merely convenient that he died in battle. The resulting country, Bolivia, took its name from the liberator Bolívar, who also provided the new country with a conservative constitution. The Venezuelan Sucre became its first president, although he was forced to surrender power after only three years. Although independent, Bolivia's economic and social structures were among the least altered in all of Spanish America.

Brazil

The arrival of the court in 1808 dramatically altered the political life and economy of Brazil. Access to the court and the possibility of gaining a title pulled the colonial elite into the monarch's orbit. Even though many Brazilians came to resent the arrogance and privileged status of the recent arrivals, this anti-Portuguese sentiment did not undermine support for the king.

John VI moved quickly to address the many long-standing grievances of the local elite. Soon after the court's arrival, he opened the colony's ports to free trade. The prohibition of colonial manufactures was removed, and some import duties were dropped. Great Britain, not the local producers, was the prime beneficiary of this more liberal commercial policy, although Brazilian consumers were able to buy imported goods more cheaply. The court also helped stimulate colonial production by dramatically increasing the demand for goods and services. More than 20,000 Portuguese and thousands of other Europeans entered the city of Rio de Janeiro alone between 1808 and 1822. As the urban population of the capital rose toward 100,000, demands for housing, food, locally manufactured goods, and services expanded as well. Even the urban masses experienced small improvements in employment and wages.

Once the peninsular war ended and Portugal was liberated from the French, John had to face the problem of whether to remain in Brazil or to return to Lisbon. His British allies and the merchant elite and nobility of Portugal expected him to return quickly to the metropolis, but the king elected to remain in Brazil. In late 1815 he granted Brazil the status of a cokingdom equal with Portugal itself. Although Brazilians applauded the decision, the role of imperial capital carried burdens as well as benefits.

The court was costly, and its expenses were paid largely through taxes and duties imposed on local producers. Portuguese emigrés who held the highest administrative and military offices largely enjoyed the high salaries and luxurious life-styles provided by royal patronage. But even though this was a period of general prosperity, some members of the Brazilian elite came to resent this forced subsidy. Because John yielded to British pressure and agreed to restrictions on the slave trade, he lost support among the sugar, cotton, and coffee producers. As slave prices rose and the price of agricultural exports fell following the return of peace to Europe, political unrest spread in Brazil's agricultural sector. Finally, the costly commitment of military forces in Uruguay in 1811 and 1816 proved unpopular in Brazil.

Despite a growing undercurrent of dissatisfaction, there was only one significant Brazilian uprising against the monarchy. In Pernambuco in 1817, some planters, merchants, and churchmen joined what was basically a military rebellion. The leaders affected the customs of the French Revolution, addressing one another as "patriot" and offering the French constitution as a model for organizing a government. This "republic" lasted less than three months. Once order was restored, additional troops from Portugal were brought in to garrison strategic points in Brazil.

Independence, however, did not result from the maturation of these colonial grievances or the spread of radical republicanism in Brazil. Rather, events in Portugal destabilized Brazil. Liberal juntas were created in Lisbon and Oporto in 1820. Committed to a constitution based on the Spanish constitution of 1812, the junta followed the Spanish precedent and summoned representatives from throughout the empire to a *cortes*. Brazil was permitted to elect approximately seventy-five of the more than two hundred delegates. Although a liberal perspective dominated the reform agenda in Portugal itself, the economic agenda was traditional imperialism. The *cortes* leadership sought to subordinate Brazil's economic interests to those of the metropolis, by reestablishing the commercial system that had existed before the French invasion.

John VI's position deteriorated when Portuguese soldiers in Belém created the first Brazilian junta in January 1821. Then in February the Portuguese garrison in Rio de Janeiro forced the king to reorganize his ministry and to accept the creation of juntas and the formulation of a liberal constitution. These events provoked a political crisis among Brazilian political leaders. Although many of them supported the ideology of the Lisbon junta, they recognized that the loss of the court would mean recolonization.

When John sailed for Portugal on July 26, 1821, he left his twenty-two-year-old son Pedro as regent in Brazil. These events made Brazilians more self-consciously nationalistic. The *cortes*'s decision to reestablish limitations on Brazilian commerce and to reinforce Brazilian garrisons with Portuguese troops fed this sense of Brazilian distinctiveness. As Portugal reasserted its domination, seven Brazilian delegates to the *cortes* fled Lisbon rather than accept the new Portuguese constitution of 1822.

Events now moved quickly. In response to intense pressure, including a petition signed by eight thousand persons, Pedro refused the *cortes*'s order to return to Portugal. The army in Brazil was then purged of those soldiers

and officers unwilling to swear allegiance to Dom Pedro, and troops sent
from Portugal were denied permission to land. With the appointment of
José Bonifácio de Andrada e Silva, a wealthy Brazilian with broad experience in Portugal, as head of a Brazilian cabinet, the break with the metropolis became inevitable. Although the other members of this advisory body
were Portuguese, they all were committed to maintaining Pedro in Brazil
in defiance of metropolitan authority.

There remained substantial disagreement over the institutional form
and political content of the developing movement toward independence.
José Bonifácio tried to prevent dramatic political or social change, believing that monarchy was the best insurance against the chaos that had
engulfed the neighboring republics of Spanish America. Although more
radical leaders forced the creation of the Constituent Assembly, the imposition of indirect elections and limited suffrage guaranteed that this body
would be compatible with the conservative vision of José Bonifácio. The
jailing or expulsion of leading radicals further strengthened the conservative leadership.

After May 1822 it was decided that decrees of the Portuguese *cortes*
would not be enforced without Pedro's permission. In the same month the
prince was given the title of perpetual protector of Brazil. Then in June all
appointees to the civil service were required to swear support for Brazilian
independence. Finally, the provincial governments were ordered to prevent individuals appointed by the *cortes* from taking office. Independence
was effectively achieved.

While the prince was traveling in São Paulo, his wife met with the Council of State to inform them what the *cortes* was planning to send troops to
Brazil, as it now regarded Dom Pedro and his advisers as traitors. Following the urging of José Bonifácio, Pedro declared Brazilian independence
on September 7, 1822. The British government guaranteed the success of
this bloodless movement by making clear to Portugal that it would not tol-
erate European military intervention in the newly independent empire.

Independence in Mexico and Central America

In the last decades of the colonial period New Spain was the wealthiest,
most productive and economically diversified, and most populous Spanish
colony. The empire's largest colony, it included the area that stretched
from Central America in the south to the vast, sparsely settled frontier
zone that is now the American Southwest. With more than 6 million hab-
itants, New Spain was home to over 40 percent of the entire Spanish American population. Its capital, Mexico City, was after Madrid the second largest city in the Spanish-speaking world, and with more than 150,000
inhabitants it was the largest city in the Western Hemisphere.

Although agriculture and grazing still absorbed nearly 80 percent of the labor force and produced nearly 40 percent of the gross domestic product, the colony had a large manufacturing sector led by the textile industry, a vigorous international trade, and, of course, its famous mining sector. Mining produced only about 10 percent of gross domestic product, but this 10 percent was disproportionally important, as it was the source of the colony's money supply and provided one of the government's most accessible sources of tax income. Society was arranged hierarchically, with a few native-born whites at the top and the Indian population at the bottom. The *casta* population, especially *mestizos* but also mulattoes, provided much of the artisan and less-skilled urban and mining work force. The majority of *castas* lived in poverty, as rural wage laborers and tenants or as urban day laborers.

Mexican society, then, was fraught with deep race and class divisions. Most of the colony's wealthiest men and women were creoles, but this native aristocracy, although granted titles and other privileges, had only limited access to the highest levels of the state and church. Peninsulars, fewer than fifteen thousand in number, enjoyed a disproportionate share of the most prestigious and lucrative posts in the state, church, and military as well as a lucrative portion of international trade. At the very top of Mexican society, the great families drew on the resources of both creole and peninsular members and formed an informal but effective elite that only a few outsiders could enter. Below the peninsular officeholders and merchants and the wealthy creole aristocrats came a large group of creole professionals—lawyers, clerics, notaries, and others. It was they who most keenly felt the weight of the colonial system. Increasingly they demonstrated an awareness in and enthusiasm for what was distinctively Mexican; the popularity of the cult of the Virgin of Guadalupe was one sign of this nascent nationalism. Another sign was the identification that a minority of creoles felt with the pre-Colombian Aztec civilization.

The Initial Challenge

On July 16, 1808, news of Ferdinand's forced abdication and the French invasion of Spain arrived in Mexico City. Delegations from competing metropolitan juntas later came to New Spain to lay claim to colonial recognition. The apparent need to choose among rival metropolitan authorities raised the level of political debate and drove a wedge between creole and peninsular members of the elite. Finally, the *cabildo*, the institutional platform for creole elite interests, passed a resolution asking Viceroy José de Iturrigaray to assume responsibility for summoning representatives from the colony's cities to an assembly. This request for what was in effect a constitutional convention was based on the premise that with the collapse of the monarchy, sovereignty had reverted to the people of New Spain.

Iturrigaray apparently supported the outline of the *cabildo*'s proposal and sponsored a series of discussions of political options by various elite groups. Fearful of where this might lead, peninsular leaders, including some members of the *audiencia* of Mexico, the archbishop, and *consulado* merchants, staged a preemptive coup on September 15, 1808. Led by Gabriel de Yermo, a rich merchant and sugar producer, they arrested the viceroy and the leading creole supporters of autonomy. The *audiencia* then sanctioned the overthrow of the viceroy, appointing an ineffectual retired field marshal, Pedro de Garibay, to replace him. Garibay was followed by two other temporary governments until a permanent replacement, Francisco Javier de Venegas, arrived in September 1810. This action by peninsular conservatives politically neutralized the creole elite centered in Mexico City. Its very success, however, encouraged political dissent in the provinces.

New Spain in 1810 had developed very low levels of regional economic integration. With the major exception of the mining sectors, regions tended to operate as nearly independent economies centered on the local cities. Guadalajara, one of the most economically expansive regions of the late colonial period, exported only 2 percent of its gross regional product in the years around 1800. Lack of integration combined with unpredictable access to international markets and heavy tax burdens to inhibit economic growth. One characteristic of this development was the regional economies' difficulty in responding to subsistence crises. For example, droughts in 1808 and 1809 led to two years of famine in the north-central region of Mexico. Because inadequate transportation, market, and credit mechanisms prevented a coherent response, the poorest sectors of society suffered greatly.

The geographic region called the Bajío, roughly the intendancy of Guanajuato, was the most modern in Mexico. Nearly half of its residents lived in cities of five thousand or more, and approximately half of the work force was employed outside agriculture. It was also a region in which a relatively small percentage of its rural population lived in traditional communities. Both sharecropping and wage labor were more common among rural residents here than in other regions, and urban workers and miners in the Bajío were more dependent on wages in 1810 than at earlier times. As a result, class consciousness—as opposed to the more typical corporate and racial identities—was also more developed.

The economic and social changes associated with the modernization of the Bajío aggravated the effects of drought and famine that coincided with the imperial political crisis. Consumers there had less access to family or village production and were, therefore, forced to buy grain in a market dominated by large-scale capitalist producers who sought to maximize their profits by holding their grain off the market to drive prices even higher. As prices rose, mine owners and other large employers had to absorb the higher costs in order to feed their livestock and consequently either laid off their workers or cut back their hours. Because of these changes in labor relations, the effects of the famine were experienced more by rural and urban workers in the Bajío and aggravated class tensions

between these groups and the rural landowning class that generally profited from the crisis.

Stage 1: The Hidalgo Revolt

A group of well-placed creoles in the textile center of Querétaro organized
a conspiracy against the conservative peninsular government imposed in
1808. Some had been involved in an earlier failed conspiracy, including
Ignacio Allende, Juan de Aldama, and Mariano Abasolo, three militia officers with ties to the merchant and landowning classes. Miguel Domínguez,
the creole *corregidor* of Querétaro, was the highest-ranking conspirator.
Also included was the parish priest of the town of Dolores, Miguel Hidalgo
y Costilla.

Hidalgo was a creole born to a modest family in 1753. His father was
the majordomo on a ranch in Guanajuato, and Hidalgo spent his early life
in the country. Determined to set him on the road to an ecclesiastical
career, his parents sent him to the Jesuit college of San Francisco Javier in
Valladolid. Two years later the school closed when the Jesuits were
expelled from the colony. Hidalgo then entered the diocesan college and
in 1774 received a bachelor's degree from the University of Mexico. He
later returned to Valladolid as lecturer at his alma mater and then became
its rector.

Hidalgo's free thinking and unbridled tongue quickly caused him problems. He was reported to the Inquisition for challenging a number of
church doctrines, including one regarding fornication, as well as questioning political orthodoxy in the imperial system. He also read and kept prohibited books and lived openly with a mistress. But these problems did not
prevent his appointment to the lucrative parish of Dolores in 1803. There
he devoted most of his time to promoting new industries—ceramics, weaving, wine making, and beekeeping, among others—and sublet his sacramental duties to another priest. Contact with Ignacio Allende drew him
into the Querétaro conspiracy.

The Querétaro conspirators planned their rising for December 8, 1810.
Apparently they had exercised little discretion while seeking additional
recruits, for the colonial authorities were informed of the plot by a number of different individuals. On September 13 the home of one of the conspirators was searched and weapons were found. As the authorities began
to arrest the conspirators in Querétaro, Doña Josefa Ortiz de Domínguez,
the wife of the *corregidor,* sent word to Allende, Aldama, and Hidalgo.
Informed of these events on September 16, Hidalgo rang the bells of his
parish church and attracted a crowd of Indians and *mestizos.* He urged his
listeners to follow him in a movement to preserve New Spain from the
peninsulars who had overthrown Viceroy Iturrigary. It is likely that he concluded his speech with an appeal to Ferdinand VII, America, and religion
and a denunciation of "bad government." That he called for independence in this famed *Grito de Dolores* is highly unprobable.

Hidalgo's followers started off without organization or training, picking up recruits as they proceeded. At Atotonilco, Hidalgo took a banner representing the Virgin of Guadalupe as a symbol of the rebellion's religious sanction. This virgin had a special place in the religious beliefs of the lower orders of Mexico and helped impart a class as well as a religious content to the uprising.

The first town the insurgents took was San Miguel, where the local militia joined the rebels. As a precursor of later events, Hidalgo's largely unarmed "army" of thousands of peasants followed up the town's peaceful surrender with a night of violence and pillage. Two days later Celaya was similarly sacked. Although Hidalgo and other leaders appeared to sanction, if not to encourage, attacks on the persons and property of peninsulars, it was clear almost immediately that the mob could not or would not distinguish between peninsulars and creoles. This was a class and race war more than a struggle over the political future of Mexico. Numbering more than 25,000, the insurgent forces reached the intendancy's capital of Guanajuato on September 23.

The intendant of Guanajuato, Juan Antonio de Riaño, had received news of the earlier atrocities perpetrated by Hidalgo's followers and refused to surrender the city. Instead he fortified the public granary and attempted to hold out until relief arrived. Inside the granary were most of the city's peninsulars and many wealthy creoles as well. Hidalgo's forces were greatly augmented by thousands of miners and urban workers who chose to join the rebellion. Hundreds of the insurgents were killed by the well-armed defenders as they rushed the granary, but soon they succeeded in burning down the wooden gates and forcing an entry. In the rout that followed, more than three hundred men and women of Guanajuato's elite were put to the knife inside the granary, and many more died in the pillage that followed.

Following Guanajuato, Hidalgo's army, mostly armed with agricultural implements and without even rudimentary military training, grew to more than sixty thousand. Its movement was more like an armed migration than a military campaign, as families and even animals trailed along. Hidalgo was the leading actor in this struggle, but the movement lacked either intellectual coherence or clear objectives. It sought an ill-defined "independence" but claimed allegiance to Ferdinand VII. As they moved across the countryside, rebels attacked directly the social and economic privileges of the colonial order, yet the leadership lacked any agreed-upon reform agenda. Hidalgo and Allende seemed unable or unwilling to impose order or to organize the movement into a clear alternative to the viceregal government. Threatened directly by the social revolutionary nature of the violence, the creole elite moved to support the viceroy. If Hidalgo understood the political ramifications of this alignment, he did little to reverse it.

Zacatecas, San Luis Potosí, and Valladolid also fell to the rebels before they threatened a frontal assault on Mexico City. With more than eighty thousand in his force, at Monte de las Cruces, Hidalgo took on a much smaller, but much better armed and trained force commanded by the royalist General Félix Mariá Calleja. The rebel victory was costly. Nearly two thousand men perished in the bitter battle alone, and in its aftermath nearly half of Hidalgo's ill-disciplined army deserted. After camping outside Mexico City for three days and futilely asking for its surrender, Hidalgo withdrew without attacking.

The reasons for this withdrawal are unclear. It might have resulted from Hidalgo's desire to spare the capital from the atrocities that had followed earlier victories, from a fear that he could not control the rural peasants once let loose amid the luxuries of the city, or from the absence of any sign of revolt or sympathy from the urban population. It is clear that outside the Bajío and some northwestern mining centers, Hidalgo received little support from urban residents of any class. In rural areas the revolt also failed in its efforts to broaden its social base. Traditional Indian communities, villages with communal lands and vestiges of self-government, were much less likely to provide recruits than were villages and small towns deeply penetrated by market-oriented production.

Following his withdrawal from his camp outside Mexico City, Hidalgo divided his forces with Allende and then proceeded to Valladolid and Guadalajara. In both places Hidalgo seemed more directly responsible for acts of violence than previously. In all, more than 400 European noncombatants were killed. In Guanajuato, Allende's followers executed 138 European prisoners before being driven from the city by royalist forces. Nearly one of every eight peninsulars in Mexico died violently during the Hidalgo revolt.

In January 1811 General Calleja's army caught up with the disintegrating rebel force at Puente de Calderón on the Lerma River. Again outnumbered, the royalists nonetheless won a devastating victory. While the battle was still in doubt, a cannon shot hit a wagon loaded with ammunition and set the grass on fire in the midst of the rebel lines. As the fire spread, the rebels broke ranks and fled in panic. This was the effective end of Hidalgo's brief challenge to Spanish power. As he, Allende, and other rebel leaders escaped northward—hoping to reestablish their movement in the chronically dissatisfied regions of Coahuila and Texas—they were captured. In Chihuahua, Allende and other laymen were executed. As a priest, Hidalgo was tried first by the Inquisition. Found guilty of heresy and treason, he was turned over to local authorities and shot on July 31, 1811. His severed head was taken to Guanajuato where it was exhibited for ten years on the burned shell of the public granary.

Stage 2: José María Morelos y Pavón

With the execution of Hidalgo and other leaders of the original movement, the rebellion continued through the efforts of a new generation of leaders. Chief among these was the priest José María Morelos y Pavón. This transfer of leadership coincided with a new stage in the character of the rebellion. The spontaneous uprising that followed Hidalgo's _Grito de Dolores_ in September 1810 lasted barely six months and never lost the character of a peasant revolt. Hidalgo and the other leaders seemed incapable of imposing anything other than destinations on the masses. But under Morelos this was changed. He organized, trained, and supplied a disciplined army. He also formed political alliances that transcended the narrow class, race, and geographic limits that so constrained the Hidalgo period. Finally, under Morelos the objectives of the revolt were clarified. Complete independence from Spain and a number of social and economic changes emerged as specific goals.

Born into a poor _mestizo_ family, Morelos worked as a muleteer in his youth before an opportunity to gain an education came along. Eventually he graduated from the University of Mexico and entered the church. Lacking powerful patrons or useful family connections, he received appointments only to poor Indian parishes in Michoacán. Born into a lower social stratum than Hidalgo was, Morelos thus was closer to the poor peasants and _mestizos_ that made up a majority of Mexico's population.

Militarily, Morelos relied on small mobile units that forced the royalists to divide their forces. Strategically, he sought to gain control of the regions surrounding Mexico City and ultimately force the capital's surrender. He also worked to develop both a clear political program and the essential elements of a national political apparatus but lacked the military resources to enforce it. His political objectives included the creation of a representative form of government, and in September 1813, he called a congress to meet in Chilpancingo. Once in place, the congress declared Mexico's independence and granted Morelos executive authority. His social program responded to the needs of the social groups that still provided the revolution's basic constituency. He promised to abolish Indian tribute (as the viceregal government had already done) and to end slavery and the discriminatory elements of the caste system. He also appeared to commit the revolution to land reform, partly accomplished by the seizure of lands belonging to his enemies. On the conservative side, he committed himself to maintaining the Catholic Church's traditional place in society and to the continuation of private property. But even with a more disciplined military campaign, an avoidance of the outrages of the Hidalgo era, and these public commitments to church and property, Morelos was only marginally more successful than Hidalgo was in attracting the support of the creole elite and the professional classes.

Having escaped a near mortal blow from the royalist commander Calleja in 1812, Morelos expanded his control over much of the region south and west of Mexico City. Forces loyal to him also controlled part of the Gulf coast region north of Vera Cruz. By late 1813, however, he began to suffer irreversible defeats that reduced his control over the congress of Chilpancingo.

Forced to move to Apatzingán, the rebel congress produced a constitution. Morelos signed the document but was not one of its principal authors. The constitution created a three-person executive and separated political and military authority. These provisions were clearly directed against Morelos, who earlier had exercised supreme military and political power. With the military balance now in the hands of the Spanish commanders, congress spent much of 1815 fleeing from one small town to the next. On November 5, Morelos was captured while attempting to provide an escort for the congress. He was taken to Mexico City and, like Hidalgo, was tried by the Inquisition and found guilty. He was executed by firing squad on December 22, 1815.

With the capture and execution of Morelos, any semblance of a national movement for independence disappeared. What remained were small regional forces, sometimes indistinguishable from bandits, that harassed the royalists with guerrilla attacks. Only two rebel leaders commanded substantial military forces: Guadalupe Victoria operated in the areas of Puebla and Vera Cruz, and Vicente Guerrero held out in Oaxaca. Although their forces could and did disrupt trade and forced the viceregal and local governments to maintain costly defenses, they were incapable of winning independence.

The defeat of Hidalgo and Morelos was accomplished largely through the organization and allocation of local resources by the viceroys of Mexico, especially Venegas and his successor Calleja. Almost all of the troops used against the rebels were recruited and trained locally; the majority, in fact, were native-born Mexicans. The war, a very costly one, was also paid for by local resources. Extraordinary taxes and forced contributions drained money from the economy and tended to exacerbate the crisis brought on by military violence. Even with these measures the viceregal government acquired a debt of nearly 50 million pesos. The economic burdens of the war effort, disproportionally borne by the creole elite, created dissatisfaction in this politically important class.

The response of the colonial administration to the reforming initiatives of the Spanish government also heightened the creole elite's dissatisfaction with Mexico's colonial status. Throughout the war years the viceroys of Mexico found the constitutional and legislative reforms put in place by the Spanish *cortes* to be inconvenient or even subversive to the prosecution of the insurgency. When the *cortes* decreed a free press, Viceroy Venegas stalled its implementation. Even when enshrined in the Constitution of 1812, freedom of the press was suspended in less than a year. The constitution's requirement of local elections also contradicted the repressive and conservative wartime regime evolved under viceroys Venegas and Calleja. When elections were held, interference and intervention by the viceroys thwarted the will of the electors. Despite the intentions of the *cortes*, Calleja operated in Mexico as a virtual military dictator. With the return of Ferdinand VII and his suspension of the constitution, Calleja moved aggressively against Mexican liberals uncovered in the struggles over free speech and elections.

Viceroy Juan Ruíz de Apodaca replaced Calleja in 1816. Apodaca decided to pursue a policy of accommodation and moderation, and his offer of amnesty further weakened the insurgent forces. But events in

Spain again provoked a crisis in Mexico. The Riego revolt in 1820 and Ferdinand's forced acceptance of the Constitution of 1812 reopened the question of Mexico's status within the empire and renewed the debate between liberals and conservatives over the structure and substance of political life. Unlike Venegas and Calleja, Apodaca permitted the constitution to be implemented in Mexico.

Many of the political changes resulting from these metropolitan events were popular in Mexico. The *cortes,* however, remained an intransigent imperial government committed to continuing the colonial relationship between Spain and Mexico. The religious reforms the *cortes* pursued, moreover, were perceived in Mexico as anticlerical and consequently were unpopular. Abolition of the ecclesiastical and military *fueros,* in particular, alienated two of the imperial regime's most valuable props.

The Final Stage: Agustín de Iturbide and the Plan of Iguala

In 1820 Viceroy Apodaca selected Colonel Agustín de Iturbide, a creole who had been an effective royalist commander, to undertake a campaign against Vicente Guerrero. In November Iturbide began his march south with 2,500 veteran troops. After some preliminary skirmishing, Iturbide arranged a series of meetings with the veteran rebel commander and proposed a compromise program that would unite the surviving insurgent forces and disaffected royalist troops.

The agreement formulated was called the Plan of Iguala. The basic platform included three provisions—religion, independence, and *unión*—guaranteed by the united army of Iturbide and Guerrero. The plan was not an antipeninsular document: Those peninsulars willing to accept its provisions were permitted to retain their property and even their positions in the government and church. In fact, the viceroy was proposed as a member of the interim governing junta. The plan also contained essential elements of the liberal Spanish constitution. Monarchist in conception, the plan proposed inviting Ferdinand VII or another Bourbon prince to take up a Mexican crown while also calling for the creation of a representative Mexican assembly to write a constitution.

By guaranteeing the traditional privileges of the church and military, Iturbide's plan won support from the two institutions that had decisively won both propaganda and battlefield victories over Hidalgo and Morelos. By guaranteeing property and avoiding a populist ideology that might promote new challenges from the Indian and *mestizo* masses, it won the support of those creoles whose ambitions had been thwarted by the peninsular coup of 1808 and the limited enforcement of the Constitution of 1812. Peninsulars, too, accepted the concept of *unión* that guaranteed their equality with creoles. Even the surviving insurgents were won over by this unexpected opportunity to achieve at least the minimum political objective of their rebellion—independence from Spain.

Soon after the publication of the Plan of Iguala, royalist military units began to announce their affiliation with Iturbide. Even peninsulars, long the intransigent bastion of the continuation of empire, seemed neutralized by and, in some cases, even enthusiastic for a proposal that freed them from a liberal Spain embarked on a campaign of destroying privilege. As garrison after garrison converted to the rebel cause, the viceroy was forced to resign by the royalist forces in the capital. When Juan de O'Donojú, appointed captain-general of New Spain by the *cortes,* arrived in Vera Cruz, he quickly recognized the inevitability of independence and signed the Treaty of Córdoba, thereby ending royalist resistance. On September 27, 1821, the thirty-nine-year-old Iturbide entered Mexico City as president of the provisional regency.

Iturbide and his closest military supporters received decorations, promotions, and financial rewards, Iturbide receiving a salary of 125,000 pesos a year, far more than the last Spanish viceroy had. The congress called to determine the nation's political future debated over republic and monarchical forms of government, but it was the troops and popular groups in the street that decided the issue. On May 18, street demonstrators demanded that Iturbide accept the crown. The next day the galleries of congress were filled with Iturbide's supporters. With the leader of independence himself present, congress declared Iturbide the constitutional emperor. In rapid order the monarchy was declared hereditary, and an elaborate court ritual was put in place. Crowned Agustín I on July 21, 1822, Iturbide found it more difficult to govern than to secure a crown.

Mexico's economy was in desperate condition by 1821. The production of silver coinage, for example, had fallen from 26 million pesos in 1809 to under 6 million in 1821. Grazing and agriculture had also been seriously damaged by the effects of more than a decade of conflict. As a result, Iturbide found it extremely difficult to meet his obligations to the army, civil service, and creditors. In these circumstances the pomp and display of the imperial court proved a political liability. Issues of paper money, forced loans applied to the Church, and other desperate expedients created more political problems than revenues.

As the effects of the government's fiscal crisis spread, liberal republicans began to find an audience in the congress and in the larger society. Impatient with the debate, Iturbide suspended congress. This provocation led to a new military mutiny led by Antonio López de Santa Anna, the commander of Vera Cruz, and other dissatisfied military leaders. The rebel leaders published the Plan of Casa Mata on February 1, 1823, which called for the establishment of a republican government. Within weeks Iturbide recognized the inevitable and abdicated. Mexico's brief experiment with an indigenous monarchy was over.

Central America

As in the other mainland colonies, the dramatic events in Europe after 1808 destabilized the kingdom of Guatemala. From his capital in Guatemala City, the captain-general ruled a large and diverse region that included Guatemala, Chiapas, El Salvador, Honduras, Nicaragua, and

Costa Rica. Indians constituted the majority of the more than one million inhabitants, and the *castas,* known as *ladinos* in the region, were the next largest group. The economy was oriented toward agricultural exports, and the social structure was among the most regressive in the empire.

When the Hidalgo revolt broke out in 1810, there was no sign of sympathy or support in Central America. The absence of militancy among the Indians and *ladinos* was particularly noteworthy. Enjoying unchallenged authority, the government of Central America was able to provide funds and other forms of support to the viceroy in Mexico City.

The Constitution of 1812 created tensions between conservatives and liberals, and given the nature of the region's social and economic relationships, these political differences took on a centrifugal regional character. The election of provincial deputies, city councils, and delegates to the Spanish *cortes* all worked to politicize the elite and middle sectors of this society. The issue of free trade proved the most divisive. The creole elite sought open ports as a means of stimulating demand for their rural products and lowering the costs of imports. Spanish authorities sided with the peninsular merchant community to oppose these popular local initiatives. Although this period witnessed an increase in political tension and even one or two ineffective conspiracies, there was no rebellion. The restoration of Ferdinand in 1814 led to the persecution of the most outspoken liberals in Central America. Newspapers were closed, and all dissent was silenced. A change in administrative leadership in 1818 was followed by more liberal trade policies and the reappearance of liberal political opinion.

In 1820, news of the restoration of the Constitution of 1812 gave rise to the new contentiousness. Contending factions became incipient political parties as issues were vented in the press. News of the Plan of Iguala led to the rapid loss of Chiapas to Mexico. In Guatemala an assembly was convened to determine future policy. In other regions of the kingdom, local elites attempted to gain the maximum benefit from the loss of authority by the capital. These centrifugal pressures were briefly quieted when Iturbide threatened to enforce Mexico City's authority militarily. *Cabildos* all over the kingdom then called *cabildos abiertos* and accepted incorporation within the Mexican Empire. By January 1822, Central America, with the exception of El Salvador, had joined Iturbide's Mexico. Soon El Salvador was compelled to join as well. The fall of Iturbide smashed this relationship, and in 1824 a federal republic was created that included all of the former kingdom of Guatemala except Chiapas. Central America had achieved independence.

Epilogue

Once independent, the former colonies of Latin America undertook the difficult process of organizing new governments, establishing internal order, and promoting economic growth. Despite the scale of these tasks, the political and intellectual leaders of the early stages of the independence era were generally optimistic about the future. The native-born elite, like the conquistadors and early European settlers, believed that Latin America was richly endowed by nature, and many foreign visitors, particularly the British, shared this belief. According to these observers, colonialism was the only major impediment to the region's material progress.

Much of this initial optimism had disappeared before the last royalist armies were defeated in Spanish America. Competing claims of regions, classes, colors, and ideologies already divided political life and promoted sectoral violence. These divisions later appeared in Brazil in the 1830s,

Map 5
LATIN AMERICA IN 1830

despite that nation's more peaceful transition to independence. The reduced authority and limited resources of independent governments, compared with those of the colonial period, led, throughout the region, to an increase in banditry and other forms of civil disorder. In response, the propertied classes encouraged, or at least supported, various forms of authoritarian rule. Early hopes for economic growth and prosperity faded quickly in the decades after independence. The wars for independence had been costly, and the loss of the established imperial commercial ties had often been economically disruptive. Even where trade had expanded and exports had increased, the benefits were not widely shared by the newly independent populations.

The Economy

The establishment of political independence in Spanish America exacted a heavy price. By 1830 nearly every region was poorer than it had been in 1800. These economic costs appear to have been greatest in the mining centers of Mexico and the Andean nations of Peru and Bolivia, where silver production fell by two-thirds. Plantation agriculture in Venezuela and Peru, the grazing industry of Argentina and Uruguay, manufacturing and cottage industries in Ecuador and Mexico, and internal trade throughout Spanish America suffered reverses. Brazil, having served as the capital of the Portuguese Empire from 1808 to 1821 and then gaining independence under the leadership of the prince-regent in 1822, avoided the economic and social dislocations that proved so costly to its neighbors.

Many of the economic problems the new nations faced were rooted in geography and natural resources or were structural legacies of centuries of colonialism. The destructive effects of the political conflicts and military campaigns that led to independence only heightened these problems. Because the international context within which Latin America's new leaders attempted to remedy these difficulties after 1825 was more dynamic, expansive, and unpredictable than before, prior experiences, existing institutions, and established practice were of only limited usefulness. The development of new technology, the rise of industrial capitalism, and the creation of an ever-more integrated world economy played a major role in shaping the countries' policy choices and determining their resource allocations. Local political leaders, however, had to live with the consequences of these potent forces.

The wars for independence were civil wars. With few exceptions, both royalist and insurgent armies were recruited locally, often at the point of a bayonet. In most cases military manpower requirements affected mining and export agriculture more than subsistence farming. Although the actual loss of life was relatively light in comparison with Europe's experience during the Napoleonic Wars, the dispersal of soldiers caused by the long-distance campaigns of San Martín and Bolívar, the migration of those seeking to avoid military service, and the depredations of invading armies multiplied the disruptive effects of enlistment and conscription.

Market scene in Rio de Janeiro at time of independence

Peninsulars made up only a small percentage of the total work force, but they were among the most experienced, best-trained sectors of the professional, commercial, and artisan classes. Through emigration, discrimination, and loss of life, their productive energy was largely lost. Losses also occurred at the bottom of the labor force. Both egalitarian ideology and practical political necessity led to attacks on all forms of compulsory labor. Both San Martín and Bolívar abolished the *mita,* and nearly all the revolutionary governments in Spanish America outlawed the African slave trade in the first decade after independence. Slavery itself had been weakened by gradualist emancipation laws and by manumissions granted as a result of military service. Few former slaves or *mita* laborers voluntarily accepted employment in the plantations or mines where they had been forced to work in the colonial period. Cacao production in Venezuela and gold production in Colombia declined, in part because of the loss of slave labor. Silver production in Peru and Bolivia also fell. Only in Brazil did slavery emerge strengthened after independence. The widespread violation of agreements to end the slave trade in the 1830s and 1840s brought nearly 500,000 new African slaves to Brazil and facilitated the large-scale expansion of coffee production. Britain's use of both naval force and diplomacy forced an end to the slave trade in the 1850s. By this time, however, Brazil had established a market advantage in coffee relative to that of its rivals.

Latin America also confronted the problem of depleted capital resources. In order to replace and restore production capacity damaged by the wars and to stimulate new growth, it was necessary to find large amounts of investment capital. The major sources of such capital during the colonial era, the church and the peninsular merchant community, were gravely weakened by expropriations, forced loans, and destruction in the wars. Many wealthy peninsulars had fled war-torn areas with their liquid capital, returning to Spain or sometimes settling in Cuba, one of the few remaining colonies. During the era of civil wars and regional conflicts that followed independence, the church remained under pressure because of its wealth. Although liberals and conservatives disagreed over the church's role in education, intellectual life, and political discourse, both groups in the end were willing to force it to subsidize government expenses. The use of deficit spending by colonial administrators in defense of the old order was imitated by numerous rebel leaders and, after independence, by new governments. As a result, customs duties and other revenues were commonly allocated to debt service rather than to internal improvements that would enable increased production. Under pressure to stretch fiscal resources, governments debased their currencies and borrowed from foreign lenders. During the 1820s, Spanish American governments placed bonds with a nominal value of 18 million pounds in Europe. After the cost of commissions and speculation was subtracted, only about 10 million pounds were delivered to the borrowers. Brazil borrowed 3 million pounds in 1824 and then another 400,000 pounds in 1825 to help service its initial debt. By 1830 many Latin American nations were in default, and their access to European credit was nearly cut off.

Other resources were also lost during the wars. Both royalist and rebel armies commonly expropriated crops and livestock. One reason that Hidalgo was able to create and sustain an army of more than fifty thousand was the coincidence of his rebellion with the grain harvest. Marauding soldiers seized horses, mules, and cattle when the opportunity presented itself. They also took wagons, carts, and tools. Sea and river transportation was devastated in a similar manner. Blockades, the spread of privateering, and the breakdown of customary tax and tariff laws led to the loss or diversion of much of Spanish America's shipping capacity. Mines deteriorated or were flooded. In Mexico it took half a century to regain the level of mineral production of 1800.

Destroyed, deteriorated, and expropriated resources contributed to a decline in exports and generally low levels of investment. Sectors of the economy tied to the imperial commercial system—cacao and sugar production and silver mining—tended to suffer most. On the other hand, exports such as livestock products, coffee, and copper expanded after independence to meet the needs of a market dominated by Great Britain. The high profits that resulted from the new European demands for coffee led Venezuelan landowners to accept an interest rate of 15 percent to aid in increasing production in the 1830s. In contrast with much of Spanish America, Brazil suffered little in the transition to independence and therefore found few impediments to expand its exports. In Chile, where mineral resources had been little exploited in the colonial era, mining production boomed after independence. The greatest growth and most rapid recoveries occurred in the mineral and agricultural exporting regions that had natural linkages with the British or other European markets. Many of these new or expanded exports were subject to periodic, often violent, price changes. While prices were rising, Latin Americans invested heavily in expanding production, often borrowing funds at high interest rates. The inevitable collapse in prices that followed the appearance of new producers or a change in European demand usually had devastating economic and political consequences for the Latin American countries. This cycle of boom and bust remains characteristic of the region.

Although by 1850 new exports and new markets had overcome the economic costs of independence in most of Latin America, the new economic order was in some ways less advanced than the colonial system it replaced. In general the economies were less integrated and interdependent. Large-scale unified political and economic systems like the viceroyalty of Río de la Plata disappeared, and as a result, formerly protected agriculture and industry disappeared as well. Manufacturing and artisan production also fell throughout the region. One measure of these changes was the relative loss of the cities' economic importance. Only cities closely tied to the new exports—Buenos Aires, Caracas, and Rio de Janeiro—escaped stagnation or decline.

Government

Brazil's transition to independence was facilitated by the presence of a Portuguese prince in Rio de Janeiro. Independence came first without a change in constitution or law. Even the highest levels of the bureaucracy experienced little change in personnel. In Spanish America, however, the transition was more dramatic and more complete. Virtually the entire edifice of the Spanish colonial order was scrapped, and few experienced high officials escaped dismissal within a few years after independence. Gone too was a monarchical system that had provided legitimacy. During the first stage of the revolutions in Spanish America, juntas claimed loyalty to Ferdinand VII while waging war against his agents. After 1814, region after region formally declared independence and began creating new constitutional and political practices.

Although monarchism found its supporters—San Martín and Iturbide being the most important—the revolutionary leadership in Spanish American was generally republican in principle. It was not, however, democratic in practice. Rivadavia, O'Higgins, Bolívar, Páez, and Sucre all accepted and exercised extraconstitutional authority. As the newly independent countries confronted centrifugal political threats—the regional political energies and economic forces that broke up Bolívar's vision of a Gran Colombia, subverted Central America's union with Mexico, and frustrated the recreation of a United Provinces of the Río de la Plata—representative institutions lost their importance. Real power was exercised by strong men,

caudillos who relied for their legitimacy on their clients and elite patronage
rather than on election or formal institutions. Some *caudillos* called themselves liberals, other conservatives, but all used personal, not constitutional, authority. Among the many important *caudillos* were Juan Manuel
de Rosas of Argentina, Diego Portales of Chile, José Antonio Páez of Venezuela, and Antonio López de Santa Anna of Mexico. Although all these
leaders appeared as "great men" to admirers of their day, it is clear that
their political importance resulted more from the relative diminution of
centralized power and the reduction of state resources during the 1820s
and 1830s than from their merits. All actors appear large on a small stage.

The state remained an important economic force after independence,
although limited resources reduced and constrained ambitions. Only the
government of Brazil retained a colonial-era ability to influence the allocation of resources. Even in this case Great Britain's preponderant position as a trading partner limited the goverment's freedom of action. The
decision to end the slave trade, for example, was effectively made in London, not in Rio de Janeiro. Virtually no independent government was able
to create and collect taxes as efficiently as its colonial predecessor had
been. Nearly the whole range of colonial-era production and consumption
taxes in Spanish America disappeared with independence. As a result, by
1850, customs duties and export taxes provided nearly 80 percent of government revenue in Latin America. These taxes and duties inhibited
regional trade—further disrupting colonial patterns such as Chilean wheat
exports to Peru—and advanced the region's integration into the European market. In an extreme but not unique case, the provincial governments in Argentina imposed tariffs on trade with one another. In such an
environment, less efficient producers in neighboring countries were relatively disadvantaged in their competition with European industry.

Nevertheless, the state remained the largest single employer and consumer in these new nations. It therefore could expand or restrict consumption and production through its budgetary decisions. The state's role
in banking, liability, and insurance was also important. Nonetheless, the
Latin American nations generally lagged far behind Europe and the
United States in providing an environment suitable to commercial and
industrial expansion. New national monetary systems also proved less stable than the silver-based colonial system had been. In Argentina, for example, paper money quickly led to inflation; in Brazil the issuance of copper
coins produced a similar result. The natural consequence of these unpredictable economies was an increasing tendency to invest in property rather
than in more risky enterprises.

After independence, the political importance of the military grew as
civilian authority declined. Although military officers or former military
officers often held executive power, political life was not militarized. In an
era of civil war, regional secessionism, and ideological conflict, political
peace could result only from the efforts of leaders capable of organizing
and asserting military force. However, few of the successful military men
of this period politicized or even professionalized the military. José Anto-

nio Páez, the Venezuelan revolutionary-era military hero and later president, actually reduced the regular army to eight hundred men in 1838. Juan Manuel de Rosas, the Argentine *caudillo* of the 1830s and 1840s, refused for fifteen years, despite inflation, to increase the nominal pay of officers and enlisted men. It was the increased importance of regional militias and other irregular military forces, not politicized regular armies, that changed political life in Latin America. This new military phase, often accompanied by violence, represented a breakdown in public order and central authority that tended to elevate the relative political weight of even small, poorly armed military forces. At root Latin American federalism was as much a military fact of life as it was an ideology.

The status of the church became a bitterly divisive issue in the decades following independence, but it is important to remember that this conflict began with Charles III's effort to subordinate the church to secular authority. Clerical immunity from secular jurisdiction in criminal and civil cases, sanctuary, and control of patronage remained unresolved when colonial rule ended. New conflicts over secular education, religious freedom, and church wealth helped separate conservatives and liberals. Finally, the papacy's efforts to reassert patronage rights in Latin America proved an incendiary issue, as new political elites sought to create a compliant and supportive episcopal structure. In many nations—Mexico and Colombia, for example—these struggles proved to be major obstacles to the development of stable national governments.

Social Change

Independence brought about significant changes, although the social hierarchy based largely on wealth and skin color remained intact. Those born in the Americas now claimed the highest positions in the civil administration and eventually the church, but these positions lost much of their prestige by the 1840s. Central governments and the church lost power and influence. Salaries and other benefits were diminished by inflation or by the policies of penurious governments. As a result, members of the elite groups produced by the export economies were less eager to place family members in these institutions than their colonial era predecessors had been. Everywhere except Brazil, where a monarchical court survived, wealth became the primary denominator of status. Colonial concerns with family, birthplace, color, and religious conformity became less important.

With the increased economic importance of export agriculture, rural social norms and manners and even the idealization of the large estate as a social entity gained wider acceptance. The owners of large estates felt less compelled to maintain urban households, and they were also less willing to acknowledge the cultural superiority of the urban groups. This process was counterbalanced, in part, by the presence of large numbers of Europeans, particularly British merchants, in the port cities and by the increased intellectual penetration of European ideas, styles, and tastes. Urban elites, especially commercial and professional groups, accepted these fashions and ideas and often asserted their superiority over indigenous customs and beliefs. These contradictory trends helped generate the liberal-conservative—or alternatively, urban-rural—conflicts of the middle decades of the nineteenth century.

Independence did not much affect the lives of the urban and rural masses. The *mita* was abolished officially, but in many countries, compulsory labor was forced on Indian communities into the twentieth century. Peru and Bolivia continued for decades to collect Indian tribute, their most important and reliable fiscal resource. In fact, this dependence on tribute led these same governments to provide minimal protection for the communal landholdings that helped the Indians pay the tax. The slave trade ended in most of Spanish America by 1830 and in Brazil in 1850, yet slavery persisted in many nations until mid-century and in Brazil until 1888.

Mixed-race officers of the revolutionary armies achieved a degree of upward social mobility. By 1850 a number of dark-skinned men had gained political and economic power, and a handful had become presidents. Yet color prejudice and active discrimination survived. Bolívar's characterization of the Mexican hero of independence Vicente Guerrero as the "vile abortion of a savage Indian and a fierce African"[3] suggests the limited racial enlightenment during this period. Despite persistent racism, every independent Latin American country experienced some social change: There was more physical and social mobility and greater ethnic and cultural diversity. A small flow of European immigrants was responsible for some societal changes. Brazil received nearly six thousand immigrants as early as 1842 and more than eighteen thousand immigrants in 1854. In Argentina, Welsh and Scottish sheepherders had an important impact. The Central American governments also promoted European immigration, although with little success. Nevertheless, the social order throughout Latin America remained rooted in the colonial past, and the persistence of white domination, particularly in rural areas, suggests that independence had brought little change to class relations.

Independence was an important watershed in the history of Latin America. In political and economic terms, the region was more dynamic and more vulnerable than before breaking with Spain and Portugal. Reduced legitimacy coupled with increased economic volatility fed the political instability of the region to 1850 and beyond. Underlying these changes were the vestigial social and economic structures inherited from the colonial era.

Notes

1. Timothy E. Anna, *The Fall of the Royal Government in Peru* (Lincoln: University of Nebraska Press, 1979), pp. 107–8.

2. John Lynch, *The Spanish-American Revolutions, 1808–1826,* 2nd ed. (New York: Norton, 1986), p. 198.

3. Tulio Halperín-Donghi, *The Aftermath of Revolution in Latin America* (New York: Harper & Row, 1973), p. 34.

Suggested for Further Reading

Anna, Timothy E. *The Fall of the Royal Government in Mexico City.* Lincoln: University of Nebraska Press, 1978.

Anna, Timothy E. *The Fall of the Royal Government in Peru.* Lincoln: University of Nebraska Press, 1979.

Anna, Timothy E. *Spain & the Loss of Empire.* Lincoln: University of Nebraska Press, 1983.

Arnada, Charles W. *The Emergence of the Republic of Bolivia.* Gainesville: University of Florida Press, 1957.

Benson, Nettie Lee, editor. *Mexico and the Spanish Cortes, 1810–1822.* Austin: University of Texas Press, 1966.

Bumgartner, Louis E. *José del Valle of Central America.* Durham, N.C.: Duke University Press, 1963.

Bushnell, David, editor. *The Liberator, Simon Bolívar: Man and Image.* New York: Knopf, 1970.

Collier, Simon. *Ideas and Politics of Chilean Independence, 1808–1833.* Cambridge, England: Cambridge University Press, 1969.

Dominguez, Jorge I. *Insurrection or Loyalty. The Breakdown of the Spanish American Empire.* Cambridge, Mass.: Harvard University Press, 1980.

Flores Caballero, Romeo. *Counterrevolution. The Role of the Spaniards in the Independence of Mexico, 1804–1838.* Translated by Jaime E. Rodríguez O. Lincoln: University of Nebraska Press, 1974.

Griffin, Charles C. *The United States and the Disruption of the Spanish Empire, 1800–1822.* New York: Columbia University Press, 1937.

Halperín-Donghi, Tulio. *The Aftermath of Revolution in Latin America.* New York: Harper & Row, 1973.

Halperín-Donghi, Tulio. *Politics Economics and Society in Argentina in the Revolutionary Period.* Cambridge, England: Cambridge University Press, 1975.

Hamill, Hugh M. Jr. *The Hidalgo Revolt: Prelude to Mexican Independence.* Gainesville: University of Florida Press, 1966.

Hamnett, Brian R. *Roots of Insurgency. Mexican Regions, 1750–1824.* Cambridge, England: Cambridge University Press, 1986.

Kaufmann, W. W. *British Policy and the Independence of Latin America, 1802–1828.* New Haven, Conn: Yale University Press, 1951.

Lynch, John, editor. *Origins of the Latin American Revolutions, 1808–1826.* New York: Knopf, 1965.

Lynch, John. *The Spanish-American Revolutions, 1808–1826.* 2nd edition. New York: Norton, 1986.

Masur, Gerhard. *Simon Bolívar.* 2nd edition. Albuquerque: University of New Mexico Press, 1969.

Metford, J. C. J. *San Martín the Liberator.* London: Longmans Green, 1950.

Ott, T. O. *The Haitian Revolution, 1789–1804.* Knoxville: University of Tennessee Press, 1973.

Robertson, William Spence. *France and Latin-American Independence.* Baltimore: Johns Hopkins University Press, 1939.

Robertson, William Spence. *Iturbide of Mexico.* Durham, N.C.: Duke University Press, 1952.

Rodríguez O, Jaime E. *The Emergence of Spanish America: Vicente Rocafuerte and Spanish Americanism, 1808–1832.* Berkeley and Los Angeles: University of California Press, 1975.

Rodríguez, Mario. *The Cádiz Experiment in Central America, 1808 to 1826.* Berkeley and Los Angeles: University of California Press, 1978.

Russell-Wood, A. J. R., editor. *From Colony to Nation: Essays on the Independence of Brazil.* Baltimore: Johns Hopkins University Press, 1975.

Stoan, Stephen K. *Pablo Morillo and Venezuela, 1815–1820.* Columbus: Ohio State University Press, 1974.

Street, John. *Artigas and the Emancipation of Uruguay.* Cambridge, England: Cambridge University Press, 1959.

Timmons, W. H. *Morelos of Mexico, Priest, Soldier, Statesman.* El Paso: Texas Western Press, 1963.

Whitaker, Arthur P. *The United States and the Independence of Latin America, 1800–1830.* Baltimore: Johns Hopkins University Press, 1941.

Worcester, Donald E. *Sea Power and Chilean Independence.* Gainesville: University of Florida Press, 1962.

A NOTE ON PERIODICAL LITERATURE

A voluminous periodical literature helped immensely in writing this book. The most useful English-language periodicals were *The Hispanic American Historical Review, The Americas,* the *Journal of Latin American Studies,* and the *Latin American Research Review.* The *Handbook of Latin American Studies* provides a good annotated guide to current books and articles. Charles C. Griffin (ed.), *Latin America: A Guide to the Historical Literature* (1971) is a landmark evaluation of materials published until the late 1960s. Valuable recent examinations of scholarship on colonial Latin America include Benjamin Keene, "Main Currents in United States Writings on Colonial Spanish America, 1884–1984," *Hispanic American Historical Review* 65:4 (November 1985), 657–82; A. J. R. Russell-Wood, "United States Scholarly Contributions to the Historiography of Colonial Brazil," *Hispanic American Historical Review* 65:44 (November 1985), 683–723; Eric Van Young, "Recent Anglophone Scholarship on Mexico and Central America in the Age of Revolution (1750–1850)," *Hispanic American Historical Review* 65:4 (November 1985), 725–43; and John E. Kicza, "The Social and Ethnic Historiography of Colonial Latin America: The Last Twenty Years," *The William and Mary Quarterly,* Third Series 45:3 (July 1988), 453–88.

GLOSSARY

Aguardiente de caña. An alcoholic beverage distilled from sugarcane.

Alcabala. A sales tax.

Alcaldía mayor. An administrative province or district.

Aldeias. In Brazil, recongregated Indian communities associated with Christian conversion.

Alternativa. The rotation of clerical offices, especially in regular orders, between peninsulars and creoles.

Asiento. A monopoly contract to import slaves to the Spanish colonies.

Audiencia. A high-court and advisory body to a regional chief executive in the Spanish colonies; similar to a relacao in Brazil. Also the territorial jurisdiction of such a court.

Auto da fé. An act of faith; a public or private event at which the Inquisition decreed punishment of transgressions.

Ayllu. The basic kin groups in the Andean region; family units claiming ties to a common ancestor.

Ayuntamiento. A municipal council, also known as a *cabildo.*

Bandeirante. A participant in slaving expeditions against Indians in Brazil. São Paulo was the most common origin.

Bandeira. A Brazilian expedition to capture Indian slaves.

Barrio. An urban neighborhood or district.

Batab. A term for a native chieftain in Yucatán.

Boucan. A grill for roasting meat over a fire.

Caballero (cavaleiro). A knight; the highest category of untitled nobles.

Cabildo. A municipal council, also known as an *ayuntamiento.*

Cabildo abierto. An extraordinary meeting of *cabildo* attended by representatives of the Church, other governmental institutions, and members of the economic elite.

Caboclos. In Brazil, a person of mixed Indian and white ancestry.

Cacique. An indian chieftain, usually hereditary. Known as a *kuraka* in the Andes and a *batab* in the Mayan region.

Calpulli. An Indian clan in Mesoamerica; the basic social and economic unit.

Capitulación. A contract between the Castilian Crown and a private citizen, usually outlining terms of exploration, conquest, and settlement.

Casa de Contratación. The House of Trade established in Seville in 1503, moved to Cádiz in 1717, and abolished in 1790. Oversaw Spanish trade with the colonies.

Casa grande. The "big house" or owner's residence on a Brazilian plantation.

Casta. A person of mixed racial background, which included African ancestry or the suspicion of it because of illegitimacy.

Chicha. An Andean alcoholic beverage often made from corn.

Cofradía. A lay religious brotherhood.

Colegio. A secondary school in the Spanish colonies and Brazil.

Comarca. A territorial jurisdiction in Brazil.

Compadrazgo. Godparentage.

Comunero. Supporters of a popular revolt. In Spanish America, rebels in Paraguay in 1720s and 1730s and in New Granada in 1780.

Congregación. Also known as a *reducción* or, in Brazil, an *aldeia*. A resettlement of Indians by Spaniards to aid in the Indians' conversion to Christianity.

Consulado. A merchant guild.

Converso. A convert to Christianity; usually applied to a converted Jew or a "New Christian."

Corregedor. A provincial administrator employed in Portugal.

Corregidor. A magistrate and chief administrative officer for a provincial jurisdiction. In much of Spanish America, the Spanish official charged with the administration of Indian communities.

Corregimiento. An administrative province or district.

Creole. A Spaniard born in the New World.

Cue. An Aztec temple.

De capa y espada. Here, a minister on the Council of the Indies who has not had university training in law.

Doctrina. An Indian parish.

Don, Doña. Lord; a title rare in the conquest but subsequently more commonly used.

Encomendero. The holder of an *encomienda* (q.v.).

Encomienda. A grant of authority over a group of Indians. It carried the obligation to Christianize and protect them in exchange for labor services and/or tribute.

Engenho (Sp. ingenio). The Portuguese term for sugar mill. Refers to the complete operation, including the physical plant, land, and slaves.

Español. A Spaniard born in the Old or New World; refers to both peninsulars and creoles.

Fazenda. The Brazilian term for *hacienda* (q.v.).

Flibustier. The French term for buccaneers.

Flota. The fleet that sailed from Spain to Vera Cruz.

Forastero. An outsider; a person residing in a region other than where born.

Fueros. Special judicial privileges enjoyed by a particular group, for example, ecclesiastical *fueros*.

Galeones. The fleet that sailed from Spain to Cartagena and Panama.

Gaucho. A cowboy, usually of mixed ancestry, in the Río de la Plata. Known as *llanero* in Venezuela and *vaqueiro* in the Brazilian backlands.

Gobernación. An administrative province or district.

Hacendado. The owner of a *hacienda* (q.v.).

Hacienda. A large estate devoted to livestock raising or agricultural activities. Known as a *fazenda* in Brazil.

Hermandad. The Holy Brotherhood; a league of law officers hired by municipalities in Spain.

Hidalgo (fidalgo). An untitled noble.

Hidalguía. A Castilian aristocratic ideal of nobility.

Huaca. A native Andean god; often thought of as an ancestor. Commonly represented as hills, stones, water, or mummies.

Ingenio. See *engenho.*

Inquilinaje. Peonage based on tenancy common in Chile.

Jefe político. The highest colonial administrative officer in reorganized system created in the Constitution of 1812, replacing the viceroy.

Jornal. A daily wage.

Khipus. Multicolored knotted strings that served as memory aids in preconquest Peru. Also known as *quipus.*

Kuraka. See *cacique.*

Labrador. The person who works the small property he owns or rents.

Ladino. The Central American term for *mestizo.*

Lavradores de cana. In Brazil, sugar cultivators who depended on an *engenho* for processing. Many were sharecroppers.

Limpieza de sangre. Blood purity; the absence of Jewish or Muslim ancestors.

Llanero. See *gaucho.*

Llanos. The southern plains of Venezuela.

Macehual. A Mexica commoner with access to land.

Mameluco. The offspring of Portuguese and Indian parents.

Máscara. A parade of costumed men and women.

Mayeque. A commoner in Aztec Mexico without access to land.

Mayorazgo. An entailed estate.

Mazombo. A Portuguese born in Brazil.

Media anata. Tax paid by officeholders, half of their first year's salary.

Mesta. The sheep owners' guild.

Mestizo. The offspring of Spanish and Indian parents.

Ministro togado. Here, a minister on the Council of the Indies who does have university training in law; so named because he wore the robe (toga) of the judiciary.

Mita. The colonial forced labor draft that provided Indian workers on a rotational basis. Most common in mining in Peru. Adapted from an Inca precedent.

Mitayo. An Indian forced to serve in *mita.*

Mitmaq. The Indian colonizers in Andean Peru sent to exploit an ecological zone or to help secure a conquered region.

Mulatto. The offspring of black and white parents.

Obraje. A primitive factory commonly used to produce textiles in Spanish colonies. Usually dependent on forced labor.

Palenque. A fortified hamlet of runaway slaves in Spanish America; called *quilombo* in Brazil.

Pampa. The plains of Río de la Plata.

Panaca. A deceased Inca's male descendants other than his chosen heir.

Pardo. A mulatto.

Patio process. A means of refining silver through its amalgamation with mercury.

Patronato real. Royal patronage over the Church. The right to nominate for Church offices and supervise Church administration.

Peninsular. A Spaniard born in Iberia.

Peso. A coin and monetary unit in Spanish America. The silver peso was valued at eight *reales* of silver.

Pieza de indias. An accounting term in the Spanish slave trade. A male slave without physical defects between fifteen and forty years of age. Women and children were calculated as fractions of a *pieza*.

Pipiltin. Hereditary Mexica nobility.

Plata. Silver.

Pochteca. Long-distance merchants in Aztec Mexico.

Presidio. A frontier garrison.

Pulpería. A small retail shop.

Pulque. An alcoholic beverage made from maguey, popular in Mexico before and after the conquest.

Quilombo. See *palenque*.

Radicado. A Spaniard long resident in the colonies. The term suggests someone who is well connected with local interests through marriage, friendship, and business associations.

Recôncavo. The area surrounding Bahia's Bay of All Saints.

Repartimiento. The allocation of an Indian chieftain and his people to a Spaniard to provide labor; a forced labor draft (known as *mita* in Peru).

Repartimiento de bienes. The forced sale of merchandise to Indians by Spanish officials.

Requerimiento. The "requirement"; a statement read to Indians before battle urging them to accept Christiantiy and allegiance to the Castilian Crown; their failure to do so justified war on them.

Residencia. The judicial review of an official's conduct in office.

Sertão. The backland of Brazil.

Tlatoani. A "king" in preconquest central Mexico.

Traza. The rectilinear core of a colonial city.

Vaqueiro. See *gaucho*.

Vecino. A citizen of a municipality.

Visita. An official inspection into the conduct of bureaucrats, usually unscheduled and unexpected.

Yanacona. A native retainer or laborer bound to an overlord in the Andean region.

Yerba. An herbal tea indigenous to Paraguay.

Yunga. An Andean term for a warm, low-altitude zone.

ILLUSTRATION SOURCES
AND CREDITS

p. 4: Neg. No. 279980, Courtesy Department Library Services, American Museum of Natural History.

p. 5: Neg. No. 330281 (Photo by Martin Lowenfish), Courtesy Department Library Services, American Museum of Natural History.

pp. 19, 29: Weinditz, Christoph. *Das Trachtenbach des C. Weinditz Reisen Noch Spanin*, edited by Theodor Hampe. Berlin: Verlag von Walter de Gruyter Co., 1927.

p. 91: Romero Flores, Jesus. *Iconografía colonial*. Mexico: Museo nacional de arqueologia, historia y ethnografia, 1940.

pp. 110, 129: Osuna, Mariano Tellez—Giron y Beaufort. *Pintura del gobernador, alcaldes, y regidores de Mexico*. Madrid: Impr. de M. G. Hernandez, 1878.

p. 130: Published with the permission of John Jay TePaske and Herbert S. Klein.

p. 132: Koster, Henry. *Voyages dans la partie septentrionale du Brésil*. 2 vols. Paris: Delauney, 1818.

p. 156: Peñafiel, Antonio. *Nombres geograficos de Mexico*. Mexico: Oficina tip. de la Secretaria de Fomento, 1885.

p. 172: Lenate, Claudio. *Costumes Civiles*. Bruxells: C. Sattanino, 1828.

pp. 173, 180, 181: Archivo General de la Nación, Buenos Aires, Argentina.

pp. 179, 224: Photographs by Asunción Lavrin.

p. 193: Guaman Poma de Ayala, Phelipe. *Nueva Coronica y Buen Gobierno*.

p. 195: O'Crouley, Pedro Alonso. *A Description of the Kingdom of New Spain*. Translated and edited by Seban Galvin. San Francisco: J. Howell, 1972.

pp. 206, 220, 231: Martínez Compañon, Baltasar Jaime. *Trujillo del Peru a fines del siglo XVIII*. Madrid, 1936.

p. 229: Romero Flores, Jesus. *Inconografía colonial*. Mexico: Museo nacional de arqueologia, historia y ethnografia, 1940.

p. 244: Debret, John Baptist. *Voyage pittoresque et historique au Brésil*. . . . 3 vols. Paris: Firmin Didot Frères, 1834–39.

p. 251: Spix, Johann Baptist von. *Reise in Brasilien*. 2 vols. Augsburg: G. Jaquet, 1846.

p. 265: Martínez Compañon, Baltasar Jaime. *Trujillo del Peru a fines del siglo XVIII*. Madrid, 1936.

p. 272: Vidal, Emeric Essex. *Picturesque Illustrations of Buenos Ayres and Monte Video, Consisting of Twenty-four Views*. London: R. Ackermann, 1820.

pp. 274, 279: Baucke, Florian. *Iconografía colonial rioplatense, 1749–1769.* Buenos Aires: Viau y Zona, 1935.

p. 281: Garnerey, Hippolite J. B. *Vues de la Havané et des environs.* Paris, Madrid, etc.: Bulla, 1836?

p. 327: Chamberlain, Sir Henry, 2nd Bart. *Views and Costumes of the City and Neighborhood of Rio de Janeiro.* London, M'Lean, 1822.

INDEX